PEARSON ALWA

Writing and Reading for ACP Composition
Second Edition

Compiled by Christine R. Farris
and Deanna M. Jessup

Taken from:
Writing and Reading Across the Curriculum,
Eleventh Edition
by Laurence Behrens and Leonard J. Rosen

Writing and Reading Across the Curriculum,
Twelfth Edition
by Laurence Behrens and Leonard J. Rosen

Cover photo: Courtesy of Seamas Culligan

Taken from:

Writing and Reading Across the Curriculum, Eleventh Edition
by Laurence Behrens and Leonard J. Rosen
Copyright © 2011 by Laurence Behrens and Leonard J. Rosen
Published by Longman
New York, New York 10036

Writing and Reading Across the Curriculum, Twelfth Edition
by Laurence Behrens and Leonard J. Rosen
Copyright © 2013 by Laurence Behrens and Leonard J. Rosen
Published by Longman

Pearson Learning Solutions, 501 Boylston Street, Suite 900, Boston, MA 02116
A Pearson Education Company
www.pearsoned.com

Printed in the United States of America

1 2 3 4 5 6 7 8 9 10   V011 18 17 16 15 14 13

0002000102717766797

ML/LC

ISBN-10: 1-269-32154-4
ISBN-13: 978-1-269-32154-9

COPYRIGHT ACKNOWLEDGMENTS

Brief Contents

INTRODUCTION
A MESSAGE FROM CHRISTINE FARRIS   xvii

PART I
ANTHOLOGY OF READINGS   1

Chapter 1
Marriage and Family in America   3

Chapter 2
Obedience   75

Chapter 3
Weight Debate   151

Chapter 4
Green Power   211

Chapter 5
The Cinderella Myth   267

Detailed Contents

INTRODUCTION
A MESSAGE FROM CHRISTINE FARRIS   xvii

PART I
ANTHOLOGY OF READINGS   1

Chapter 1
Marriage and Family in America   3

A Pop Quiz on Marriage; The Radical Idea of Marrying for Love   3
Stephanie Coontz

The Radical Idea of Marrying for Love   4

The State of Our Unions   16
David Popenoe and Barbara Dafoe Whitehead

A Debate on Gay Marriage   29

For Gay Marriage   29
Andrew Sullivan

Against Gay Marriage   33
William J. Bennett

*The Satisfactions of Housewifery and Motherhood/Paradise Lost
    (Domestic Division)   36*
Terry Martin Hekker

Paradise Lost (Domestic Division)   38

A Mother's Day Kiss-Off   41
Leslie Bennetts

Understanding Mom   44
Deborah Tannen

American Marriage in Transition   46
Andrew J. Cherlin

The Myth of Co-Parenting: How It Was Supposed to Be. How It Was.   50
Hope Edelman

My Problem with Her Anger   57
Eric Bartels

Will Your Marriage Last?   63
Aviva Patz

The Arbus Factor   69
Lore Segal

Answer Key to "A Pop Quiz on Marriage"   71

Chapter 2
Obedience   75

The Abu Ghraib Prison Scandal: Sources of Sadism   75
Marianne Szegedy-Maszak

The Perils of Obedience   77
Stanley Milgram

Review of Stanley Milgram's Experiments on Obedience   89
Diana Baumrind

Obedience   95
Ian Parker

The Stanford Prison Experiment   105
Philip G. Zimbardo

The Genocidal Killer in the Mirror   117
Crispin Sartwell

Just Do What the Pilot Tells You   119
Theodore Dalrymple

Disobedience as a Psychological and Moral Problem   123
Erich Fromm

Time to Think About Torture   128
Jonathan Alter

The My Lai Massacre: A Military Crime of Obedience   131
Herbert C. Kelman and V. Lee Hamilton

Opinions and Social Pressure   142
Solomon E. Asch

The Power of Situations   147
Lee Ross and Richard E. Nisbett

Chapter 3
Weight Debate 151

Prevalence of Obesity Among U.S. Adults, by Characteristics and by State 151
Centers for Disease Control and Prevention

Rethinking Weight 154
Amanda Spake

Too Much of a Good Thing 160
Greg Critser

Fat and Happy: In Defense of Fat Acceptance 163
Mary Ray Worley

Too "Close to the Bone": The Historical Context for Women's Obsession with Slenderness 167
Roberta Seid

Fat and Happy? 179
Hillel Schwartz

The Man Who Couldn't Stop Eating 186
Atul Gawande

Thinking Sociologically about Sources of Obesity in the United States 200
Robert L. Peralta

Chapter 4
Green Power 211

Going Green: A Wedge Issue 211

National Security Consequences of U.S. Oil Dependence 212
Report of an Independent Task Force

The Dangerous Delusions of Energy Independence 215
Robert Bryce

A Debate on the Future of Nuclear Power, Post-Fukushima 222

The Future of Nukes, and of Japan 224
Holman W. Jenkins, Jr.

No Fail-Safe Option 226
Eugene Robinson

Why I Still Support Nuclear Power, Even After Fukushima   228
William Tucker

If the Japanese Can't Build a Safe Nuclear Reactor, Who Can?   229
Anne Applebaum

Solar Power   231

State Solar Plans Are as Big as All Outdoors   232
Marla Dickerson

Here Comes the Sun   235
Paul Krugman

Solar Is Getting Cheaper, but How Far Can It Go?   237
Brad Plumer

Wind Power   238

The Island in the Wind   240
Elizabeth Kolbert

Wind Power Puffery   247
H. Sterling Burnett

Electric Cars   248

The Great Electric Car Experiment   250
Daniel Yergin

Why the Gasoline Engine Isn't Going Away Any Time Soon   260
Joseph B. White

Chapter 5
The Cinderella Myth   267

Universality of the Folktale   267
Stith Thompson

Walt Disney's "Cinderella"   270
Adapted by Campbell Grant

Cinderella   273
Charles Perrault

"Cinderella": A Story of Sibling Rivalry and Oedipal Conflicts   277
Bruno Bettelheim

Fairy Tales and a Dose of Reality   284
Catherine Orenstein

Cinderella: Not So Morally Superior   286
Elisabeth Panttaja

"Cinderella" and the Loss of Father-Love   *289*
Jacqueline M. Schectman

Fairy Tales and Modern Stories   *303*
Bruno Bettelheim

An Introduction to Fairy Tales   *306*
Maria Tatar

The Truth about Cinderella   *313*
Martin Daly and Margo Wilson

The Rise of Perrault's "Cinderella"   *318*
Bonnie Cullen

The Princess Paradox   *323*
James Poniewozik

Cinderella and Princess Culture   *326*
Peggy Orenstein

Introduction

As part of writing in English W131, you will examine the claims and evidence at work in source materials. This course aims to build sequentially on your abilities to read closely and critically and to analyze the perspectives and rhetorical strategies of experts in a variety of disciplines and professions.

Some of the units and readings your instructor will assign offer multiple perspectives that can be put in conversation with one another. Some readings offer new lenses for considering or reconsidering issues and phenomena beyond just what the author is specifically writing about. Some will function as jumping off points for further inquiry and research. Still others are themselves examples of the sort of analytical and argumentative moves we want you to use in your own writing.

You can expect your instructor to ask that you read the essays in this book closely and more than once in order to understand an author's main argument, sub-points, key vocabulary, and concepts. Expect to work on summarizing and paraphrasing throughout the course in order to engage with the author's ideas on his or her as well as your terms. In addition, your instructor will invite you to "talk back" to the readings, but in constructive ways that uncover their assumptions and test and extend their ideas as part of formulating positions and analyses of your own.

CHRISTINE FARRIS
Indiana University
Bloomington

Part I

Anthology of Readings

Marriage and Family in America

A Pop Quiz on Marriage;
The Radical Idea of Marrying for Love
Stephanie Coontz

Our chapter selections begin with a "pop quiz" designed to ferret out your assumptions about marriage. There's no penalty for getting the answers wrong; but you may be interested to discover that you know less about the subject than you thought. After taking the quiz (and checking the correct answers), you'll proceed to an in-depth historical survey of love, as it relates to marriage.

One of the bedrock assumptions of modern marriage is the once-radical idea that newlyweds be in love. Marriage and love have existed through the ages, of course. But according to historian Stephanie Coontz, only in the relatively recent past, beginning in the eighteenth century, did the political and economic institution of marriage take on romantic associations. Reminding us through historical and cultural examples that many people were (and still are) horrified by the idea of marrying for love, and loving the one you marry, Coontz traces the intellectual development of this subversive notion back to the Enlightenment. She then hints at the long-term consequences it held for the institution of marriage.

Stephanie Coontz teaches history and family studies at The Evergreen State College in Olympia, Washington, and has written numerous books on marriage and family in America, including The Way We Never Were: American Families and the Nostalgia Trap *(1992) and* The Way We Really Are: Coming to Terms with America's Changing Families *(1998). The following selection first appeared in* Marriage: A History: From Obedience to Intimacy, or How Love Conquered Marriage *(2005).*

1. Women are more eager to marry than men. *True or False?*
2. Men are threatened by women who are their intellectual and occupational equals, preferring to be with much younger, less accomplished women. *True or False?*
3. There are more long-term marriages today than in the past. *True or False?*
4. Americans have become much more tolerant of all sexual activity. *True or False?*
5. The growth in the number of couples living together and even having children without formal marriage ceremonies or licenses reflects a sharp break with centuries old tradition. *True or False?*
6. Educated married women are increasingly "opting out" of work to stay home with their children. *True or False?*

7. Men and women who hold nontraditional views about gender roles are less likely to marry and more likely to divorce than those with traditional values. *True or False?*
8. Divorce rates in the 1950's were lower than at any other time in the 20th century. *True or False?*
9. Throughout history, philosophers and theologians have always believed that strong marital commitments form the foundation of a virtuous society. *True or False?*
10. American women have more positive attitudes toward marriage than Japanese women do. *True or False?*
11. Divorce has always been a disaster for women and children. *True or False?*
12. The preferred form of marriage through the ages has been between one man and one woman. *True or False?*
13. Born-again Christians are just as likely to divorce as more secular Americans. *True or False?**

The Radical Idea of Marrying for Love

1   George Bernard Shaw described marriage as an institution that brings together two people "under the influence of the most violent, most insane, most delusive, and most transient of passions. They are required to swear that they will remain in that excited, abnormal, and exhausting condition continuously until death do them part."

2   Shaw's comment was amusing when he wrote it at the beginning of the twentieth century, and it still makes us smile today, because it pokes fun at the unrealistic expectations that spring from a dearly held cultural ideal— that marriage should be based on intense, profound love and a couple should maintain their ardor until death do them part. But for thousands of years the joke would have fallen flat.

3   For most of history it was inconceivable that people would choose their mates on the basis of something as fragile and irrational as love and then focus all their sexual, intimate, and altruistic desires on the resulting marriage. In fact, many historians, sociologists, and anthropologists used to think romantic love was a recent Western invention. This is not true. People have always fallen in love, and throughout the ages many couples have loved each other deeply.

4   But only rarely in history has love been seen as the main reason for getting married. When someone did advocate such a strange belief, it was no laughing matter. Instead, it was considered a serious threat to social order.

*For Answer key, please turn to p. 71.

5   In some cultures and times, true love was actually thought to be incompatible with marriage. Plato believed love was a wonderful emotion that led men to behave honorably. But the Greek philosopher was referring not to the love of women, "such as the meaner men feel," but to the love of one man for another.

6   Other societies considered it good if love developed after marriage or thought love should be factored in along with the more serious considerations involved in choosing a mate. But even when past societies did welcome or encourage married love, they kept it on a short leash. Couples were not to put their feelings for each other above more important commitments, such as their ties to parents, siblings, cousins, neighbors, or God.

7   In ancient India, falling in love before marriage was seen as a disruptive, almost antisocial act. The Greeks thought lovesickness was a type of insanity, a view that was adopted by medieval commentators in Europe. In the Middle Ages the French defined love as a "derangement of the mind" that could be cured by sexual intercourse, either with the loved one or with a different partner. This cure assumed, as Oscar Wilde once put it, that the quickest way to conquer yearning and temptation was to yield immediately and move on to more important matters.

8   In China, excessive love between husband and wife was seen as a threat to the solidarity of the extended family. Parents could force a son to divorce his wife if her behavior or work habits didn't please them, whether or not he loved her. They could also require him to take a concubine if his wife did not produce a son. If a son's romantic attachment to his wife rivaled his parents' claims on the couple's time and labor, the parents might even send her back to her parents. In the Chinese language the term *love* did not traditionally apply to feelings between husband and wife. It was used to describe an illicit, socially disapproved relationship. In the 1920s a group of intellectuals invented a new word for love between spouses because they thought such a radical new idea required its own special label.

9   In Europe, during the twelfth and thirteenth centuries, adultery became idealized as the highest form of love among the aristocracy. According to the Countess of Champagne, it was impossible for true love to "exert its powers between two people who are married to each other."

10   In twelfth-century France, Andreas Capellanus, chaplain to Countess Marie of Troyes, wrote a treatise on the principles of courtly love. The first rule was that "marriage is no real excuse for not loving." But he meant loving someone outside the marriage. As late as the eighteenth century the French essayist Montaigne wrote that any man who was in love with his wife was a man so dull that no one else could love him.

11   Courtly love probably loomed larger in literature than in real life. But for centuries, noblemen and kings fell in love with courtesans rather than the wives they married for political reasons. Queens and noblewomen had to be more discreet than their husbands, but they too looked beyond marriage for love and intimacy.

12   This sharp distinction between love and marriage was common among the lower and middle classes as well. Many of the songs and stories popular among peasants in medieval Europe mocked married love.

13   The most famous love affair of the Middle Ages was that of Peter Abelard, a well-known theologian in France, and Héloïse, the brilliant niece of a fellow churchman at Notre Dame. The two eloped without marrying, and she bore him a child. In an attempt to save his career but still placate Héloïse's furious uncle, Abelard proposed they marry in secret. This would mean that Héloïse would not be living in sin, while Abelard could still pursue his church ambitions. But Héloïse resisted the idea, arguing that marriage would not only harm his career but also undermine their love.

"Nothing Is More Impure than to Love One's Wife as If She Were a Mistress"

14 Even in societies that esteemed married love, couples were expected to keep it under strict control. In many cultures, public displays of love between husband and wife were considered unseemly. A Roman was expelled from the Senate because he had kissed his wife in front of his daughter. Plutarch conceded that the punishment was somewhat extreme but pointed out that everyone knew that it was "disgraceful" to kiss one's wife in front of others.

15   Some Greek and Roman philosophers even said that a man who loved his wife with "excessive" ardor was "an adulterer." Many centuries later Catholic and Protestant theologians argued that husbands and wives who loved each other too much were committing the sin of idolatry. Theologians chided wives who used endearing nicknames for their husbands, because such familiarity on a wife's part undermined the husband's authority and the awe that his wife should feel for him. Although medieval Muslim thinkers were more approving of sexual passion between husband and wife than were Christian theologians, they also insisted that too much intimacy between husband and wife weakened a believer's devotion to God. And, like their European counterparts, secular writers in the Islamic world believed that love thrived best outside marriage.

16   Many cultures still frown on placing love at the center of marriage. In Africa, the Fulbe people of northern Cameroon do not see love as a legitimate emotion, especially within marriage. One observer reports that in conversations with their neighbors, Fulbe women "vehemently deny emotional attachment to a husband." In many peasant and working-class communities, too much love between husband and wife is seen as disruptive because it encourages the couple to withdraw from the wider web of dependence that makes the society work.

17   As a result, men and women often relate to each other in public, even after marriage, through the conventions of a war between the sexes, disguising the fondness they may really feel. They describe their marital behavior, no matter how exemplary it may actually be, in terms of convenience, compulsion, or self-interest rather than love or sentiment. In Cockney rhyming slang, the term for *wife* is *trouble and strife*.

18   Whether it is valued or not, love is rarely seen as the main ingredient for marital success. Among the Taita of Kenya, recognition and approval of married love are widespread. An eighty-year-old man recalled that his

fourth wife "was the wife of my heart. . . . I could look at her and no words would pass, just a smile." In this society, where men often take several wives, women speak wistfully about how wonderful it is to be a "love wife." But only a small percentage of Taita women experience this luxury, because a Taita man normally marries a love wife only after he has accumulated a few more practical wives.

19   In many cultures, love has been seen as a desirable outcome of marriage but not as a good reason for getting married in the first place. The Hindu tradition celebrates love and sexuality in marriage, but love and sexual attraction are not considered valid reasons for marriage. "First we marry, then we'll fall in love" is the formula. As recently as 1975, a survey of college students in the Indian state of Karnataka found that only 18 percent "strongly" approved of marriages made on the basis of love, while 32 percent completely disapproved.

20   Similarly, in early modern Europe most people believed that love developed after marriage. Moralists of the sixteenth and seventeenth centuries argued that if a husband and wife each had a good character, they would probably come to love each other. But they insisted that youths be guided by their families in choosing spouses who were worth learning to love. It was up to parents and other relatives to make sure that the woman had a dowry or the man had a good yearly income. Such capital, it was thought, would certainly help love flower.

"[I]t Made Me Really Sick, Just as I Have Formerly Been When in Love with My Wife"

21 I don't believe that people of the past had more control over their hearts than we do today or that they were incapable of the deep love so many individuals now hope to achieve in marriage. But love in marriage was seen as a bonus, not as a necessity. The great Roman statesman Cicero exchanged many loving letters with his wife, Terentia, during their thirty-year marriage. But that didn't stop him from divorcing her when she was no longer able to support him in the style to which he had become accustomed.

22   Sometimes people didn't have to make such hard choices. In seventeenth-century America, Anne Bradstreet was the favorite child of an indulgent father who gave her the kind of education usually reserved for elite boys. He later arranged her marriage to a cherished childhood friend who eventually became the governor of Massachusetts. Combining love, duty, material security, and marriage was not the strain for her that it was for many men and women of that era. Anne wrote love poems to her husband that completely ignored the injunction of Puritan ministers not to place one's spouse too high in one's affections. "If ever two were one," she wrote him, "then surely we; if ever man were loved by wife, then thee. . . . I prize thy love more than whole mines of gold, or all the riches that the East doth hold; my love is such that rivers cannot quench, nor ought but love from thee, give recompense."

23   The famous seventeenth-century English diarist Samuel Pepys chose to marry for love rather than profit. But he was not as lucky as Anne. After hearing a particularly stirring piece of music, Pepys recorded that it "did

wrap up my soul so that it made me really sick, just as I have formerly been when in love with my wife." Pepys would later disinherit a nephew for marrying under the influence of so strong yet transient an emotion.

24   There were always youngsters who resisted the pressures of parents, kin, and neighbors to marry for practical reasons rather than love, but most accepted or even welcomed the interference of parents and others in arranging their marriages. A common saying in early modern Europe was "He who marries for love has good nights and bad days." Nowadays a bitter wife or husband might ask, "Whatever possessed me to think I loved you enough to marry you?" Through most of the past, he or she was more likely to have asked, "Whatever possessed me to marry you just because I loved you?"

"Happily Ever After"

25 Through most of the past, individuals hoped to find love, or at least "tranquil affection," in marriage. But nowhere did they have the same recipe for marital happiness that prevails in most contemporary Western countries. Today there is general agreement on what it takes for a couple to live "happily ever after." First, they must love each other deeply and choose each other unswayed by outside pressure. From then on, each must make the partner the top priority in life, putting that relationship above any and all competing ties. A husband and wife, we believe, owe their highest obligations and deepest loyalties to each other and the children they raise. Parents and in-laws should not be allowed to interfere in the marriage. Married couples should be best friends, sharing their most intimate feelings and secrets. They should express affection openly but also talk candidly about problems. And of course they should be sexually faithful to each other.

26   This package of expectations about love, marriage, and sex, however, is extremely rare. When we look at the historical record around the world, the customs of modern America and Western Europe appear exotic and exceptional.

27   Leo Tolstoy once remarked that all happy families are alike, while every unhappy family is unhappy in its own way. But the more I study the history of marriage, the more I think the opposite is true. Most unhappy marriages in history share common patterns, leaving their tear-stained—and sometimes bloodstained—records across the ages. But each happy, successful marriage seems to be happy in its own way. And for most of human history, successful marriages have not been happy in *our* way.

28   A woman in ancient China might bring one or more of her sisters to her husband's home as backup wives. Eskimo couples often had cospousal arrangements, in which each partner had sexual relations with the other's spouse. In Tibet and parts of India, Kashmir, and Nepal, a woman may be married to two or more brothers, all of whom share sexual access to her.

29   In modern America, such practices are the stuff of trash TV: "I caught my sister in bed with my husband"; "My parents brought their lovers into our home"; "My wife slept with my brother"; "It broke my heart to share my husband with another woman." In other cultures, individuals often find such practices normal and comforting. The children of Eskimo

cospouses felt that they shared a special bond, and society viewed them as siblings. Among Tibetan brothers who share the same wife, sexual jealousy is rare.

30   In some cultures, cowives see one another as allies rather than rivals. In Botswana, women add an interesting wrinkle to the old European saying "Woman's work is never done." There they say: "Without cowives, a woman's work is never done." A researcher who worked with the Cheyenne Indians of the United States in the 1930s and 1940s told of a chief who tried to get rid of two of his three wives. All three women defied him, saying that if he sent two of them away, he would have to give away the third as well.

31   Even when societies celebrated the love between husband and wife as a pleasant by-product of marriage, people rarely had a high regard for marital intimacy. Chinese commentators on marriage discouraged a wife from confiding in her husband or telling him about her day. A good wife did not bother her husband with news of her own activities and feelings but treated him "like a guest," no matter how long they had been married. A husband who demonstrated open affection for his wife, even at home, was seen as having a weak character.

32   In the early eighteenth century, American lovers often said they looked for "candor" in each other. But they were not talking about the soul-baring intimacy idealized by modern Americans, and they certainly did not believe that couples should talk frankly about their grievances. Instead candor meant fairness, kindliness, and good temper. People wanted a spouse who did *not* pry too deeply. The ideal mate, wrote U.S. President John Adams in his diary, was willing "to palliate faults and Mistakes, to put the best Construction upon Words and Action, and to forgive Injuries."

33   Modern marital advice books invariably tell husbands and wives to put each other first. But in many societies, marriage ranks very low in the hierarchy of meaningful relationships. People's strongest loyalties and emotional connections may be reserved for members of their birth families. On the North American plains in the 1930s, a Kiowa Indian woman commented to a researcher that "a woman can always get another husband, but she has only one brother." In China it was said that "you have only one family, but you can always get another wife." In Christian texts prior to the seventeenth century, the word *love* usually referred to feelings toward God or neighbors rather than toward a spouse.

34   In Confucian philosophy, the two strongest relationships in family life are between father and son and between elder brother and younger brother, not between husband and wife. In thirteenth-century China the bond between father and son was so much stronger than the bond between husband and wife that legal commentators insisted a couple do nothing if the patriarch of the household raped his son's wife. In one case, although the judge was sure that a woman's rape accusation against her father-in-law was true, he ordered the young man to give up his sentimental desire "to grow old together" with his wife. Loyalty to parents was paramount, and therefore the son should send his wife back to her own father, who could then marry her to someone else. Sons were sometimes ordered beaten for

siding with their wives against their father. No wonder that for 1,700 years women in one Chinese province guarded a secret language that they used to commiserate with each other about the griefs of marriage.

35   In many societies of the past, sexual loyalty was not a high priority. The expectation of mutual fidelity is a rather recent invention. Numerous cultures have allowed husbands to seek sexual gratification outside marriage. Less frequently, but often enough to challenge common preconceptions, wives have also been allowed to do this without threatening the marriage. In a study of 109 societies, anthropologists found that only 48 forbade extramarital sex to both husbands and wives.

36   When a woman has sex with someone other than her husband and he doesn't object, anthropologists have traditionally called it wife loaning. When a man does it, they call it male privilege. But in some societies the choice to switch partners rests with the woman. Among the Dogon of West Africa, young married women publicly pursued extramarital relationships with the encouragement of their mothers. Among the Rukuba of Nigeria, a wife can take a lover at the time of her first marriage. This relationship is so embedded in accepted custom that the lover has the right, later in life, to ask his former mistress to marry her daughter to his son.

37   Among the Eskimo of northern Alaska, as I noted earlier, husbands and wives, with mutual consent, established comarriages with other couples. Some anthropologists believe cospouse relationships were a more socially acceptable outlet for sexual attraction than was marriage itself. Expressing open jealousy about the sexual relationships involved was considered boorish.

38   Such different notions of marital rights and obligations made divorce and remarriage less emotionally volatile for the Eskimo than it is for most modern Americans. In fact, the Eskimo believed that a remarried person's partner had an obligation to allow the former spouse, as well as any children of that union, the right to fish, hunt, and gather in the new spouse's territory.

39   Several small-scale societies in South America have sexual and marital norms that are especially startling for Europeans and North Americans. In these groups, people believe that any man who has sex with a woman during her pregnancy contributes part of his biological substance to the child. The husband is recognized as the primary father, but the woman's lover or lovers also have paternal responsibilities, including the obligation to share food with the woman and her child in the future. During the 1990s researchers taking life histories of elderly Bari women in Venezuela found that most had taken lovers during at least one of their pregnancies. Their husbands were usually aware and did not object. When a woman gave birth, she would name all the men she had slept with since learning she was pregnant, and a woman attending the birth would tell each of these men: "You have a child."

40   In Europe and the United States today such an arrangement would be a surefire recipe for jealousy, bitter breakups, and very mixed-up kids. But among the Bari people this practice was in the best interests of the child. The secondary fathers were expected to provide the child with fish and game, with the result that a child with a secondary father was twice as likely to live to the age of fifteen as a brother or sister without such a father.

41   Few other societies have incorporated extramarital relationships so successfully into marriage and child rearing. But all these examples of differing marital and sexual norms make it difficult to claim there is some universal model for the success or happiness of a marriage.

42   About two centuries ago Western Europe and North America developed a whole set of new values about the way to organize marriage and sexuality, and many of these values are now spreading across the globe. In this Western model, people expect marriage to satisfy more of their psychological and social needs than ever before. Marriage is supposed to be free of the coercion, violence, and gender inequalities that were tolerated in the past. Individuals want marriage to meet most of their needs for intimacy and affection and all their needs for sex.

43   Never before in history had societies thought that such a set of high expectations about marriage was either realistic or desirable. Although many Europeans and Americans found tremendous joy in building their relationships around these values, the adoption of these unprecedented goals for marriage had unanticipated and revolutionary consequences that have since come to threaten the stability of the entire institution.

. . .

44   [B]y the beginning of the seventeenth century a distinctive marriage system had taken root in Western Europe, with a combination of features that together not only made it different from marriage anywhere else in the world but also made it capable of very rapid transformation. Strict divorce laws made it difficult to end a marriage, but this was coupled with more individual freedom to choose or refuse a partner. Concubinage had no legal status. Couples tended to marry later and to be closer to each other in age. And upon marriage a couple typically established an independent household.

45   During the eighteenth century the spread of the market economy and the advent of the Enlightenment wrought profound changes in record time. By the end of the 1700s personal choice of partners had replaced arranged marriage as a social ideal, and individuals were encouraged to marry for love. For the first time in five thousand years, marriage came to be seen as a private relationship between two individuals rather than one link in a larger system of political and economic alliances. The measure of a successful marriage was no longer how big a financial settlement was involved, how many useful in-laws were acquired, or how many children were produced, but how well a family met the emotional needs of its individual members. Where once marriage had been seen as the fundamental unit of work and politics, it was now viewed as a place of refuge from work, politics, and community obligations.

46   The image of husbands and wives was also transformed during the eighteenth century. The husband, once the supervisor of the family labor force, came to be seen as the person who, by himself, provided for the family. The wife's role was redefined to focus on her emotional and moral contributions to family life rather than her economic inputs. The husband was the family's economic motor, and the wife its sentimental core.

47   Two seismic social changes spurred these changes in marriage norms. First, the spread of wage labor made young people less dependent on their parents for a start in life. A man didn't have to delay marriage until he inherited land or took over a business from his father. A woman could more readily earn her own dowry. As day labor replaced apprenticeships and provided alternatives to domestic service, young workers were no longer obliged to live in a master's home for several years. They could marry as soon as they were able to earn sufficient wages.

48   Second, the freedoms afforded by the market economy had their parallel in new political and philosophical ideas. Starting in the mid-seventeenth century, some political theorists began to challenge the ideas of absolutism. Such ideas gained more adherents during the eighteenth-century Enlightenment, when influential thinkers across Europe championed individual rights and insisted that social relationships, including those between men and women, be organized on the basis of reason and justice rather than force. Believing the pursuit of happiness to be a legitimate goal, they advocated marrying for love rather than wealth or status. Historian Jeffrey Watts writes that although the sixteenth-century Reformation had already "enhanced the dignity of married life by denying the superiority of celibacy," the eighteenth-century Enlightenment "exalted marriage even further by making love the most important criterion in choosing a spouse."

49   The Enlightenment also fostered a more secular view of social institutions than had prevailed in the sixteenth and seventeenth centuries. Marriage came to be seen as a private contract that ought not be too closely regulated by church or state. After the late eighteenth century, according to one U.S. legal historian, marriage was increasingly defined as a private agreement with public consequences, rather than as a public institution whose roles and duties were rigidly determined by the family's place in the social hierarchy.

50   The new norms of the love-based, intimate marriage did not fall into place all at once but were adopted at different rates in various regions and social groups. In England, the celebration of the love match reached a fever pitch as early as the 1760s and 1770s, while the French were still commenting on the novelty of "marriage by fascination" in the mid-1800s. Many working-class families did not adopt the new norms of marital intimacy until the twentieth century.

51   But there was a clear tipping point during the eighteenth century. In England, a new sentimentalization of wives and mothers pushed older anti-female diatribes to the margins of polite society. Idealization of marriage reached such heights that the meaning of the word *spinster* began to change. Originally an honorable term reserved for a woman who spun yarn, by the 1600s it had come to mean any woman who was not married. In the 1700s the word took on a negative connotation for the first time, the flip side of the new reverence accorded to wives.

52   In France, the propertied classes might still view marriage as "a kind of joint-stock affair," in the words of one disapproving Englishwoman, but the common people more and more frequently talked about marriage as the route to "happiness" and "peace." One study found that before the 1760s fewer than

10 percent of French couples seeking annulments argued that a marriage should be based on emotional attachment to be fully valid, but by the 1770s more than 40 percent thought so.

53   Romantic ideals spread in America too. In the two decades after the American Revolution, New Englanders began to change their description of an ideal mate, adding companionship and cooperation to their traditional expectations of thrift and industriousness.

54   These innovations spread even to Russia, where Tsar Peter the Great undertook westernizing the country's army, navy, bureaucracy, and marriage customs all at once. In 1724 he outlawed forced marriages, requiring bride and groom to swear that each had consented freely to the match. Russian authors extolled "the bewitchment and sweet tyranny of love."

55   The court records of Neuchâtel, in what is now Switzerland, reveal the sea change that occurred in the legal norms of marriage. In the sixteenth and seventeenth centuries, judges had followed medieval custom in forcing individuals to honor betrothals and marriage contracts that had been properly made, even if one or both parties no longer wanted the match. In the eighteenth century, by contrast, judges routinely released people from unwanted marriage contracts and engagements, so long as the couple had no children. It was no longer possible for a man to force a woman to keep a marriage promise.

56   In contrast to the stories of knightly chivalry that had dominated secular literature in the Middle Ages, late eighteenth-century and early nineteenth-century novels depicted ordinary lives. Authors and audiences alike were fascinated by domestic scenes and family relations that had held no interest for medieval writers. Many popular works about love and marriage were syrupy love stories or melodramatic tales of betrayals. But in the hands of more sophisticated writers, such as Jane Austen, clever satires of arranged marriages and the financial aspects of courtship were transformed into great literature.

57   One result of these changes was a growing rejection of the legitimacy of domestic violence. By the nineteenth century, male wife-beaters rather than female "scolds" had become the main target of village shaming rituals in much of Europe. Meanwhile, middle- and upper-class writers condemned wife beating as a "lower-class" vice in which no "respectable" man would indulge.

58   Especially momentous for relations between husband and wife was the weakening of the political model upon which marriage had long been based. Until the late seventeenth century the family was thought of as a miniature monarchy, with the husband king over his dependents. As long as political absolutism remained unchallenged in society as a whole, so did the hierarchy of traditional marriage. But the new political ideals fostered by the Glorious Revolution in England in 1688 and the even more far-reaching revolutions in America and France in the last quarter of the eighteenth century dealt a series of cataclysmic blows to the traditional justification of patriarchal authority.

59   In the late seventeenth century John Locke argued that governmental authority was simply a contract between ruler and ruled and that if a ruler exceeded the authority his subjects granted him, he could be replaced. In 1698 he suggested that marriage too could be seen as a contract between equals. Locke still believed that men would normally rule their families because of their greater strength and ability, but another English writer, Mary Astell, pushed Locke's theories to what she thought was their logical conclusion, "If Absolute Sovereignty be not necessary in a State," Astell asked, "how comes it to be so in a Family?" She answered that not only was absolutism unnecessary within marriage, but it was actually "more mischievous in Families than in kingdomes," by exactly the same amount as "100,000 tyrants are worse than one."

60   During the eighteenth century people began to focus more on the mutual obligations required in marriage. Rejecting analogies between the absolute rights of a husband and the absolute rights of a king, they argued that marital order should be based on love and reason, not on a husband's arbitrary will. The French writer the Marquis de Condorcet and the British author Mary Wollstonecraft went so far as to call for complete equality within marriage.

61   Only a small minority of thinkers, even in "enlightened" circles, endorsed equality between the sexes. Jean Jacques Rousseau, one of the most enthusiastic proponents of romantic love and harmonious marriage, also wrote that a woman should be trained to "docility . . . for she will always be in subjection to a man, or to man's judgment, and she will never be free to set her own opinion above his." The German philosopher J. G. Fichte argued in 1795 that a woman could be "free and independent only as long as she had no husband." Perhaps, he opined, a woman might be eligible to run for office if she promised not to marry. "But no rational woman can give such a promise, nor can the state rationally accept it. For woman is destined to love, and . . . when she loves, it is her duty to marry."

62   In the heady atmosphere of the American and French revolutions of 1776 and 1789, however, many individuals dared draw conclusions that anticipated feminist demands for marital reform and women's rights of the early twentieth century. And even before that, skeptics warned that making love and companionship the core of marriage would open a Pandora's box.

The Revolutionary Implications of the Love Match

63 The people who pioneered the new ideas about love and marriage were not, by and large, trying to create anything like the egalitarian partnerships that modern Westerners associate with companionship, intimacy, and "true love." Their aim was to make marriage more secure by getting rid of the cynicism that accompanied mercenary marriage and encouraging couples to place each other first in their affections and loyalties.

64   But basing marriage on love and companionship represented a break with thousands of years of tradition. Many contemporaries immediately recognized the dangers this entailed. They worried that the unprecedented idea of basing marriage on love would produce rampant individualism.

65   Critics of the love match argued—prematurely, as it turns out, but correctly—that the values of free choice and egalitarianism could easily spin out of control. If the choice of a marriage partner was a personal decision, conservatives asked, what would prevent young people, especially women, from choosing unwisely? If people were encouraged to expect marriage to be the best and happiest experience of their lives, what would hold a marriage together if things went "for worse" rather than "for better"?

66   If wives and husbands were intimates, wouldn't women demand to share decisions equally? If women possessed the same faculties of reason as men, why would they confine themselves to domesticity? Would men still financially support women and children if they lost control over their wives' and children's labor and could not even discipline them properly? If parents, church, and state no longer dictated people's private lives, how could society make sure the right people married and had children or stop the wrong ones from doing so?

67   Conservatives warned that "the pursuit of happiness," claimed as a right in the American Declaration of Independence, would undermine the social and moral order. Preachers declared that parishioners who placed their husbands or wives before God in their hierarchy of loyalty and emotion were running the risk of becoming "idolaters." In 1774 a writer in England's *Lady Magazine* commented tartly that "the idea of matrimony" was not "for men and women to be always taken up with each other" or to seek personal self-fulfillment in their love. The purpose of marriage was to get people "to discharge the duties of civil society, to govern their families with prudence and to educate their children with discretion."

68   There was a widespread fear that the pursuit of personal happiness could undermine self-discipline. One scholar argues that this fear explains the extraordinary panic about masturbation that swept the United States and Europe at the end of the eighteenth century and produced thousands of tracts against "the solitary vice" in the nineteenth. The threat of female masturbation particularly repelled and fascinated eighteenth-century social critics. To some it seemed a short step from two people neglecting their social duties because they were "taken up with each other" to one person pleasuring herself without fulfilling a duty to anyone else at all.

69   As it turned out, it took another hundred years for the contradictions that gave rise to these fears to pose a serious threat to the stability of the new system of marriage.

The State of Our Unions
David Popenoe and Barbara Dafoe Whitehead

At the end of the previous selection, Stephanie Coontz hinted at the consequences that the rise of the "love match" would have for the institution of marriage. So how is marriage faring? In the following selection, the codirectors of the National Marriage Project at Rutgers State University warn that the institutions of marriage and family are in a state of crisis. David Popenoe is a professor of sociology at Rutgers University in New Brunswick, New Jersey. An expert in the study of marriage and family life, he has written or edited ten books, most recently War Over the Family *(2005). Barbara Dafoe Whitehead lectures and writes on the well-being of families and children for scholarly and popular audiences. She is the author of* The Divorce Culture: Rethinking Our Commitment to Marriage and Family *(1997). The following selection combines sections of Popenoe and Whitehead's 2002 and 2005 reports on marriage, presented here in three parts: Marriage, Divorce, and Unmarried Cohabitation. The earlier report appeared in* USA Today Magazine *in July 2002. The later report appears on the National Marriage Project Web site at http://marriage.rutgers.edu/Publications/SOOO/TEXTSOOU2005.htm. Data in figures have been updated to reflect those contained in the authors' 2007 report.*

1 Each year, the National Marriage Project at Rutgers University publishes an assessment of the health of marriage and marital relationships in America entitled "The State of Our Unions." It is based on a thorough review and evaluation of the latest statistics and research findings about marriage, family, and courtship trends, plus our own special surveys.

2   Americans haven't given up on marriage as a cherished ideal. Indeed, most continue to prize and value it as an important life goal, and the vast majority (an estimated 85%) will marry at least once in a lifetime. Almost all couples enter marriage with a strong desire and determination for a lifelong, loving partnership, and this desire may even be increasing among the young. Since the 1980s, the percentage of high school seniors who say that having a good marriage is extremely important to them as a life goal has gone up, though only slightly.

· · ·

Marriage

3 Key Finding: Marriage trends in recent decades indicate that Americans have become less likely to marry, and the most recent data show that the marriage rate in the United States continues to decline. Of those who do marry, there has been a moderate drop since the 1970s in the percentage of couples who consider their marriages to be "very happy," but in the past decade this trend has swung in a positive direction.

4   Americans have become less likely to marry. This is reflected in a decline of nearly 50 percent, from 1970 to 2004, in the annual number of marriages per 1,000 unmarried adult women (Figure 1). Some of this decline—it is not

FIGURE 1 Number of Marriages per 1,000 Unmarried Women Age 15 and Older, by Year, United States[a]	
Year	Number[b]
1960	73.5
1970	76.5
1975	66.9
1980	61.4
1985	56.2
1990	54.5
1995	50.8
2000	46.5
2005	40.7

a. We have used the number of marriages per 1,000 unmarried women age 15 and older, rather than the Crude Marriage Rate of marriages per 1,000 population to help avoid the problem of compositional changes in the population, that is, changes which stem merely from there being more or less people in the marriageable ages. Even this more refined measure is somewhat susceptible to compositional changes.

b. Per 1,000 unmarried women age 14 and older.

Source: U.S. Department of the Census, Statistical Abstract of the United States, 2001, Page 87, Table 117; and Statistical Abstract of the United States, 1986, Page 79, Table 124. Figure for 2004 was obtained using data from the Current Population Surveys, March 2004 Supplement, as well as Births, Marriages, Divorces, and Deaths: Provisional Data for 2004, National Vital Statistics Report 53:21, June 26, 2005, Table 3. (http://www.cdc.gov/nchs/data/nvsr/nvsr53/nvsr53_21.pdf) The CPS, March Supplement, is based on a sample of the U.S. population, rather than an actual count such as those available from the decennial census. See sampling and weighting notes at http://www.bis.census.gov:80/cps/ads/2002/ssampwgt.htm

clear just how much—results from the delaying of first marriages until older ages: the median age at first marriage went from 20 for females and 23 for males in 1960 to about 26 and 27, respectively, in 2004. Other factors accounting for the decline are the growth of unmarried cohabitation and a small decrease in the tendency of divorced persons to remarry.

5   The decline also reflects some increase in lifelong singlehood, though the actual amount cannot be known until current young and middle-aged adults pass through the life course.

6   The percentage of adults in the population who are currently married has also diminished. Since 1960, the decline of those married among all persons age 15 and older has been 14 percentage points—and over 29 points among black females (Figure 2). It should be noted that these data include both people who have never married and those who have married and then divorced. (For some economic implications of the decline of marriage, see the accompanying box: "The Surprising Economic Benefits of Marriage.")

FIGURE 2   Percentage of All Persons Age 15 and Older Who Were Married, by Sex and Race, 1960–2006, United States[a]

Year	Total Males	Black Males	White Males	Total Females	Black Females	White Females
1960	69.3	60.9	70.2	65.9	59.8	66.6
1970	66.7	56.9	68	61.9	54.1	62.8
1980	63.2	48.8	65	58.9	44.6	60.7
1990	60.7	45.1	62.8	56.9	40.2	59.1
2000	57.9	42.8	60	54.7	36.2	57.4
2006[b]	56.3	40.9	58.5	53.4	34.3	56.3

a. Includes races other than Black and White.

b. In 2003, the U.S. Census Bureau expanded its racial categories to permit respondents to identify themselves as belonging to more than one race. This means that racial data computations beginning in 2004 may not be strictly comparable to those in prior years.

Source: U.S. Bureau of the Census, Current Population Reports, Series P20-506; America's Families and Living Arrangements: March 2000 and earlier reports; and data calculated from the Current Population Surveys, March 2004 Supplement.

7   In order partially to control for a decline in married adults simply due to delayed first marriages, we have looked at changes in the percentage of persons age 35 through 44 who were married (Figure 3). Since 1960, there has been a drop of 22 percentage points for married men and 20 points for married women.

8   Marriage trends in the age range of 35 to 44 are suggestive of lifelong singlehood. In times past and still today, virtually all persons who were going to marry during their lifetimes had married by age 45. More than 90 percent of women have married eventually in every generation for which records exist, going back to the mid-1800s. By 1960, 94 percent of women then alive had been married at least once by age 45—probably an historical high point.[1] For the generation of 1995, assuming a continuation of then current marriage rates, several demographers projected that 88 percent of women and 82 percent of men would ever marry.[2] If and when these figures are recalculated for the early years of the 21st century, the percentage of women and men ever marrying will almost certainly be lower.

9   It is important to note that the decline in marriage does not mean that people are giving up on living together with a sexual partner. On the contrary, with the incidence of unmarried cohabitation increasing

[1]Andrew J. Cherlin, *Marriage, Divorce, and Remarriage* (Cambridge, MA: Harvard University Press, 1992): 10; Michael R. Haines, "Long-Term Marriage Patterns in the United States from Colonial Times to the Present," *The History of the Family* 1-1 (1996): 15–39.

[2]Robert Schoen and Nicola Standish, "The Retrenchment of Marriage: Results from Marital Status Life Tables for the United States, 1995." *Population and Development Review* 27-3 (2001): 553–563.

FIGURE 3   Percentage of Persons Age 35 through 44 Who Were Married, by Sex, 1960–2006, United States

Year	Males	Females
1960	88.0	87.4
1970	89.3	86.9
1980	84.2	81.4
1990	74.1	73.0
2000	69.0	71.6
2006	67.9	69.5

Source: U.S. Bureau of the Census, Statistical Abstract of the United States, 1961, Page 34, Table 27; Statistical Abstract of the United States, 1971, Page 32, Table 38; Statistical Abstract of the United States, 1981, Page 38, Table 49; and U.S. Bureau of the Census, General Population Characteristics, 1990, Page 45, Table 34; and Statistical Abstract of the United States, 2001, Page 48, Table 51; internet tables (http://www.census.gov/population/socdemo/hh-fam/cps2003/tabA1-all.pdf) and data calculated from the Current Population Surveys, March 2004 Supplement. Figure for 2004 was obtained using data from the Current Population Surveys rather than data from the census. The CPS, March Supplement, is based on a sample of the U.S. population, rather than an actual count such as those available from the decennial census. See sampling and weighting notes at http://www.bls .census.gov:80/cps/ads/2002/ssampwgt.htm

rapidly, marriage is giving ground to unwed unions. Most people now live together before they marry for the first time. An even higher percentage of those divorced who subsequently remarry live together first. And a growing number of persons, both young and old, are living together with no plans for eventual marriage.

10   There is a common belief that, although a smaller percentage of Americans are now marrying than was the case a few decades ago, those who marry have marriages of higher quality. It seems reasonable that if divorce removes poor marriages from the pool of married couples and cohabitation "trial marriages" deter some bad marriages from forming, the remaining marriages on average should be happier. The best available evidence on the topic, however, does not support these assumptions. Since 1973, the General Social Survey periodically has asked representative samples of married Americans to rate their marriages as either "very happy," "pretty happy," or "not too happy."[3] As Figure 4 indicates, the percentage of both men and women saying "very happy" has declined moderately over the past 25 years.[4] This trend, however, is now heading in a positive direction.

---

[3]Conducted by the National Opinion Research Center of the University of Chicago, this is a nationally representative study of the English-speaking, non-institutionalized population of the United States age 18 and over.

[4]Using a different data set that compared marriages in 1980 with marriages in 1992, equated in terms of marital duration, Stacy J. Rogers and Paul Amato found similarly that the 1992 marriages had less marital interaction, more marital conflict, and more marital problems. "Is Marital Quality Declining? The Evidence from Two Generations," *Social Forces* 75 (1997): 1089.

FIGURE 4   Percentage of Married Persons Age 18 and Older Who Said Their Marriages Were "Very Happy," by Period, United States

Period	Men	Women
1973–1976	69.6	68.6
1977–1981	68.3	64.2
1982–1986	62.9	61.7
1987–1991	66.4	59.6
1993–1996	63.2	59.7
1998–2004	64.4	60.4

Source: The General Social Survey, conducted by the National Opinion Research Center of the University of Chicago. The trend for both men and women is statistically significant (p < .01 on a two-tailed test).

THE SURPRISING ECONOMIC BENEFITS OF MARRIAGE

When thinking of the many benefits of marriage, the economic aspects are often overlooked. Yet the economic benefits of marriage are substantial, both for individuals and for society as a whole. Marriage is a wealth generating institution. Married couples create more economic assets on average than do otherwise similar singles or cohabiting couples. A 1992 study of retirement data concluded that "individuals who are not continuously married have significantly lower wealth than those who remain married throughout their lives." Compared to those continuously married, those who never married have a reduction in wealth of 75% and those who divorced and didn't remarry have a reduction of 73%.[a]

One might think that the explanation for why marriage generates economic assets is because those people who are more likely to be wealth creators are also more likely to marry and stay married. And this is certainly true, but only in part. The institution of marriage itself provides a wealth-generation bonus. It does this through providing economies of scale (two can live more cheaply than one), and as implicitly a long-term personal contract it encourages economic specialization. Working as a couple, individuals can develop those skills in which they excel, leaving others to their partner.

Also, married couples save and invest more for the future, and they can act as a small insurance pool against life uncertainties such as illness and job loss.[b] Probably because of marital social norms that encourage healthy, productive behavior, men tend to become more economically productive after marriage; they earn between 10 and 40% more than do single men with similar education and job histories.[c] All of these benefits are independent of the fact that married couples receive more work-related and government-provided support, and also more help and support from their extended families (two sets of in-laws) and friends.[d]

Beyond the economic advantages of marriage for the married couples themselves, marriage has a tremendous economic impact on society. It is a major contributor to family income levels and inequality. After more than doubling between 1947 and 1977, the growth of median family income has slowed over the past 20 years, increasing by just 9.6%. A big reason is that married couples, who fare better economically than their single counterparts, have been a rapidly decreasing proportion of total families. In this same 20 year period, and largely because of changes in family structure, family income inequality has increased significantly.[e]

Research has shown consistently that both divorce and unmarried childbearing increase child poverty. In recent years the majority of children who grow up outside of married families have experienced at least one year of dire poverty.[f] According to one study, if family structure had not changed between 1960 and 1998, the black child poverty rate in 1998 would have been 28.4% rather than 45.6%, and the white child poverty rate would have been 11.4% rather than 15.4%.[g] The rise in child poverty, of course, generates significant public costs in health and welfare programs.

Marriages that end in divorce also are very costly to the public. One researcher determined that a single divorce costs state and federal governments about $30,000, based on such things as the higher use of food stamps and public housing as well as increased bankruptcies and juvenile delinquency. The nation's 1.4 million divorces in 2002 are estimated to have cost the taxpayers more than $30 billion.[h]

Notes

a. Janet Wilmoth and Gregor Koso, "Does Marital History Matter? Marital Status and Wealth Outcomes Among Preretirement Adults," *Journal of Marriage and the Family* 64:254–68, 2002.

b. Thomas A. Hirschl, Joyce Altobelli, and Mark R. Rank, "Does Marriage Increase the Odds of Affluence? Exploring the Life Course Probabilities," *Journal of Marriage and the Family* 65-4 (2003): 927–938; Joseph Lupton and James P. Smith, "Marriage, Assets and Savings," in Shoshana A. Grossbard-Schectman (ed.) *Marriage and the Economy* (Cambridge: Cambridge University Press, 2003): 129–152.

c. Jeffrey S. Gray and Michael J. Vanderhart, "The Determination of Wages: Does Marriage Matter?," in Linda Waite, et al. (eds.) *The Ties that Bind: Perspectives on Marriage and Cohabitation* (New York: Aldine de Gruyter, 2000): 356–367; S. Korenman and D. Neumark, "Does Marriage Really Make Men More Productive?" *Journal of Human Resources* 26-2 (1991): 282–307; K. Daniel, "The Marriage Premium," in M. Tomassi and K. Ierulli (eds.) *The New Economics of Human Behavior* (Cambridge: Cambridge University Press, 1995) 113–125.

d. Lingxin Hao, "Family Structure, Private Transfers, and the Economic Well-Being of Families with Children," *Social Forces* 75 (1996): 269–292.

e. U.S. Bureau of the Census, Current Population Reports, P60-203, *Measuring 50 Years of Economic Change Using the March Current Population Survey*, U.S. Government Printing Office, Washington, DC, 1998; John Iceland, "Why Poverty Remains High: The Role of Income Growth, Economic Inequality, and Changes in Family Structure, 1949–1999," *Demography* 40-3:499–519, 2003.

f. Mark R. Rank and Thomas A. Hirschl, "The Economic Risk of Childhood in America: Estimating the Probability of Poverty Across the Formative Years," *Journal of Marriage and the Family* 61:1058–1067, 1999.

g. Adam Thomas and Isabel Sawhill, "For Richer or For Poorer: Marriage as an Antipoverty Strategy," *Journal of Policy Analysis and Management* 21:4, 2002.

h. David Schramm, "The Costly Consequences of Divorce in Utah: The Impact on Couples, Community, and Government," Logan, UT: Utah State University, 2003. Unpublished preliminary report.

Divorce

11 Key Finding: The American divorce rate today is nearly twice that of 1960, but has declined slightly since hitting the highest point in our history in the early 1980s. For the average couple marrying in recent years, the lifetime probability of divorce or separation remains between 40 and 50 percent.

12   The increase in divorce, shown by the trend reported in Figure 5, probably has elicited more concern and discussion than any other family-related trend in the United States. Although the long-term trend in divorce has been upward since colonial times, the divorce rate was level for about two decades after World War II during the period of high fertility known as the baby boom. By the middle of the 1960s, however, the incidence of divorce started to increase and it more than doubled over the next fifteen years to reach an historical high point in the early 1980s. Since then the divorce rate has modestly declined, a trend described by many experts as "leveling off at a high level." The decline apparently represents a slight increase in marital stability.[5] Two probable reasons for this are an increase in the age at which people marry for the first time, and a higher educational level of those marrying, both of which are associated with greater marital stability.[6]

13   Although a majority of divorced persons eventually remarry, the growth of divorce has led to a steep increase in the percentage of all adults who are currently divorced (Figure 6). This percentage, which was only 1.8 percent

---

[5]Joshua R. Goldstein, "The Leveling of Divorce in the United States," *Demography* 36 (1999): 409–414.

[6]Tim B. Heaton, "Factors Contributing to Increased Marital Stability in the United States," *Journal of Family Issues* 23 (2002): 392–409.

FIGURE 5   Number of Divorces per 1,000 Married Women Age 15 and Older, by Year, United States[a]

Year	Divorces
1960	9.2
1965	10.6
1970	14.9
1975	20.3
1980	22.6
1985	21.7
1990	20.9
1995	19.8
2000	18.8
2005	16.4

a. We have used the number of divorces per 1,000 married women age 15 and older, rather than the Crude Divorce Rate of divorces per 1,000 population to help avoid the problem of compositional changes in the population. Even this more refined measure is somewhat susceptible to compositional changes.

Source: Statistical Abstract of the United States, 2001, Page 87, Table 117; National Vital Statistics Reports, August 22, 2001; California Current Population Survey Report: 2000, Table 3, March 2001; Births, Marriages, Divorces, and Deaths: Provisional Data for 2004, National Vital Statistics Report 53:21, June 26, 2005, Table 3, (http://www.cdc.gov/nchs/data/nvsr/nvsr53/nvsr53_21.pdf) and calculations by the National Marriage Project for the U.S. [not including] California, Georgia, Hawaii, Indiana, Louisiana and Oklahoma using the Current Population Surveys, 2004.

FIGURE 6   Percentage of All Persons Age 15 and Older Who Were Divorced, by Sex and Race, 1960–2006, United States

Year	Males			Females		
	Total	Blacks	Whites	Total	Blacks	Whites
1960	1.8	2	1.8	2.6	4.3	2.5
1970	2.2	3.1	2.1	3.5	4.4	3.4
1980	4.8	6.3	4.7	6.6	8.7	6.4
1990	6.8	8.1	6.8	8.9	11.2	8.6
2000	8.3	9.5	8.4	10.2	11.8	10.2
2006[a]	8.6	9.4	8.7	10.9	12.9	10.9

a. In 2003, the U.S. Census Bureau expanded its racial categories to permit respondents to identify themselves as belonging to more than one race. This means that racial data computations beginning in 2004 may not be strictly comparable to those of prior years.

Source: U.S. Bureau of the Census, Current Population Reports, Series P20-537; America's Families and Living Arrangements: March 2000 and earlier reports; and Current Population Surveys, March 2004 supplement, raw data.

for males and 2.6 percent for females in 1960, quadrupled by the year 2000. The percentage of divorce is higher for females than for males primarily because divorced men are more likely to remarry than divorced women. Also, among those who do remarry, men generally do so sooner than women.

14   Overall, the chances remain very high—estimated between 40 and 50 percent—that a marriage started in recent years will end in either divorce or separation before one partner dies.[7] (But see the accompanying box: "Your Chances of Divorce May Be Much Lower Than You Think.") The likelihood of divorce has varied considerably among different segments of the American population, being higher for Blacks than for Whites, for instance, and higher in the West than in other parts of the country. But these variations have been diminishing. The trend toward a greater similarity of divorce rates between Whites and Blacks is largely attributable to the fact that fewer blacks are marrying.[8] Divorce rates in the South and Midwest have come to resemble those in the West, for reasons that are not well understood, leaving only the Eastern Seaboard and the Central Plains with significantly lower divorce.

15   At the same time, there has been little change in such traditionally large divorce rate differences as between those who marry when they are teenagers compared to those who marry after age 21, high-school drop outs versus college graduates, and the non-religious compared to the religiously committed. Teenagers, high-school drop outs, and the non-religious who marry have considerably higher divorce rates.[9]

Unmarried Cohabitation

16 Key Finding: The number of unmarried couples has increased dramatically over the past four decades, and the increase is continuing. Most younger Americans now spend some time living together outside of marriage, and unmarried cohabitation commonly precedes marriage.

17   Between 1960 and 2004, as indicated in Figure 7, the number of unmarried couples in America increased by nearly 1200 percent. Unmarried cohabitation—the status of couples who are sexual partners, not married to each other, and sharing a household—is particularly common among the young. It is estimated that about a quarter of unmarried women age 25 to 39 are currently living with a partner and

---

[7]Robert Schoen and Nicola Standish, "The Retrenchment of Marriage: Results from Marital Status Life Tables for the United States, 1995," *Population and Development Review* 27-3 (2001): 553–563; R. Kelly Raley and Larry Bumpass, "The Topography of the Divorce Plateau: Levels and Trends in Union Stability in the United States after 1980," *Demographic Research* 8-8 (2003): 245–259.

[8]Jay D. Teachman, "Stability across Cohorts in Divorce Risk Factors," *Demography* 39-2 (2002): 331–351.

[9]Raley and Bumpass, 2003.

YOUR CHANCES OF DIVORCE MAY BE MUCH LOWER THAN YOU THINK

By now almost everyone has heard that the national divorce rate is close to 50% of all marriages. This is true, but the rate must be interpreted with caution and several important caveats. For many people, the actual chances of divorce are far below 50/50.

The background characteristics of people entering a marriage have major implications for their risk of divorce. Here are some percentage point decreases in the risk of divorce or separation *during the first ten years of marriage*, according to various personal and social factors:[a]

Factors	Percent Decrease in Risk of Divorce
Annual income over $50,000 (vs. under $25,000)	−30
Having a baby seven months or more after marriage (vs. before marriage)	−24
Marrying over 25 years of age (vs. under 18)	−24
Own family of origin intact (vs. divorced parents)	−14
Religious affiliation (vs. none)	−14
Some college (vs. high-school dropout)	−13

So if you are a reasonably well-educated person with a decent income, come from an intact family and are religious, and marry after age twenty-five without having a baby first, your chances of divorce are very low indeed.

Also, it should be realized that the "close to 50%" divorce rate refers to the percentage of marriages entered into during a particular year that are projected to end in divorce or separation before one spouse dies. Such projections assume that the divorce and death rates occurring that year will continue indefinitely into the future—an assumption that is useful more as an indicator of the instability of marriages in the recent past than as a predictor of future events. In fact, the divorce rate has been dropping, slowly, since reaching a peak around 1980, and the rate could be lower (or higher) in the future than it is today.[b]

Notes

a. Matthew D. Bramlett and William D. Mosher, *Cohabitation, Marriage, Divorce and Remarriage in the United States*, National Center for Health Statistics, Vital and Health Statistics, 23 (22), 2002. The risks are calculated for women only.

b. Rose M. Kreider and Jason M. Fields, "Number, Timing and Duration of Marriages and Divorces, 1996," *Current Population Reports*, P70–80, Washington, DC: U.S. Census Bureau, 2002.

FIGURE 7 Number, in Thousands, of Cohabiting, Unmarried, Adult Couples of the Opposite Sex, by Year, United States	
Year	Number
1960	439
1970	523
1980	1,589
1990	2,856
2000	4,736
2006	5,368

Source: U.S. Bureau of the Census, Current Population Reports, Series P20–537; America's Families and Living Arrangements: March 2000; and U.S. Bureau of the Census, Population Division, Current Population Survey, 2004 Annual Social and Economic Supplement (http://www.census.gov/population/socdemo/hh-fam/cps2004).

an additional quarter have lived with a partner at some time in the past. Over half of all first marriages are now preceded by living together, compared to virtually none 50 years ago.[10]

18   For many, cohabitation is a prelude to marriage, for others, simply an alternative to living alone, and for a small but growing number, it is considered an alternative to marriage. Cohabitation is more common among those of lower educational and income levels. Recent data show that among women in the 19 to 44 age range, 60 percent of high-school dropouts have cohabited compared to 37 percent of college graduates.[11] Cohabitation is also more common among those who are less religious than their peers, those who have been divorced, and those who have experienced parental divorce, fatherlessness, or high levels of marital discord during childhood. A growing percentage of cohabiting couple households, now over 40 percent, contain children.

19   The belief that living together before marriage is a useful way "to find out whether you really get along," and thus avoid a bad marriage and an eventual divorce, is now widespread among young people. But the available data on the effects of cohabitation fail to confirm this belief. In fact, a substantial body of evidence indicates that those who live together before marriage are more likely to break up after marriage. This evidence is controversial, however, because it is difficult to distinguish the "selection effect" from the "experience of cohabitation effect." The selection effect refers to the fact that people who cohabit before marriage have different characteristics from those who do not, and it may be these characteristics, and not the experience of cohabitation, that leads to mar-

---

[10]Larry Bumpass and Hsien-Hen Lu, "Trends in Cohabitation and Implications for Children's Family Contexts in the U. S.," *Population Studies* 54 (2000) 29–41.

[11]Bumpass and Lu, 2000.

ital instability. There is some empirical support for both positions. Also, a recent study based on a nationally representative sample of women concluded that premarital cohabitation (and premarital sex), when limited to a woman's future husband, is not associated with an elevated risk of marital disruption.[12] What can be said for certain is that no evidence has yet been found that those who cohabit before marriage have stronger marriages than those who do not.[13]

Conclusions

20 As a **stage in the life course of adults,** marriage is shrinking. Americans are living longer, marrying later, exiting marriages more quickly, and choosing to live together before marriage, after marriage, in between marriages, and as an alternative to marriage. A small but growing percentage, an estimated 15% [as of 2002], will never marry, compared to about five percent during the 1950s. As a consequence, marriage gradually is giving way to partnered and unpartnered singlehood, with or without children. Since 1960, the percentage of persons age 35 through 44 who were married has dropped from 88% to 68% for men and 87% to 70% for women.

21   As an **institution,** marriage has lost much of its legal, social, economic, and religious meaning and authority. The marital relationship once consisted of an economic bond of mutual dependency, a social bond supported by the extended family and larger community, and a spiritual bond upheld by religious doctrine, observance, and faith. Today, there are many marriages that have none of these elements. The older ideal of marriage as a permanent contractual union, strongly supported by society and designed for procreation and childrearing, is giving way to a new reality of it as a purely individual contract between two adults. Moreover, marriage is also quietly losing its place in the language and in popular culture. Unmarried people now tend to speak inclusively about "relationships" and "intimate partners." In the entertainment industry—including films, television, and music—marriage is often neglected or discredited.

22   If these have been the main changes, what, then, has marriage become in 21st-century America? First, let us not forget that many of the marriage-related trends of recent decades have been positive. The legal, sexual, and financial emancipation of women has become a reality as never before in history. With few restrictions on divorce, a married woman who

---

[12]Jay Teachman, "Premarital Sex, Premarital Cohabitation, and the Risk of Subsequent Marital Disruption among Women," *Journal of Marriage and the Family* 65 (2003): 444–455.

[13]For a full review of the research on cohabitation see: Pamela J. Smock, "Cohabitation in the United States," *Annual Review of Sociology* 26 (2000); and David Popenoe and Barbara Dafoe Whitehead, *Should We Live Together? What Young Adults Need to Know About Cohabitation Before Marriage—A Comprehensive Review of Recent Research,* 2nd Edition (New Brunswick, NJ: The National Marriage Project, Rutgers University, 2002).

is seriously abused by her husband can get out of the relationship, which she previously might have been stuck in for life. Due to great tolerance of family diversity, adults and children who through no fault of their own end up in nontraditional families are not marked for life by social stigma. Moreover, based on a companionship of equals, many marriages today may be more emotionally satisfying than ever before.

23   We have described the new marriage system as "emotionally deep, but socially shallow." For most Americans, marriage is a "couples relationship" designed primarily to meet the sexual and emotional needs of the spouses. Increasingly, happiness in marriage is measured by each partner's sense of psychological well-being, rather than the more-traditional measures of getting ahead economically, boosting children up to a higher rung on the educational ladder than the parents, or following religious teachings on marriage. People tend to be puzzled or put off by the idea that marriage has purposes or benefits that extend beyond fulfilling individual adult needs for intimacy and satisfaction. Eight out of 10 of the young adults in our survey agreed that "marriage is nobody's business, but that of the two people involved."

24   It is a sign of the times that the overwhelming majority (94%) of never-married singles in our survey agreed that "when you marry, you want your spouse to be your soul mate, first and foremost." This perspective, surely encouraged not only by the changing nature of marriage, but by the concern about divorce and therefore the seeming necessity of finding the one right person, is something that most people in the older generation would probably consider surprising. In times past, people married to start a new family, and therefore they looked for a competent and reliable mate to share life's tasks. To the degree that a soul mate was even considered, it was more likely to have been thought of as the end result of a lifetime of effort put into making a marriage work, not something you start out with.

25   Of course, having a soul mate as a marriage partner would be wonderful. In many ways, it is reassuring that today's young people are looking for a marriage that is both meaningful and lasting. Yet, there is a danger that the soul mate expectation sets a standard so high it will be hard to live up to. Also, if people believe that there is just one soul mate waiting somewhere out there for them, as most of today's youths in fact do according to our survey, doesn't it seem more likely that a marriage partner will be dropped when the going gets rough? Isn't it easier to say, "I must have picked the wrong person"? In other words, perhaps we have developed a standard for marriage that tends to destabilize the institution.

26   There are some hopeful signs in the recent statistics that may bode well for the future of marriage. The divorce rate has slowly been dropping since the early 1980s. Since the early 1990s, the teen birthrate has decreased by about 20%, with some indications that teenagers have become sexually more conservative. Overall, the percentage of unwed births has remained at its current level for the past five years. Indeed, due to fewer divorces and stabilized unwed births, the percentage of children living in single-parent families dropped slightly in the past few years, after having increased rapidly and continuously since 1960.

27   Moreover, one can see glimmers of hope here and there on the cultural scene. There are stirrings of a grassroots "marriage movement." Churches in several hundred communities have joined together to establish a common set of premarital counseling standards and practices for engaged couples. Marriage education has emerged as a prominent theme among some family therapists, family life educators, schoolteachers, and clergy. In several states, legislatures have passed bills promoting marriage education in the schools and even seeking ways to cut the divorce rate, mainly through educational means. More books are being published with the theme of how to have a good marriage, and seemingly fewer with the theme of divorcing to achieve personal liberation. Questions are being raised more forcefully by members of Congress, on both sides of the aisle, about the "family values" of the entertainment industry. These positive trends bear watching and are encouraging, but it is too soon to tell whether they will persist or result in the revitalization of this critical social institution.

A DEBATE ON GAY MARRIAGE

There are few more hot-button topics in American politics today than gay marriage. In the Defense of Marriage Act of 1996, the federal government defined marriage as the legal union of a man as husband and a woman as wife. Similar legislation has been passed in 38 states. In November 2003, however, the Massachusetts Supreme Court ruled that denying marriage licenses to gay couples violated the state's Equal Protection Clause. The following year, the city of San Francisco began issuing marriage licenses to gay couples. Hundreds of same-sex couples were legally married in the aftermath of these rulings. Responding in outrage, many conservative state legislatures rushed to pass or reaffirm laws banning gay marriage. In July 2006, court rulings in New York, Nebraska, and Washington limited marriage to unions between a man and a woman. In November 2008, Proposition 8, an initiative to ban gay marriage in California, was passed by 52% of voters; the initiative was subsequently upheld by California's Supreme Court.

For Gay Marriage
Andrew Sullivan

The debate over gay marriage highlights a vast cultural divide that typically hinges on core beliefs regarding the nature of marriage itself. In the following selection from Andrew Sullivan's book Virtually Normal: An Argument about Homosexuality *(1995), Sullivan articulates a vision of marriage as a public contract that should be available to any two citizens. Andrew Sullivan is a former editor of the* New Republic *magazine who writes on a wide range of political and social topics, including gay and lesbian issues. He lives in Washington, D.C.*

1   Marriage is not simply a private contract; it is a social and public recognition of a private commitment. As such, it is the highest public recognition of personal integrity. Denying it to homosexuals is the most public affront possible to their public equality.

2   This point may be the hardest for many heterosexuals to accept. Even those tolerant of homosexuals may find this institution so wedded to the notion of heterosexual commitment that to extend it would be to undo its very essence. And there may be religious reasons for resisting this that, within certain traditions, are unanswerable. But I am not here discussing what churches do in their private affairs. I am discussing what the allegedly neutral liberal state should do in public matters. For liberals, the case for homosexual marriage is overwhelming. As a classic public institution, it should be available to any two citizens.

3   Some might argue that marriage is by definition between a man and a woman; and it is difficult to argue with a definition. But if marriage is articulated beyond this circular fiat, then the argument for its exclusivity to one man and one woman disappears. The center of the public contract is an emotional, financial, and psychological bond between two people; in this respect, heterosexuals and homosexuals are identical. The heterosexuality of marriage is intrinsic only if it is understood to be intrinsically procreative; but that definition has long been abandoned in Western society. No civil marriage license is granted on the condition that the couple bear children; and the marriage is no less legal and no less defensible if it remains childless. In the contemporary West, marriage has become a way in which the state recognizes an emotional commitment by two people to each other for life. And within that definition, there is no public way, if one believes in equal rights under the law, in which it should legally be denied homosexuals.

4   Of course, no public sanctioning of a contract should be given to people who cannot actually fulfill it. The state rightly, for example, withholds marriage from minors, or from one adult and a minor, since at least one party is unable to understand or live up to the contract. And the state has also rightly barred close family relatives from marriage because familial emotional ties are too strong and powerful to enable a marriage contract to be entered into freely by two autonomous, independent individuals, and because incest poses a uniquely dangerous threat to the trust and responsibility that the family needs to survive. But do homosexuals fall into a similar category? History and experience strongly suggest they don't. Of course, marriage is characterized by a kind of commitment that is rare—and perhaps declining—even among heterosexuals. But it isn't necessary to prove that homosexuals or lesbians are less—or more—able to form long-term relationships than straights for it to be clear that at least *some* are. Moreover, giving these people an equal right to affirm their commitment doesn't reduce the incentive for heterosexuals to do the same.

5   In some ways, the marriage issue is exactly parallel to the issue of the military. Few people deny that many homosexuals are capable of the sacrifice, the commitment, and the responsibilities of marriage. And indeed,

for many homosexuals and lesbians, these responsibilities are already enjoined—as they have been enjoined for centuries. The issue is whether these identical relationships should be denied equal legal standing, not by virtue of anything to do with the relationships themselves but by virtue of the internal, involuntary nature of the homosexuals involved. Clearly, for liberals, the answer to this is clear. Such a denial is a classic case of unequal protection of the laws.

6   But perhaps surprisingly, . . . one of the strongest arguments for gay marriage is a conservative one. It's perhaps best illustrated by a comparison with the alternative often offered by liberals and liberationists to legal gay marriage, the concept of "domestic partnership." Several cities in the United States have domestic partnership laws, which allow relationships that do not fit into the category of heterosexual marriage to be registered with the city and qualify for benefits that had previously been reserved for heterosexual married couples. In these cities, a variety of interpersonal arrangements qualify for health insurance, bereavement leave, insurance, annuity and pension rights, housing rights (such as rent-control apartments), adoption, and inheritance rights. Eventually, the aim is to include federal income tax and veterans' benefits as well. Homosexuals are not the only beneficiaries; heterosexual "live-togethers" also qualify.

7   The conservative's worries start with the ease of the relationship. To be sure, potential domestic partners have to prove financial interdependence, shared living arrangements, and a commitment to mutual caring. But they don't need to have a sexual relationship or even closely mirror old-style marriage. In principle, an elderly woman and her live-in nurse could qualify, or a pair of frat buddies. Left as it is, the concept of domestic partnership could open a Pandora's box of litigation and subjective judicial decision making about who qualifies. You either are or you're not married; it's not a complex question. Whether you are in a domestic partnership is not so clear.

8   More important for conservatives, the concept of domestic partnership chips away at the prestige of traditional relationships and undermines the priority we give them. Society, after all, has good reasons to extend legal advantages to heterosexuals who choose the formal sanction of marriage over simply living together. They make a deeper commitment to one another and to society; in exchange, society extends certain benefits to them. Marriage provides an anchor, if an arbitrary and often weak one, in the maelstrom of sex and relationships to which we are all prone. It provides a mechanism for emotional stability and economic security. We rig the law in its favor not because we disparage all forms of relationship other than the nuclear family, but because we recognize that not to promote marriage would be to ask too much of human virtue.

9   For conservatives, these are vital concerns. There are virtually no conservative arguments either for preferring no social incentives for gay relationships or for preferring a second-class relationship, such as domestic partnership, which really does provide an incentive for the decline of traditional marriage. Nor, if conservatives are concerned by the collapse of

stable family life, should they be dismayed by the possibility of gay parents. There is no evidence that shows any deleterious impact on a child brought up by two homosexual parents, and considerable evidence that such a parental structure is clearly preferable to single parents (gay or straight) or no effective parents at all, which, alas, is the choice many children now face. Conservatives should not balk at the apparent radicalism of the change involved, either. The introduction of gay marriage would not be some sort of leap in the dark, a massive societal risk. Homosexual marriages have always existed, in a variety of forms; they have just been euphemized. Increasingly they exist in every sense but the legal one. As it has become more acceptable for homosexuals to acknowledge their loves and commitments publicly, more and more have committed themselves to one another for life in full view of their families and friends. A law institutionalizing gay marriage would merely reinforce a healthy trend. Burkean conservatives should warm to the idea.

10   It would also be an unqualified social good for homosexuals. It provides role models for young gay people, who, after the exhilaration of coming out can easily lapse into short-term relationships and insecurity with no tangible goal in sight. My own guess is that most homosexuals would embrace such a goal with as much (if not more) commitment as heterosexuals. Even in our society as it is, many lesbian and gay male relationships are virtual textbooks of monogamous commitment; and for many, "in sickness and in health" has become a vocation rather than a vow. Legal gay marriage could also help bridge the gulf often found between homosexuals and their parents. It could bring the essence of gay life—a gay couple—into the heart of the traditional family in a way the family can most understand and the gay offspring can most easily acknowledge. It could do more to heal the gay-straight rift than any amount of gay rights legislation.

11   More important, perhaps, as gay marriage sank into the subtle background consciousness of a culture, its influence would be felt quietly but deeply among gay children. For them, at last, there would be some kind of future; some older faces to apply to their unfolding lives, some language in which their identity could be properly discussed, some rubric by which it could be explained—not in terms of sex, or sexual practices, or bars, or subterranean activity, but in terms of their future life stories, their potential loves, their eventual chance at some kind of constructive happiness. They would be able to feel by the intimation of myriad examples that in this respect their emotional orientation was not merely about pleasure, or sin, or shame, or otherness (although it might always be involved in many of those things), but about the ability to love and be loved as complete, imperfect human beings. Until gay marriage is legalized, this fundamental element of personal dignity will be denied a whole segment of humanity. No other change can achieve it.

12   Any heterosexual man who takes a few moments to consider what his life would be like if he were never allowed a formal institution to cement his relationships will see the truth of what I am saying. Imagine life with-

out a recognized family; imagine dating without even the possibility of marriage. Any heterosexual woman who can imagine being told at a young age that her attraction to men was wrong, that her loves and crushes were illicit, that her destiny was singlehood and shame, will also appreciate the point. Gay marriage is not a radical step; it is a profoundly humanizing, traditionalizing step. It is the first step in any resolution of the homosexual question—more important than any other institution, since it is the most central institution to the nature of the problem, which is to say, the emotional and sexual bond between one human being and another. If nothing else were done at all, and gay marriage were legalized, 90 percent of the political work necessary to achieve gay and lesbian equality would have been achieved. It is ultimately the only reform that truly matters.

13   So long as conservatives recognize, as they do, that homosexuals exist and that they have equivalent emotional needs and temptations as heterosexuals, then there is no conservative reason to oppose homosexual marriage and many conservative reasons to support it. So long as liberals recognize, as they do, that citizens deserve equal treatment under the law, then there is no liberal reason to oppose it and many liberal reasons to be in favor of it. So long as intelligent people understand that homosexuals are emotionally and sexually attracted to the same sex as heterosexuals are to the other sex, then there is no human reason on earth why it should be granted to one group and not the other.

Against Gay Marriage
William J. Bennett

In the following selection, William J. Bennett, a prominent cultural conservative, explains why he thinks that allowing gays to marry would damage the institution of marriage. Note that Bennett attempts to rebut Andrew Sullivan's pro-gay marriage arguments. Bennett served as chairman of the National Endowment for the Humanities (1981–85) and secretary of education (1985–88) under President Ronald Reagan, and as President George H. W. Bush's "drug czar" (1989–90). His writings on cultural issues in America include The Book of Virtues *(1997) and* The Broken Hearth: Reversing the Moral Collapse of the American Family *(2001). He has served as senior editor of the conservative journal* National Review *and is codirector of Empower America, a conservative advocacy organization. This piece first appeared as an op-ed column in the* Washington Post *on May 21, 1996.*

1   We are engaged in a debate which, in a less confused time, would be considered pointless and even oxymoronic: the question of same-sex marriage.

2   But we are where we are. The Hawaii Supreme Court has discovered a new state constitutional "right"—the legal union of same-sex couples. Unless a "compelling state interest" can be shown against them, Hawaii will become the first state to sanction such unions. And if Hawaii legalizes

same-sex marriages, other states might well have to recognize them because of the Constitution's Full Faith and Credit Clause. Some in Congress recently introduced legislation to prevent this from happening.*

3   Now, anyone who has known someone who has struggled with his homosexuality can appreciate the poignancy, human pain and sense of exclusion that are often involved. One can therefore understand the effort to achieve for homosexual unions both legal recognition and social acceptance. Advocates of homosexual marriages even make what appears to be a sound conservative argument: Allow marriage in order to promote faithfulness and monogamy. This is an intelligent and politically shrewd argument. One can even concede that it might benefit some people. But I believe that overall, allowing same-sex marriages would do significant, long-term social damage.

4   Recognizing the legal union of gay and lesbian couples would represent a profound change in the meaning and definition of marriage. Indeed, it would be the most radical step ever taken in the deconstruction of society's most important institution. It is not a step we ought to take.

5   The function of marriage is not elastic; the institution is already fragile enough. Broadening its definition to include same-sex marriages would stretch it almost beyond recognition—and new attempts to broaden the definition still further would surely follow. On what principled grounds could the advocates of same-sex marriage oppose the marriage of two consenting brothers? How could they explain why we ought to deny a marriage license to a bisexual who wants to marry two people? After all, doing so would be a denial of that person's sexuality. In our time, there are more (not fewer) reasons than ever to preserve the essence of marriage.

6   Marriage is not an arbitrary construct; it is an "honorable estate" based on the different, complementary nature of men and women—and how they refine, support, encourage and complete one another. To insist that we maintain this traditional understanding of marriage is not an attempt to put others down. It is simply an acknowledgment and celebration of our most precious and important social act.

7   Nor is this view arbitrary or idiosyncratic. It mirrors the accumulated wisdom of millennia and the teaching of every major religion. Among worldwide cultures, where there are so few common threads, it is not a coincidence that marriage is almost universally recognized as an act meant to unite a man and a woman.

8   To say that same-sex unions are not comparable to heterosexual marriages is not an argument for intolerance, bigotry or lack of compassion (although I am fully aware that it will be considered so by some). But it is an argument for making distinctions in law about relationships that are themselves distinct. Even Andrew Sullivan, among the most intelligent

---

*As of September 2009, six states (Massachusetts, Connecticut, Vermont, New Hampshire, Maine and Iowa) and the District of Columbia have recognized the right of same-sex couples to marry. Nine states (including Oregon, Washington, and New Jersey) recognize some form of civil union for same-sex couples. Legislatures in several other states are actively debating the issue.

advocates of same-sex marriage, has admitted that a homosexual marriage contract will entail a greater understanding of the need for "extramarital outlets." He argues that gay male relationships are served by the "openness of the contract," and he has written that homosexuals should resist allowing their "varied and complicated lives" to be flattened into a "single, moralistic model."

9   But this "single, moralistic model" is precisely the point. The marriage commitment between a man and a woman does not—it cannot—countenance extramarital outlets. By definition it is not an open contract; its essential idea is fidelity. Obviously that is not always honored in practice. But it is normative, the ideal to which we aspire precisely because we believe some things are right (faithfulness in marriage) and others are wrong (adultery). In insisting that marriage accommodate the less restrained sexual practices of homosexuals, Sullivan and his allies destroy the very thing that supposedly has drawn them to marriage in the first place.

10   There are other arguments to consider against same-sex marriage—for example, the signals it would send, and the impact of such signals on the shaping of human sexuality, particularly among the young. Former Harvard professor E. L. Pattullo has written that "a very substantial number of people are born with the potential to live either straight or gay lives." Societal indifference about heterosexuality and homosexuality would cause a lot of confusion. A remarkable 1993 article in *The Post* supports this point. Fifty teenagers and dozens of school counselors and parents from the local area were interviewed. According to the article, teenagers said it has become "cool" for students to proclaim they are gay or bisexual—even for some who are not. Not surprisingly, the caseload of teenagers in "sexual identity crisis" doubled in one year. "Everything is front page, gay and homosexual," according to one psychologist who works with the schools. "Kids are jumping on it . . . [counselors] are saying, 'What are we going to do with all these kids proclaiming they are bisexual or homosexual when we know they are not?' "

11   If the law recognizes homosexual marriages as the legal equivalent of heterosexual marriages, it will have enormous repercussions in many areas. Consider just two: sex education in the schools and adoption. The sex education curriculum of public schools would have to teach that heterosexual and homosexual marriage are equivalent. "Heather Has Two Mommies" would no longer be regarded as an anomaly; it would more likely become a staple of a sex education curriculum. Parents who want their children to be taught (for both moral and utilitarian reasons) the privileged status of heterosexual marriage will be portrayed as intolerant bigots; they will necessarily be at odds with the new law of matrimony and its derivative curriculum.

12   Homosexual couples will also have equal claim with heterosexual couples in adopting children, forcing us (in law at least) to deny what we know to be true: that it is far better for a child to be raised by a mother and a father than by, say, two male homosexuals.

13   The institution of marriage is already reeling because of the effects of the sexual revolution, no-fault divorce and out-of-wedlock births. We have reaped the consequences of its devaluation. It is exceedingly imprudent to conduct a radical, untested and inherently flawed social experiment on an institution that is the keystone in the arch of civilization. That we have to debate this issue at all tells us that the arch has slipped. Getting it firmly back in place is, as the lawyers say, a "compelling state interest."

The Satisfactions of Housewifery and Motherhood/Paradise Lost (Domestic Division)
Terry Martin Hekker

We begin with a matched set of op-ed columns written nearly 30 years apart for the New York Times *by the same author. At the time her December 20, 1977, column "The Satisfactions of Housewifery and Motherhood" was published, Terry Martin Hekker was a housewife living in South Nyack, New York, who had been married 22 years to her husband, John Hekker, a lawyer and South Nyack village judge. The column deals with Hekker's experiences as a "stay-at-home" mom at a time—the late 1970s—when many women were opting to enter the workforce rather than stay home to raise their children. As a result of the extraordinary response to Hekker's column—some of which she describes in her follow-up 2006 piece, "Paradise Lost"—she expanded the essay into a book,* Ever Since Adam and Eve, *published by William Morrow in 1979. "Paradise Lost" was published on January 1, 2006. Like her first column, it aroused much comment in op-ed pieces and blogs around the nation.*

(1977)

1   My son lied about it on his college application. My husband mutters it under his breath when asked. And I had grown reluctant to mention it myself.

2   The problem is my occupation. But the statistics on women that have come out since the Houston conference have given me a new outlook. I have ceased thinking of myself as obsolete and begun to see myself as I really am—an endangered species. Like the whooping crane and the snow leopard, I deserve attentive nurturing and perhaps a distinctive metal tag on my foot. Because I'm one of the last of the dying breed of human females designated, "Occupation: Housewife."

3   I know it's nothing to crow about. I realize that when people discuss their professions at parties I am more of a pariah than a hooker or a loan shark is. I have been castigated, humiliated and scorned. In an age of do-your-own-thing, it's clear no one meant me. I've been told (patiently and a little louder than necessary, as one does with a small child) that I am an anachronism (except that they avoid such a big word). I have been made to feel so outmoded that I wouldn't be surprised to discover that, like a carton of yogurt, I have an expiration date stamped on my bottom.

4   I once treasured a small hope that history might vindicate me. After all, nursing was once just such a shameful occupation, suitable for only the lowest women. But I abandoned any thought that my occupation would ever become fashionable again, just as I had to stop counting on full-figured women coming back into style. I'm a hundred years too late on both counts.

5   Now, however, thanks to all these new statistics, I see a brighter future for myself. Today, fewer than 16 percent of American families have a full-time housewife-mother. Comparing that with previous figures, at the rate it's going I calculate I am less than eight years away from being the last housewife in the country. And then I intend to be impossible.

6   I shall demand enormous fees to go on talk shows, and will charge for my autograph. Anthropologists will study my feeding and nesting habits through field glasses and keep notebooks detailing my every move. That is, if no one gets the bright idea that I'm so unique that I must be put behind sealed glass like the Book of Kells. In any event, I can expect to be a celebrity and to be pampered. I cannot, though, expect to get even.

7   There's no getting even for years of being regarded as stupid or lazy, or both. For years of being considered unproductive (unless you count five children, which no one does). For years of being viewed as a parasite, living off a man (except by my husband whose opinion doesn't seem to matter). For years of fetching other women's children after they'd thrown up in the lunchroom, because I have nothing better to do, or probably there is nothing I do better, while their mothers have "careers." (Is clerking in a drug store a bona fide career?) For years of caring for five children and a big house and constantly being asked when I'm going to work.

8   I come from a long line of women, most of them more Edith Bunker[*] than Betty Friedan,[†] who never knew they were unfulfilled. I can't testify that they were happy, but they *were* cheerful. And if they lacked "meaningful relationships," they cherished relations who meant something. They took pride in a clean, comfortable home and satisfaction in serving a good meal because no one had explained to them that the only work worth doing is that for which you get paid.

9   They enjoyed rearing their children because no one ever told them that little children belonged in church basements and their mothers belonged somewhere else. They lived, very frugally, on their husbands' paychecks because they didn't realize that it's more important to have a bigger house and a second car than it is to rear your own children. And they were so incredibly ignorant that they died never suspecting they'd been failures.

---

[*]Edith Bunker (wife of Archie Bunker) was a character in the 1970s sitcom *All in the Family;* in the first few years of the series, she was a traditional stay-at-home housewife.

[†]Betty Friedan (1921–2006) was an author and activist; her 1963 book *The Feminine Mystique,* documenting the stifling and vaguely dissatisfied lot of the mid-20th century traditional housewife, launched the "second wave" feminist revolution.

10   That won't hold true for me. I don't yet perceive myself as a failure, but it's not for want of being told I am.

11   The other day, years of condescension prompted me to fib in order to test a theory. At a party where most of the guests were business associates of my husband, a Ms. Putdown asked me who I was. I told her I was Jack Hekker's wife. That had a galvanizing effect on her. She took my hand and asked if that was all I thought of myself—just someone's wife? I wasn't going to let her in on the five children but when she persisted I mentioned them but told her that they weren't mine, that they belonged to my dead sister. And then I basked in the glow of her warm approval.

12   It's an absolute truth that whereas you are considered ignorant to stay home to rear *your* children, it is quite heroic to do so for someone else's children. Being a housekeeper is acceptable (even to the Social Security office) as long as it's not *your* house you're keeping. And treating a husband with attentive devotion is altogether correct as long as he's not *your* husband.

13   Sometimes I feel like Alice in Wonderland. But lately, mostly, I feel like an endangered species.

Paradise Lost (Domestic Division)

(2006)

1   A while back, at a baby shower for a niece, I overheard the expectant mother being asked if she intended to return to work after the baby was born. The answer, which rocked me, was, "Yes, because I don't want to end up like Aunt Terry."

2   That would be me.

3   In the continuing case of Full-Time Homemaker vs. Working Mother, I offer myself as Exhibit A. Because more than a quarter-century ago I wrote an Op-Ed article for *The New York Times* on the satisfaction of being a full-time housewife in the new age of the liberated woman. I wrote it from my heart, thoroughly convinced that homemaking and raising my children was the most challenging and rewarding job I could ever want.

4   "I come from a long line of women," I wrote, "most of them more Edith Bunker than Betty Friedan, who never knew they were unfulfilled. I can't testify that they were happy, but they were cheerful. They took pride in a clean, comfortable home and satisfaction in serving a good meal because no one had explained that the only work worth doing is that for which you get paid."

5   I wasn't advocating that mothers forgo careers to stay home with their children; I was simply defending my choice as a valid one. The mantra of the age may have been "Do your own thing," but as a full-time homemaker, that didn't seem to mean me.

6   The column morphed into a book titled *Ever Since Adam and Eve*, followed by a national tour on which I, however briefly, became the authority on homemaking as a viable choice for women. I ultimately told my story on *Today* and to Dinah Shore, Charlie Rose and even to Oprah, when she was the host of a local TV show in Baltimore.

7   In subsequent years I lectured on the rewards of homemaking and housewifery. While others tried to make the case that women like me were parasites and little more than legalized prostitutes, I spoke to rapt audiences about the importance of being there for your children as they grew up, of the satisfactions of "making a home," preparing family meals and supporting your hard-working husband.

8   So I was predictably stunned and devastated when, on our 40th wedding anniversary, my husband presented me with a divorce. I knew our first anniversary would be paper, but never expected the 40th would be papers, 16 of them meticulously detailing my faults and flaws, the reason our marriage, according to him, was over.

9   We had been married by a bishop with a blessing from the pope in a country church filled with honeysuckle and hope. Five children and six grandchildren later we were divorced by a third-rate judge in a suburban courthouse reeking of dust and despair.

10   Our long marriage had its full share of love, complications, illnesses, joy and stress. Near the end we were in a dismal period, with my husband in treatment for alcoholism. And although I had made more than my share of mistakes, I never expected to be served with divorce papers. I was stunned to find myself, at this stage of life, marooned. And it was small comfort that I wasn't alone. There were many other confused women of my age and circumstance who'd been married just as long, sharing my situation.

11   I was in my teens when I first read Dickens's *Great Expectations*, with the tale of Miss Haversham, who, stood up by her groom-to-be, spent decades in her yellowing wedding gown, sitting at her cobweb-covered bridal banquet table, consumed with plotting revenge. I felt then that to be left waiting at the altar with a church full of people must be the most crushing thing that could happen to a woman.

12   I was wrong. No jilted bride could feel as embarrassed and humiliated as a woman in her 60's discarded by her husband. I was confused and scared, and the pain of being tossed aside by the love of my life made bitterness unavoidable. In those first few bewildering months, as I staggered and wailed through my life, I made Miss Haversham look like a good sport.

13   Sitting around my kitchen with two friends who had also been dumped by their husbands, I figured out that among the three of us we'd been married 110 years. We'd been faithful wives, good mothers, cooks and housekeepers who'd married in the 50's, when "dress for success" meant a wedding gown and "wife" was a tenured position.

14   Turns out we had a lot in common with our outdated kitchen appliances. Like them we were serviceable, low maintenance, front loading, self-cleaning and (relatively) frost free. Also like them we had warranties that

had run out. Our husbands sought sleeker models with features we lacked who could execute tasks we'd either never learned or couldn't perform without laughing.

15   Like most loyal wives of our generation, we'd contemplated eventual widowhood but never thought we'd end up divorced. And "divorced" doesn't begin to describe the pain of this process. "Canceled" is more like it. It began with my credit cards, then my health insurance and checkbook, until, finally, like a used postage stamp, I felt canceled too.

16   I faced frightening losses and was overwhelmed by the injustice of it all. He got to take his girlfriend to Cancun, while I got to sell my engagement ring to pay the roofer. When I filed my first nonjoint tax return, it triggered the shocking notification that I had become eligible for food stamps.

17   The judge had awarded me alimony that was less than I was used to getting for household expenses, and now I had to use that money to pay bills I'd never seen before: mortgage, taxes, insurance and car payments. And that princely sum was awarded for only four years, the judge suggesting that I go for job training when I turned 67. Not only was I unprepared for divorce itself, I was utterly lacking in skills to deal with the brutal aftermath.

18   I read about the young mothers of today—educated, employed, self-sufficient—who drop out of the work force when they have children, and I worry and wonder. Perhaps it is the right choice for them. Maybe they'll be fine. But the fragility of modern marriage suggests that at least half of them may not be.

19   Regrettably, women whose husbands are devoted to their families and are good providers must nevertheless face the specter of future abandonment. Surely the seeds of this wariness must have been planted, even if they can't believe it could ever happen to them. Many have witnessed their own mothers jettisoned by their own fathers and seen divorced friends trying to rear children with marginal financial and emotional support.

20   These young mothers are often torn between wanting to be home with their children and the statistical possibility of future calamity, aware that one of the most poverty-stricken groups in today's society are divorced older women. The feminine and sexual revolutions of the last few decades have had their shining victories, but have they, in the end, made things any easier for mothers?

21   I cringe when I think of that line from my Op-Ed article about the long line of women I'd come from and belonged to who were able to find fulfillment as homemakers "because no one had explained" to us "that the only work worth doing is that for which you get paid." For a divorced mother, the harsh reality is that the work for which you do get paid is the only work that will keep you afloat.

22   These days couples face complex negotiations over work, family, child care and housekeeping. I see my children dealing with these issues in their marriages, and I understand the stresses and frustrations. It becomes evident that where traditional marriage through the centuries had been a partnership based on mutual dependency, modern marriage demands greater self-sufficiency.

23   While today's young women know from the start they'll face thorny decisions regarding careers, marriage and children, those of us who married in the 50's anticipated lives similar to our mothers' and grandmothers'. Then we watched with bewilderment as all the rules changed, and the goal posts were moved.

24   If I had it to do over again, I'd still marry the man I married and have my children: they are my treasure and a powerful support system for me and for one another. But I would have used the years after my youngest started school to further my education. I could have amassed two doctorates using the time and energy I gave to charitable and community causes and been better able to support myself.

25   But in a lucky twist, my community involvement had resulted in my being appointed to fill a vacancy on our Village Board. I had been serving as titular deputy mayor of my hometown (Nyack, N.Y.) when my husband left me. Several weeks later the mayor chose not to run again because of failing health, and I was elected to succeed him, becoming the first female mayor.

26   I held office for six years, a challenging, full-time job that paid a whopping annual salary of $8,000. But it consumed me and gave me someplace to go every day and most nights, and as such it saved my sanity. Now, mostly retired except for some part-time work, I am kept on my toes by 12 amazing grandchildren.

27   My anachronistic book was written while I was in a successful marriage that I expected would go on forever. Sadly, it now has little relevance for modern women, except perhaps as a cautionary tale: never its intended purpose. So I couldn't imagine writing a sequel. But my friend Elaine did come up with a perfect title: "Disregard First Book."

A Mother's Day Kiss-Off
Leslie Bennetts

Hekker's bitter experience in the wake of her divorce, particularly her sense of abandonment and lack of preparedness to enter the world of work and earn her own living, is all too typical of many women in her situation. In the following selection, Leslie Bennetts, a contributing editor at Vanity Fair *since 1988, and the author of* The Feminine Mistake (2008) *further explores these issues. Echoing Hekker, Bennetts has written of the "millions of women [who] continue to be misled by the fairy-tale version of life, in which Prince Charming comes along and takes care of you forever."*

This passage first appeared as an op-ed in the Los Angeles Times *on Mother's Day 2007 (May 13), alongside the Deborah Tannen piece that immediately follows.*

1 This morning, millions of proud mothers will be presented with special, homemade breakfasts by their beaming children. There will be Mother's

Day presents and cards, including precious handmade creations from the kids and joking or romantic ones from Dad.

2 But then the world, having made its annual perfunctory nod to the contributions of American mothers, will move on, leaving us once again to cope with our inordinate responsibilities, largely on our own.

3 Those responsibilities—and the personal sacrifices they typically entail—generate a permanent state of simmering anger in all too many women. Some deny it even to themselves. But the evidence is everywhere.

4 Last month, a *Washington Post* review of my new book asked why it is that so many mothers are so angry. After noting that lack of sleep doesn't fully explain this pervasive phenomenon, the writer suggested that motherhood represents the first time most women run headfirst into fundamental inequities—not just the biological differences between men and women but also the disproportionate burdens imposed by a culture that still regards the raising of children as the mother's responsibility.

5 The result is often a painful collision between family needs and workplace realities. Even all these years after the women's movement emerged, working mothers must still confront the intransigence of a corporate culture whose extreme hours, inflexible structures and hostility toward caretaking needs can make the juggling act very difficult. Most husbands still view child care and household chores as women's work, even when those women are working full time.

6 Stressed and resentful, the majority of women nonetheless continue to work, many out of financial necessity. Others quit their jobs to stay home, although the price may include conflicted feelings about having had to make such a "choice."

7 Both working mothers and stay-at-home moms have good reason for resentment, but it's the latter group that is most at risk. Although our culture tends to romanticize full-time motherhood, forgoing an independent income can make mothers and their children profoundly vulnerable to economic hardship, among other problems.

8 If a breadwinner dies, divorces his wife or becomes unemployed, homemakers often cannot find decent jobs to support their families. Years later, they often remain shocked and furious as well as grief-stricken, feeling deeply betrayed.

9 But even among women who enjoy stable marriages with employed spouses, many wives who give up their careers to stay home are also angry. While researching a book about the dangers of economic dependency and the rewards of work, I interviewed a woman who had wanted to be a lawyer since she was in second grade. As a successful commercial litigator, she regarded stay-at-home wives with disdain—until she had children and found that her employer's unforgiving demands made it impossible for her to continue to excel at her own job, and that her husband's heavy travel schedule and brutal work hours made it equally impossible for him to share the child-care duties with her.

10 "It was horrible," she said. "My husband understood my stress level, but his answer was, 'Then *you* leave work.' It was my problem."

11   So she became a stay-at-home mother, even as she continued to seethe about the sacrifice she had been forced to make. Months after our interview, when she received a pre-publication copy of my book, she was so upset by the explosiveness of her own words on the page that she asked me to change her name, which I did.

12   But her decision made me sad. Having given up a career she loved to accept domestic responsibilities she often found to be thankless, she then gave up even her right to sound off about it without hiding behind a pseudonym. Her retreat seemed like a powerful metaphor for the ways in which women sacrifice parts of themselves that they shouldn't have to give up. Frightened by the toxic feelings that result, they then sacrifice their own voices, feeling that they must even refrain from admitting how angry they really are.

13   But their resentment often festers just below the surface of their lives, erupting into full-blown rage at the slightest provocation. Sometimes it's directed against their husbands for not sharing the domestic burdens in a remotely equitable manner. Often, however, this anger is directed against other women, as in the vicious back-and-forth of the so-called Mommy Wars.

14   Since publishing my book, I have been pilloried in print and in cyberspace by hundreds of enraged stay-at-home mothers who have attacked everything from my appearance to my marriage and children. Their rage is genuinely frightening, as is their choice of targets. Ridiculing my weight or writing that my kids must be "scarred and dysfunctional" because I'm a working mother doesn't exactly advance the public debate over important work-family issues.

15   And yet the real problems are systemic, not personal. Women are indeed giving up too much, which may be why so many are so angry.

16   We accept unacceptable inequities in the workplace, quitting and retiring to our homes instead of organizing to demand reforms. Why do any of us accept the fact that childless women earn 10% less than their male counterparts, or that women with children earn 27% less, or that single mothers earn up to 44% less?

17   We accommodate our husbands' careers at the expense of our own interests, thereby leaving ourselves and our children vulnerable to future hardship. Can any of us defend the fact that women's standard of living drops by 36% after divorce, whereas that of men rises by 28%?

18   We put up with elected officials who pay lip service to family values but do little or nothing to address the real needs of American families, from flexible work schedules to affordable, quality child care.

19   Compared with other Western nations, the family-related policies of the United States are a disgrace. The United States and Australia are the only industrialized countries that don't provide paid maternity leave by law.

20   But nothing will change here until we insist on it. And men won't truly commit themselves to the effort until they too must be responsive to family needs. It's only when fathers as well as mothers get the call from the school nurse at 11:30 a.m. that their 6-year-old is vomiting and has to be picked up

immediately that men will understand the need for workplace flexibility—
and the imperative to make it happen.

21   It's long past time for women to stop venting their anger on each other
and redirect it to changing the institutions, policies and practices that
oppress us all. We need solutions, not scapegoats.

22   Mother's Day would be an even happier occasion if it didn't leave so
many women feeling that their most important concerns had been kissed
off by a greeting card holiday.

Understanding Mom
Deborah Tannen

Professional women often confront a generational gap when discussing their life choices with their mothers, who grew up assuming that the highest calling of a woman was to marry, raise children, and run a household. In the following piece, Deborah Tannen stands her ground as she justifies her choice to divorce her husband and return to school; at the same time, she makes a generous and touching effort to understand the worlds of gender and marriage from her mother's perspective.

Deborah Tannen is a linguist who teaches at George Washington University in Washington, D.C. She has published numerous articles and books on interpersonal communication, social interaction, and public discourse. Her book You Just Don't Understand: Women and Men in Conversation *(1990) remained on the* New York Times *Best Sellers list for four years. She has written nine other books, including* That's Not What I Meant! How Conversational Style Makes or Breaks Relationships *(1986) and* You're Wearing That?: Mothers and Daughters in Conversation *(2006).*

This article first appeared as an op-ed in the Los Angeles Times *on Mother's Day 2007 (May 13), opposite Leslie Bennetts's, which precedes it in this chapter.*

1   "My mother never saw me," several women have told me.

2   I think they meant that their mothers didn't perceive—or didn't value—
the qualities these women most valued in themselves. But I wonder how
many of us really saw our mothers.

3   My mother wanted for me the gifts of an ordinary life—a husband, children, a comfortable home. What I wanted was anything but. As a teenager, I identified with the heroine of "The Fantasticks," who whispered,
"Please God, don't let me be ordinary."

4   Growing up in the 1960s, I disdained makeup even as my mother insisted, "Put on a little lipstick when you go out with me." My passion for
books was so consuming that I frequently read while walking home from
school—so engrossed that I didn't see my mother standing on the porch,
worrying that I'd trip and fall on the sidewalk. And when I divorced at 29,

my mother was not pleased that I decided to enroll in graduate school and work toward a doctorate instead of working toward finding a replacement husband.

5   All that time, I was convinced that it was unfair of my mother to scorn my values. It didn't occur to me that it was unfair of me to scorn hers.

6   Soon after I received my doctorate and joined the faculty at Georgetown University, my mother visited me. I was eager to prove to her that my life was good even though I hadn't remarried. I showed her my office with my name on the door and my publications on the shelf, hoping that she'd be proud of my success. And she was. But then she asked, "Do you think you would have accomplished all this if you'd stayed married?"

7   "I'm sure I wouldn't have," I replied. "If I'd stayed married, I wouldn't have gone back to school to get a PhD."

8   My mother thought for a moment, then said, "Well, if you'd stayed married, you wouldn't have had to."

9   I have told this story often, knowing my listeners would groan or gasp at how my mother hurtfully denigrated my professional success, caring only about my marital state. More recently, however, I tell this story for a different purpose: to understand her point of view.

10   My mother was born in Russia in 1911 and came to the United States before she turned 12. She left high school without graduating because she had to go to work to help support her family. What on Earth was she to make of a woman getting a doctorate and becoming a university professor—and of this unimaginable fate befalling her own daughter?

11   Surely every mother is proud of a daughter who soars. But from the perspective of the earthbound onlooker, a soaring daughter is receding in the sky, heading toward a universe her mother cannot know. Along with pride must come the pain of separation and of loss—plus the jolt of seeing the child she reared behaving as if she were an entirely different species.

12   Faced with the trappings of my professional life, my mother was probably trying to figure out how it all had happened. In her world, marriage ensured a woman's financial stability. An unmarried woman had to achieve that goal by going to work. "If you had stayed married, you wouldn't have had to" reflects this view.

13   Thinking of my mother's perspective reminds me of a remark a woman once made to me. "The shock of my life," she said, "was that my daughter didn't turn out exactly like me."

14   Though my mother would not have put that insight into words, I'll bet it describes what she was grappling with: trying to make sense of a life so different from any she could have imagined for herself.

15   We want our mothers to see us and love us for who we are, but we are often disappointed in them for falling short of who we think they should be. Mother's Day is a good time to try to see our mothers and love them for who they are: creations of their lives and their worlds, which doubtless are different from our own.

American Marriage in Transition
Andrew J. Cherlin

How has the institution of marriage changed in the United States during the past sixty years? In the following selection—originally titled "The Deinstitutionalization of American Marriage," Andrew J. Cherlin, a sociologist at Johns Hopkins University, attempts to answer this question. Cherlin defines "deinstitutionalization" as "the weakening of the social norms that define people's behavior in a social institution such as marriage." These norms include such tacit or explicit understandings regarding which partner assumes the role of chief breadwinner, which assumes the role of chief homemaker; which is the chief source of authority, which is the "loyal and supportive spouse."

Andrew Cherlin specializes in the sociology of families and public policy. He has published numerous books and articles on marriage and divorce, children's well-being, intergenerational relations, family policy, and welfare policy. The following is an excerpted version of an article that first appeared in the Journal of Marriage and Family *in November 2004.*

1 By 1978, the changing division of labor in the home and the increase in childbearing outside marriage were undermining the *institutionalized* basis of marriage. The distinct roles of homemaker and breadwinner were fading as more married women entered the paid labor force. Looking into the future, I thought that perhaps an equitable division of household labor might become institutionalized. But what happened instead was the "stalled revolution," in Hochschild's (1989) well-known phrase. Men do somewhat more home work than they used to do, but there is wide variation, and each couple must work out their own arrangement without clear guidelines. In addition, in 1978 1 out of 6 births in the United States occurred outside marriage, already a much higher ratio than at midcentury (U.S. National Center for Health Statistics, 1982). Today, the comparable figure is 1 out of 3 (U.S. National Center for Health Statistics, 2003). The percentage is similar in Canada (Statistics Canada, 2003) and in the United Kingdom and Ireland (Kiernan, 2002). In the Nordic countries of Denmark, Iceland, Norway, and Sweden, the figure ranges from about 45% to about 65% (Kiernan). Marriage is no longer the nearly universal setting for childbearing that it was a half century ago.

. . .

Two Transitions in the Meaning of Marriage

2 In a larger sense, the changing division of labor, childbearing outside of marriage, cohabitation, and gay marriage are the result of long-term cultural and material trends that altered the meaning of marriage during the 20th century. The cultural trends included, first, an emphasis on emotional satisfaction and romantic love that intensified early in the century. Then, during the last few decades of the century, an ethic of expressive individualism—which Bellah, Marsden, Sullivan, Swidler, &

Tipton (1985) describe as the belief that "each person has a unique core of feeling and intuition that should unfold or be expressed if individuality is to be realized" (p. 334)—became more important. On the material side, the trends include the decline of agricultural labor and the corresponding increase in wage labor; the decline in child and adult mortality; rising standards of living; and, in the last half of the 20th century, the movement of married women into the paid workforce.

3   These developments, along with historical events such as the Depression and World War II, produced two great changes in the meaning of marriage during the 20th century. Ernest Burgess famously labeled the first one as a transition "from an institution to a companionship" (Burgess & Locke, 1945). In describing the rise of the *companionate marriage,* Burgess was referring to the single-earner, breadwinner-homemaker marriage that flourished in the 1950s. Although husbands and wives in the companionate marriage usually adhered to a sharp division of labor, they were supposed to be each other's companions—friends, lovers—to an extent not imagined by the spouses in the institutional marriages of the previous era. The increasing focus on bonds of sentiment within nuclear families constituted an important but limited step in the individualization of family life. Much more so than in the 19th century, the emotional satisfaction of the spouses became an important criterion for marital success. However, through the 1950s, wives and husbands tended to derive satisfaction from their participation in a marriage-based nuclear family (Roussel, 1989). That is to say, they based their gratification on playing marital roles well: being good providers, good homemakers, and responsible parents.

4   During this first change in meaning, marriage remained the only socially acceptable way to have a sexual relationship and to raise children in the United States, Canada, and Europe, with the possible exception of the Nordic countries. In his history of British marriages, Gillis (1985) labeled the period from 1850 to 1960 the "era of mandatory marriage." In the United States, marriage and only marriage was one's ticket of admission to a full family life. Prior to marrying, almost no one cohabited with a partner except among the poor and the avant garde. As recently as the 1950s, premarital cohabitation in the United States was restricted to a small minority (perhaps 5%) of the less educated (Bumpass, Sweet, & Cherlin, 1991). In the early 1950s, only about 4% of children were born outside marriage (U.S. National Center for Health Statistics, 1982). In fact, during the late 1940s and the 1950s, major changes that increased the importance of marriage occurred in the life course of young adults. More people married—about 95% of young adults in the United States in the 1950s, compared with about 90% early in the century (Cherlin, 1992)—and they married at younger ages. Between 1900 and 1960, the estimated median age at first marriage in the United States fell from 26 to 23 for men, and from 22 to 20 for women (U.S. Census Bureau, 2003a). The birth rate, which had been falling for a century or more, increased sharply, creating the "baby boom." The post-World War II increase in marriage and childbearing also occurred in many European countries (Roussel, 1989).

5   But beginning in the 1960s, marriage's dominance began to diminish, and the second great change in the meaning of marriage occurred. In the United States, the median age at marriage returned to and then exceeded the levels of the early 1900s. In 2000, the median age was 27 for men and 25 for women (U.S. Census Bureau, 2003a). Many young adults stayed single into their mid to late 20s, some completing college educations and starting careers. Cohabitation prior to (and after) marriage became much more acceptable. Childbearing outside marriage became less stigmatized and more accepted. Birth rates resumed their long-term declines and sunk to all-time lows in most countries. Divorce rates rose to unprecedented levels. Same-sex unions found greater acceptance as well.

6   During this transition, the companionate marriage lost ground not only as the demographic standard but also as a cultural ideal. It was gradually overtaken by forms of marriage (and non-marital, families) that Burgess had not foreseen, particularly marriages in which both the husband and the wife worked outside the home. Although women continued to do most of the housework and child care, the roles of wives and husbands became more flexible and open to negotiation. And an even more individualistic perspective on the rewards of marriage took root. When people evaluated how satisfied they were with their marriages, they began to think more in terms of the development of their own sense of self and the expression of their feelings, as opposed to the satisfaction they gained through building a family and playing the roles of spouse and parent. The result was a transition from the companionate marriage to what we might call the *individualized marriage.*

7   The transition to the individualized marriage began in the 1960s and accelerated in the 1970s, as shown by an American study of the changing themes in popular magazine articles offering marital advice in every decade between 1900 and 1979 (Cancian, 1987). The author identified three themes that characterized beliefs about the post-1960-style marriage. The first was self-development: Each person should develop a fulfilling, independent self instead of merely sacrificing oneself to one's partner. The second was that roles within marriage should be flexible and negotiable. The third was that communication and openness in confronting problems are essential. She then tallied the percentage of articles in each decade that contained one or more of these three themes. About one third of the articles in the first decade of the century, and again at mid-century, displayed these themes, whereas about two thirds displayed these themes in the 1970s. The author characterized this transition as a shift in emphasis "from role to self" (Cancian).

8   During this second change in the meaning of marriage, the role of the law changed significantly as well. This transformation was most apparent in divorce law. In the United States and most other developed countries, legal restrictions on divorce were replaced by statutes that recognized consensual and even unilateral divorce. The transition to "private ordering" (Mnookin & Kornhauser, 1979) allowed couples to negotiate the details of their divorce agreements within broad limits. Most European nations experienced similar legal developments (Glendon, 1989; Théry,

1993). Indeed, French social demographer Louis Roussel (1989) wrote of a "double deinstitutionalization" in behavior and in law: a greater hesitation of young adults to enter into marriage, combined with a loosening of the legal regulation of marriage.

9   Sociological theorists of late modernity (or postmodernity) such as Anthony Giddens (1991, 1992) in Britain and Ulrich Beck and Elisabeth Beck-Gemsheim in Germany (1995, 2002) also have written about the growing individualization of personal life. Consistent with the idea of deinstitutionalization, they note the declining power of social norms and laws as regulating mechanisms for family life, and they stress the expanding role of personal choice. They argue that as traditional sources of identity such as class, religion, and community lose influence, one's intimate relationships become central to self-identity. Giddens (1991, 1992) writes of the emergence of the "pure relationship": an intimate partnership entered into for its own sake, which lasts only as long as both partners are satisfied with the rewards (mostly intimacy and love) that they get from it. It is in some ways the logical extension of the increasing individualism and the deinstitutionalization of marriage that occurred in the 20th century. The pure relationship is not tied to an institution such as marriage or to the desire to raise children. Rather, it is "free-floating," independent of social institutions or economic life. Unlike marriage, it is not regulated by law, and its members do not enjoy special legal rights. It exists primarily in the realms of emotion and self-identity.

10   Although the theorists of late modernity believe that the quest for intimacy is becoming the central focus of personal life, they do not predict that *marriage* will remain distinctive and important. Marriage, they claim, has become a choice rather than a necessity for adults who want intimacy, companionship, and children. According to Beck and Beck-Gernsheim (1995), we will see "a huge variety of ways of living together or apart which will continue to exist side by side" (pp. 141–142). Giddens (1992) even argues that marriage has already become "just one life-style among others" (p. 154), although people may not yet realize it because of institutional lag.

The Current Context of Marriage

11 Overall, research and writing on the changing meaning of marriage suggest that it is now situated in a very different context than in the past. This is true in at least two senses. First, individuals now experience a vast latitude for choice in their personal lives. More forms of marriage and more alternatives to marriage are socially acceptable. Moreover, one may fit marriage into one's life in many ways: One may first live with a partner, or sequentially with several partners, without an explicit consideration of whether a marriage will occur. One may have children with one's eventual spouse or with someone else before marrying. One may, in some jurisdictions, marry someone of the same gender and build a shared marital world with few guidelines to rely on. Within marriage, roles are more flexible and negotiable, although women still do more than their share of the household work and childrearing.

12   The second difference is in the nature of the rewards that people seek through marriage and other close relationships. Individuals aim for personal growth and deeper intimacy through more open communication and mutually shared disclosures about feelings with their partners. They may feel justified in insisting on changes in a relationship that no longer provides them with individualized rewards. In contrast, they are less likely than in the past to focus on the rewards to be found in fulfilling socially valued roles such as the good parent or the loyal and supportive spouse. The result of these changing contexts has been a deinstitutionalization of marriage, in which social norms about family and personal life count for less than they did during the heyday of the companionate marriage, and far less than during the period of the institutional marriage. Instead, personal choice and self-development loom large in people's construction of their marital careers.

· · ·

The Symbolic Significance of Marriage

13 What has happened is that although the practical importance of being married has declined, its symbolic importance has remained high, and may even have increased. Marriage is at once less dominant and more distinctive than it was. It has evolved from a marker of conformity to a marker of prestige. Marriage is a status one builds up to, often by living with a partner beforehand, by attaining steady employment or starting a career, by putting away some savings, and even by having children. Marriage's place in the life course used to come before those investments were made, but now it often comes afterward. It used to be the foundation of adult personal life; now it is sometimes the capstone. It is something to be achieved through one's own efforts rather than something to which one routinely accedes.

The Myth of Co-Parenting: How It Was Supposed to Be. How It Was.
Hope Edelman

The previous selections in the chapter (Hekker excepted) have dealt with issues of modern marriage from a journalistic, scholarly, or activist viewpoint. In the following two essays, two professional writers—a woman and a man—offer personal perspectives on their own marriages. You are already familiar with some of the issues they will discuss. What is distinctive about these selections is their tone: The writing is by turns raw, wounded, angry, and defensive and offers an unflinchingly honest, if brutal, assessment of each writer's marriage. These essays strikingly reveal the miscommunication and resentment that can afflict even mature, thoughtful, dedicated couples. In the first, Hope Edelman describes the disillusionment and anger she felt when, after the birth of their child, her husband immersed himself in his career, leaving her to run their household alone.

Hope Edelman has written three nonfiction books, including Motherless Daughters *(1995). Her essays and articles have appeared in the* New York Times, *the* Chicago Tribune, *the* San Francisco Chronicle, *and* Seventeen *magazine. She lives with her husband and two children in Los Angeles. This essay was written for the anthology* The Bitch in the House *(2002).*

1 Throughout much of 1999 and 2000, my husband spent quite a lot of time at work. By "quite a lot" I mean the kind of time Fermilab scientists spent trying to split the atom, which is to say, every waking moment. The unofficial count one week came in at ninety-two hours, which didn't include cell phone calls answered on grocery checkout lines or middle-of-the-night brainstorms that had to be e-mailed before dawn. Often I would wake at 3:00 A.M. and find him editing a business plan down in the living room, drinking herbal tea in front of his laptop's ethereal glow. If he had been a lawyer tallying billable hours, he would have made some firm stinking rich.

2   He was launching an Internet company back then, and these were the kind of hours most people in his industry were putting in. Phrases like "window of opportunity" and "ensuring our long-term security" were bandied about our house a lot, usually during the kind of exasperating late-night conversations that began with "The red-eye to New York? *Again?*" and included "I mean, it's not like you're trying to find a cure for cancer," somewhere within. I was working nearly full-time myself, though it soon became clear this would have to end. Our daughter was a year and a half old, and the phrase "functionally orphaned" was also getting thrown around our house a lot, usually by me.

3   So as my husband's work hours exponentially increased, I started cutting back on mine. First a drop from thirty-five per week to twenty-five, and then a dwindle down to about eighteen. At first I didn't really mind. With the exception of six weeks postpartum, this was the first time since high school that I had a good excuse not to work like a maniac, and I was grateful for the break. Still, there was something more than vaguely unsettling about feeling that my choice hadn't been much of an actual choice. When one parent works ninety-two hours a week, the other one, by necessity, has to start picking up the slack. Otherwise, some fairly important things—like keeping the refrigerator stocked, or filing income taxes, or finding a reliable baby-sitter, not to mention giving a child some semblance of security and consistency around this place, for God's sake— won't get done. A lot of slack was starting to pile up around our house. And because I was the only parent spending any real time there, the primary de-slacker was me.

4   How did I feel about this? I don't mind saying. I was extremely pissed off.

5   Like virtually every woman friend I have, I entered marriage with the belief that co-parenting was an attainable goal. In truth, it was more of a vague assumption, a kind of imagined parity I had superimposed on the idea of marriage without ever really thinking it through. *If I'm going to contribute half of the income, then he'll contribute half of the housework and child care.* Like that. If you'd asked me to elaborate, I would have said something impassioned and emphatic, using terms like "shared responsibility" and

"equal division of labor." The watered-down version of feminism I identified with espoused those catchphrases, and in lieu of a more sophisticated blueprint for domestic life, I co-opted the talk as my own. But really, I
didn't know what I was talking about beyond the fact that I didn't want to
be the dominant parent in the house.

6   When I was growing up in suburban New York, my mother seemed to
do everything. *Everything.* Carpooling, haircuts, vet appointments, ice
cream cakes, dinners in the Crock-Pot, book-report dioramas—the whole
roll call for a housewife of the 1960s and 1970s. My father, from my child's
point of view, did three things. He came home from work in time for
dinner. He sat at the kitchen table once a month and paid the bills. And, on
weekend trips, he drove the car. Certainly he did much more than that,
including earn all of our family's income, but my mother's omnipresence
in our household meant that anyone else felt, well, incidental in comparison. The morning after she died, of breast cancer at forty-two, my younger
siblings and I sat at the kitchen table with our father as dawn filtered
through the yellow window shades. I looked at him sitting there, in a polo
shirt and baseball cap, suddenly so small beneath his collapsed shoulders.
I was barely seventeen. He was fifty-one. *Huh,* I thought. *Who are* you?

7   There were no chore charts taped to the refrigerator, no family pow-
wows, no enthusiastic TV nannies suddenly materializing outside our
front door. My father taught himself to use a microwave and I started driving my siblings for their haircuts and that, as they say, was that.

8   My cousin Lorraine, a devout Baha'i, once told me it doesn't matter how
many orgasms a potential husband gives you; what really matters is the
kind of father he'll be. At first I thought she said this because Baha'is dis-
avow premarital sex, but the more men I dated, the more I realized
Lorraine was right. Loyalty and devotion are undoubtedly better traits to
have in a spouse than those fleeting moments of passion, though I can't
deny the importance of the latter. When I met John, it was like winning the
boyfriend jackpot. He was beautiful and sexy, and devoted and smart, *so*
smart, and he had the kindest green eyes. The first time I saw those eyes,
when I was negotiating an office sublease from him in New York, he
smiled right at me and it happened, just the way you dream about when
you're twelve: I knew this was someone I would love. *And* he wanted children, which immediately separated him from a cool three-quarters of the
men I'd dated before. I was thirty-two when we started dating, and just
becoming acutely aware that I didn't have unlimited time to wait.

9   What happened next happened fast. Within two years, John and I were
parents and homeowners in a canyon outside Los Angeles. By then he was
deep into the process of starting his own company, which left us with barely
an hour to spend together at the end of each day. And even though I so badly
wanted him to succeed, to get the acclaim a smart, hardworking, honest
person deserves—and even though I was grateful that his hard, honest work
earned enough to support us both—well, let me put it bluntly. Back there
when I was single and imagining the perfect partnership? This wasn't what
I had in mind.

10   When John became so scarce around our house, I had to compensate by being utterly present in every way: as a kisser of boo-boos; a dispenser of discipline; an employer of baby-sitters; an assembler of child furniture; a scary-monster slayer, mortgage refinancer, reseeder of dying backyards. And that's before I even opened my office door for the day. Balancing act? I was the whole damn circus, all three rings.

11   It began to make me spitting mad, the way the daily duties of parenting and home ownership started to rest entirely on me. It wasn't even the additional work I minded as much as the total responsibility for every decision made. The frustration I felt after researching and visiting six preschools during my so-called work hours, trying to do a thorough job for both of us, and then having John offhandedly say, "Just pick the one you like best." Or the irritation I felt when, after three weeks of weighing the options, I finally made the choice, and then he raised his eyebrows at the cost. *I didn't sign up for this!* I began shouting at my sister over the phone.

12   How does it happen, I wondered both then and now, that even today, in this post–second wave, post-superwoman, dual-income society we're supposed to live in, the mother nearly always becomes the primary parent, even when she, too, works full-time—the one who meets most or all of the children's and the household's minute-by-minute needs? We start out with such grand intentions for sharing the job, yet ultimately how many fathers handle the dental appointments, shop for school clothes, or shuttle pets to and from the vet? Nine times out of ten, it's still the mother who plans and emcees the birthday parties, the mother who cuts the meeting short when the school nurse calls. Women have known about this Second Shift for years, the way the workday so often starts up again for women when they walk through the door at the end of the *other* workday—a time mandated perhaps by the baby-sitter's deadline, but also by their own guilt, sense of responsibility, tendency to prioritize their husband's job first, or a combination of all three. Still, I—like many other enlightened, equality-oriented women having babies in this era—had naïvely thought that a pro-feminist partner, plus my own sheer will power, would prevent this from happening to me. I hadn't bargained for how deeply the gender roles of "nurturer" and "provider" are ingrained in us all, or—no matter how much I love being a mother to my daughter—how much I would grow to resent them.

13   When it became clear that my husband and I were not achieving the kind of co-parenting I'd so badly wanted us to achieve, I felt duped and infuriated and frustrated and, beneath it all, terribly, impossibly sad. Sad for myself, and sad for my daughter, who—just like me as a child—had so little one-on-one time with her father. No matter how sincerely John and I tried to buck convention, no matter how often I was the one who sat down at the kitchen table to pay the bills, there we were: he absorbed in his own world of work, me consumed by mine at home. My parents all over again.

14   The intensity of John's workplace was, originally, supposed to last for six months, then for another six months, then for only about three months more. But there was always some obstacle on the horizon: first-round fund-

ing, second-round funding, hirings, firings, had to train a sales force, had to meet a new goal. And meetings, all those meetings. Seven in the morning, nine at night. How were all those other dot-com wives managing?

15   There was no time together for anything other than the most pragmatic exchanges. When he walked through the door at 10:00 P.M., I'd lunge at him with paint chips to approve, or insurance forms to sign, or leaks to examine before I called the plumber first thing in the morning. Fourteen hours of conversation compressed into twenty highly utilitarian minutes before we fell, exhausted, into bed. A healthy domestic situation, it was not.

16   I was angry with the kind of anger that had nothing to do with rationality. A lot of the time, I was mad at Gloria Steinem for having raised women's expectations when I was just a toddler—but at least she lived by her principles, marrying late and never trying to raise kids; so then I got mad at Betty Friedan for having started it all with *The Feminine Mystique*, and when that wasn't satisfying enough, I got mad at all the women in my feminist criticism class in graduate school, the ones who'd sat there and so smugly claimed it was impossible for a strong-willed woman to ever have an equal partnership with a man. Because it was starting to look as if they'd been right.

17   But mostly I was mad at John, because he'd never actually sat down with me to say, "This is what starting a dot-com company will involve," or even, "I'd like to do this—what do you think?"—the way I imagine I would have with him before taking on such a demanding project (which, of course, we'd then have realized together was not feasible unless he quit his job or cut back dramatically, which—of course—was out of the question). Legitimate or not, I felt that at least partly because he was "the husband" and his earning power currently eclipsed mine, his career took precedence, and I had to pick up the household slack, to the detriment of my own waning career—or in addition to it. Before our marriage, I had never expected that. I don't remember the conversation where I asked him to support me financially in exchange for me doing everything else. In fact, I'd never wanted that and still decidedly didn't. I was not only happy to put in my portion of the income (though it would inevitably be less than usual during any year I birthed and breast-fed an infant), I expected to and *wanted* to contribute as much as I could: Part of who I was—what defined me and constituted a main source of my happiness and vitality—was my longtime writing and teaching career. I didn't want to give it up, but I also didn't want hired professionals running my household and raising my child. It felt like an impossible catch-22.

. . .

18 Face-to-face, John and I didn't give ultimatums. At first, we didn't even argue much out loud. Instead we engaged in a kind of low-level quibbling where the stakes were comfortably low. Little digs that didn't mean much in isolation but eventually started to add up. Like bickering about whose fault it was we never took vacations. (He said mine, I said his.) And whether we should buy our daughter a swing set. (I said yes, he said not now.) And about who forgot to roll the trash cans to the bottom of the driveway, again. (Usually him.)

19   I'd been through therapy. I knew the spiel. How you were supposed to
say, "When you're gone all the time, it makes me feel angry and resentful
and lonely," instead of, "How much longer do you realistically think I'm
going to put up with this crap?" I tried that first approach, and there was
something to it, I admit. John listened respectfully. He asked what he could
do to improve. Then it was his turn. He told me how he'd begun to feel like
a punching bag in our home. How my moods ruled our household, how
sometimes he felt like wilting when he heard that sharp edge in my voice.
Then he said he was sorry and I said I was sorry, and he said he'd try to be
home more and I said I'd try to lighten up. And this would work, for a while.
Until the night John would say he'd be home at eight to put Maya to bed but
would forget to call about the last-minute staff meeting that started at six,
and when he'd walk through the door at ten I'd be too pissed off to even say
hello. Instead, I'd snap, "How much longer do you realistically think I'm
going to put up with this crap?" And the night would devolve from there.

20   Neither of us was "wrong." Neither was completely right. The culpability was shared. Both of us were stuck together on that crazy carousel,
where the more time John spent away from home, the more pissed off I got,
and the more pissed off I got, the less he wanted to be around.

. . .

21 One day I said fuck it, and I took John's credit card and bought a swing set.
Not one of those fancy redwood kinds that look like a piece of the Alamo,
but a sturdy wood one nonetheless with a tree house at the top of the slide,
and I paid for delivery and assembly, too. On the way home I stopped at
one of those places that sell the fancy redwood kind and ordered a play-
ground-quality bucket swing for another seventy bucks.

22   Fuck it.

23   There were other purchases I'd made like this, without John's
involvement—the silk bedroom curtains, the Kate Spade wallet I didn't
really need—each one thrilling me with a momentary, devilish glee. But
the swing set: the swing set was my gutsiest act of rebellion thus far.
Still, when it was fully installed on our side lawn, the cloth roof of the
tree house gently flapping in the breeze, I felt oddly unfulfilled. Because,
after all, what had I really achieved? My daughter had a swing set, but
I was still standing on the grass by myself, furiously poking at gopher
holes with my foot, thinking about whether I'd have time on Thursday
to reseed the lawn alone. When what I really wanted was for my husband to say, "Honey, let me help you with that reseeding, and then we'll
all three go out for dinner together." I just wanted him to come home, to
share with me—and Maya—all the joys and frustrations and responsibilities of domestic life.

24   On bad days, when the baby-sitter canceled or another short-notice
business trip had just been announced, he would plead with me to hire a
full-time nanny—we'd cut corners elsewhere, we'd go into savings, whatever it took, he said. I didn't want to hear it. "I don't need a nanny, I need
a husband!" I shouted. Didn't he understand? My plan hadn't been to hire
someone to raise our child. My plan had been to do it together: two respon-

sible parents with two fulfilling jobs, in an egalitarian marriage with a well-adjusted kid who was equally bonded to us both.

25   In writing class I tell my students there are just two basic human motivators: desire and fear. Every decision we make, every action we take, springs from this divided well. Some characters are ruled by desire. Others are ruled by fear. So what was my story during the year and a half that John spent so much time at work? He claimed that I was fear-driven, that I was threatened by the loss of control, which may in fact have been true. When I try to dissect my behavior then, reaching beneath all the months of anger and complaints, I do find fear: the fear that I'd never find a way to balance work and family life without constantly compromising one, the other, or both. But mostly what I find is desire. For my daughter to have a close relationship with her father, for my husband to have more time to spend with me, for me to find a way to have some control over my time, even with a husband and a child factored into the mix. And then there was the big one: for my husband to fulfill the promise I felt he made to me on our wedding day, which was to be my partner at home and in life. Somewhere along the way, we'd stopped feeling like a team, and I wanted that fellowship back.

26   I wish, if only to inject a flashy turning point into this story right about now, that I could say some climactic event occurred from which we emerged dazed yet transformed, or that one of us delivered an ultimatum the other couldn't ignore and our commitment to each other was then renewed. But in reality, the way we resolved all this was gradual, and—in retrospect—surprisingly simple. John got the company stabilized and, as he'd promised, finally started working fewer hours. And I, knowing he would be home that much more, slowly started adding hours to my workday. With the additional income, we hired a live-in nanny, who took over much of the housework as well. And then, a few months after Francis arrived, Maya started preschool two mornings a week. Those became blessed writing hours for me, time when I was fully released of the guilt of paying others to watch my child. Between 9:00 A.M. and 12:30 P.M. Maya was exactly where she was supposed to be and, within that time frame, so was I.

27   With Francis came an additional benefit: a baby-sitter on Friday nights. For the first time since Maya's birth, John and I had a set night each week to devote to each other, and as we split combination sushi plates and did side-by-side chatarangas in a 6:00 P.M. yoga class, we began to slowly build upon the foundation we'd laid with our marriage—and, thankfully, even in the darkest months, we'd always trusted hadn't disappeared. Yes, there were still some Friday nights when I watched TV alone because John was flying back from New York, and other Fridays when I had to sit late in front of the computer to meet a deadline. And there were some weekend days when John still had to take meetings, though they became fewer and fewer over time.

. . .

28 It has taken real effort for me to release the dream of completely equal co-parenting, or at least to accept that we may not be the family to make it real.

We're still quite a distance from that goal, and even further when you factor in the amount of household support we now have. Does John do 50 percent of the remaining child care? No. But neither do I contribute 50 percent of the income, as I once did. Ours is still an imbalanced relationship in some ways, but imbalance I've learned to live with—especially after the extreme inequity we once had.

29   What really matters now—more than everything being absolutely equal, more than either my husband or me "striking it rich"—is that John is home before Maya's bedtime almost every night now to join the pileup on her bed, and that we took our first real family vacation last December. This is the essence of what I longed for during those bleak, angry months of my daughter's first two years. It was a desire almost embarrassing in its simplicity, yet one so strong that, in one of the greatest paradoxes of my marriage, it might have torn my husband and me apart: the desire to love and be loved, with reciprocity and conviction, with fairness and respect; the desire to capture that elusive animal we all grow up believing marriage is, and never stop wanting it to be.

My Problem with Her Anger
Eric Bartels

In the previous selection, Hope Edelman describes how her husband's absence made her feel "angry and resentful and lonely." In the following essay, Eric Bartels writes about what it is like to be on the receiving end of such spousal anger. Eric Bartels is a feature writer for the Portland Tribune *in Portland, Oregon, where he lives with his wife and two children. This is a revised version of the essay by this title that appeared in* The Bastard on the Couch: 27 Men Try Really Hard to Explain Their Feelings About Love, Loss, Fatherhood, and Freedom *(2004), an anthology edited by Daniel Jones.*

1   My wife and kids were sleeping when I finished the dishes the other night, shook the water off my hands and smudged them dry with one of the grimy towels hanging on the door to the oven. I gave the kitchen floor a quick sweep, clearing it of all but the gossamer tufts of cat hair that always jet away from the broom as if under power.

2   I turned to shut the lights, but then I noticed the two metal grills I had left to soak in the basin. They're the detachable, (cast iron type) (stove-top kind) that we occasionally use to affect a kind of indoor, open-flame cooking experience. Submerging them in water for awhile makes it easier to remove the carbonized juices and bits of flesh that get welded on during use. It's a good, sensible way to save labor.

3   The problem was that they'd been in the sink for several days now. And then it occurred to me: What I was staring at was the dark heart of the divide between men and women.

4   It's unlikely I was any less harried or less tired the previous few nights as I went about my kitchen duties, a responsibility that has fallen to me more or less exclusively of late. No, my energy level is fairly constant—that is to say depleted—at that particular point of just about any day. I could, and probably should have finished the grill-cleaning project sooner. Just as I should make the bed every morning instead of occasionally. Just as I should always throw my underwear into the hamper before showering, rather than leaving them on top of it, or on the floor next to it.

5   These are the things men do that quietly annoy the living shit out of a woman. Until she becomes a mother. Then they inspire a level of fury unlike anything she has ever experienced. And that fury won't be kept secret. On the receiving end, the husband will be left to wonder why the punishment is so wildly out of line with the crime. This is the kind of vitriol that should be reserved for lying politicians, corporate greed and hitters who don't take a pitch when their team trails in the late innings—not a dedicated marriage partner with garden-variety human foibles.

6   Yet here we are, my wife and me. We're both good people. We have lots of friends. We make a decent living at relatively satisfying professional jobs: She, half-time at a small advertising firm; I, as a newspaper writer. And we're dedicated, attentive parents to a six-year old daughter and a two-year old son.

7   We don't use profanity in front of the children, unless we're arguing angrily. We don't talk to each other disrespectfully, except when arguing angrily. And we don't say bad things about each other to the kids, unless, of course, we just finished arguing angrily.

8   I know my wife's life is hard. She spends more time with the kids than I do and is almost completely responsible for running them around to day care and school. I contribute regularly and earnestly to the shopping, cooking and cleaning, but a fair amount of it still falls to her. And her job, although part-time for the last six years, presents her with Hell's own revolving door of guilt over neglecting her work for kids and vice versa.

9   I work hard to take pressure off her and have given up some freedoms myself since our first child was born: time with friends, regular pickup basketball games, beer. And I honestly don't mind living without these things. What gets me, though, is how little credit I get for the effort. My wife gets tired. She gets frustrated. She gets angry. And she seems to want to take it out on me.

10   Then logic starts moving backward in an ugly zigzag pattern. If, in her mind, my shortcomings provide the justification for her anger, then the perception of my behavior must be groomed like the playing field of a game I can't seem to win. The things I do that don't conform to my new loser image—and to think this woman once thought I was cooler than sliced bread—don't even show up on the scoreboard. Until, finally, nothing I do is right.

11   My efforts to organize the contents of the armoire one day—a project she had suggested—led to a screaming fight. The clutter I was planning to move to the basement would just create more junk down there, she said.

But we hardly use the basement, I thought, and besides, why couldn't we just make another, separate project of sorting out the basement later? Doesn't it solve the more pressing armoire problem in the meantime? Isn't that logical?

12   Evidently not.

13   One night she stomped into the kitchen as I was cleaning up after a dinner that I may well have cooked and served and announced in angry tones that she needed more help getting the kids ready for bed than I had been providing, as if she had just found me drinking beer and playing video games. Isn't that something we could discuss rationally, I asked her, when we're not both right in the middle of our respective (unpleasant) (demanding) nightly routines?

14   It didn't occur to her, I guess.

15   And a few nights later, after bathing the kids in succession, putting them in their pajamas and feeding them their vitamins, I was rocking our son to sleep when I heard my wife approach. I think she had been downstairs doing laundry. She walks into the bathroom and scornfully asks no one in particular "Why is there still water in the bathtub?"

16   I missed it.

17   I make a nice dinner after a long day at work, broiled pork chops with steamed zuccini, perhaps, and she asks why I made rice instead of pasta. At the grocery store, I try to buy food that's somewhere between not entirely toxic and prohibitively expensive, but I often disappoint her. I wash clothes the wrong way, not separating them properly by color. I spend too much time rinsing off dishes before loading them into the dishwasher.

18   If this is my castle, it is under siege. From within.

19   At times, the negativity threatens to grind my spirit into dust. I make it through an arduous week, gleeful to have it behind me, only to come home to the sound of her loudly and impatiently scolding our son for standing on a chair or turning on the TV or dumping his cheese puffs on the floor, exactly the stuff two-year old boys are supposed to do. Okay, children need to learn "no," and my wife does a lot of the teaching, but I'm certain there's a gentler way to pronounce the word.

20   I try to make this point calmly, and when that doesn't work, I make it more forcefully. Then we fight, until the (shame and) futility of that leaves me feeling deflated and distant, in a place where passion of any kind has slipped into a coma. And then it's time to start all over.

21   At times I watch my wife's mercury rise steadily, predictably to that point where she lashes out, almost as if she wanted to get there. I tell her, in the quietest, most reasonable tone I can manage, to please relax. Choose: "(You, Your Daughter, Your Son) did/did not do (this, that, the other)," she replies, her ire mounting. But, I think to myself, I didn't ask her what she's angry about, I asked her to stay calm. Aren't those different things?

22   I think it's fairly well established by now that marriage is a challenge, a creaky, old institution that may not have fully adapted itself to modern life, one that now fails in this country more often than not. Put children in the picture and you have an exponentially higher degree of difficulty.

23   Motherhood asks the modern woman, who has grown up seeing professional success as hers for the taking, to add the loss of a linear career path to an already considerable burden: child rearing, body issues, a shifting self-image and a husband who fell off his white horse long, long ago. I suppose this would make anyone angry.

24   Perhaps for women of recent generations, anger has replaced the quiet desperation of the past. That seems like a healthy development to me. But that doesn't mean there aren't several good reasons why, having seen the frustrated, angry, resentful place that the demands of modern motherhood will almost certainly take them, women shouldn't take the next logical, evolutionary step.

25   It seems to me that a woman should now focus only secondarily on what the world, and more specifically, her partner can do for her during the challenging early years of child rearing. She must now truly empower herself by turning to the more important issue: Controlling the monstrous effects that motherhood can have on her own emotional landscape.

26   In other words, buck up.

27   For better or worse, men don't experience life the way women do. Absent the degree of intuition and empathy that seem an integral (natural) part of a woman's nurturing instinct, men grow up in a simpler milieu in which challenges are to be quickly surmounted, without a great deal of fanfare. Something breaks, you fix it and move on. (But don't throw it out, it could come in handy at some point.)

28   It's not a mindset that lends itself to a great deal of introspection and deep thought. That's not to say that women can't fix things or that men are shallow-minded. These (just seem like) are philosophical tendencies propelled by disparate biological imperatives. The result in men is an inclination not to worry about things before they happen. This imbues them with a confidence that, however vexing a problem might seem, it can and will be resolved.

29   I don't think most women share this confidence. A friend of mine says that everything in a woman's world starts with fear. Everything becomes tied in some way to fears of disapproval and abandonment and loss of control and God knows what else. To make matters worse, a man's more measured response to (in) certain situations is likely to suggest to his wife that he is not sufficiently engaged. Indifferent. Oblivious.

30   Am I the only guy who feels like he forever stands accused of not understanding the pressures my wife is under? That I can't possibly fathom her frustrations? After all, what would a man know about controlling his impulses?

31   What would he know? I like that one. Remember, we're talking about men here, the people with the built-in testosterone factory. The ones whose favorite childhood entertainments run to breaking windows, starting fires and dismembering small animals. The ones who instantly want to know if their first car will do 100 mph. The ones who attend beery high school parties with the goal of getting laid, but who'll settle for a good fistfight. Women should be eager to learn what most men know about managing anger.

32   For many years, I made a living as a bartender. I was good at it and loved the challenge of having to nimbly beat back the surging, immediate gallery of tasks that a big crowd and a busy night present. But it's a job where things go wrong pretty much constantly and I would occasionally lose my cool, kicking a cooler door closed or angrily sending an empty bottle smashing into a bin with an ear-splitting explosion. I imagined I was just blowing off a little steam.

33   I didn't know what I was really doing until I was a patron at someone else's bar one night. I watched a bartender momentarily capture everyone's attention with a loud fit of pique and realized quickly that witnesses saw the whole thing as landing somewhere between laughable and pathetic. We didn't care what was bothering him. We were having drinks and a good time. Too bad he wasn't enjoying the evening himself.

34   Was the guy under a lot of pressure? Yes. Was he being vexed by all manner of impediments to his ability to do his job? Almost certainly. Did anybody care? No.

35   I did a lot less kicking doors and throwing things after that.

36   Of course I care about my wife's happiness. Whether we're bothered by the same things or react to challenges the same way is irrelevant. She is my partner and I love her. We have important things to do together. The life we've built depends heavily on her ability to find contentment.

37   But she's not the only one in the family who has tough days. I have my own stuff to deal with and so do our kids, young as they are. When my wife decides it's okay to look darkly at her self or the day she's having, she's giving herself permission to ignore what's going on in other's lives. However little she regards the obligations and pressures of my existence, the fact is that I have some less than radiant days myself.

38   Women could try to accept that it is theoretically possible for a man to be tired, feel stress and even need a bit of emotional support himself. The children can certainly provide a lift, but they are also notoriously inconsistent about refraining from imperfect, untimely behaviors: talking in loud, excited voices, soiling themselves and moving at high speed in close proximity to valued objects and unforgiving hardwood furniture.

39   An overworked wife is certainly within her rights, as ever, to express her concerns and wishes at these moments. But that is not the same as a bilious, ill-timed attack that suggests her husband, through arrogance and selfishness, knows absolutely nothing of the realities of her world. In fact, he probably has a pretty good idea. He's probably even willing to meet any reasonable request to help. He'd just like it if someone would ask him nicely.

40   I'm amazed at how willing my wife is to push my buttons sometimes. And it's not like she's unfamiliar with the instrument panel. She evidently hasn't noticed that I occasionally ignite like dry kindling.

41   I should probably admit about now that I'm not always a model of decorum. I'm a personable, intelligent guy, but I'm not one of those wise, super-evolved aliens with the massive cranium from science fiction. I've said unkind things to people. I've thrown elbows on the basketball court. Gripped by paroxysmic anger, I've sent any number of small appliances to the promised land. And I do like to win. But this is about not fighting.

42 Anyone who's ever watched a young child's face crumple in fear and bewilderment as parents unleash their anger, in any direction, knows instantly what the stakes are. Parents do not need the toxic stew of anger coursing through them while in charge of small, impressionable children. And partners who are struggling to remember what particular disease of the brain led to their union won't be helped back to the right path by the rotating wheel of frustration, resentment and blame.

43 I fear that when anger is allowed to manifest itself regularly, it becomes less and less necessary to question its origins. No need to examine it, no need to work backward in the hope of identifying and defusing the triggers to the fast-replicating chain of events. And what is the hope of altering a behavior if you don't know where it came from and never see it coming?

44 It baffles me that someone of my wife's intelligence would shout at our son to stop yelling or demand in a voice twisted with exasperation that our daughter stop whining. Can't she see what she's doing? It's like hitting someone to curb his or her violent tendencies. Of course I understand her frustration. But to let the expression of that frustration take any form, however inappropriate or unproductive, is indefensible.

45 Anger can spread quickly and I don't want us to poison the house where our kids are growing up. I don't know for a fact that whiney, self-centered children are always the product of undisciplined, self-indulgent parents, but what reasonable person would want to take that chance? Isn't a bit of restraint a rather small price to pay?

46 Anger is not power. Managing anger is power. A good friend of many years, with whom I've had many passionate debates on all manner of issues, used to tell me how his father would sit impassively during their own lively exchanges. His father, a university department head, would never lose his temper, never so much as raise his voice. I think I dismissed it as humanly impossible. My friend said it drove him crazy. But he is now an eloquent, engaging orator who runs a weekly literary discussion group out of his home. Then again, he also has two young sons and is divorced.

47 The level of discipline my friend learned from his father doesn't generally reside where my wife grew up. Individually, my in-laws are charming, intelligent, accomplished people. But together, they struggle mightily to break old habits. You can get one or another of them to acknowledge the familiar cycle of intolerance, blame and recrimination that often cripples their dealings with each other, but no one seems to have the will to fix it. As if the patience it would require would be seen as weakness.

48 My wife is the black sheep of that family. She has a quick mind, both analytical and imaginative. She has no love for convention and looks easily through hypocrisy of all kinds. She also has big-time Type A tendencies, character traits that make her the choice for many of the organizational and administrative duties in our shared life like paying bills and scheduling the kids' activities.

49 But these proclivities also work against her. The chaotic, unpredictable reality of having two small children threatens and at times overwhelms her

compulsion for order. She breaks down. Traveling, with the on-the-fly time-management it requires, makes her crazy. I watched her walk face-first into a glass door at the airport. Another time, near the baggage carousel, she distractedly pushed our son's stroller into another child. The child was seated at the time. A pointless quarrel over a trip to the Home Depot led to her backing out of the driveway and into a parked mail truck one morning.

50 My wife and I need to fix this anger thing. We knew, or should have known, what we were getting into. We signed the contract. Shook on it. Kissed, actually. But I think we missed some of the small print. We wanted kids and had a vague idea that it would involve some work. Well, I have a news flash: It can be really, really hard.

51 And that goes for guys, too. I don't recall being told about spending more money each year than I actually earn, with no exotic vacations, nice cars or fancy anything else to show for it. I wasn't informed that I would give up golf altogether, just as I was pushing my handicap down toward single digits. And I'm certain I was not warned that sex would become a rarer commodity than at any time in the thirty years since I learned to participate in it.

52 But I've gotten used to all that. I do what most men do. I take a deep breath and push ahead, fairly confident that if I can just soldier on, the things I've sacrificed and more will be my reward down the road.

53 I suppose the anger issues in our household loom as large as they do, in part, because of my fervor to confront (defeat) them. It's been a battlefield at times. My wife and I have been mean and fought dirty and we've hurt each other. We need to recognize that and make up our minds to change, no matter how much work it requires.

54 But hey, we're still here. Our children, who we love so dearly, are growing up and every day we can count on the reassuring rhythms of life: the sun rises in the morning, a weather system slips over the Oregon Cascades and blots it out, cats barf up hairballs on the carpet. I'm optimistic. I don't think we've done any permanent damage. I don't think it's anything we can't fix.

55 But that's just me.

Will Your Marriage Last?
Aviva Patz

Every newly wedded couple expects—or at least hopes—that their marriage will endure the test of time. But in most parts of the world the statistics are not encouraging. As of 2002, the highest divorce rate was found in Sweden, where 55 percent of new marriages ended in divorce; Guatemala had the lowest rate: 0.13 percent. The divorce rate in the United States is on the high end of the scale: 46 percent.

Is it possible to predict, in the early stages of a marriage, whether it will likely succeed or fail? In the following selection, Aviva Patz, executive editor of Psychology Today, *reports on a study designed to answer that intriguing question. Ted Huston, a professor of human ecology and psychology at the University of Texas at Austin, designed and conducted the PAIR Project (Processes of Adaptation in Intimate Relationships), which followed the experiences of 168 couples from their wedding day through the next thirteen years. The results should surprise you and may overturn some of your assumptions about what makes for a successful marriage.*

This article first appeared in the Los Angeles Times *on March 15, 2000, and, in slightly different form, in* Psychology Today *on April 23 of that year. The present selection is drawn from both versions of the article.*

1   What if I told you that there is a man in America who can predict, from the outset, whether your marriage will last? He doesn't need to hear you arguing; he doesn't need to know what you argue about. He doesn't even care whether you argue at all.

2   I was dubious, too, but I was curious enough to attend a lecture on the subject at the most recent American Psychological Association convention in Boston. Ted Huston, a professor of human ecology and psychology at the University of Texas at Austin, was showcasing the results of a long-term study of married couples that pierces the heart of social-psychological science: the ability to forecast whether a husband and wife, two years after taking their vows, will stay together and whether they will be happy.

3   My press pass notwithstanding, I went to the seminar for reasons of my own. Fresh out of college I had gotten married—and burned. Some part of me was still reeling from three years of waking up angry every morning, not wanting to go home after work, feeling lonely even as my then-husband sat beside me. I went because I have recently remarried and just celebrated my one-year anniversary. Needless to say, I'd like to make this one work. So I scribbled furiously in my notebook, drinking in the graphs and charts—for psychology, for husbands and wives everywhere, but mostly for myself.

4   Huston, a pioneer in the psychology of relationships, launched the Processes of Adaptation in Intimate Relationships (the "PAIR Project") in 1981, in which he followed 168 couples—drawn from marriage license records in four counties in a rural and working-class area of Pennsylvania—from their wedding day through thirteen years of marriage.

Examining a Marriage's Early Stages

5   Through multiple interviews, Huston looked at the way partners related to one another during courtship, as newlyweds and through the early years of marriage. Were they "gaga"? Comfortable? Unsure? He measured their positive and negative feelings for each other and observed how those feelings changed over time. Are newlyweds who hug and kiss more likely than other couples to have a happy marriage, he wondered, or are they particularly susceptible to divorce if their romance dissipates? Are newlyweds who bicker destined to part ways?

6   Since one in two marriages ends in divorce in this country, there ought to be tons of research explaining why. But the existing literature provides only pieces of the larger puzzle.

7   Past research has led social scientists to believe that newlyweds begin their life together in romantic bliss and can then be brought down by their inability to navigate the issues that inevitably crop up during the marriage. When Benjamin Karny and Thomas Bradbury did a comprehensive review of the literature in 1995, they confirmed studies such as those of John Gottman and Neil Jacobson, maintaining that the best predictors of divorce are interactive difficulties, such as frequent expressions of antagonism, lack of respect for each other's ideas and similar interpersonal issues.

8   But most of this research was done on couples who had been married a number of years, with many of them already well on their way to divorce. It came as no surprise, then, that researchers thought their hostility toward one another predicted the further demise of the relationship.

9   Huston's study was unique in that it looked at couples much earlier, when they were courting and during the initial years of marriage, thus providing the first complete picture of the earliest stages of distress. Its four main findings were quite surprising.

10   First, contrary to popular belief, Huston found that many newlyweds are far from blissfully in love. Second, couples whose marriages begin in romantic bliss are particularly divorce-prone because such intensity is too hard to maintain. Believe it or not, marriages that start out with less "Hollywood romance" usually have more promising futures.

11   Accordingly, and this is the third major finding, spouses in lasting but lackluster marriages are not prone to divorce, as one might suspect; their marriages are less fulfilling to begin with, so there is no erosion of a Western-style romantic ideal. Lastly, and perhaps most important, it is the loss of love and affection, not the emergence of interpersonal issues, that sends couples journeying toward divorce.

12   By the end of Huston's study in 1994, the couples looked a lot like the rest of America, falling into four groups. They were either married and happy; married and unhappy; divorced early, within seven years; or divorced later, after seven years—and each category showed a distinct pattern.

Satisfied Spouses Were Happy Newlyweds

13 Those who remained happily married were very "in love" and affectionate as newlyweds. They showed less ambivalence, expressed negative feelings less often and viewed their mate more positively than other couples. Most important, these feelings remained stable over time. By contrast, although many couples who divorced later were very affectionate as newlyweds, they gradually became less loving, more negative and more critical of their spouse.

14   Indeed, Huston found that how well spouses got along as newlyweds affected their future, but the major distinguishing factor between those who divorced and those who remained married was the amount of change in the relationship over its first two years.

15   "The first two years are key—that's when the risk of divorce is particularly high," he says. "And the changes that take place during this time tell us a lot about where the marriage is headed."

16   What surprised Huston most was the nature of the changes that led to divorce: The experiences of the 56 participating couples who divorced showed that loss of initial levels of love and affection, rather than conflict, was the most salient predictor of distress and divorce. This loss sends that relationship into a downward spiral, leading to increased bickering and fighting, and to the collapse of the union.

17   "This ought to change the way we think about the early roots of what goes wrong in marriage," Huston said. "The dominant approach has been to work with couples to resolve conflict, but it should focus on preserving the positive feelings. That's a very important take-home lesson."

Feelings May Determine a Union's Fate

18 "Huston's research fills an important gap in the literature by suggesting that there is more to a successful relationship than simply managing conflict," said Harry Reis, of the University of Rochester, a leading social psychologist.

19   "My own research speaks to 'loss of intimacy,' in the sense that when people first become close they feel a tremendous sense of validation from each other, like their partner is the only other person on earth who sees things as they do. That feeling sometimes fades, and when it does, it can take a heavy toll on the marriage."

20   Social science has a name for that fading dynamic—"disillusionment": Lovers initially put their best foot forward, ignoring each other's—and the relationship's—shortcomings. But after they tie the knot, hidden aspects of their personalities emerge, and idealized images give way to more realistic ones. This can lead to disappointment, loss of love and, ultimately, distress and divorce.

When Marriage Fails

21 The story of Peter and Suzie, participants in the PAIR Project, shows classic disillusionment. When they met, Suzie was 24, a new waitress at the golf course where Peter, then 26, played. He was "awed" by her beauty. After a month, the two considered themselves an exclusive couple. Peter said Suzie "wasn't an airhead; she seemed kind of smart, and she's pretty." Suzie said Peter "cared a lot about me as a person, and was willing to overlook things."

22   By the time they strolled down the aisle on Valentine's Day in 1981, Peter and Suzie had dated only nine months, experiencing many ups and downs along the way.

23   Huston says couples are most vulnerable to disillusionment when their courtship is brief. In a whirlwind romance, it's easy to paint an unrealistically rosy picture of the relationship, one that cannot be sustained.

24   Sure enough, reality soon set in for Peter and Suzie. Within two years, Suzie was less satisfied with almost every aspect of their marriage. She

expressed less affection for Peter and felt her love decline continuously. She considered him to have "contrary" traits, such as jealousy and possessiveness, and resented his propensity to find fault with her.

25 Peter, for his part, was disappointed that his wife did not become the flawless parent and homemaker he had envisioned.

26 Another danger sign for relationships is a courtship filled with drama and driven by external circumstances. For this pair, events related to Peter's jealousy propelled the relationship forward. He was the force behind their destroying letters and pictures from former lovers. It was a phone call between Suzie and an old flame that prompted him to bring up the idea of marriage in the first place. And it was a fit of jealousy—over Suzie's claiming to go shopping and then coming home suspiciously late—that convinced Peter he was ready to marry.

27 Theirs was a recipe for disaster: A short courtship, driven largely by Peter's jealousy, enabled the pair to ignore flaws in the relationship and in each other, setting them up for disappointment. That disappointment eroded their love and affection, which soured their perception of each other's personalities, creating feelings of ambivalence.

28 Ten years after saying "I do," the disaffected lovers were in the midst of divorce. When Suzie filed the papers, she cited as the primary reason a gradual loss of love.

29 The parallels between Peter and Suzie's failed marriage and my own are striking: My courtship with my first husband was short, also about nine months. Like Peter, I had shallow criteria: This guy was cool; he had long hair, wore a leather jacket, played guitar and adored the same obscure band that I did.

30 When it came time to build a life together, however, we were clearly mismatched. I wanted a traditional family with children; he would have been happy living on a hippie commune. In college, when we wanted to move in together, we thought our parents would be more approving if we got engaged first. So we did, even though we weren't completely sold on the idea of marriage.

31 The road to divorce was paved early, by the end of the first year: I had said I wanted us to spend more time together; he accused me of trying to keep him from his hobbies, and told me, in so many words, to "get a life." Well I did, and two years later, he wasn't in it.

When Marriage Succeeds

32 While the disillusionment model best describes those who divorce, Huston found that another model suits those who stay married, whether or not they are happy: The "enduring dynamics model," in which partners establish patterns of behavior early and maintain them over time, highlights stability in the relationship—the feature that distinguishes those who remain together from those who eventually split up.

33 The major difference between the unhappily married couples and their happy counterparts is simply a lower level of satisfaction across the

board. Yet, oddly enough, this relative unhappiness by itself does not doom the marriage. "We have a whole group of people who are stable in unhappy marriages and not necessarily dissatisfied," Huston said. "It's just a different model of marriage. It's not that they're happy about their marriage; it's just that the discontent doesn't spill over and soil the rest of their lives."

34   And while all married couples eventually lose a bit of that honeymoon euphoria, Huston notes, those who remain married don't consider this a crushing blow, but rather a natural transition from "romantic relationship" to "working partnership." And when conflict does arise, they diffuse it with various constructive coping mechanisms.

35   Nancy and John, participants in Huston's study, are a shining example of happy, healthy balance. They met in February 1978 and were immediately attracted to each other. John said Nancy was "fun to be with" and he "could take her anywhere." Nancy said John always complimented her and liked to do things she enjoyed, things "other guys wouldn't do."

36   During their courtship, they spent a lot of time together, going to dances at their high school and hanging out with friends. They became comfortable with each other and began to openly disclose their opinions and feelings, realizing they had a lot in common and enjoyed each other's company.

37   John paid many surprise visits to Nancy and bought her a number of gifts. Toward the end of the summer, John gave Nancy a charm necklace with a "genuine diamond." She recalls his saying: "This isn't your ring, honey, but you're going to get one." And she did. The two married on Jan. 17, 1981, nearly three years after they began dating.

38   The prognosis for this relationship is good. Nancy and John have a solid foundation of love and affection, built on honesty and intimacy. A three-year courtship enabled them to paint realistic portraits of one another.

39   In 1994, when they were last interviewed, Nancy and John were highly satisfied with their marriage. They were very compatible, disagreeing only about politics. Both felt they strongly benefited from the marriage and said they had no desire to leave.

40   When the seminar ends, I can't get to a pay phone fast enough. After two rings, the phone is answered. He's there, of course. Dependable. Predictable. That's one of the things that first set my husband apart. At the close of one date, he'd lock in the next. "Can I see you tomorrow for lunch?"

41   "Will you have dinner with me next week?"

42   Unlike the fantasy-quality of my first marriage, I felt a deep sense of comfort and companionship with him, and did not harbor outrageous expectations. We exchanged vows 3 1/2 years later, in August, 1998.

43   There at the convention center, I try to tell my husband about Huston's study, about the critical first few years, about "enduring dynamics," it all comes out in a jumble.

44   "You're saying we have a good marriage, that we're not going to get divorced?" he asks.

45   "Yes," I say breathlessly, relieved of the burden of explanation.

46   "Well I'm glad to hear that," he says, "but I wasn't really worried."

47 Sometimes I wonder: Knowing what I know now, could I have saved my first marriage? Probably not. Huston's research suggests that the harbingers of disaster were present even before my wedding day.

48 And he blames our culture. Unlike many other world cultures, he says Western society makes marriage the key adult relationship, which puts pressure on people to marry. "People feel they have to find a way to get there and one way is to force it, even if it only works for the time being," he says.

49 Our culture is also to blame, Huston says, for perpetuating the myth of storybook romance, which is more likely to doom a marriage than strengthen it. He has few kind words for Hollywood, which brings us unrealistic passion.

50 So if your new romance starts to resemble a movie script, try to remember: The audience never sees what happens after the credits roll.

51 Are you headed for bliss or a bust-up?

The Arbus Factor
Lore Segal

We conclude our chapter on marriage and family with a poignant short story—a miniature gem. To tease out its meaning, relate your discussions about it to some of the other discussions provoked by earlier selections in this chapter.

Born in Vienna, Lore Segal subsequently lived in England (where she received her B.A. in English from the University of London in 1948), the Dominican Republic, and (starting in 1951), New York. She has taught writing at Columbia University's School of the Arts, Princeton, Bennington College, the University of Illinois at Chicago, and Ohio State University. A prolific writer, her novels include Other People's Houses *(1964),* Lucinella *(1978), and* Her First American *(1985). Her children's books include* Tell Me a Mitzi *(1970),* Morris the Artist *(2003), and* Why Mole Shouted and Other Stories *(2004). Thirteen interrelated stories, seven of which appeared in the* New Yorker, *were collected into* Shakespeare's Kitchen *(2007). "The Arbus Factor" appeared in the Winter Fiction issue of the* New Yorker *on December 24 and 31, 2007.*

1 On one of the first days of the New Year, Jack called Hope. "Let's have lunch," he said. "I've got an agenda." No need to specify the Café Provence on upper Broadway, or the time—fifteen minutes before noon, when they were sure of getting their table by the window.

2 They did the menu, heard the specials. Hope said, "I'm always going to order something different," but ordered the onion soup. Jack ordered the cassoulet, saying, "I *should* have the fish.

3 "And a bottle of your Merlot," he told the unsmiling proprietress, "which we will have right away."

4 "We'll share a salad," Hope said. She saw Jack watch the proprietress walk off in the direction of the bar, in a remarkably short skirt for a woman

of fifty. Hope saw the long, brown, athletic legs, bare even in January, with Jack's eyes. Jack, a large man, with a heavy, dark face, turned to Hope. "So?"

5   "O.K., I guess. You?"

6   Jack said, "My agenda: if we were still making resolutions, what would yours be?"

7   Hope's interest pricked right up. "I'm thinking. You go first."

8   Jack said, "I'm going to watch what I eat. It's not the weight; it's the constantly thinking of eating. I don't eat real meals unless Jeremy comes over." Jeremy was Jack's son.

9   Hope said, "I'm going to watch what I watch and then I'm going to turn the TV off. It's ugly waking mornings with the thing flickering. It feels debauched."

10   Jack said, "I'm not going to order books from Amazon till I've read the ones on my shelves."

11   Hope said, "I'm going to hang up my clothes even when nobody is coming over. Nora is very severe with me." Nora was Hope's daughter.

12   The wine arrived. Jack did the label-checking, cork-sniffing, tasting, and nodding. The salad came. Hope served their two plates. Jack indicated Hope's hair, which she had done in an upsweep. "Very fetching," he commented.

13   "Thank you. Here's an old new resolution: Going to learn French. What was the name of my teacher when we got back from Paris? I once counted eleven years of school French, but it was you who always had to do the talking."

14   Jack said, "I want to learn how to pray."

15   Hope looked across the table to see if he was being cute. Jack was concentrating on folding a whole lettuce leaf into his mouth.

16   Hope said, "I'll never understand the principle of not cutting it into bite size."

17   The onion soup came, the cassoulet came. Jack asked Hope if she would like to go back.

18   "Go back? Back to Paris!" Jack and Hope had lived together before marrying two other people. Jack subsequently divorced his wife, who had subsequently died. Hope was widowed.

19   "To Paris. To Aix," Jack said.

20   "Something I've been meaning to ask you," Hope said. "Were you and I ever together in an old, old garden? Did we walk under century-old trees? Did we lie down in the grass and look into tree crowns in France, or was that in England? Was it an old English garden or is this a garden in a book?"

21   "What's to keep us?" Jack said.

22   There were a lot of reasons, of course, to keep them from going back. Two of the littlest were at this moment flattening their noses against the outside of the restaurant window. Ten-year-old Benjamin stuck his thumbs in his ears and wiggled his fingers at his grandfather. Hope made as if to catch her granddaughter's hand through the glass. This made little

Miranda laugh. And there was Hope's daughter, Nora, with baby Julie in a stroller, and Jack's son, Jeremy, standing out on the sidewalk.

23   "I'm just going to the bathroom," Hope mouthed to her daughter.

24   "What?" Nora mouthed back, her face sharpened with irritation. The baby was crying.

25   "She knows I can't hear her through the glass," Nora said to Jeremy.

26   Jeremy said, "You stay with the kids. I'll go in and get him. I'll see what your mother wants." Jeremy walked into the restaurant, passing Jack and Hope on his way to the corner where, an hour ago, he had folded up his father's wheelchair. Hope stood and came around the table to kiss Jack and be kissed goodbye.

27   "On the double, Dad," Jeremy said. "I need to get back to the office."

28   "I'll call you," Jack said to Hope. "We'll have lunch."

29   Hope was mouthing through the window again and Nora said, "Julie, shut up, please! Mom, *what*?" The baby had started screeching.

30   Hope pointed in the direction of the ladies' room. Nora signalled, You need me to go with you? Hope shook her head no. One of the reasons for the Café Provence was that its bathrooms were on the street floor, not in the basement, down a long stair.

31   Gathering her coat and bag, Hope opened the door to the ladies' room and saw, in the mirror above the basins, that her hair was coming out of its pins. She removed all the pins and stood gazing at the crone with the gray, shoulder-length hair girlishly loosened. Hope saw what Diane Arbus might have seen and was appalled, and being appalled pricked her interest right up. "I've got an agenda: the Arbus factor of old age," Hope looked forward to saying to Jack the next time it would be convenient for Jeremy and Nora to arrange lunch for them at the Café Provence.

Answer Key to "A Pop Quiz on Marriage"

1. **FALSE.** From 1970 to the late 1990s, men's attitudes toward marriage became more favorable, while women's became less so. By the end of the century, more men than women said that marriage was their ideal lifestyle. And on average, men become more content with their marriages over time, while women grow less so. A majority of divorced men and women report that the wife was the one who wanted out of the marriage. A recent study of divorces that occurred after age 40 found that wives initiated two-thirds of them.

2. **FALSE.** The difference in the ages of men and women at first marriage has been narrowing for the past 80 years and is now at a historic low. By the end of the 1990s, 39 percent of women age 35 to 44 lived with younger men. Men still rate youth and good looks higher than women do when looking for a mate, but those criteria no longer outweigh all others. Men are much more likely

now to seek a mate who has the same level of education and similar earnings potential. College educated women are more likely to marry and less likely to divorce than women with less education.

3. **TRUE.** Although divorce rates have risen, death rates have fallen even more steeply, so that more couples will celebrate their 40th wedding anniversaries now than at any time in the past. Furthermore, the divorce rate reached its height more than 25 years ago. It has fallen by more than 25 percent since 1981.

4. **FALSE.** Americans are now more tolerant of consenting sexual relations between unmarried adults than in the past. But surveys show that disapproval of adultery, sexual coercion, rape and sex with minors has increased over the past 30 years and is now at a historic high. In 1889, a girl could legally consent to sex at 10, 11 or 12 in half the states, and in Delaware the age of consent was 7. There were many more prostitutes per capita in late 19th century America than there are today—resulting in a high incidence of venereal disease among respectably married women infected by their husbands.

5. **FALSE.** For the first thousand years of its existence, the church held that a marriage was valid if a couple claimed they had exchanged words of consent—even if there were no witnesses and no priest to officiate. Not until 1754 did England require issuance of a license for a marriage to be valid. Informal marriage and cohabitation were so common in early 19th-century America that one judge estimated that one third of all children were born to couples who were not legally married.

6. **FALSE.** The likelihood that college-educated women will drop out of the labor force because of having children declined by half from 1984 to 2004. And among all mothers with children under 6, the most highly educated are the least likely to leave their jobs, with that likelihood declining with each level of educational attainment.

7. **TRICK QUESTION.** Women with nontraditional values are indeed more likely to divorce than women with traditional views, but they are also more likely to get married in the first place. As for men, those with traditional values about gender are more likely to marry than nontraditional men, but they are also more likely to divorce. We don't precisely know why this discrepancy exists, but it probably has something to do with the fact that women's views on gender are changing more rapidly than men's.

8. **FALSE.** Aside from a huge spike in divorce immediately after World War II, divorce rates in the 1950s were higher than in any previous decade aside from the Depression, and almost one in three marriages formed in the 1950s eventually ended in divorce. Divorce rates rose

steadily from the 1890s through the 1960s (with a dip in the Depression and a spike after World War II), soared in the 1970s, and have fallen since 1981. Marriage rates, however, have also fallen significantly in the past 25 years.

9. **FALSE.** Ancient Roman philosophers and medieval theologians thought that loving your spouse too much was a form of "adultery," a betrayal of one's obligations to country or God. The ancient Greeks held that the purest form of love was between two men. In China, Confucian philosophers ranked the relationship between husband and wife as second from the bottom on their list of the most important family ties, with the father-eldest son relationship topping the list. Early Christians thought marriage was inescapably tainted by the presence of sex. According to the medieval church, virgins ranked highest in godliness, widows were second and wives a distant third.

10. **TRUE.** In 2001 schoolgirls around the world were asked whether they agreed with the statement that everyone needed to marry. Three-quarters of American schoolgirls agreed. But in Japan, 88 percent of schoolgirls disagreed.

11. **FALSE.** Divorce in modern America often does cause a sharp drop in the economic standard of living for women and children. But states that legalize no-fault divorce experienced an average 10 percent decline in suicide rates among married women over the following five years. And a recent study suggests that while divorce worsens the emotional well being of 55 percent to 60 percent of children, it improves the well-being of 40 percent to 45 percent.

12. **FALSE.** The form of marriage that has been approved by more societies than any other through the ages has been polygamy—one man and many women. That family form is the one mentioned most often in the first five books of the Bible. In some societies, one woman could marry several men. In others, two families could forge an alliance by marrying off a son or daughter to the "ghost" of the other family's dead child. For most of history; the main impetus for marriage was getting in-laws and managing property, not love or sex.

13. **TRUE.** Thirty-five percent of born-again Christians in this country have divorced, almost the same as the 37 percent of atheists and agnostics who have divorced—and 23 percent of born-again Christians have divorced twice. Among Pentecostals, the divorce rate is more than 40 percent. The region with the highest divorce rate is the Bible Belt.

Obedience

2

The Abu Ghraib Prison Scandal: Sources of Sadism

Marianne Szegedy-Maszak

In January 2004, a military investigator in Baghdad found on his cot a disk containing images of horrific physical abuse and humiliation committed by American military guards against Iraqi detainees at Abu Ghraib prison. A whistleblower, who (along with his family) was subsequently placed in protective custody because of death threats, found the images so disturbingly at odds with standards of military conduct and basic decency that he reported the abuse, which quickly grew into an international scandal. President Bush strongly condemned the "disgraceful conduct by a few American troops who dishonored our country and disregarded our values." Others, recalling abuses in Vietnam and Nazi Germany, wondered whether the military's culture of obedience and the extreme circumstances of war can turn otherwise decent people into agents of terror. At stake are the questions at the heart of this chapter: What if these "few" American soldiers weren't monsters? What if they were typical men and women who, caught in the wrong circumstances, found themselves committing atrocities? Faced with similar pressures, might the most ordinary person (of any nation) be capable of heinous acts?

At press time (August 2004), criminal charges had been brought against seven enlisted soldiers from the 372nd Military Police Company. Specialist Jeremy C. Sivits pleaded guilty and was sentenced to a year in prison; he is now cooperating with authorities in building the case against the other defendants. Pfc. Lynndie England, prominent in many of the photos (including one that shows her dragging a naked Iraqi man on a leash), will face trial at Fort Bragg, NC. The other five await hearings in Iraq and Germany, and their attorneys have already indicated that they will employ a "following orders" defense. An investigative report by a panel chaired by Maj. Gen. George Fay (which some critics have labeled a "whitewash"), due for release at the end of August, names some officers from the 205th Military Intelligence Brigade as bearing culpability for what happened. The commander of this unit, Col. Thomas Pappas, was reprimanded for failing to assure that his officers followed the Geneva Conventions at Abu Ghraib. Additionally, a separate Pentagon investigation chaired by former CIA director James Schlesinger is expected to criticize Secretary of Defense Donald Rumsfeld and his senior aides, though the Schlesinger report is prohibited from entering into "matters of personal responsibility."

In "Sources of Sadism," which first appeared in the 24 May 2004 edition of U.S. News & World Report, Marianne Szegedy-Maszak explores some of the reasons psychologists have offered to explain how American soldiers (at least one of whom was college-aged at the time of the abuses) could have knowingly degraded and tortured Iraqi detainees. The author refers directly to two experiments you will read about at some length in this chapter: Philip Zimbardo's Stanford Prison Experiment and Stanley Milgram's experiments in obedience.

If you have not yet seen the Abu Ghraib photos and wish to do so (be warned—they are disturbing), you can readily find them on the Internet.

1   Those hoping to see a flicker of anger or remorse or conscience on the faces of the American soldiers photographed tormenting Iraqi prisoners in Abu Ghraib are likely to be disappointed. Evidence of how these young recruits apparently became gleeful sadists can be found in neither their faces nor their biographies.

2   While many theories have been advanced about the forces that tragically came together at Abu Ghraib—inadequate training, overzealous intelligence gathering, failure of leadership—none can adequately account for the hardening of heart necessary for such sadism. So the question is: Are there particular conditions in Iraq today that might shed light on why these soldiers committed these unconscionable acts?

3   The usual points of reference in psychology are two classic studies that attempted to explore the capacity for evil residing in "normal" people. In 1971, Stanford psychologist Philip Zimbardo created a simulated prison and randomly assigned students to be either guards or prisoners. With astonishing speed, the "guards" indulged in forms of torture and humiliation not unlike those horrifying us today. This followed on earlier experiments by Yale psychologist Stanley Milgram on obedience to authority. Milgram recruited volunteers to participate in what he described as a study on learning. An actor sat in a chair that students believed was wired with electricity. Each time this actor would give an incorrect answer, the students would be directed by Milgram to deliver a larger shock. As the subject in the electric chair seemed to suffer more and more, 2 out of 3 of the unwitting students administered shocks that would have been lethal in real life.

4   These experiments demonstrate that Everyman is a potential torturer. But what relevance does that have to Baghdad today? Robert Okin, a professor of psychiatry at the University of California-San Francisco who has worked with victims of torture, says that while there are lessons to be learned from these studies, the particulars of the soldiers' life in Abu Ghraib also need to be taken into account. In Iraq, Okin says, the abuse became "an inexcusable way of working off their rage, anxiety about their own safety, and their sense of helplessness."

5   The anxiety and helplessness are exacerbated by difficult living conditions and constant danger—including the unfavorable odds of 450 military guards overseeing 7,000 often hostile prisoners. Then there is the issue of sex: One of the least discussed aspects of the occupation in Iraq has been the lack of a reliable local brothel where male soldiers are able to unwind. Experts have long appreciated the fact that sexual activity can often be a way of relieving the anxiety of war.

6   Abu Ghraib also has three traits that psychologist Herbert Kelman has described as necessary for torture: authorization, routinization, and dehumanization. To translate the jargon, authorization means that someone with power needs to say that extreme measures are acceptable. (Pfc. Lynndie England said in an interview last week that her superiors said, "Hey, you're doing great; keep it up.")

7   Authorization leads to routinization, a kind of division of labor. In Nazi Germany, for example, one person had responsibility for writing the orders

to deport the Jews, someone else for shaving their heads, and so on. The guards at Abu Ghraib were told they were merely "softening up" the prisoners for interrogation. Such parceling out of responsibility, says Boston psychiatrist Jonathan Shay, "seems to tantalize someone's moral compass, making it possible to do things that might be personally distasteful."

8   Dehumanization follows. In Vietnam the enemy became "slopes," and in Iraq they're "towel heads." Covering prisoners' faces with hoods, Okin adds, makes it possible for the soldiers "to sever any empathic human connection with them."

9   The protected walls of Abu Ghraib made it an island where conventional morality no longer applied. When these soldiers testify at court-martial, perhaps their testimony will contribute to the psychological theories on blind obedience to authority. However, Okin says, "The ethical questions just don't go away; horror doesn't go away by being able to explain it." And indeed, as the explanations always fall short, the horror continues to loom large.

The Perils of Obedience
Stanley Milgram

In 1963, a Yale psychologist conducted one of the classic studies on obedience. Stanley Milgram designed an experiment that forced participants either to violate their conscience by obeying the immoral demands of an authority figure or to refuse those demands. Surprisingly, Milgram found that few participants could resist the authority's orders, even when the participants knew that following these orders would result in another person's pain. Were the participants in these experiments incipient mass murderers? No, said Milgram. They were "ordinary people, simply doing their jobs." The implications of Milgram's conclusions are immense.

Consider these questions: Where does evil reside? What sort of people were responsible for the Holocaust, and for the long list of other atrocities that seem to blight the human record in every generation? Is it a lunatic fringe, a few sick but powerful people who are responsible for atrocities? If so, then we decent folk needn't ever look inside ourselves to understand evil since (by our definition) evil lurks out there, in "those sick ones." Milgram's study suggested otherwise: that under a special set of circumstances the obedience we naturally show authority figures can transform us into agents of terror.

The article that follows is one of the longest in this book, and it may help you to know in advance the author's organization. In paragraphs 1–11, Milgram discusses the larger significance and the history of dilemmas involving obedience to authority; he then summarizes his basic experimental design and follows with a report of one experiment. Milgram organizes the remainder of his article into sections, which he has subtitled "An Unexpected Outcome," "Peculiar Reactions," "The Etiquette of Submission," and "Duty Without Conflict." He begins his conclusion in paragraph 108. If you find the article too long or complex to complete in a single sitting, then plan to read sections at a time, taking notes on each until you're done. Anticipate the article that immediately follows this one: It reviews Milgram's work and largely concerns the ethics of his experimental design. Consider these ethics as you read so that you, in turn, can respond to Milgram's critics.

Stanley Milgram (1933–1984) taught and conducted research at Yale and Harvard universities and at the Graduate Center, City University of New York. He was named Guggenheim Fellow in 1972–1973 and a year later was nominated for the National Book Award for Obedience to Authority. *His other books include* Television and Antisocial Behavior *(1973),* The City and the Self *(1974),* Human Aggression *(1976), and* The Individual in the Social World *(1977).*

1   Obedience is as basic an element in the structure of social life as one can point to. Some system of authority is a requirement of all communal living, and it is only the person dwelling in isolation who is not forced to respond, with defiance or submission, to the commands of others. For many people, obedience is a deeply ingrained behavior tendency, indeed a potent impulse overriding training in ethics, sympathy, and moral conduct.

2   The dilemma inherent in submission to authority is ancient, as old as the story of Abraham, and the question of whether one should obey when commands conflict with conscience has been argued by Plato, dramatized in *Antigone,* and treated to philosophic analysis in almost every historical epoch. Conservative philosophers argue that the very fabric of society is threatened by disobedience, while humanists stress the primacy of the individual conscience.

3   The legal and philosophic aspects of obedience are of enormous import, but they say very little about how most people behave in concrete situations. I set up a simple experiment at Yale University to test how much pain an ordinary citizen would inflict on another person simply because he was ordered to by an experimental scientist. Stark authority was pitted against the subjects' strongest moral imperatives against hurting others, and with the subjects' ears ringing with the screams of the victims, authority won more often than not. The extreme willingness of adults to go to almost any lengths on the command of an authority constitutes the chief finding of the study and the fact most urgently demanding explanation.

4   In the basic experimental design, two people come to a psychology laboratory to take part in a study of memory and learning. One of them is designated as a "teacher" and the other a "learner." The experimenter explains that the study is concerned with the effects of punishment on learning. The learner is conducted into a room, seated in a kind of miniature electric chair; his arms are strapped to prevent excessive movement, and an electrode is attached to his wrist. He is told that he will be read lists of simple word pairs, and that he will then be tested on his ability to remember the second word of a pair when he hears the first one again. Whenever he makes an error, he will receive electric shocks of increasing intensity.

5   The real focus of the experiment is the teacher. After watching the learner being strapped into place, he is seated before an impressive shock generator. The instrument panel consists of thirty level switches set in a horizontal line. Each switch is clearly labeled with a voltage designation ranging from 15 to 450 volts. The following designations are

clearly indicated for groups of four switches, going from left to right: Slight Shock, Moderate Shock, Strong Shock, Very Strong Shock, Intense Shock, Extreme Intensity Shock, Danger: Severe Shock. (Two switches after this last designation are simply marked XXX.)

6   When a switch is depressed, a pilot light corresponding to each switch is illuminated in bright red; an electric buzzing is heard; a blue light, labeled "voltage energizer," flashes; the dial on the voltage meter swings to the right; and various relay clicks sound off.

7   The upper left-hand corner of the generator is labeled SHOCK GENERATOR, TYPE ZLB, DYSON INSTRUMENT COMPANY, WALTHAM, MASS. OUTPUT 15 VOLTS—450 VOLTS.

8   Each subject is given a sample 45-volt shock from the generator before his run as teacher, and the jolt strengthens his belief in the authenticity of the machine.

9   The teacher is a genuinely naive subject who has come to the laboratory for the experiment. The learner, or victim, is actually an actor who receives no shock at all. The point of the experiment is to see how far a person will proceed in a concrete and measurable situation in which he is ordered to inflict increasing pain on a protesting victim.

10   Conflict arises when the man receiving the shock begins to show that he is experiencing discomfort. At 75 volts, he grunts; at 120 volts, he complains loudly; at 150, he demands to be released from the experiment. As the voltage increases, his protests become more vehement and emotional. At 285 volts, his response can be described only as an agonized scream. Soon thereafter, he makes no sound at all.

11   For the teacher, the situation quickly becomes one of gripping tension. It is not a game for him; conflict is intense and obvious. The manifest suffering of the learner presses him to quit; but each time he hesitates to administer a shock, the experimenter orders him to continue. To extricate himself from this plight, the subject must make a clear break with authority.*

12   The subject, Gretchen Brandt,† is an attractive thirty-one-year-old medical technician who works at the Yale Medical School. She had emigrated from Germany five years before.

13   On several occasions when the learner complains, she turns to the experimenter coolly and inquires, "Shall I continue?" She promptly returns to her task when the experimenter asks her to do so. At the administration of 210 volts, she turns to the experimenter, remarking firmly, "Well, I'm sorry, I don't think we should continue."

14   EXPERIMENTER: The experiment requires that you go on until he has learned all the word pairs correctly.

---

* The ethical problems of carrying out an experiment of this sort are too complex to be dealt with here, but they receive extended treatment in the book from which this article is adapted.

† Names of subjects described in this piece have been changed.

15   BRANDT: He has a heart condition. I'm sorry. He told you that before.

16   EXPERIMENTER: The shocks may be painful but they are not dangerous.

17   BRANDT: Well, I'm sorry, I think when shocks continue like this, they *are* dangerous. You ask him if he wants to get out. It's his free will.

18   EXPERIMENTER: It is absolutely essential that we continue. . . .

19   BRANDT: I'd like you to ask him. We came here of our free will. If he wants to continue I'll go ahead. He told you he had a heart condition. I'm sorry. I don't want to be responsible for anything happening to him. I wouldn't like it for me either.

20   EXPERIMENTER: You have no other choice.

21   BRANDT: I think we are here on our own free will. I don't want to be responsible if anything happens to him. Please understand that.

22   She refuses to go further and the experiment is terminated.

23   The woman is firm and resolute throughout. She indicates in the interview that she was in no way tense or nervous, and this corresponds to her controlled appearance during the experiment. She feels that the last shock she administered to the learner was extremely painful and reiterates that she "did not want to be responsible for any harm to him."

24   The woman's straightforward, courteous behavior in the experiment, lack of tension, and total control of her own action seem to make disobedience a simple and rational deed. Her behavior is the very embodiment of what I envisioned would be true for almost all subjects.

An Unexpected Outcome

25 Before the experiments, I sought predictions about the outcome from various kinds of people—psychiatrists, college sophomores, middle-class adults, graduate students, and faculty in the behavioral sciences. With remarkable similarity, they predicted that virtually all subjects would refuse to obey the experimenter. The psychiatrists, specifically, predicted that most subjects would not go beyond 150 volts, when the victim makes his first explicit demand to be freed. They expected that only 4 percent would reach 300 volts, and that only a pathological fringe of about one in a thousand would administer the highest shock on the board.

26   These predictions were unequivocally wrong. Of the forty subjects in the first experiment, twenty-five obeyed the orders of the experimenter to the end, punishing the victim until they reached the most potent shock available on the generator. After 450 volts were administered three times, the experimenter called a halt to the session. Many obedient subjects then heaved sights of relief, mopped their brows, rubbed their fingers over their eyes, or nervously fumbled cigarettes. Others displayed only minimal signs of tension from beginning to end.

27   When the very first experiments were carried out, Yale undergraduates were used as subjects, and about 60 percent of them were fully obedient. A colleague of mine immediately dismissed these findings as having no relevance to "ordinary" people, asserting that Yale undergraduates are a highly aggressive, competitive bunch who step on each other's necks on the slightest provocation. He assured me that when "ordinary" people

were tested, the results would be quite different. As we moved from the pilot studies to the regular experimental series, people drawn from every stratum of New Haven life came to be employed in the experiment: professionals, white-collar workers, unemployed persons, and industrial workers. *The experiment's total outcome was the same as we had observed among the students.*

28   Moreover, when the experiments were repeated in Princeton, Munich, Rome, South Africa, and Australia, the level of obedience was invariably somewhat *higher* than found in the investigation reported in this article. Thus one scientist in Munich found 85 percent of his subjects to be obedient.

29   Fred Prozi's reactions, if more dramatic than most, illuminate the conflicts experienced by others in less visible form. About fifty years old and unemployed at the time of the experiment, he has a good-natured, if slightly dissolute, appearance, and he strikes people as a rather ordinary fellow. He begins the session calmly but becomes tense as it proceeds. After delivering the 180-volt shock, he pivots around in his chair and, shaking his head, addresses the experimenter in agitated tones:

30   PROZI: I can't stand it. I'm not going to kill that man in there. You hear him hollering?

31   EXPERIMENTER: As I told you before, the shocks may be painful, but . . .

32   PROZI: But he's hollering. He can't stand it. What's going to happen to him?

33   EXPERIMENTER (*his voice patient, matter-of-fact*): The experiment requires that you continue, Teacher.

34   PROZI: Aaah, but unh, I'm not going to get that man sick in there—know what I mean?

35   EXPERIMENTER: Whether the learner likes it or not, we must go on, through all the word pairs.

36   PROZI: I refuse to take the responsibility. He's in there hollering!

37   EXPERIMENTER: It's absolutely essential that you continue, Prozi.

38   PROZI (*indicating the unused questions*): There's too many left here. I mean, Jeez, if he gets them wrong, there's too many of them left. I mean, who's going to take the responsibility if anything happens to that gentleman?

39   EXPERIMENTER: I'm responsible for anything that happens to him. Continue, please.

40   PROZI: All right. (*Consults list of words.*) The next one's "Slow—walk, truck, dance, music." Answer, please (*A buzzing sound indicates the learner has signaled his answer.*) Wrong. A hundred and ninety-five volts. "Dance." (*Zzumph!*)

41   LEARNER (*yelling*): Let me out of here! My heart's bothering me! (*Teacher looks at experimenter.*)

42   EXPERIMENTER: Continue, please.

43   LEARNER (*screaming*): Let me out of here! You have no right to keep me here! Let me out of here, my heart's bothering me, let me out!

44   PROZI (*shakes head, pats the table nervously*): You see, he's hollering. Hear that? Gee, I don't know.

45   EXPERIMENTER: The experiment requires . . .

46   PROZI (*interrupting*): I know it does, sir, but I mean—hunh! He don't know what he's getting in for. He's up to 195 volts! (*Experiment continues, through 210 volts, 225 volts, 240 volts, 255 volts, 270 volts, at which point Prozi, with evident relief, runs out of word-pair questions.*)

47   EXPERIMENTER: You'll have to go back to the beginning of that page and go through them again until he's learned them all correctly.

48   PROZI: Aw, no. I'm not going to kill that man. You mean I've got to keep going up with the scale? No sir. He's hollering in there. I'm not going to give him 450 volts.

49   EXPERIMENTER: The experiment requires that you go on.

50   LEARNER: Ohhh. I absolutely refuse to answer anymore. (*Shouting urgently now.*) Let me out of here! You can't hold me here! Get me out. Get-me-out-of-here!

51   EXPERIMENTER: Continue. The next word is "Green," please.

52   PROZI: "Green—grass, hat, ink, apple." (*Nothing happens. No answering buzz. Just gloomy silence.*)

53   PROZI: I don't think he is going to answer.

54   EXPERIMENTER: If the learner doesn't answer in a reasonable time, about four or five seconds, consider the answer wrong. And follow the same procedures you have been doing for wrong answers. Say, "Wrong," tell him the number of volts, give him the punishment, read him the correct answer. Continue, please.

55   PROZI: "Green—grass, hat, ink, apple." Answer, please. (*More silence. Subject just sits there.*)

56   EXPERIMENTER: Go on with the procedure, please.

57   PROZI: Three hundred and fifteen volts. The answer is "ink." (*Zzumph!*)

58   LEARNER: Ohh. Ooohh.

59   PROZI (*relieved to hear response*): Next one . . .

60   LEARNER: I absolutely refuse to answer.

61   PROZI: You got to. You get a shock if you don't answer. (*Experiment continues with learner refusing to answer, and finally, failing even to grunt or groan. At 375 volts, the subject stands up.*)

62   PROZI: I think something's happened to that fellow in there. I don't get no answer. He was hollering at less voltage. Can't you check in and see if he's all right, please?

63   EXPERIMENTER: (*with same detached calm*): Not once we've started. Please continue, Teacher.

64   PROZI (*sits down, sighs deeply*): "Cool—day, shade, water, paint." Answer, please. Are you all right in there? Are you all right?

65   EXPERIMENTER: Please continue, Teacher. Continue, please. (*Subject pushes lever. Zzumph!*)

66   PROZI (*swiveling around in his chair*): Something's happened to that man in there. (*Swiveling back.*) Next one. "Low—dollar, necklace, moon, paint." (*Turning around again.*) Something's happened to that man in there. You better check on him, sir. He won't answer or nothing.

67   EXPERIMENTER: Continue. Go on, please.

68   PROZI: You accept all responsibility?

69   EXPERIMENTER: The responsibility is mine. Correct. Please go on. (*Subject returns to his list, starts running through words as rapidly as he can read them, works through to 450 volts.*)

70   PROZI: That's that.

71   EXPERIMENTER: Continue using the 450 switch for each wrong answer. Continue, please.

72   PROZI: But I don't get anything!

73   EXPERIMENTER: Please continue. The next word is "white."

74   PROZI: Don't you think you should look in on him, please?

75   EXPERIMENTER: Not once we've started the experiment.

76   PROZI: What if he's dead in there? (*Gestures toward the room with the electric chair.*) I mean, he told me he can't stand the shock, sir. I don't mean to be rude, but I think you should look in on him. All you have to do is look in on him. All you have to do is look in the door. I don't get no answer, no noise. Something might have happened to the gentleman in there, sir.

77   EXPERIMENTER: We must continue. Go on, please.

78   PROZI: You mean keep giving him what? Four-hundred-fifty volts, what he's got now?

79   EXPERIMENTER: That's correct. Continue. The next word is "white."

80   PROZI (*now at a furious pace*): "White—cloud, horse, rock, house." Answer, please. The answer is "horse." Four hundred and fifty volts. (*Zzumph!*) Next word, "Bag—paint, music, clown, girl." The answer is "paint." Four hundred and fifty volts. (*Zzumph!*) Next word is "Short—sentence, movie . . ."

81   EXPERIMENTER: Excuse me, Teacher. We'll have to discontinue the experiment.

Peculiar Reactions

82   Morris Braverman, another subject, is a thirty-nine-year-old social worker. He looks older than his years because of his bald head and serious demeanor. His brow is furrowed, as if all the world's burdens were carried on his face. He appears intelligent and concerned.

83   When the learner refuses to answer and the experimenter instructs Braverman to treat the absence of an answer as equivalent to a wrong answer, he takes his instruction to heart. Before administering 300 volts he asserts officiously to the victim, "Mr. Wallace, your silence has to be considered as a wrong answer." Then he administers the shock. He offers half-heartedly to change places with the learner, then asks the experimenter, "Do I have to follow these instructions literally?" He is satisfied with the experimenter's answer that he does. His very refined and authoritative manner of speaking is increasingly broken up by wheezing laughter.

84   The experimenter's notes on Mr. Braverman at the last few shocks are:

> Almost breaking up now each time gives shock. Rubbing face to hide laughter. Squinting, trying to hide face with hand, still laughing. Cannot control his laughter at this point no matter what he does. Clenching fist, pushing it onto table.

85   In an interview after the session, Mr. Braverman summarizes the experiment with impressive fluency and intelligence. He feels the experiment may have been designed also to "test the effects on the teacher of being in an essentially sadistic role, as well as the reactions of a student to a learning situation that was authoritative and punitive." When asked how painful the last few shocks administered to the learner were, he indicates that the most extreme category on the scale is not adequate (it read EXTREMELY PAINFUL) and places his mark at the edge of the scale with an arrow carrying it beyond the scale.

86   It is almost impossible to convey the greatly relaxed, sedate quality of his conversation in the interview. In the most relaxed terms, he speaks about his severe inner tension.

87   EXPERIMENTER: At what point were you most tense or nervous?

88   MR. BRAVERMAN: Well, when he first began to cry out in pain, and I realized this was hurting him. This got worse when he just blocked and refused to answer. There was I. I'm a nice person, I think, hurting somebody, and caught up in what seemed a mad situation . . . and in the interest of science, one goes through with it.

89   When the interviewer pursues the general question of tension, Mr. Braverman spontaneously mentions his laughter.

90   "My reactions were awfully peculiar. I don't know if you were watching me, but my reactions were giggly, and trying to stifle laughter. This isn't the way I usually am. This was a sheer reaction to a totally impossible situation. And my reaction was to the situation of having to hurt somebody. And being totally helpless and caught up in a set of circumstances where I just couldn't deviate and I couldn't try to help. This is what got me."

91   Mr. Braverman, like all subjects, was told the actual nature and purpose of the experiment, and a year later he affirmed in a questionnaire that he had learned something of personal importance: "What appalled me was that I could possess this capacity for obedience and compliance to a central idea, i.e., the value of a memory experiment, even after it became clear that continued adherence to this value was at the expense of violation of another value, i.e., don't hurt someone who is helpless and not hurting you. As my wife said, 'You can call yourself Eichmann.'* I hope I deal more effectively with any future conflicts of values I encounter."

The Etiquette of Submission

92 One theoretical interpretation of this behavior holds that all people harbor deeply aggressive instincts continually pressing for expression, and that the experiment provides institutional justification for the release of these impulses. According to this view, if a person is placed in a situation in

---

* *Adolf Eichmann* (1906–1962), the Nazi official responsible for implementing Hitler's "Final Solution" to exterminate the Jews, escaped to Argentina after World War II. In 1960, Israeli agents captured him and brought him to Israel, where he was tried as a war criminal and sentenced to death. At his trial, Eichmann maintained that he was merely following orders in arranging murders of his victims.

which he has complete power over another individual, whom he may punish as much as he likes, all that is sadistic and bestial in man comes to the fore. The impulse to shock the victim is seen to flow from the potent aggressive tendencies, which are part of the motivational life of the individual, and the experiment, because it provides social legitimacy, simply opens the door to their expression.

93   It becomes vital, therefore, to compare the subject's performance when he is under orders and when he is allowed to choose the shock level.

94   The procedure was identical to our standard experiment, except that the teacher was told that he was free to select any shock level on any of the trials. (The experimenter took pains to point out that the teacher could use the highest levels on the generator, the lowest, any in between, or any combination of levels.) Each subject proceeded for thirty critical trials. The learner's protests were coordinated to standard shock levels, his first grunt coming at 75 volts, his first vehement protest at 150 volts.

95   The average shock used during the thirty critical trials was less than 60 volts—lower than the point at which the victim showed the first signs of discomfort. Three of the forty subjects did not go beyond the very lowest level on the board, twenty-eight went no higher than 75 volts, and thirty-eight did not go beyond the first loud protest at 150 volts. Two subjects provided the exception, administering up to 325 and 450 volts, but the overall result was that the great majority of people delivered very low, usually painless, shocks when the choice was explicitly up to them.

96   This condition of the experiment undermines another commonly offered explanation of the subjects' behavior—that those who shocked the victim at the most severe levels came only from the sadistic fringe of society. If one considers that almost two-thirds of the participants fall into the category of "obedient" subjects, and that they represented ordinary people drawn from working, managerial, and professional classes, the argument becomes very shaky. Indeed, it is highly reminiscent of the issue that arose in connection with Hannah Arendt's 1963 book, *Eichmann in Jerusalem.* Arendt contended that the prosecution's efforts to depict Eichmann as a sadistic monster was fundamentally wrong, that he came closer to being an uninspired bureaucrat who simply sat at his desk and did his job. For asserting her views, Arendt became the object of considerable scorn, even calumny. Somehow, it was felt that the monstrous deeds carried out by Eichmann required a brutal, twisted personality, evil incarnate. After witnessing hundreds of ordinary persons submit to the authority in our own experiments, I must conclude that Arendt's conception of the banality of evil comes closer to the truth than one might dare imagine. The ordinary person who shocked the victim did so out of a sense of obligation—an impression of his duties as a subject—and not from any peculiarly aggressive tendencies.

97   This is, perhaps, the most fundamental lesson of our study: ordinary people, simply doing their jobs, and without any particular hostility on their part, can become agents in a terrible destructive process. Moreover, even

when the destructive effects of their work become patently clear, and they are asked to carry out actions incompatible with fundamental standards of morality, relatively few people have the resources needed to resist authority.

98   Many of the people were in some sense against what they did to the learner, and many protested even while they obeyed. Some were totally convinced of the wrongness of their actions but could not bring themselves to make an open break with authority. They often derived satisfaction from their thoughts and felt that—within themselves, at least—they had been on the side of the angels. They tried to reduce strain by obeying the experimenter but "only slightly," encouraging the learner, touching the generator switches gingerly. When interviewed, such a subject would stress that he had "asserted my humanity" by administering the briefest shock possible. Handling the conflict in this manner was easier than defiance.

99   The situation is constructed so that there is no way the subject can stop shocking the learner without violating the experimenter's definitions of his own competence. The subject fears that he will appear arrogant, untoward, and rude if he breaks off. Although these inhibiting emotions appear small in scope alongside the violence being done to the learner, they suffuse the mind and feelings of the subject, who is miserable at the prospect of having to repudiate the authority to his face. (When the experiment was altered so that the experimenter gave his instructions by telephone instead of in person, only a third as many people were fully obedient through 450 volts.) It is a curious thing that a measure of compassion on the part of the subject—an unwillingness to "hurt" the experimenter's feelings—is part of those binding forces inhibiting his disobedience. The withdrawal of such deference may be as painful to the subject as to the authority he defies.

Duty Without Conflict

100 The subjects do not derive satisfaction from inflicting pain, but they often like the feeling they get from pleasing the experimenter. They are proud of doing a good job, obeying the experimenter under difficult circumstances. While the subjects administered only mild shocks on their own initiative, one experimental variation showed that, under orders, 30 percent of them were willing to deliver 450 volts even when they had to forcibly push the learner's hand down on the electrode.

101   Bruno Batta is a thirty-seven-year-old welder who took part in the variation requiring the use of force. He was born in New Haven, his parents in Italy. He has a rough-hewn face that conveys a conspicuous lack of alertness. He has some difficulty in mastering the experimental procedure and needs to be corrected by the experimenter several times. He shows appreciation for the help and willingness to do what is required. After the 150-volt level, Batta has to force the learner's hand down on the shock plate, since the learner himself refuses to touch it.

102   When the learner first complains, Mr. Batta pays no attention to him. His face remains impassive, as if to dissociate himself from the learner's disruptive behavior. When the experimenter instructs him to force the learner's hand down, he adopts a rigid, mechanical procedure. He tests the generator switch. When it fails to function, he immediately forces the learner's hand onto the shock plate. All the while he maintains the same rigid mask. The learner, seated alongside him, begs him to stop, but with robotic impassivity he continues the procedure.

103   What is extraordinary is his apparent total indifference to the learner; he hardly takes cognizance of him as a human being. Meanwhile, he relates to the experimenter in a submissive and courteous fashion.

104   At the 330-volt level, the learner refuses not only to touch the shock plate but also to provide any answers. Annoyed, Batta turns to him, and chastises him: "You better answer and get it over with. We can't stay here all night." These are the only words he directs to the learner in the course of an hour. Never again does he speak to him. The scene is brutal and depressing, his hard, impassive face showing total indifference as he subdues the screaming learner and gives him shocks. He seems to derive no pleasure from the act itself, only quiet satisfaction at doing his job properly.

105   When he administers 450 volts, he turns to the experimenter and asks, "Where do we go from here, Professor?" His tone is deferential and expresses his willingness to be a cooperative subject, in contrast to the learner's obstinacy.

106   At the end of the session he tells the experimenter how honored he has been to help him, and in a moment of contrition, remarks, "Sir, sorry it couldn't have been a full experiment."

107   He has done his honest best. It is only the deficient behavior of the learner that has denied the experimenter full satisfaction.

108   The essence of obedience is that a person comes to view himself as the instrument for carrying out another person's wishes, and he therefore no longer regards himself as responsible for his actions. Once this critical shift of viewpoint has occurred, all of the essential features of obedience follow. The most far-reaching consequence is that the person feels responsible *to* the authority directing him but feels no responsibility *for* the content of the actions that the authority prescribes. Morality does not disappear—it acquires a radically different focus: the subordinate person feels shame or pride depending on how adequately he has performed the actions called for by authority.

109   Language provides numerous terms to pinpoint this type of morality: *loyalty, duty, discipline* all are terms heavily saturated with moral meaning and refer to the degree to which a person fulfills his obligations to authority. They refer not to the "goodness" of the person per se but to the adequacy with which a subordinate fulfills his socially defined role. The most frequent defense of the individual who has performed a heinous act under command of authority is that he has simply done his duty. In asserting this

defense, the individual is not introducing an alibi concocted for the moment but is reporting honestly on the psychological attitude induced by submission to authority.

110   For a person to feel responsible for his actions, he must sense that the behavior has flowed from "the self." In the situation we have studied, subjects have precisely the opposite view of their actions—namely, they see them as originating in the motives of some other person. Subjects in the experiment frequently said, "If it were up to me, I would not have administered shocks to the learner."

111   Once authority has been isolated as the cause of the subject's behavior, it is legitimate to inquire into the necessary elements of authority and how it must be perceived in order to gain compliance. We conducted some investigations into the kinds of changes that would cause the experimenter to lose his power and to be disobeyed by the subject. Some of the variations revealed that:

- *The experimenter's physical presence has a marked impact on his authority.* As cited earlier, obedience dropped off sharply when orders were given by telephone. The experimenter could often induce a disobedient subject to go on by returning to the laboratory.
- *Conflicting authority severely paralyzes action.* When two experimenters of equal status, both seated at the command desk, gave incompatible orders, no shocks were delivered past the point of their disagreement.
- *The rebellious action of others severely undermines authority.* In one variation, three teachers (two actors and a real subject) administered a test and shocks. When the two actors disobeyed the experimenter and refused to go beyond a certain shock level, thirty-six of the forty subjects joined their disobedient peers and refused as well.

112   Although the experimenter's authority was fragile in some respects, it is also true that he had almost none of the tools used in ordinary command structures. For example, the experimenter did not threaten the subjects with punishment—such as loss of income, community ostracism, or jail—for failure to obey. Neither could he offer incentives. Indeed, we should expect the experimenter's authority to be much less than that of someone like a general, since the experimenter has no power to enforce his imperatives, and since participation in a psychological experiment scarcely evokes the sense of urgency and dedication found in warfare. Despite these limitations, he still managed to command a dismaying degree of obedience.

113   I will cite one final variation of the experiment that depicts a dilemma that is more common in everyday life. The subject was not ordered to pull the lever that shocked the victim, but merely to perform a subsidiary task (administering the word-pair test) while another person administered the shock. In this situation, thirty-seven of forty adults continued to the highest level on the shock generator. Predictably, they excused their behavior

by saying that the responsibility belonged to the man who actually pulled the switch. This may illustrate a dangerously typical arrangement in a complex society: it is easy to ignore responsibility when one is only an intermediate link in a chain of action.

114   The problem of obedience is not wholly psychological. The form and shape of society and the way it is developing have much to do with it. There was a time, perhaps, when people were able to give a fully human response to any situation because they were fully absorbed in it as human beings. But as soon as there was a division of labor things changed. Beyond a certain point, the breaking up of society into people carrying out narrow and very special jobs takes away from the human quality of work and life. A person does not get to see the whole situation but only a small part of it, and is thus unable to act without some kind of overall direction. He yields to authority but in doing so is alienated from his own actions.

115   Even Eichmann was sickened when he toured the concentration camps, but he had only to sit at a desk and shuffle papers. At the same time the man in the camp who actually dropped Cyclon-b into the gas chambers was able to justify *his* behavior on the ground that he was only following orders from above. Thus there is a fragmentation of the total human act; no one is confronted with the consequences of his decision to carry out the evil act. The person who assumes responsibility has evaporated. Perhaps this is the most common characteristic of socially organized evil in modern society.

Review of Stanley Milgram's Experiments on Obedience
Diana Baumrind

Many of Milgram's colleagues saluted him for providing that "hard information" about human nature. Others attacked him for violating the rights of his subjects. Still others faulted his experimental design and claimed he could not, with any validity, speculate on life outside the laboratory based on the behavior of his subjects within.

In the following excerpted review, psychologist Diana Baumrind excoriates Milgram for "entrapping" his subjects and potentially harming their "self-image or ability to trust adult authorities in the future." In a footnote at the end of this selection (page 331), we summarize Milgram's response to Baumrind's critique.

Diana Baumrind is a psychologist who, when writing this review, worked at the Institute of Human Development, University of California, Berkeley. The review appeared in American Psychologist *shortly after Milgram published the results of his first experiments in 1963.*

1 . . . The dependent, obedient attitude assumed by most subjects in the experimental setting is appropriate to that situation. The "game" is defined by the experimenter and he makes the rules. By volunteering, the subject agrees implicitly to assume a posture of trust and obedience. While the experimental conditions leave him exposed, the subject has the right to assume that his security and self-esteem will be protected.

2   There are other professional situations in which one member—the patient or client—expects help and protection from the other—the physician or psychologist. But the interpersonal relationship between experimenter and subject additionally has unique features which are likely to provoke initial anxiety in the subject. The laboratory is unfamiliar as a setting and the rules of behavior ambiguous compared to a clinician's office. Because of the anxiety and passivity generated by the setting, the subject is more prone to behave in an obedient, suggestible manner in the laboratory than elsewhere. Therefore, the laboratory is not the place to study degree of obedience or suggestibility, as a function of a particular experimental condition, since the base line for these phenomena as found in the laboratory is probably much higher than in most other settings. Thus experiments in which the relationship to the experimenter as an authority is used as an independent condition are imperfectly designed for the same reason that they are prone to injure the subjects involved. They disregard the special quality of trust and obedience with which the subject appropriately regards the experimenter.

3   Other phenomena which present ethical decisions, unlike those mentioned above, *can* be reproduced successfully in the laboratory. Failure experience, conformity to peer judgment, and isolation are among such phenomena. In these cases we can expect the experimenter to take whatever measures are necessary to prevent the subject from leaving the laboratory more humiliated, insecure, alienated, or hostile than when he arrived. To guarantee that an especially sensitive subject leaves a stressful experimental experience in the proper state sometimes requires special clinical training. But usually an attitude of compassion, respect, gratitude, and common sense will suffice, and no amount of clinical training will substitute. The subject has the right to expect that the psychologist with whom he is interacting has some concern for his welfare, and the personal attributes and professional skill to express his good will effectively.

4   Unfortunately, the subject is not always treated with the respect he deserves. It has become more commonplace in sociopsychological laboratory studies to manipulate, embarrass, and discomfort subjects. At times the insult to the subject's sensibilities extends to the journal reader when the results are reported. Milgram's (1963) study is a case in point. The following is Milgram's abstract of his experiment:

> This article describes a procedure for the study of destructive obedience in the laboratory. It consists of ordering a naive S to administer increasingly more severe punishment to a victim in the context of a learning experiment.* Punishment is administered by means of a

shock generator with 30 graded switches ranging from Slight Shock to Danger: Severe Shock. The victim is a confederate of E. The primary dependent variable is the maximum shock the S is willing to administer before he refuses to continue further.** 26 Ss obeyed the experimental commands fully, and administered the highest shock on the generator. 14 Ss broke off the experiment at some point after the victim protested and refused to provide further answers. The procedure created extreme levels of nervous tension in some Ss. Profuse sweating, trembling, and stuttering were typical expressions of this emotional disturbance. One unexpected sign of tension—yet to be explained—was the regular occurrence of nervous laughter, which in some Ss developed into uncontrollable seizures. The variety of interesting behavioral dynamics observed in the experiment, the reality of the situation for the S, and the possibility of parametric variations† within the framework of the procedure point to the fruitfulness of further study [p. 371].

5   The detached, objective manner in which Milgram reports the emotional disturbance suffered by his subjects contrasts sharply with his graphic account of that disturbance. Following are two other quotes describing the effects on his subjects of the experimental conditions:

> I observed a mature and initially poised businessman enter the laboratory smiling and confident. Within 20 minutes he was reduced to a twitching, stuttering wreck, who was rapidly approaching a point of nervous collapse. He constantly pulled on his earlobe, and twisted his hands. At one point he pushed his fist into his forehead and muttered: "Oh God, let's stop it." And yet he continued to respond to every word of the experimenter, and obeyed to the end [p. 377].

> In a large number of cases the degree of tension reached extremes that are rarely seen in sociopsychological laboratory studies. Subjects were observed to sweat, tremble, stutter, bite their lips, groan, and dig their fingernails into their flesh. These were characteristic rather than exceptional responses to the experiment.
>   One sign of tension was the regular occurrence of nervous laughing fits. Fourteen of the 40 subjects showed definite signs of nervous laughter and smiling. The laughter seemed entirely out of place, even bizarre. Full-blown, uncontrollable seizures were observed for 3 subjects. On one occasion we observed a seizure so violently convulsive that it was necessary to call a halt to the experiment. . . [p. 375].

---

* In psychological experiments, S is an abbreviation for *subject*; E is an abbreviation for *experimenter*.

** In the context of a psychological experiment, a *dependent variable* is a behavior that is expected to change as a result of changes in the experimental procedure.

† *Parametric variation* is a statistical term that describes the degree to which information based on data for one experiment can be applied to data for a slightly different experiment.

Milgram does state that,

> After the interview, procedures were undertaken to assure that the
> subject would leave the laboratory in a state of well being. A friendly
> reconciliation was arranged between the subject and the victim, and an
> effort was made to reduce any tensions that arose as a result of the
> experiment [p. 374].

It would be interesting to know what sort of procedures could dissipate the
type of emotional disturbance just described. In view of the effects on subjects, traumatic to a degree which Milgram himself considers nearly
unprecedented in sociopsychological experiments, his casual assurance
that these tensions were dissipated before the subject left the laboratory is
unconvincing.

6   What could be the rational basis for such a posture of indifference?
Perhaps Milgram supplies the answer himself when he partially explains
the subject's destructive obedience as follows, "Thus they assume that the
discomfort caused the victim is momentary, while the scientific gains
resulting from the experiment are enduring" [p. 378]. Indeed such a ratio-
nale might suffice to justify the means used to achieve his end if that end
were of inestimable value to humanity or were not itself transformed by
the means by which it was attained.

7   The behavioral psychologist is not in as good a position to objectify his
faith in the significance of his work as medical colleagues at points of
breakthrough. His experimental situations are not sufficiently accurate
models of real-life experience; his sampling techniques are seldom of a
scope which would justify the meaning with which he would like to
endow his results; and these results are hard to reproduce by colleagues
with opposing theoretical views. Unlike the Sabin vaccine,* for example,
the concrete benefit to humanity of his particular piece of work, no
matter how competently handled, cannot justify the risk that real harm
will be done to the subject. I am not speaking of physical discomfort,
inconvenience, or experimental deception per se, but of permanent harm,
however slight. I do regard the emotional disturbance described by
Milgram as potentially harmful because it could easily effect an alteration
in the subject's self-image or ability to trust adult authorities in the
future. It is potentially harmful to a subject to commit, in the course of an
experiment, acts which he himself considers unworthy, particularly when
he has been entrapped into committing such acts by an individual he has
reason to trust. The subject's personal responsibility for his actions is not
erased because the experimenter reveals to him the means which he used
to stimulate these actions. The subject realizes that he would have hurt
the victim if the current were on. The realization that he also made a fool
of himself by accepting the experimental set results in additional loss of

---

* The Sabin vaccine provides immunization against polio.

self-esteem. Moreover, the subject finds it difficult to express his anger outwardly after the experimenter in a self-acceptant but friendly manner reveals the hoax.

8   A fairly intense corrective interpersonal experience is indicated wherein the subject admits and accepts his responsibility for his own actions, and at the same time gives vent to his hurt and anger at being fooled. Perhaps an experience as distressing as the one described by Milgram can be integrated by the subject, provided that careful thought is given to the matter. The propriety of such experimentation is still in question even if such a reparational experience were forthcoming. Without it I would expect a naive, sensitive subject to remain deeply hurt and anxious for some time, and a sophisticated, cynical subject to become even more alienated and distrustful.

9   In addition the experimental procedure used by Milgram does not appear suited to the objectives of the study because it does not take into account the special quality of the set which the subject has in the experimental situation. Milgram is concerned with a very important problem, namely, the social consequences of destructive obedience. He says,

> Gas chambers were built, death camps were guarded, daily quotas of corpses were produced with the same efficiency as the manufacture of appliances. These inhumane policies may have originated in the mind of a single person, but they could only be carried out on a massive scale if a very large number of persons obeyed orders [p. 371].

But the parallel between authority-subordinate relationships in Hitler's Germany and in Milgram's laboratory is unclear. In the former situation the SS man or member of the German Officer Corps, when obeying orders to slaughter, had no reason to think of his superior officer as benignly disposed towards himself or their victims. The victims were perceived as subhuman and not worthy of consideration. The subordinate officer was an agent in a great cause. He did not need to feel guilt or conflict because within his frame of reference he was acting rightly.

10   It is obvious from Milgram's own description that most of his subjects were concerned about their victims and did trust the experimenter, and that their distressful conflict was generated in part by the consequences of these two disparate but appropriate attitudes. Their distress may have resulted from shock at what the experimenter was doing to them as well as from what they thought they were doing to their victims. In any case there is not a convincing parallel between the phenomena studied by Milgram and destructive obedience as the concept would apply to the subordinate-authority relationship demonstrated in Hitler's Germany. If the experiments were conducted "outside of New Haven and without any visible ties to the university," I would still question their validity on similar although not identical grounds. In addition, I would question the representativeness of a sample of subjects who would voluntarily participate within a noninstitutional setting.

11   In summary, the experimental objectives of the psychologist are seldom incompatible with the subject's ongoing state of well being, provided that the experimenter is willing to take the subject's motives and interests into consideration when planning his methods and correctives. Section 4b in *Ethical Standards of Psychologists* (APA, undated) reads in part:

> Only when a problem is significant and can be investigated in no other way is the psychologist justified in exposing human subjects to emotional stress or other possible harm. In conducting such research, the psychologist must seriously consider the possibility of harmful aftereffects, and should be prepared to remove them as soon as permitted by the design of the experiment. Where the danger of serious aftereffects exists, research should be conducted only when the subjects or their responsible agents are fully informed of this possibility and volunteer nevertheless [p. 12].

From the subject's point of view procedures which involve loss of dignity, self-esteem and trust in rational authority are probably most harmful in the long run and require the most thoughtfully planned reparations, if engaged in at all. The public image of psychology as a profession is highly related to our own actions, and some of these actions are changeworthy. It is important that as research psychologists we protect our ethical sensibilities rather than adapt our personal standards to include as appropriate the kind of indignities to which Milgram's subjects were exposed. I would not like to see experiments such as Milgram's proceed unless the subjects were fully informed of the dangers of serious aftereffects and his correctives were clearly shown to be effective in restoring their state of well being.*

References

American Psychological Association (n.d.). *Ethical standards of psychologists: A summary of ethical principles.* Washington, DC: APA.

Milgram, S. (1963). Behavioral study of obedience. *Journal of Abnormal and Social Psychology. 67,* 371–378.

---

* Stanley Milgram replied to Baumrind's critique in a lengthy critique of his own [From Stanley Milgram, "Issues in the Study of Obedience: A Reply to Baumrind," *American Psychologist* 19, 1964, pp. 848–851]. Following are his principal points:

• Milgram believed that the experimental findings were in large part responsible for Baumrind's criticism. He writes:

Is not Baumrind's criticism based as much on the unanticipated findings as on the method? The findings were that some subjects performed in what appeared to be a shockingly immoral way. If, instead, every one of the subjects had broken off at "slight shock," or at the first sign of the learner's discomfort, the results would have been pleasant, and reassuring, and who would protest?

• Milgram objected to Baumrind's assertion that those who participated in the experiment would have trouble justifying their behavior. Milgram conducted follow-up questionnaires. The results, summarized in Table 1, indicate that 84 percent of the subjects claimed they were pleased to have been a part of the experiment.

TABLE 1 Excerpt from Questionnaire Used in a Follow-up Study of the Obedience Research			
Now That I Have Read the Report, and All Things Considered . . .	Defiant	Obedient	All
1. I am very glad to have been in the experiment	40.0%	47.8%	43.5%
2. I am glad to have been in the experiment	43.8%	35.7%	40.2%
3. I am neither sorry nor glad to have been in the experiment	15.3%	14.8%	15.1%
4. I am sorry to have been in the experiment	0.8%	0.7%	0.8%
5. I am very sorry to have been in the experiment	0.0%	1.0%	0.5%

Note—Ninety-two percent of the subjects returned the questionnaire. The characteristics of the nonrespondents were checked against the respondents. They differed from the respondents only with regard to age; younger people were overrepresented in the nonresponding group.

- Baumrind objected that studies of obedience cannot meaningfully be carried out in a laboratory setting, since the obedience occurred in a context where it was appropriate. Milgram's response: "I reject Baumrind's argument that the observed obedience does not count because it occurred where it is appropriate. That is precisely why it *does* count. A soldier's obedience is no less meaningful because it occurs in a pertinent military context."

- Milgram concludes his critique in this way: "If there is a moral to be learned from the obedience study, it is that every man must be responsible for his own actions. This author accepts full responsibility for the design and execution of the study. Some people may feel it should not have been done. I disagree and accept the burden of their judgment."

Obedience
Ian Parker

As Ian Parker points out, Milgram's experiment became "the most cited, celebrated—and reviled—experiment in the history of social psychology." Parker also explains, however, that for Milgram himself the experiment was a mixed blessing: it would both "make his name and destroy his reputation."

Milgram was fascinated by the Asch experiment, but when all was said and done, this experiment was only about lines. He wondered if it were possible "to make Asch's conformity experiment more humanely significant." Milgram's breakthrough, his "incandescent moment," came when he asked himself "Just how far would a person go under the experimenter's orders?" We have seen the results in the experiment he describes and discusses in an earlier selection.

In the following selection, Ian Parker, a British writer who lives in New York, focuses on both the immediate and the long-term reaction to Milgram's experiments among both the general public and Milgram's professional colleagues and also of the effect of the experiment upon the experimenter himself. This selection is excerpted from an article that

Parker wrote for the Autumn 2000 issue of Granta. *Parker writes regularly for the* New Yorker *and has also written for* Human Sciences, History of the Human Sciences, Political Studies, *and* Human Relations.

1 Milgram had a world exclusive. He had caught evil on film. He had invented a kind of torture machine. But it was not immediately clear what he should do with his discovery. When he began the study, he had no theory, nor was he planning to test another man's theory. His idea had sprung from contemplation of Solomon Asch, but the "incandescent" moment at Princeton was a shift away from theory into experimental practice. He had had an idea for an experiment. Now, he was in an odd situation: he had caused something extraordinary to happen, but, technically, his central observation counted for nothing. With no provocation, a New Haven man had hit a fellow citizen with 450 volts. To the general observer, this will come as a surprise, but it is not a social scientific discovery, as Edward E. Jones, the distinguished editor of the *Journal of Personality,* made clear to Milgram when he declined the invitation to publish Milgram's first paper. "The major problem," Jones wrote to Milgram, "is that this is really the report of some pilot research on a method for inducing stress or conflict . . . your data indicate a kind of triumph of social engineering . . . we are led to no conclusions about obedience, really, but rather are exhorted to be impressed with the power of your situation as an influence context." The *Journal of Abnormal and Social Psychology* also rejected the paper on its first submission, calling it a "demonstration" rather than an experiment.

2 Milgram had described only one experimental situation. When he resubmitted the paper to the same journal, he now included experimental variables, and it was publishable. In the rewrite, Milgram put the emphasis on the way in which differences in situation had caused differences in degrees of obedience: the closer the learner to the teacher, the greater the disobedience, and so on. These details were later lost as the experiment moved out of social psychology into the larger world. But it could hardly have happened otherwise. The thought that people were zapping each other in a Yale laboratory is bound to be more striking than the thought that zapping occurs a little less often when one is looking one's victim in the eye. The unscientific truth, perhaps, is that the central comparison in Milgram's study is not between any two experimental variables: it is between what happened in the laboratory, and what we thought would happen. The experimental control in Milgram's model is our hopelessly flawed intuition.

3 "Somehow," Milgram told a friend in 1962, "I don't write as fast or as easily as I run experiments. I have done about all the experiments I plan to do on Obedience, am duly impressed with the results, and now find myself acutely constipated." Milgram found it hard to knock the experiment into social scientific shape. It would be another decade before he incorporated his findings into a serious theory of the sources of human obedience. When he did so, in the otherwise absorbing and beautifully written book *Obedience to Authority* (1974), his thoughts about an "agen-

tic state"—a psychological zone of abandoned autonomy—were not widely admired or developed by his peers, not least because they were so evidently retrospective. Most readers of *Obedience to Authority* are more likely to take interest in the nods of acknowledgment made to Arthur Koestler's *The Ghost in the Machine,* and to Alex Comfort, the English anarchist poet, novelist, and author of *The Joy of Sex.* Most readers will take more pleasure—and feel Milgram took more pleasure—in the novelistic and strikingly unscientific descriptions of his experimental subjects. ("Mrs Dontz," he wrote, "has an unusually casual, slow-paced way of speaking, and her tone expresses constant humility; it is as if every assertion carries the emotional message: 'I'm just a very ordinary person, don't expect a lot from me.' Physically, she resembles Shirley Booth in the film *Come Back, Little Sheba.*")

4   But while Milgram was struggling to place his findings in a proper scientific context, they seemed to have found a natural home elsewhere. Stanley Milgram—a young social psychology professor at the start of his career—appeared to be in a position to contribute to one of the late twentieth century's most pressing intellectual activities: making sense of the Holocaust. Milgram always placed the experiments in this context, and the figure of Adolf Eichmann, who was seized in Buenos Aires in the spring of 1960, and whose trial in Jerusalem began a year later, loomed over his proceedings. (In a letter that urged Alan Elms to keep up the supply of experimental volunteers, Milgram noted that this role bore "some resemblance to Mr. Eichmann's position.") The trial, as Peter Novick has recently written in *The Holocaust in American Life,* marked "the first time that what we now call the Holocaust was presented to the American public as an entity in its own right, distinct from Nazi barbarism in general." When Milgram published his first paper on the obedience studies in 1963, Hannah Arendt's articles about the trial had just appeared in the *New Yorker,* and in her book, *Eichmann in Jerusalem,* and they had given widespread currency to her perception about "the banality of evil." Milgram put Eichmann's name in the first paragraph of his first obedience paper, and so claimed a place in a pivotal contemporary debate. His argument was this: his study showed how ordinary people are surprisingly prone to destructive obedience; the crimes of the Holocaust had been committed by people obeying orders; those people, therefore, could now be thought ordinary. The argument had its terrifying element and its consoling element: according to Milgram, Americans had to see themselves as potential murderers; at the same time we could understand Nazis to be no more unusual than any New Haven guy in a check shirt.

5   It may seem bizarre now: Milgram returned to ordinary Nazis their Nuremberg defense, nicely polished in an American laboratory. But the idea struck a chord, and news quickly spread of Milgram's well-meaning, all-American torturers. "Once the [Holocaust] connection was in place," said Arthur G. Miller, a leading Milgram scholar, "then the experiments took on a kind of a larger-than-life quality." Milgram's work was reported

in the *New York Times* (65% IN TEST BLINDLY OBEY ORDER TO INFLICT PAIN), and the story was quickly picked up by *Life, Esquire*, ABC television, UPI, and the British press. The fame of the experiments spread, and as the Sixties acquired their defining spirit, Holocaust references were joined by thoughts of My Lai; this was a good moment in history to have things to say about taking orders. By the time Milgram had published his book and released a short film of the experiment, his findings had spread into popular culture, and into theological, medical, and legal discussions. Thomas Blass, a social psychologist at the University of Maryland, Baltimore County, who is preparing a Milgram biography, has a large collection of academic references, including a paper in the context of accountancy ethics. (Is it unthinking obedience that causes accountants to act unlawfully on behalf of clients?) Outside the academy, Dannie Abse published an anti-Milgram play, *The Dogs of Pavlov*, in 1973, and two years later, in America, CBS broadcast a television movie, *The Tenth Level*, that made awkward melodrama out of the obedience experiments, and starred William Shatner as a spookily obsessed and romantically disengaged version of Professor Milgram. ("You may know your social psychology, Professor, but you have a lot to learn about the varieties of massage.") Peter Gabriel sang "We Do What We're Told (Milgram's 37)" in 1986. And there would be more than a whiff of Milgram in the 1990 episode of *The Simpsons*, "There's No Disgrace Like Home," in which the family members repeatedly electrocute one another until the lights across Springfield flicker and dim. Last year, "The Stanley Milgram Experiment"—a comedy sketch duo—made its off-off-Broadway debut in New York. Robbie Chafitz, one of the pair, had been startled and amused by the Milgram film as a teenager, and had always vowed to use the name one way or another. Besides, as he told me, "anything with electricity and people is funny."

6   But however celebrated the experiments became, there was a question they could never shake off. It was an ethical issue: had Stanley Milgram mistreated his subjects? Milgram must have seen the storm coming, at least from the moment when Herbert Winer marched into his office, talking of heart attacks. In the summer of 1962, other subjects recorded their feelings about the experiment in response to a questionnaire sent out by Milgram along with a report explaining the true purpose of the experiment. Replies were transferred on to index cards and are now held—unpublished and anonymous—at Yale. "Since taking part in the experiment," reads one card, "I have suffered a mild heart attack. The one thing my doctor tells me that I must avoid is any form of tension." Another card: "Right now I'm in group therapy. Would it be OK if I showed this report to [the] group and the doctors at the clinic?"

7   Since then, the experiment has been widely attacked from within the profession and from outside. To many, Milgram became a social psychological demon; Alan Elms has met people at parties who have recoiled at the news that he was a Milgram lieutenant. The psychologist Bruno Bettelheim described Milgram's work as "vile" and "in line with the human experiments of the Nazis." In his defense, Milgram would always highlight the results of

post-experimental psychological studies—which had reported "no evidence of any traumatic reactions"—and the fact of the debriefings in Linsly-Chittenden Hall, in which care had been taken to give obedient subjects reasons not to feel bad about themselves. They were told to remember, for example, that doctors routinely hurt people in a thoroughly good cause. (Alan Elms wonders if this debriefing was *too* effective, and that subjects should have been obliged to confront their actions more fully.)

8   But Milgram never quite won the ethical argument. And the controversy was immediately damaging to his career. Someone—perhaps a Yale colleague, according to Thomas Blass—quickly brought the experiment to the attention of the American Psychological Association, and Milgram's application for APA membership was delayed while the case against him was considered. Today, although the APA is happy to include Milgram's shock generator in a traveling psychology exhibition, it is careful to describe the experiments as "controversial" in its accompanying literature. As the APA points out, modern ethical guidelines (in part inspired by Milgram) would prevent the obedience studies from being repeated today.

9   The controversy followed him. In 1963 Milgram left Yale for Harvard. He was happy there. This is where his two children were born. And when a tenured job came up, he applied. But he needed the unanimous support of his colleagues, and could not secure it. He was blackballed by enemies of the obedience work. (According to Alexandra Milgram, her husband once devised a board game based on the tenure of university professors.) The late Roger Brown, a prominent Harvard psychologist, told Thomas Blass that there had been those in the department who thought of Milgram as "sort of manipulative, or the mad doctor. They felt uneasy about him."

10   So in 1967 Stanley Milgram left Harvard to become head of the social psychology programme in the psychology department in the Graduate Center of the City University of New York (CUNY). In one sense, it was a promotion; he was a full professor at thirty-three. "But after Yale and Harvard, it was the pits," said Milgram's friend and fellow social psychologist, Philip Zimbardo. "Most people I know who didn't get tenure, it had a permanent effect on their lives. You don't get to Yale or Harvard unless you've been number one from kindergarten on, you've been top— so there's this discontinuity. It's the first time in your life you've failed. You're Stanley Milgram, and people all over the world are talking about your research, and you've failed." Milgram was the most cited man in social psychology—Roger Brown, for example, considered his research to be of "profound importance and originality"—yet in later life, he was able to tell Zimbardo that he felt under-appreciated.

11   The ethical furor preyed on Milgram's mind—in the opinion of Arthur G. Miller, it may have contributed to his premature death—but one of its curious side effects was to reinforce the authenticity of his studies in the world outside psychology departments. Among those with a glancing knowledge of Milgram, mistreatment of experimental subjects became the

only Milgram controversy. The studies remained intellectually sound, a minor building block of Western thought, a smart conversational gambit at cocktail parties. "People identified the problem with Milgram as just a question of ethics," says Henderikus Stam, of the University of Calgary in Canada, who trained as a social psychologist, but who lost faith and is now a psychological theoretician and historian. "So in a way people never got beyond that. Whereas there's a deeper epistemological question, which is: what can we actually know when we've done an experiment like that, what are we left with? What have we learned about obedience?"

12   Within the academy, there was another, quieter, line of criticism against Milgram: this was methodological. In a paper in 1968 the social psychologists Martin Orne and Charles Holland raised the issue of incongruity, pointing out that Milgram's subjects had been given two key pieces of information: a man in apparent danger, and another man—a man in a lab coat—whose lack of evident concern suggested there was no danger. It seemed possible that obedient subjects had believed in the more plausible piece of information (no danger), and thus concluded, at some conscious or semi-conscious level, that the experiment was a fake, and—in a "pact of ignorance"—been generous enough to role-play for the sake of science. In other words, they were only obeying the demands of amateur dramatics.

13   Perhaps forgetting that people weep in the theatre, Milgram's response was to argue that the subjects' signs of distress or tension—the twitching and stuttering and racing heartbeats—could be taken as evidence that they had accepted the experiment's reality. He also drew upon the questionnaire he had sent out in 1962, in which his volunteers—now entirely in the know—had been asked to agree with one of five propositions, running from, "I fully believed the learner was getting painful shocks" to "I was certain the learner was not getting the shocks." Milgram was pleased to note that three-quarters of the subjects said they believed the learner was definitely or probably getting the shocks. (He added, reasonably, "It would have been an easy out at this point to deny that the hoax had been accepted.")

14   Herbert Winer reports that he was fully duped, and Alan Elms told me that, watching through the mirror during the summer of 1961, he saw very little evidence of widespread disbelief. But it is worth pointing out that Milgram could have reported his questionnaire statistics rather differently. He could have said that only fifty-six per cent accepted his first proposition: "I fully believed the learner was getting painful shocks." Forty-four per cent of Milgram's subjects claimed to be at least partially unpersuaded. (Indeed, on his own questionnaire, Winer said he had some doubts.) These people do not have much of a presence in Milgram's writings, but you catch a glimpse of them in the Yale Library index cards. One reads: "I was quite sure 'grunts and screams' were electrically reproduced from a speaker mounted in [the] students' room." (They were.) "If [the learner] was making the sounds I should have heard the screams from under the door—which was a poorly fit [*sic*] thin door. I'm sorry that I didn't have enough something to get up and open this door. Which was not locked. To

see if student was still there." On another card: "I think that one of the main reasons I continued to the end was that . . . I just couldn't believe that Yale would concoct anything that would be [as] dangerous as the shocks were supposed to be." Another subject had noticed how the experimenter was watching him rather than the learner. Another hadn't understood why he was not allowed to volunteer to be the learner. And another wrote, "I had difficulty describing the experiment to my wife as I was so overcome with laughter—haven't had such a good laugh since the first time I saw the 4 Marx Bros—some 25 years ago."

15   For an experiment supposed to involve the undeserved torture of an innocent Irish-American man, there was a lot of laughter in Yale's Interaction Laboratory. Frequently, Milgram's subjects could barely contain themselves as they moved up the shock board. ("On one occasion," Milgram later wrote, "we observed a seizure so violently convulsive that it was necessary to call a halt to the experiment.") Behind their one-way mirror, Milgram and Elms were at times highly amused. And when students are shown the Milgram film today, there tends to be loud laughter in the room. People laugh, and—despite the alleged revelation of a universal heart of darkness—they go home having lost little faith in their friends and their families.

16   According to Henderikus Stam, the laughter of the students, and per-haps that of the subjects, is a reasonable response to an absurd situation. It's a reaction to the notion that serious and complex moral issues, and the subtleties of human behaviour, can reasonably be illuminated through play-acting in a university laboratory. The experiment does nothing but illuminate itself. "What it does is it says, 'Aren't we clever?' If you wanted to demonstrate obedience to authority wouldn't you be better showing a film about the Holocaust, or news clips about Kosovo? Why do you need an experiment, that's the question? What does the experiment do? The experiment says that if we really want to know about obedience to author-ity we need an abstract representation of that obedience, removed from all real forms of the abuse of authority. But what we then do is to use that rep-resentation to refer back to the real historical examples."

17   What happens when we refer back to historical examples? Readers of *Hitler's Willing Executioners*, Daniel Jonah Goldhagen's study of the complic-ity of ordinary German citizens in the Holocaust, will learn within one para-graph of a German policeman, Captain Wolfgang Hoffmann, a "zealous executioner of Jews," who "once stridently disobeyed a superior order that he deemed morally objectionable." The order was that he and members of his company should sign a declaration agreeing not to steal from Poles. Hoffmann was affronted that anyone would think the declaration necessary, that anyone would imagine his men capable of stealing. "I feel injured," he wrote to his superiors, "in my sense of honour." The genocidal killing of thou-sands of Jews was one thing, but plundering from Poles was another. Here was an order to which he was opposed, and which he felt able to disobey.

18   Goldhagen is impatient with what he calls "the paradigm of external compulsion," which sets the actions of the Holocaust's perpetrators in the context of social-psychological or totalitarian state forces. His book aims to

show how the crimes of the Holocaust were carried out by people obeying their own consciences, not blindly or fearfully obeying orders. "If you think that certain people are evil," he told me, "and that it's necessary to do away with them—if you hate them—and then someone orders you to kill them, you're not carrying out the deed only because of the order. You're carrying it out because you think it's right. So in all those instances where people are killing people they hate—their enemies or their perceived enemies—then Milgram is just completely inapplicable."

19   Goldhagen wonders if the Milgram take on the Holocaust met a particular need, during the Cold War, for America's new German allies "to be thought well of." He also wonders if, by robbing people of their agency, "of the fact that they're moral beings," the experiment tapped into the kind of reductive universalism by which, he says, Americans are easily seduced— the belief that all men are created equal, and in this case equally obedient. Goldhagen has no confidence in the idea that Milgram was measuring obedience at all. The experimental conditions did not properly control for other variables, such as trust, nor did they allow for the way decisions are made in the real world—over time, after consultation. Besides, said Goldhagen, in a tone close to exasperation, "people disobey all the time! Look around the world. Do people always pay all their taxes? Do what their bosses tell them? Or quietly accept what any government decides? Even with all kinds of sanctions available, one of the greatest problems that institutions face is to get their members to comply with rules and orders." Milgram's findings, he says, "are roundly, repeatedly and glaringly falsified by life."

20   In the opinion of Professor Stam, this comes close to defining the problems of social psychology itself. It is a discipline, he says, that makes the peculiar claim that "if you want to ask questions about the social world, you have to turn them into abstract technical questions." The Milgram experiment, he says, "has the air of scientificity about it. But it's not scientific, it's . . . *scientistic.*"

21   And there is Milgram's problem: he devised an intensely powerful piece of tragicomic laboratory theatre, and then had to smuggle it into the faculty of social science. His most famous work—which had something to say about trust, embarrassment, low-level sadism, willingness to please, exaggerated post-war respect for scientific research, the sleepy, heavy-lidded pleasure of being asked to *take part,* and, perhaps, too, the desire of a rather awkward young academic to secure attention and respect—had to pass itself off as an event with a single, steady meaning. And that disguise has not always been convincing. It's odd to hear Arthur G. Miller—one of the world's leading Milgram scholars—acknowledge that there have been times when he has wondered, just for a moment, if the experiments perhaps mean nothing at all.

22   But the faculty of social psychology is not ready to let Milgram go. And there may be a new way to rescue the experiments from their ungainly ambiguity. This is the route taken by Professors Lee Ross and Richard E. Nisbett (at Stanford and the University of Michigan respectively), whose recent synthesis of social psychological thinking aims to give the subject new power. According to Professor Ross, the experiments may be "performance,"

but they still have social psychological news to deliver. If that is true, then we can do something that the late professor was not always able to do himself: we can make a kind of reconciliation between the artist and the scientist in Stanley Milgram.

23   Ross and Nisbett find a seat for Stanley Milgram at social psychology's high table. They do this slyly, by taking the idea of obedience—Milgram's big idea—and putting it quietly to one side. When Ross teaches Milgram at Stanford, he makes a point of giving his students detailed instructions on how to prepare for the classes—instructions that he knows will be thoroughly ignored. He is then able to stand in front of his students and examine their disobedience. "I asked you to do something that's good for you rather than bad for you," he tells them. "And I'm a legitimate authority rather than an illegitimate one, and I actually have power that the Milgram experimenter doesn't have. And yet you didn't obey. So the study can't just be about obedience." What it is primarily about, Ross tells his students—and it may be about other things too—is the extreme power of a situation that has been built without obvious escape routes. (As Herbert Winer said: "At no time was there a pause or a break when anything could be raised. . . . ") "There was really no exit," Ross told me, "there was no channel for disobedience. People who were discomforted, who wanted to disobey, didn't quite know how to do it. They made some timid attempts, and it got them nowhere. In order to disobey they have to step out of the whole situation, and say to the experimenter, 'Go to hell! You can't tell me what to do!' As long as they continue to function within that relationship, they're asking the experimenter for permission not to give shocks, and as long as the experimenter denies them that permission, they're stuck. They don't know how to get out of it." Ross suspects that things would have turned out very differently given one change to the situation. It's a fairly big change: the addition of a prominent red button in the middle of the table, combined with a clearly displayed notice signed by the "Human Subjects' Committee" explaining that the button could be pressed "by any subject in any experiment at any time if he or she absolutely refuses to continue."

24   According to Ross and Nisbett (who are saying something that Milgram surely knew, but something he allowed to become obscured), the Obedience Experiments point us towards a great social psychological truth, perhaps *the* great truth, which is this: people tend to do things because of where they are, not who they are, and we are slow to see it. We look for character traits to explain a person's actions—he is clever, shy, generous, arrogant—and we stubbornly underestimate the influence of the situation, the way things *happened to be* at that moment. So, if circumstances had been even only subtly different (if she hadn't been running late; if he'd been *told* the film was a comedy), the behaviour might have been radically different. Under certain controlled circumstances, then, people can be induced to behave unkindly: to that extent, Milgram may have something to say about a kind of destructive obedience. But under other circumstances, Professor Ross promised me, the same people would

be nice. Given the correct situation, he said, we could be led to do "terrifically altruistic and self-sacrificing things that we would never have agreed to before we started."

25   So the experiment that has troubled us for nearly forty years (that buzzing and howling), and which caused Milgram to have dark thoughts about America's vulnerability to fascism, suddenly has a new complexion. Now, it is about the influence of *any* situation on behaviour, good or bad: "You stop on the highway to help someone," Professor Ross said, "and then the help you try to give doesn't prove to be enough, so you give the person a ride, and then you end up lending them money or letting them stay in your house. It wasn't because that was the person in the world you cared about the most, it was just one thing led to another. Step by step."

26   That's the Milgram situation. "We can take ordinary people," Ross said, "and make them show a degree of obedience or conformity—or for that matter altruism or bravery, whatever—to a degree that we would normally assume you would only see in the rare few. And that's relevant to telling us what we're capable of making people do, but it also tells us that when we observe the world, we are often going to be making an attribution error, because lots of times, the situational factors have been opaque to us, and therefore we are making erroneous inferences about people. The South African government says, 'Can we deal with this fellow Mandela?' and the answer is, 'No, he's a terrorist.' But a social psychologist would say, 'Mandela, in *one* context, given *one* set of situations, was a terrorist.'" According to Ross, that's the key lesson of social psychology; that's how the discipline can be useful in education, the work place, and law. "Our emphasis," he says, "should be on creating situations that promote what we want to promote, rather than searching endlessly for the right person. Don't assume that people who commit atrocities are atrocious people, or people who do heroic things are heroic. Don't get overly carried away; don't think, because you observed someone under one set of discrete situational factors, that you know *what they're like,* and therefore can predict what they would do in a very different set of circumstances."

27   It's hard not to think of Stanley Milgram in another set of circumstances—to imagine the careers he did not have in films or in the theatre, and to wonder how things would have turned out if his work had appeared at another time, or had been read a little differently. It may now be possible to place the Obedience Experiments somewhere near the center of the social psychological project, but that's not how it felt in the last years of Milgram's life. He had failed to secure tenure at Harvard. Disappointed, he moved to New York, assuming he would soon be leaving again, to take up a post at a more glamorous institution. But he was still at CUNY seventeen years later, at the time of his premature death. "He had hoped it would be just for five years," Alexandra Milgram told me, "But things got much more difficult to move on to other places. You were glad to have what you had. And he was happy to do the work that he did. I don't think he was as happy at the university as he was at, say, Harvard, but he was a very independent person: he had his ideas, he had his research."

28   The research pushed Milgram into a kind of internal exile. Confirming his reputation as social psychology's renegade, he pursued work that, although often brilliantly conceived and elegantly reported, could look eccentric and old-fashioned to colleagues, and that ran the risk of appearing to place method ahead of meaning. "It would flash and then burn out," says Professor Miller, "and then he'd go on to something else." He sent his (young, able-bodied) students on to the New York subway to ask people to give up their seats. He co-wrote a paper about *Candid Camera*'s virtues as an archive for students of human behaviour. Pre-empting the play *Six Degrees of Separation,* he studied the "small world" phenomenon, investigating the chains of acquaintance that link two strangers. He took photographs of rail commuters and showed them to those who travelled on the same route, to explore the notion of the "familiar stranger." In an expensive, elaborate, and ultimately inconclusive experiment in 1971, he explored the links between antisocial acts seen on television and similar acts in real life by getting CBS to produce and air two versions of a hit hospital drama, *Medical Center.* He asked students to try to give away money on the street. He tested how easy it was for people to walk between a pavement photographer and his subject. And when he was recuperating from one of a series of heart attacks, he made an informal study of the social psychology of being a hospital patient. He was only fifty-one when he died.

29   Once, shortly before the Obedience Experiments had begun, Milgram had written from Yale about his fear of having made the wrong career move. "Of course," he told a friend, "I am glad that the present job sometimes engages my genuine interests, or at least, a part of my interests, but there is another part that remains submerged and somehow, perhaps because it is not expressed, seems most important." He described his routine: pulling himself out of bed, dragging himself to the lecture room "where I misrepresent myself for two hours as an efficient and persevering man of science . . . I should not be here, but in Greece shooting films under a Mediterranean sun, hopping about in a small boat from one Aegean isle to the next." He added, in a spirit of comic self-laceration, "Fool!"

The Stanford Prison Experiment
Philip G. Zimbardo

As well known—and as controversial—as the Milgram obedience experiments, the Stanford Prison Experiment (1973) raises troubling questions about the ability of individuals to resist authoritarian or obedient roles, if the social setting requires these roles. Philip G. Zimbardo, professor of psychology at Stanford University, set out to study the process by which prisoners and guards "learn" to become compliant and authoritarian, respectively. To find subjects for the experiment, Zimbardo placed an advertisement in a local newspaper:

Male college students needed for psychological study of prison life. $15 per day for 1–2 weeks beginning Aug. 14. For further information & applications, come to Room 248, Jordan Hall, Stanford U.

The ad drew seventy-five responses. From these Zimbardo and his colleagues selected twenty-one college-age men, half of whom would become "prisoners" in the experiment, the other half "guards." The elaborate role-playing scenario, planned for two weeks, had to be cut short due to the intensity of subjects' responses. This article first appeared in the New York Times Magazine *(8 April 1973).*

In prison, those things withheld from and denied to the prisoner become precisely what he wants most of all.
—Eldridge Cleaver, "Soul on Ice"

Our sense of power is more vivid when we break a man's spirit than when we win his heart.
—Eric Hoffer, "The Passionate State of Mind"

Every prison that men build / Is built with bricks of shame, / And bound with bars lest Christ should see / How men their brothers maim.
—Oscar Wilde, "The Ballad of Reading Gaol"

Wherever anyone is against his will that is to him a prison.
—Epictetus, "Discourses"

1   The quiet of a summer morning in Palo Alto, Calif., was shattered by a screeching squad car siren as police swept through the city picking up college students in a surprise mass arrest. Each suspect was charged with a felony, warned of his constitutional rights, spread-eagled against the car, searched, handcuffed, and carted off in the back seat of the squad car to the police station for booking.

2   After fingerprinting and the preparation of identification forms for his "jacket" (central information file), each prisoner was left isolated in a detention cell to wonder what he had done to get himself into this mess. After a while, he was blindfolded and transported to the "Stanford County Prison." Here he began the process of becoming a prisoner—stripped naked, skin-searched, deloused, and issued a uniform, bedding, soup, and towel.

3   The warden offered an impromptu welcome:

4   "As you probably know, I'm your warden. All of you have shown that you are unable to function outside in the real world for one reason or another—that somehow you lack the responsibility of good citizens of this great country. We of this prison, your correctional staff, are going to help you learn what your responsibilities as citizens of this country are. Here are the rules. Sometime in the near future there will be a copy of the rules posted in each of the cells. We expect you to know them and to be able to

recite them by number. If you follow all of these rules and keep your hands clean, repent for your misdeeds, and show a proper attitude of penitence, you and I will get along just fine."

5   There followed a reading of the 16 basic rules of prisoner conduct, "Rule Number One: Prisoners must remain silent during rest periods, after lights are out, during meals, and whenever they are outside the prison yard. Two: Prisoners must eat at mealtimes and only at mealtimes. Three: Prisoners must not move, tamper, deface, or damage walls, ceilings, windows, doors, or other prison property. . . . Seven: Prisoners must address each other by their ID number only. Eight: Prisoners must address the guards as 'Mr. Correctional Officer.' . . . Sixteen: Failure to obey any of the above rules may result in punishment."

6   By late afternoon these youthful "first offenders" sat in dazed silence on the cots in their barren cells trying to make sense of the events that had transformed their lives so dramatically.

7   If the police arrests and processing were executed with customary detachment, however, there were some things that didn't fit. For these men were now part of a very unusual kind of prison, an experimental mock prison, created by social psychologists to study the effects of imprisonment upon volunteer research subjects. When we planned our two-week-long simulation of prison life, we sought to understand more about the process by which people called "prisoners" lose their liberty, civil rights, independence, and privacy, while those called "guards" gain social power by accepting the responsibility for controlling and managing the lives of their dependent charges.

8   Why didn't we pursue this research in a real prison? First, prison systems are fortresses of secrecy, closed to impartial observation, and thereby immune to critical analysis from anyone not already part of the correctional authority. Second, in any real prison, it is impossible to separate what each individual brings into the prison from what the prison brings out in each person.

9   We populated our mock prison with a homogeneous group of people who could be considered "normal-average" on the basis of clinical interviews and personality tests. Our participants (10 prisoners and 11 guards) were selected from more than 75 volunteers recruited through ads in the city and campus newspapers. The applicants were mostly college students from all over the United States and Canada who happened to be in the Stanford area during the summer and were attracted by the lure of earning $15 a day for participating in a study of prison life. We selected only those judged to be emotionally stable, physically healthy, mature, law-abiding citizens.

10   The sample of average, middle-class, Caucasian, college-age males (plus one Oriental student) was arbitrarily divided by the flip of a coin. Half were randomly assigned to play the role of guards, the others of prisoners. There were no measurable differences between the guards and the prisoners at the start of the experiment. Although initially warned that as prisoners their privacy and other civil rights would be violated and that they might be subjected to harassment, every subject was completely confident of his ability to endure whatever the prison had to offer for the full two-week

experimental period. Each subject unhesitatingly agreed to give his "informed consent" to participate.

11   The prison was constructed in the basement of Stanford University's psychology building, which was deserted after the end of the summer-school session. A long corridor was converted into the prison "yard" by partitioning off both ends. Three small laboratory rooms opening onto this corridor were made into cells by installing metal barred doors and replacing existing furniture with cots, three to a cell. Adjacent offices were refurnished as guards' quarters, interview-testing rooms, and bedrooms for the "warden" (Jaffe) and the "superintendent" (Zimbardo). A concealed video camera and hidden microphones recorded much of the activity and conversation of guards and prisoners. The physical environment was one in which prisoners could always be observed by the staff, the only exception being when they were secluded in solitary confinement (a small, dark storage closet, labeled "The Hole").

12   Our mock prison represented an attempt to simulate the psychological state of imprisonment in certain ways. We based our experiment on an in-depth analysis of the prison situation, developed after hundreds of hours of discussion with Carlo Prescott (our ex-con consultant), parole officers, and correctional personnel, and after reviewing much of the existing literature on prisons and concentration camps.

13   "Real" prisoners typically report feeling powerless, arbitrarily controlled, dependent, frustrated, hopeless, anonymous, dehumanized, and emasculated. It was not possible, pragmatically or ethically, to create such chronic states in volunteer subjects who realize that they are in an experiment for only a short time. Racism, physical brutality, indefinite confinement, and enforced homosexuality were not features of our mock prison. But we did try to reproduce those elements of the prison experience that seemed most fundamental.

14   We promoted anonymity by seeking to minimize each prisoner's sense of uniqueness and prior identity. The prisoners wore smocks and nylon stocking caps; they had to use their ID numbers; their personal effects were removed and they were housed in barren cells. All of this made them appear similar to each other and indistinguishable to observers. Their smocks, which were like dresses, were worn without undergarments, causing the prisoners to be restrained in their physical actions and to move in ways that were more feminine than masculine. The prisoners were forced to obtain permission from the guard for routine and simple activities such as writing letters, smoking a cigarette, or even going to the toilet; this elicited from them a childlike dependency.

15   Their quarters, though clean and neat, were small, stark, and without esthetic appeal. The lack of windows resulted in poor air circulation, and persistent odors arose from the unwashed bodies of the prisoners. After 10 P.M. lockup, toilet privileges were denied, so prisoners who had to relieve themselves would have to urinate and defecate in buckets provided by the guards. Sometimes the guards refused permission to have them cleaned out, and this made the prison smell.

16   Above all, "real" prisons are machines for playing tricks with the human conception of time. In our windowless prison, the prisoners often did not even know whether it was day or night. A few hours after falling asleep, they were roused by shrill whistles for their "count." The ostensible purpose of the count was to provide a public test of the prisoners' knowledge of the rules and of their ID numbers. But more important, the count, which occurred at least once on each of the three different guard shifts, provided a regular occasion for the guards to relate to the prisoners. Over the course of the study, the duration of the counts was spontaneously increased by the guards from their initial perfunctory 10 minutes to a seemingly interminable several hours. During these confrontations, guards who were bored could find ways to amuse themselves, ridiculing recalcitrant prisoners, enforcing arbitrary rules, and openly exaggerating any dissension among the prisoners.

17   The guards were also "deindividualized": They wore identical khaki uniforms and silver reflector sunglasses that made eye contact with them impossible. Their symbols of power were billy clubs, whistles, handcuffs, and the keys to the cells and the "main gate." Although our guards received no formal training from us in how to be guards, for the most part they moved with apparent ease into their roles. The media had already provided them with ample models of prison guards to emulate.

18   Because we were as interested in the guards' behavior as in the prisoners', they were given considerable latitude to improvise and to develop strategies and tactics of prisoner management. Our guards were told that they must maintain "law and order" in this prison, that they were responsible for handling any trouble that might break out, and they were cautioned about the seriousness and potential dangers of the situation they were about to enter. Surprisingly, in most prison systems, "real" guards are not given much more psychological preparation or adequate training than this for what is one of the most complex, demanding, and dangerous jobs our society has to offer. They are expected to learn how to adjust to their new employment mostly from on-the-job experience, and from contacts with the "old bulls" during a survival-of-the-fittest orientation period. According to an orientation manual for correctional officers at San Quentin, "the only way you really get to know San Quentin is through experience and time. Some of us take more time and must go through more experiences than others to accomplish this; some really never do get there."

19   You cannot be a prisoner if no one will be your guard, and you cannot be a prison guard if no one takes you or your prison seriously. Therefore, over time a perverted symbiotic relationship developed. As the guards became more aggressive, prisoners became more passive; assertion by the guards led to dependency in the prisoners; self-aggrandizement was met with self-deprecation, authority with helplessness, and the counterpart of the guards' sense of mastery and control was the depression and hopelessness witnessed in the prisoners. As these differences in behavior, mood, and perception became more evident to all, the need for the now "righteously" powerful guards to rule the obviously inferior and powerless inmates became a sufficient reason to support almost any further indignity of man against man:

20   Guard K: "During the inspection, I went to cell 2 to mess up a bed which the prisoner had made and he grabbed me, screaming that he had just made it, and he wasn't going to let me mess it up. He grabbed my throat, and although he was laughing I was pretty scared. . . . I lashed out with my stick and hit him in the chin (although not very hard), and when I freed myself I became angry. I wanted to get back in the cell and have a go with him, since he attacked me when I was not ready."

21   Guard M: "I was surprised at myself . . . I made them call each other names and clean the toilets out with their bare hands. I practically considered the prisoners cattle, and I kept thinking: 'I have to watch out for them in case they try something.'"

22   Guard A: "I was tired of seeing the prisoners in their rags and smelling the strong odors of their bodies that filled the cells. I watched them tear at each other on orders given by us. They didn't see it as an experiment. It was real and they were fighting to keep their identity. But we were always there to show them who was boss."

23   Because the first day passed without incident, we were surprised and totally unprepared for the rebellion that broke out on the morning of the second day. The prisoners removed their stocking caps, ripped off their numbers, and barricaded themselves inside the cells by putting their beds against the doors. What should we do? The guards were very much upset because the prisoners also began to taunt and curse them to their faces. When the morning shift of guards came on, they were upset at the night shift who, they felt, must have been too permissive and too lenient. The guards had to handle the rebellion themselves, and what they did was startling to behold.

24   At first they insisted that reinforcements be called in. The two guards who were waiting on stand-by call at home came in, and the night shift of guards voluntarily remained on duty (without extra pay) to bolster the morning shift. The guards met and decided to treat force with force. They got a fire extinguisher that shot a stream of skin-chilling carbon dioxide and forced the prisoners away from the doors; they broke into each cell, stripped the prisoners naked, took the beds out, forced the prisoners who were the ringleaders into solitary confinement, and generally began to harass and intimidate the prisoners.

25   After crushing the riot, the guards decided to head off further unrest by creating a privileged cell for those who were "good prisoners" and then, without explanation, switching some of the troublemakers into it and some of the good prisoners out into the other cells. The prisoner ringleaders could not trust these new cellmates because they had not joined in the riot and might even be "snitches." The prisoners never again acted in unity against the system. One of the leaders of the prisoner revolt later confided:

26   "If we had gotten together then, I think we could have taken over the place. But when I saw the revolt wasn't working, I decided to toe the line. Everyone settled into the same pattern. From then on, we were really controlled by the guards."

27   It was after this episode that the guards really began to demonstrate their inventiveness in the application of arbitrary power. They made the

prisoners obey petty, meaningless, and often inconsistent rules, forced them to engage in tedious, useless work, such as moving cartons back and forth between closets and picking thorns out of their blankets for hours on end. (The guards had previously dragged the blankets through thorny bushes to create this disagreeable task.) Not only did the prisoners have to sing songs or laugh or refrain from smiling on command; they were also encouraged to curse and vilify each other publicly during some of the counts. They sounded off their numbers endlessly and were repeatedly made to do pushups, on occasion with a guard stepping on them or a prisoner sitting on them.

28   Slowly the prisoners became resigned to their fate and even behaved in ways that actually helped to justify their dehumanizing treatment at the hands of the guards. Analysis of the tape-recorded private conversations between prisoners and of remarks made by them to interviewers revealed that fully half could be classified as nonsupportive of other prisoners. More dramatic, 85 percent of the evaluative statements by prisoners about their fellow prisoners were uncomplimentary and deprecating.

29   This should be taken in the context of an even more surprising result. What do you imagine the prisoners talked about when they were alone in their cells with each other, given a temporary respite from the continual harassment and surveillance by the guards? Girl friends, career plans, hobbies or politics?

30   No, their concerns were almost exclusively riveted to prison topics. Their monitored conversations revealed that only 10 percent of the time was devoted to "outside" topics, while 90 percent of the time they discussed escape plans, the awful food, grievances or ingratiating tactics to use with specific guards in order to get a cigarette, permission to go to the toilet, or some other favor. Their obsession with these immediate survival concerns made talk about the past and future an idle luxury.

31   And this was not a minor point. So long as the prisoners did not get to know each other as people, they only extended the oppressiveness and reality of their life as prisoners. For the most part, each prisoner observed his fellow prisoners allowing the guards to humiliate them, acting like compliant sheep, carrying out mindless orders with total obedience, and even being cursed by fellow prisoners (at a guard's command). Under such circumstances, how could a prisoner have respect for his fellows, or any self-respect for what *he* obviously was becoming in the eyes of all those evaluating him?

32   The combination of realism and symbolism in this experiment had fused to create a vivid illusion of imprisonment. The illusion merged inextricably with reality for at least some of the time for every individual in the situation. It was remarkable how readily we all slipped into our roles, temporarily gave up our identities, and allowed these assigned roles and the social forces in the situation to guide, shape, and eventually to control our freedom of thought and action.

33   But precisely where does one's "identity" end and one's "role" begin? When the private self and the public role behavior clash, what direction

will attempts to impose consistency take? Consider the reactions of the parents, relatives, and friends of the prisoners who visited their forlorn sons, brothers, and lovers during two scheduled visitors' hours. They were taught in short order that they were our guests, allowed the privilege of visiting only by complying with the regulations of the institution. They had to register, were made to wait half an hour, were told that only two visitors could see any one prisoner; the total visiting time was cut from an hour to only 10 minutes, they had to be under the surveillance of a guard, and before any parents could enter the visiting area, they had to discuss their son's case with the warden. Of course they complained about these arbitrary rules, but their conditioned, middle-class reaction was to work within the system to appeal privately to the superintendent to make conditions better for their prisoners.

34   In less than 36 hours, we were forced to release prisoner 8612 because of extreme depression, disorganized thinking, uncontrollable crying, and fits of rage. We did so reluctantly because we believed he was trying to "con" us—it was unimaginable that a volunteer prisoner in a mock prison could legitimately be suffering and disturbed to that extent. But then on each of the next three days another prisoner reacted with similar anxiety symptoms, and we were forced to terminate them, too. In a fifth case, a prisoner was released after developing a psychosomatic rash over his entire body (triggered by rejection of his parole appeal by the mock parole board). These men were simply unable to make an adequate adjustment to prison life. Those who endured the prison experience to the end could be distinguished from those who broke down and were released early in only one dimension—authoritarianism. On a psychological test designed to reveal a person's authoritarianism, those prisoners who had the highest scores were best able to function in this authoritarian prison environment.

35   If the authoritarian situation became a serious matter for the prisoners, it became even more serious—and sinister—for the guards. Typically, the guards insulted the prisoners, threatened them, were physically aggressive, used instruments (night sticks, fire extinguishers, etc.) to keep the prisoners in line, and referred to them in impersonal, anonymous, deprecating ways: "Hey, you," or "You [obscenity], 5401, come here." From the first to the last day, there was a significant increase in the guards' use of most of these domineering, abusive tactics.

36   Everyone and everything in the prison was defined by power. To be a guard who did not take advantage of this institutionally sanctioned use of power was to appear "weak," "out of it," "wired up by the prisoners," or simply a deviant from the established norms of appropriate guard behavior. Using Erich Fromm's definition of sadism, as "the wish for absolute control over another living being," all of the mock guards at one time or another during this study behaved sadistically toward the prisoners. Many of them reported—in their diaries, on critical-incident report forms, and during post-experimental interviews—being delighted in the new-found power and control they exercised and sorry to see it relinquished at the end of the study.

37   Some of the guards reacted to the situation in the extreme and behaved with great hostility and cruelty in the forms of degradation they invented for the prisoners. But others were kinder; they occasionally did little favors for the prisoners, were reluctant to punish them, and avoided situations where prisoners were being harassed. The torment experienced by one of these good guards is obvious in his perceptive analysis of what if felt like to be responded to as a "guard":

38   "What made the experience most depressing for me was the fact that we were continually called upon to act in a way that just was contrary to what I really feel inside. I don't feel like I'm the type of person that would be a guard, just constantly giving out [orders] . . . and forcing people to do things, and pushing and lying—it just didn't seem like me, and to continually keep up and put on a face like that is just really one of the most oppressive things you can do. It's almost like a prison that you create yourself—you get into it, and it becomes almost the definition you make of yourself, it almost becomes like walls, and you want to break out and you want just to be able to tell everyone that 'this isn't really me at all, and I'm not the person that's confined in there—I'm a person who wants to get out and show you that I am free, and I do have my own will, and I'm not the sadistic type of person that enjoys this kind of thing.'"

39   Still, the behavior of these good guards seemed more motivated by a desire to be liked by everyone in the system than by a concern for the inmates' welfare. No guard ever intervened in any direct way on behalf of the prisoners, ever interfered with the orders of the cruelest guards, or ever openly complained about the subhuman quality of life that characterized this prison.

40   Perhaps the most devastating impact of the more hostile guards was their creation of a capricious, arbitrary environment. Over time the prisoners began to react passively. When our mock prisoners asked questions, they got answers about half the time, but the rest of the time they were insulted and punished—and it was not possible for them to predict which would be the outcome. As they began to "toe the line," they stopped resisting, questioning and, indeed, almost ceased responding altogether. There was a general decrease in all categories of response as they learned the safest strategy to use in an unpredictable, threatening environment from which there is no physical escape—do nothing, except what is required. Act not, want not, feel not, and you will not get into trouble in prisonlike situations.

41   Can it really be, you wonder, that intelligent, educated volunteers could have lost sight of the reality that they were merely acting a part in an elaborate game that would eventually end? There are many indications not only that they did, but that, in addition, so did we and so did other apparently sensible, responsible adults.

42   Prisoner 819, who had gone into an uncontrollable crying fit, was about to be prematurely released from the prison when a guard lined up the prisoners and had them chant in unison, "819 is a bad prisoner. Because of what 819 did to prison property we all must suffer. 819 is a bad prisoner."

Over and over again. When we realized 819 might be overhearing this, we rushed into the room where 819 was supposed to be resting, only to find him in tears, prepared to go back into the prison because he could not leave as long as the others thought he was a "bad prisoner." Sick as he felt, he had to prove to them he was not a "bad" prisoner. He had to be persuaded that he was not a prisoner at all, that the others were also just students, that this was just an experiment and not a prison and the prison staff were only research psychologists. A report from the warden notes, "While I believe that it was necessary for *staff* [me] to enact the warden role, at least some of the time, I am startled by the ease with which I could turn off my sensitivity and concern for others for 'a good cause.'"

43   Consider our overreaction to the rumor of a mass escape plot that one of the guards claimed to have overheard. It went as follows: Prisoner 8612, previously released for emotional disturbance, was only faking. He was going to round up a bunch of his friends, and they would storm the prison right after visiting hours. Instead of collecting data on the pattern of rumor transmission, we made plans to maintain the security of our institution. After putting a confederate informer into the cell 8612 had occupied to get specific information about the escape plans, the superintendent went back to the Palo Alto Police Department to request transfer of our prisoners to the old city jail. His impassioned plea was only turned down at the last minute when the problem of insurance and city liability for our prisoners was raised by a city official. Angered at this lack of cooperation, the staff formulated another plan. Our jail was dismantled, the prisoners, chained and blindfolded, were carted off to a remote storage room. When the conspirators arrived, they would be told the study was over, their friends had been sent home, there was nothing left to liberate. After they left, we would redouble the security features of our prison making any future escape attempts futile. We even planned to lure ex-prisoner 8612 back on some pretext and imprison him again, because he had been released on false pretenses! The rumor turned out to be just that—a full day had passed in which we collected little or no data, worked incredibly hard to tear down and then rebuilt our prison. Our reaction, however, was as much one of relief and joy as of exhaustion and frustration.

44   When a former prison chaplain was invited to talk with the prisoners (the grievance committee had requested church services), he puzzled everyone by disparaging each inmate for not having taken any constructive action in order to get released. "Don't you know you must have a lawyer in order to get bail, or to appeal the charges against you?" Several of them accepted his invitation to contact their parents in order to secure the services of an attorney. The next night one of the parents stopped at the superintendent's office before visiting time and handed him the name and phone number of her cousin who was a public defender. She said that a priest had called her and suggested the need for a lawyer's services! We called the lawyer. He came, interviewed the prisoners, discussed sources of bail money, and promised to return again after the weekend.

45   But perhaps the most telling account of the insidious development of this new reality, of the gradual Kafkaesque metamorphosis of good into evil, appears in excerpts from the diary of one of the guards, Guard A:

46   *Prior to start of experiment:* "As I am a pacifist and nonaggressive individual. I cannot see a time when I might guard and/or maltreat other living things."

47   *After an orientation meeting:* "Buying uniforms at the end of the meeting confirms the gamelike atmosphere of this thing. I doubt whether many of us share the expectations of 'seriousness' that the experimenters seem to have."

48   *First Day:* "Feel sure that the prisoners will make fun of my appearance and I evolve my first basic strategy—mainly not to smile at anything they say or do which would be admitting it's all only a game. . . . At cell 3 I stop and setting my voice hard and low say to 5486, 'What are you smiling at?' 'Nothing, Mr. Correctional Officer.' 'Well, see that you don't.' (As I walk off I feel stupid.)"

49   *Second Day:* "5704 asked for a cigarette and I ignored him—because I am a non-smoker and could not empathize. . . . Meanwhile since I was feeling empathetic towards 1037, I determined not to talk with him. . . . After we had count and lights out [Guard D] and I held a loud conversation about going home to our girl friends and what we were going to do to them."

50   *Third Day (preparing for the first visitors' night):* "After warning the prisoners not to make any complaints unless they wanted the visit terminated fast, we finally brought in the first parents. I made sure I was one of the guards on the yard, because this was my first chance for the type of manipulative power that I really like—being a very noticed figure with almost complete control over what is said or not. While the parents and prisoners sat in chairs, I sat on the end of the table dangling my feet and contradicting anything I felt like. This was the first part of the experiment I was really enjoying. . . . 817 is being obnoxious and bears watching."

51   *Fourth Day:* ". . . The psychologist rebukes me for handcuffing and blindfolding a prisoner before leaving the [counseling] office, and I resentfully reply that it is both necessary security and my business anyway."

52   *Fifth Day:* "I harass 'Sarge' who continues to stubbornly overrespond to all commands. I have singled him out for the special abuse both because he begs for it and because I simply don't like him. The real trouble starts at dinner. The new prisoner (416) refuses to eat his sausage . . . we throw him into the Hole ordering him to hold sausages in each hand. We have a crisis of authority; this rebellious conduct potentially undermines the complete control we have over the others. We decide to play upon prisoner solidarity and tell the new one that all the others will be deprived of visitors if he does not eat his dinner. . . . I walk by and slam my stick into the Hole door. . . . I am very angry at this prisoner for causing discomfort and trouble for the others. I decided to force-feed him, but he wouldn't eat. I let the food slide down his face. I didn't believe it was me doing it. I hated myself for making him eat but I hated him more for not eating."

53 *Sixth Day:* "The experiment is over. I feel elated but am shocked to find some other guards disappointed somewhat because of the loss of money and some because they are enjoying themselves."

54 We were no longer dealing with an intellectual exercise in which a hypothesis was being evaluated in the dispassionate manner dictated by the canons of the scientific method. We were caught up in the passion of the present, the suffering, the need to control people, not variables, the escalation of power, and all the unexpected things that were erupting around and within us. We had to end this experiment: So our planned two-week simulation was aborted after only six (was it only six?) days and nights.

55 Was it worth all the suffering just to prove what everybody knows—that some people are sadistic, others weak, and prisons are not beds of roses? If that is all we demonstrated in this research, then it was certainly not worth the anguish. We believe there are many significant implications to be derived from this experience, only a few of which can be suggested here.

56 The potential social value of this study derives precisely from the fact that normal, healthy, educated young men could be so radically trans-formed under the institutional pressures of a "prison environment." If this could happen in so short a time, without the excesses that are possi-ble in real prisons, and if it could happen to the "cream-of-the-crop of American youth," then one can only shudder to imagine what society is doing both to the actual guards and prisoners who are at this very moment participating in that unnatural "social experiment."

57 The pathology observed in this study cannot be reasonably attributed in preexisting personality differences of the subjects, that option being elimi-nated by our selection procedures and random assignment. Rather, the sub-jects' abnormal social and personal reactions are best seen as a product of their transaction with an environment that supported the behavior that would be pathological in other settings, but was "appropriate" in this prison. Had we observed comparable reactions in a real prison, the psychiatrist undoubtedly would have been able to attribute any prisoner's behavior to character defects or personality maladjustment, while critics of the prison system would have been quick to label the guards as "psychopathic." This tendency to locate the source of behavior disorders inside a particular person or group underestimates the power of situational forces.

58 Our colleague, David Rosenhan, has very convincingly shown that once a sane person (pretending to be insane) gets labeled as insane and com-mitted to a mental hospital, it is the label that is the reality which is treat-ed and not the person. This dehumanizing tendency to respond to other people according to socially determined labels and often arbitrarily assigned roles is also apparent in a recent "mock hospital" study designed by Norma Jean Orlando to extend the ideas in our research.

59 Personnel from the staff of Elgin State Hospital in Illinois role-played either mental patients or staff in a weekend simulation on a ward in the hos-pital. The mock mental patients soon displayed behavior indistinguishable from that we usually associate with the chronic pathological syndromes of

acute mental patients: Incessant pacing, uncontrollable weeping, depression, hostility, fights, stealing from each other, complaining. Many of the "mock staff" took advantage of their power to act in ways comparable to our mock guards by dehumanizing their powerless victims.

60   During a series of encounter debriefing sessions immediately after our experiment, we all had an opportunity to vent our strong feelings and to reflect upon the moral and ethical issues each of us faced, and we considered how we might react more morally in future "real-life" analogues to this situation. Year-long follow-ups with our subjects via questionnaires, personal interviews, and group reunions indicate that their mental anguish was transient and situationally specific, but the self-knowledge gained has persisted.

61   By far the most disturbing implication of our research comes from the parallels between what occurred in that basement mock prison and daily experiences in our own lives—and we presume yours. The physical institution of prison is but a concrete and steel metaphor for the existence of more pervasive, albeit less obvious, prisons of the mind that all of us daily create, populate, and perpetuate. We speak here of the prisons of racism, sexism, despair, shyness, "neurotic hang-ups," and the like. The social convention of marriage, as one example, becomes for many couples a state of imprisonment in which one partner agrees to be prisoner or guard, forcing or allowing the other to play the reciprocal role—invariably without making the contract explicit.

62   To what extent do we allow ourselves to become imprisoned by docilely accepting the roles others assign us or, indeed, choose to remain prisoners because being passive and dependent frees us from the need to act and be responsible for our actions? The prison of fear constructed in the delusions of the paranoid is no less confining or less real than the cell that every shy person erects to limit his own freedom in anxious anticipation of being ridiculed and rejected by his guards—often guards of his own making.

The Genocidal Killer in the Mirror
Crispin Sartwell

Upon first learning of such experiments as those conducted by Asch, Milgram, and Zimbardo, many of us are apt to shake our heads at the obedient participants, confident that we would behave differently—that is, independently and ethically—under the same circumstances. But how can we be so sure? In this essay on the phenomenon that novelist Joseph Conrad called the "heart of darkness," Crispin Sartwell reviews recent history to help persuade us that we should not be so smug about our own capacity to resist corrupt authority and to commit heinous acts. Among Sartwell's books are The Art of Living: Aesthetics of the Ordinary in World Spiritual Traditions *(1995),*

Obscenity, Anarchy, Reality *(1996),* Act Like You Know: African-American Autobiography and White Identity *(1998), and* Extreme Virtue: Truth and Leadership in Five Great American Lives *(2003). The following essay appeared as an op-ed column in the* Los Angeles Times *on 11 April 2004.*

1 Ten years ago this month, the Hutu government of Rwanda mobilized its citizenry into a killing machine and started stacking corpses toward the sky. It's been 30 years since the Cambodian killing fields, 40 since the start of the Cultural Revolution, 60 since the height of the Nazi Holocaust, 100 since the Belgians started murdering Congolese, 500 since the beginnings of the African slave trade and the systematic annihilation of the native peoples of the Western Hemisphere.

2 There are various things we ought to have learned from the history of genocide. One, surely, is that no problem is as profound and no evil as prevalent as state power: The rise of genocide coincides with the rise of the modern political state, and every single one of these events is inconceivable without the bland bureaucracy of death.

3 But another is this: We—and by this I mean you and I—are deeply evil. I would like to believe that I am too good, too smart, too decent to hop on the genocide bandwagon. But I know better. It's obvious, and it's a familiar point, that average Germans, average Hutus, average Americans have been mobilized for genocide. I am not profoundly different than these people, and if you think you are, then you are either a moral hero or you are profoundly self-deluded.

4 Are you a moral hero? The qualities that are needed to recruit a person to genocide are widely shared.

- *Deference to authority.* This would be the state, the experts—under normal conditions. Ponder, perhaps, how you react to a school principal or a police officer or a president. Do you often believe what the authorities tell you just because they are authorities?
- *Response to social consensus.* People are herd animals; they seek to associate themselves with a consensus of their acquaintances. If you hate being excluded by a clique, or dress in terms of trends, you are responding in this way.
- *Willingness to respond to people as members of groups, and to expect groups, overall, to display certain qualities.* I might not want to do this, but I do. I know a lot about gay people, for example: How they talk, where they live, what they do.
- *Desire for your own security and that of your family and friends, to the extent you are willing to make moral compromises to preserve it.* These are qualities found in greater or lesser degree in everyone, and they're more than enough. You, like me, are a genocidal killer, only you (probably), like me, haven't had the opportunity to display your enthusiasm. Your goodness, like mine, has little to do with who you are and everything to do with the social conditions you happen to find yourself in.

5   In Rwanda, the Hutu government claimed falsely that it was under attack from Tutsis—a claim repeated incessantly on the state-run radio—and mobilized the population into "civilian self-defense forces." It created squads dedicated to "obligatory labor for the public good" and armed them with firearms or machetes. It rewarded those who were zealous killers with houses or cars, punished those who hesitated and killed those who sheltered the intended victims. Just two months later, 800,000 people were dead.

6   Hitler didn't kill 6 million Jews, or King Leopold 10 million Africans. They used a bureaucracy and a media machine and, finally, people just like me and you. They mobilized a society. I remember staring at Rwanda on my television, reading about Cambodia in my newspaper as the killing continued. I shook my head and did absolutely nothing—basically the same approach taken by the world in each instance. I fear that if the same thing were happening in my town to people "not like me" in some identifiable way, I would take the same approach.

7   Many decent people have.

Just Do What the Pilot Tells You
Theodore Dalrymple

Most of the readings in this chapter have illustrated the dangers of unthinking obedience to either individual or group authority. But we don't mean to suggest that disobedience is always the best, the wisest, the most moral, or the most logical choice. As even Stanley Milgram acknowledged at the beginning of his article, "Some system of authority is a requirement of all communal living, and it is only the person living in isolation who is not forced to respond, with defiance or submission, to the commands of others" (page 314). Were we to routinely defy the authority of parents, teachers, police officers, employers, clients, etc., what we call civilization could not continue to function. We would be living in a Darwinian world where only the strong would survive. The law would not provide authority, but it would also not provide protection. In fact, we need to obey most orders that we are given for our own safety and welfare.

In the following article first published in the July 5, 1999, New Statesman, Theodore *Dalrymple, a British physician, reminds us of those occasions when we should do what we are told. "Blind disobedience to authority," he observes, "is no more to be encouraged than blind obedience." In the course of his discussion Dalrymple attempts to find a reasonable balance between these two poles.*

1 Some people think a determined opposition to authority is principled and romantic.

2   It is a quarter of a century since the psychologist Stanley Milgram published his masterpiece, *Obedience to Authority*. It is one of the few books of academic psychological research that can be read with as much

pleasure as a novel and which suggest almost as much about the human condition as great literature. Only someone who had no interest whatever in the genocidal upheavals of our century could fail to be gripped, and horrified, by it.

3   Milgram asked ordinary people to come to the psychology laboratories of Yale University to take part in an experiment to determine the effects of punishment on learning. The subjects were told to deliver electric shocks of increasing severity, from 15 to 450 volts, whenever a man who was supposed to learn pairs of words made a mistake. In fact the man was an actor who received no shocks at all, but who simply acted as if he had.

4   Milgram discovered that about two-thirds of his subjects (who were probably representative of the population as a whole) were quite prepared to give a complete stranger electric shocks that they believed to be painful, dangerous and even possibly fatal, despite the stranger's screams of protest, simply because they were told by someone apparently in authority—the psychologist overseeing the experiment—that the test had to go on.

5   By a series of clever manipulations, Milgram proved that it was obedience to authority that led people to behave in this fashion, rather than, say, the unleashing of a latent sadistic urge to inflict pain on people. Although Milgram was restrained in his discussion of the significance of his findings, he nevertheless suggested that they helped to explain how, in certain circumstances, even decent people might become torturers and killers.

6   It is not difficult to see how someone might draw anarchist or antiauthority conclusions from Milgram's horrifying experimental results. Indeed the title alone sometimes seems to produce this effect. As I was re-reading it, after an interval of 20 years, on a plane to Dublin, the woman next to me—a social worker in a Dublin hospital—said: "I've always been against all authority."

7   "All?" I asked.

8   "All," she replied. "We've suffered a lot in Ireland from the authority of the Catholic Church."

9   "What about the pilot of this aircraft?" I asked. "I assume you would prefer him to continue to fly it, rather than, say, for me to take over, and that were I to attempt to do so, he should exert his authority over me as captain?"

10   She readily agreed that in this instance his authority was necessary, though only for a short time, and was legitimate because she had granted it to him. I pointed out that even the brief authority that she had been so kind as to bestow upon him actually depended upon a whole chain, or network, of other authority, such as licensing boards, medical examiners and so forth, upon whose competence, honesty and diligence she could not possibly pronounce. She was not against all authority, therefore: on the contrary, she trusted much of it implicitly, even blindly. And necessarily so in a complex, technologically advanced society.

11   But her initial response to the question of obedience to authority was far from unusual. She probably thought a blanket opposition to authority was a heroic moral stance, indeed the only possible decent attitude towards it. To oppose authority is always romantic and principled, to uphold it prosaic and cowardly.

12   Yet civilization requires a delicate balance between stability and change. Neither mulish support for what exists simply because it already exists nor Bukharinite opposition* to it for much the same reason is a sufficient guide to action. Disobedience to authority is not inherently more glorious than obedience. It rather depends on the nature of the orders given or the behaviour demanded. As Milgram himself wrote, "Some system of authority is a requirement of all communal living. . . . "

13   The psychological advantage to a person of decrying authority altogether and of adopting a mental attitude of invariant opposition is that it allows him to think himself virtuous without having to engage with the necessary, messy compromises of real life.

14   Like many another young doctor, I came across the problem of authority early in my career. I worked for a physician who was far more dedicated to the welfare of her patients than I knew that I should ever be, and whom I esteemed greatly both as a doctor and as a person; yet it seemed to me that in her zeal to help her patients, to leave no stone unturned on their behalf, she often carried the investigation and treatment of moribund patients far beyond what common sense dictated. Alas, this entailed suffering, for medical investigations are often uncomfortable or painful. In my opinion, unnecessary and fruitless hardship was inflicted upon patients in their last days of life; and it fell to my lot to inflict it.

15   I was, of course, only obeying orders. I sometimes questioned those orders, but in the end I obeyed them. I was a young and inexperienced man; I knew a fiftieth as much medicine as my superior and had a thousandth of her experience. She was haunted by the fear of not doing all that could be done to save a life, while I was haunted by the unpleasantness of taking another useless blood test from a dying patient. I was never sure in any individual case that she, not I, was right.

16   Besides, I believed that the interests of patients were served by the existence of a hierarchy among doctors. Someone had to take ultimate responsibility for the care of patients, and if junior doctors were to disobey their superiors every time they disagreed with them, the system would fall apart. Clearly a point might be reached in which it was a junior doctor's duty to disobey, but there was no general rule to guide him in the estimation of when that point had come. The exercise of judgement was, and will always remain, necessary.

---

*Nikolai Bukharin, a theoretician of the Russian Revolution of 1917, became the editor of the official revolutionary newspaper *Pravda* and subsequently, a member of the ruling Politboro. Originally allied with Stalin, Bukharin differed with the Stalinist majority on the pace of agricultural collectivization and industrialization; his position became that of the "right opposition." Dismissed from his posts, Bukharin was eventually tried for treason and executed.

17   The social worker's attitude towards authority was, in practice, far more nuanced than she admitted, but there is nevertheless a danger in the disjunction between her attitude in theory and her attitude in practice. For the idea that revolt against authority is everywhere and always a noble stance is one that can soon be communicated to people who are prepared to take it literally.

18   For example, teachers tell me that if they mention to parents that their children are misbehaving, sometimes in grotesquely antisocial ways, the parents will turn unpleasant—towards the teachers, who in this instance represent authority. Recently I met a stepfather who was sent to prison for attacking a teacher who complained about his stepson. The security men in my hospital tell me that when they catch a boy stealing a car in the hospital grounds and return him to his parents, the parents start shouting—at the security men, who again represent authority. Indeed some security men now refuse to take the car thieves home, for fear of parental violence directed at them.

19   Blind disobedience to authority is no more to be encouraged than blind obedience. It is far from pleasant when encountered. Among my patients are quite a number who admit to having always had "a problem with authority." They confess it coyly, as if it were a sign of spiritual election, when it is no such thing: it is, rather, a sign of unbridled egotism. Unable to apply themselves at school, they are unable to take orders at work, and their personal relationships are almost always stormy and violent. They accept no rules, not even the informal ones that grow up between people who live closely together. For people who have a problem with authority, their whim is law. The only consideration that moderates their conduct is the threat of superior, but essentially arbitrary, violence by others.

20   It is not difficult to guess the kind of parental upbringing that results in a problem with authority. Discipline in the home is without principle or consistency, but is rather experienced by the child as the arbitrary expression of the brute power of others over himself. The conduct that on one occasion results in a slap results on another occasion in a Mars bar. The child therefore learns that discipline is an expression not of a rule that has a social purpose, but of a stronger person's momentary emotional state. He therefore comes to the conclusion that the important determinants of a relationship with others are first how you feel, and second what you can get away with by virtue of your comparative strength. Nothing else is involved.

21   To such a person, all human relationships are essentially expressions of power. An order given by another person is thus a threat to his ego, because following orders is submission to power and nothing else: there can be no other reason for it. The distinction between service and slavery collapses. To obey is to extinguish your existence as an autonomous being.

22   While obedience to authority has its dangers—as this century above all others testifies—disobedience to authority likewise has its dangers. There are hidden ironies in Milgram's great work, a work that has generally been taken as a tract against obedience to authority.

23   His experimental design depended upon deceiving his experimental subjects, upon his not asking for their informed consent to take part in his experiments. Had Milgram applied modern ethical standards to the conduct of his experiments, they could never have been performed at all, and we should never have been horrified by their results.

24   Against this, Milgram might urge two considerations. First, that the experimental subjects retrospectively approved of their participation, once they had been fully informed of the experiment's purpose and design. But this does not in the least answer the ethical objection.

25   Second, that the knowledge gained from the experiments was so important that it was worth a little light deception of the subjects to obtain it. This argument turns upon the estimation by somebody—in this case, Milgram himself—that the light was worth the candle: in short, it depends upon our old friend, authority.

Disobedience as a Psychological and Moral Problem
Erich Fromm

Erich Fromm (1900–1980) was one of the twentieth century's distinguished writers and thinkers. Psychoanalyst and philosopher, historian and sociologist, he ranged widely in his interests and defied easy characterization. Fromm studied the works of Freud and Marx closely, and published on them both, but he was not aligned strictly with either. In much of his voluminous writing, he struggled to articulate a view that could help bridge ideological and personal conflicts and bring dignity to those who struggled with isolation in the industrial world. Author of more than thirty books and contributor to numerous edited collections and journals, Fromm is best known for Escape from Freedom *(1941),* The Art of Loving *(1956), and* To Have or To Be? *(1976).*

In the essay that follows, first published in 1963, Fromm discusses the seductive comforts of obedience, and he makes distinctions among varieties of obedience, some of which he believes are destructive, and others, life affirming. His thoughts on nuclear annihilation may seem dated in these days of post–Cold War cooperation, but it is worth remembering that Fromm wrote his essay just after the Cuban missile crisis, when fears of a third world war ran high. (We might note that despite the welcome reductions of nuclear stockpiles, the United States and Russia still possess, and retain battle plans for, thousands of warheads.) And in the wake of the 9/11 attacks, the threat of terrorists acquiring and using nuclear weapons against the United States seems very real. On the major points of his essay, concerning the psychological and moral problems of obedience, Fromm remains as pertinent today as when he wrote some forty years ago.

1   For centuries kings, priests, feudal lords, industrial bosses, and parents have insisted that *obedience is a virtue* and that *disobedience is a vice.* In order

to introduce another point of view, let us set against this position the following statement: *human history began with an act of disobedience, and it is not unlikely that it will be terminated by an act of obedience.*

2   Human history was ushered in by an act of disobedience according to the Hebrew and Greek myths. Adam and Eve, living in the Garden of Eden, were part of nature; they were in harmony with it, yet did not transcend it. They were in nature as the fetus is in the womb of the mother. They were human, and at the same time not yet human. All this changed when they disobeyed an order. By breaking the ties with earth and mother, by cutting the umbilical cord, man emerged from a prehuman harmony and was able to take the first step into independence and freedom. The act of disobedience set Adam and Eve free and opened their eyes. They recognized each other as strangers and the world outside them as strange and even hostile. Their act of disobedience broke the primary bond with nature and made them individuals. "Original sin," far from corrupting man, set him free; it was the beginning of history. Man had to leave the Garden of Eden in order to learn to rely on his own powers and to become fully human.

3   The prophets, in their messianic concept, confirmed the idea that man had been right in disobeying; that he had not been corrupted by his "sin," but freed from the fetters of pre-human harmony. For the prophets, *history* is the place where man becomes human; during its unfolding he develops his powers of reason and of love until he creates a new harmony between himself, his fellow man, and nature. This new harmony is described as "the end of days," that period of history in which there is peace between man and man, between man and nature. It is a "new" paradise created by man himself, and one which he alone could create because he was forced to leave the "old" paradise as a result of his disobedience.

4   Just as the Hebrew myth of Adam and Eve, so the Greek myth of Prometheus sees all human civilization based on an act of disobedience. Prometheus, in stealing the fire from the gods, lays the foundation for the evolution of man. There would be no human history were it not for Prometheus' "crime." He, like Adam and Eve, is punished for his disobedience. But he does not repent and ask for forgiveness. On the contrary, he proudly says: "I would rather be chained to this rock than be the obedient servant of the gods."

5   Man has continued to evolve by acts of disobedience. Not only was his spiritual development possible only because there were men who dared to say no to the powers that be in the name of their conscience or their faith, but also his intellectual development was dependent on the capacity for being disobedient—disobedient to authorities who tried to muzzle new thoughts and to the authority of long-established opinions which declared a change to be nonsense.

6   If the capacity for disobedience constituted the beginning of human history, obedience might very well, as I have said, cause the end of human history. I am not speaking symbolically or poetically. There is

the possibility, or even the probability, that the human race will destroy civilization and even all life upon earth within the next five to ten years. There is no rationality or sense in it. But the fact is that, while we are living technically in the Atomic Age, the majority of men—including most of those who are in power—still live emotionally in the Stone Age; that while our mathematics, astronomy, and the natural sciences are of the twentieth century, most of our ideas about politics, the state, and society lag far behind the age of science. If mankind commits suicide it will be because people will obey those who command them to push the deadly buttons; because they will obey the archaic passions of fear, hate, and greed; because they will obey obsolete clichés of State sovereignty and national honor. The Soviet leaders talk much about revolutions, and we in the "free world" talk much about freedom. Yet they and we discourage disobedience—in the Soviet Union explicitly and by force, in the free world implicitly and by the more subtle methods of persuasion.

7   But I do not mean to say that all disobedience is a virtue and all obedience is a vice. Such a view would ignore the dialectical relationship between obedience and disobedience. Whenever the principles which are obeyed and those which are disobeyed are irreconcilable, an act of obedience to one principle is necessarily an act of disobedience to its counterpart and vice versa. Antigone is the classic example of this dichotomy. By obeying the inhuman laws of the State, Antigone necessarily would disobey the laws of humanity. By obeying the latter, she must disobey the former. All martyrs of religious faiths, of freedom, and of science have had to disobey those who wanted to muzzle them in order to obey their own consciences, the laws of humanity, and of reason. If a man can only obey and not disobey, he is a slave; if he can only disobey and not obey, he is a rebel (not a revolutionary); he acts out of anger, disappointment, resentment, yet not in the name of a conviction or a principle.

8   However, in order to prevent a confusion of terms an important qualification must be made. Obedience to a person, institution, or power (heteronomous obedience) is submission; it implies the abdication of my autonomy and the acceptance of a foreign will or judgment in place of my own. Obedience to my own reason or conviction (autonomous obedience) is not an act of submission but one of affirmation. My conviction and my judgment, if authentically mine, are part of me. If I follow them rather than the judgment of others, I am being myself; hence the word *obey* can be applied only in a metaphorical sense and with a meaning which is fundamentally different from the one in the case of "heteronomous obedience."

9   But this distinction still needs two further qualifications, one with regard to the concept of conscience and the other with regard to the concept of authority.

10   The word *conscience* is used to express two phenomena which are quite distinct from each other. One is the "authoritarian conscience" which is

the internalized voice of an authority whom we are eager to please and afraid of displeasing. This authoritarian conscience is what most people experience when they obey their conscience. It is also the conscience which Freud speaks of, and which he called "Super-Ego." This Super-Ego represents the internalized commands and prohibitions of father, accepted by the son out of fear. Different from the authoritarian conscience is the "humanistic conscience"; this is the voice present in every human being and independent from external sanctions and rewards. Humanistic conscience is based on the fact that as human beings we have an intuitive knowledge of what is human and inhuman, what is conducive of life and what is destructive of life. This conscience serves our functioning as human beings. It is the voice which calls us back to ourselves, to our humanity.

11   Authoritarian conscience (Super-Ego) is still obedience to a power outside of myself, even though this power has been internalized. Consciously I believe that I am following *my* conscience; in effect, however, I have swallowed the principles of *power*; just because of the illusion that humanistic conscience and Super-Ego are identical, internalized authority is so much more effective than the authority which is clearly experienced as not being part of me. Obedience to the "authoritarian conscience," like all obedience to outside thoughts and power, tends to debilitate "humanistic conscience," the ability to be and to judge oneself.

12   The statement, on the other hand, that obedience to another person is *ipso facto* submission needs also to be qualified by distinguishing "irrational" from "rational" authority. An example of rational authority is to be found in the relationship between student and teacher; one of irrational authority in the relationship between slave and master. Both relationships are based on the fact that the authority of the person in command is accepted. Dynamically, however, they are of a different nature. The interests of the teacher and the student, in the ideal case, lie in the same direction. The teacher is satisfied if he succeeds in furthering the student; if he has failed to do so, the failure is his and the student's. The slave owner, on the other hand, wants to exploit the slave as much as possible. The more he gets out of him the more satisfied he is. At the same time, the slave tries to defend as best he can his claims for a minimum of happiness. The interests of slave and master are antagonistic, because what is advantageous to the one is detrimental to the other. The superiority of the one over the other has a different function in each case; in the first it is the condition for the furtherance of the person subjected to the authority, and in the second it is the condition for his exploitation. Another distinction runs parallel to this: rational authority is rational because the authority, whether it is held by a teacher or a captain of a ship giving orders in an emergency, acts in the name of reason which, being universal, I can accept without submitting. Irrational authority has to use force or suggestion, because no one would let himself be exploited if he were free to prevent it.

(13)   Why is man so prone to obey and why is it so difficult for him to disobey? As long as I am obedient to the power of the State, the Church, or
public opinion, I feel safe and protected. In fact it makes little difference
what power it is that I am obedient to. It is always an institution, or men,
who use force in one form or another and who fraudulently claim omni-
science and omnipotence. My obedience makes me part of the power
I worship, and hence I feel strong. I can make no error, since it decides for
me; I cannot be alone, because it watches over me; I cannot commit a sin,
because it does not let me do so, and even if I do sin, the punishment is
only the way of returning to the almighty power.

14   In order to disobey, one must have the courage to be alone, to err, and
to sin. But courage is not enough. The capacity for courage depends on a
person's state of development. Only if a person has emerged from
mother's lap and father's commands, only if he has emerged as a fully
developed individual and thus has acquired the capacity to think and
feel for himself, only then can he have the courage to say "no" to power,
to disobey.

15   A person can become free through acts of disobedience by learning to
say no to power. But not only is the capacity for disobedience the condition
for freedom; freedom is also the condition for disobedience. If I am afraid
of freedom, I cannot dare to say "no," I cannot have the courage to be disobedient. Indeed, freedom and the capacity for disobedience are inseparable; hence any social, political, and religious system which proclaims
freedom, yet stamps out disobedience, cannot speak the truth.

16   There is another reason why it is so difficult to dare to disobey, to say
"no" to power. During most of human history obedience has been identified with virtue and disobedience with sin. The reason is simple: thus
far throughout most of history a minority has ruled over the majority.
This rule was made necessary by the fact that there was only enough of
the good things of life for the few, and only the crumbs remained for the
many. If the few wanted to enjoy the good things and, beyond that, to
have the many serve them and work for them, one condition was necessary: the many had to learn obedience. To be sure, obedience can be
established by sheer force. But this method has many disadvantages. It
constitutes a constant threat that one day the many might have the means
to overthrow the few by force; furthermore there are many kinds of work
which cannot be done properly if nothing but fear is behind the obedience. Hence the obedience which is only rooted in the fear of force must
be transformed into one rooted in man's heart. Man must want and even
need to obey, instead of only fearing to disobey. If this is to be achieved,
power must assume the qualities of the All Good, of the All Wise; it must
become All Knowing. If this happens, power can proclaim that disobedience is sin and obedience virtue; and once this has been proclaimed, the
many can accept obedience because it is good and detest disobedience
because it is bad, rather than to detest themselves for being cowards.
From Luther to the nineteenth century one was concerned with overt and

explicit authorities. Luther, the pope, the princes, wanted to uphold it; the middle class, the workers, the philosophers, tried to uproot it. The fight against authority in the State as well as in the family was often the very basis for the development of an independent and daring person. The fight against authority was inseparable from the intellectual mood which characterized the philosophers of the enlightenment and the scientists. This "critical mood" was one of faith in reason, and at the same time of doubt in everything which is said or thought, inasmuch as it is based on tradition, superstition, custom, power. The principles *sapere aude* and *de omnibus est dubitandum*—"dare to be wise" and "of all one must doubt"—were characteristic of the attitude which permitted and furthered the capacity to say "no."

17   The case of Adolf Eichmann [see note, page 320] is symbolic of our situation and has a significance far beyond the one in which his accusers in the courtroom in Jerusalem were concerned with. Eichmann is a symbol of the organization man, of the alienated bureaucrat for whom men, women and children have become numbers. He is a symbol of all of us. We can see ourselves in Eichmann. But the most frightening thing about him is that after the entire story was told in terms of his own admissions, he was able in perfect good faith to plead his innocence. It is clear that if he were once more in the same situation he would do it again. And so would we—and so do we.

18   The organization man has lost the capacity to disobey, he is not even aware of the fact that he obeys. At this point in history the capacity to doubt, to criticize, and to disobey may be all that stands between a future for mankind and the end of civilization.

Time to Think About Torture
Jonathan Alter

Born and raised in Chicago, Jonathan Alter (1957–) received a B.A. in history (with honors) from Harvard University in 1979. After working for several years at The Washington Monthly, *he joined* Newsweek *in 1983, first as associate editor of the Nation section and later as a media critic and senior writer. Alter has been a senior editor and columnist at* Newsweek *since 1996, covering presidential campaigns and writing two columns: "Between the Lines" on political and social issues, and the humorous "Conventional Wisdom Watch" on current news. He has also written for a wide range of publications including* Rolling Stone, The New Republic, Esquire, *and the* New York Times. *His book on Franklin Delano Roosevelt's first three months in office,* The Defining Moment: FDR's Hundred Days and the Triumph of Hope,

*was published in 2006. Alter has also worked in television news. A contributing correspon-
dent for NBC for more than a decade, he can be seen on both NBC and MSNBC news and
on* Today. *In 1987 Alter won both the Lowell Mellett Award for outstanding media criticism
and the Gerald Loeb Award for distinguished business reporting. A series of awards followed,
including a National Headliner Award, several National Magazine Awards for General
Excellence, two New York State Bar Association Media Awards, a Clarion Award from Women
in Communications, and a John Bartlow Martin Award for public interest magazine journal-
ism. In this* Newsweek *column written in November 2001, Alter argues that in the aftermath
of the September 11 attacks, the U.S. government should reconsider its ban on torture.*

1   In this autumn of anger, even a liberal can find his thoughts turning to . . .
torture. OK, not cattle prods or rubber hoses, at least not here in the United
States, but *something* to jump-start the stalled investigation of the greatest
crime in American history. Right now, four key hijacking suspects aren't
talking at all.

2   Couldn't we at least subject them to psychological torture, like tapes
of dying rabbits or high-decibel rap? (The military has done that in
Panama and elsewhere.) How about truth serum, administered with a
mandatory IV? Or deportation to Saudi Arabia, land of beheadings?
(As the frustrated FBI has been threatening.) Some people still argue
that we needn't rethink any of our old assumptions about law enforce-
ment, but they're hopelessly "Sept. 10"—living in a country that no
longer exists.

3   One sign of how much things have changed is the reaction to the anti-
terrorism bill, which cleared the Senate last week by a vote of 98–1.
While the ACLU felt obliged to quibble with a provision or two, the
opposition was tepid, even from staunch civil libertarians. That great
quote from the late Chief Justice Robert Jackson—"The Constitution is
not a suicide pact"—is getting a good workout lately. "This was incom-
parably more sober and sensible than what some of our revered presi-
dents did," says Floyd Abrams, the First Amendment lawyer, referring
to the severe restrictions on liberty imposed during the Civil War and
World War I.

4   Fortunately, the new law stops short of threatening basic rights like free
speech, which is essential in wartime to hold the government accountable.
The bill makes it easier to wiretap (under the old rules, you had to get a
warrant for each individual phone, an anachronism in a cellular age),
easier to detain immigrants who won't talk and easier to follow money
through the international laundering process. A welcome "sunset" provision means the expansion of surveillance will expire after four years. That's
an important precedent, though odds are these changes will end up being
permanent. It's a new world.

5   Actually, the world hasn't changed as much as we have. The Israelis
have been wrestling for years with the morality of torture. Until 1999 an
interrogation technique called "shaking" was legal. It entailed holding
a smelly bag over a suspect's head in a dark room, then applying scary

psychological torment. (To avoid lessening the potential impact on terrorists, I won't specify exactly what kind.) Even now, Israeli law leaves a little room for "moderate physical pressure" in what are called "ticking time bomb" cases, where extracting information is essential to saving hundreds of lives. The decision of when to apply it is left in the hands of law-enforcement officials.

6   For more than 20 years Harvard Law School professor Alan Dershowitz has argued to the Israelis that this is terribly unfair to the members of the security services. In a forthcoming book, "Shouting Fire," he makes the case for what he calls a "torture warrant," where judges would balance competing claims and make the call, as they do in issuing search warrants. Dershowitz says that as long as the fruits of such interrogation are used for investigation, not to convict the detainee (a violation of the Fifth Amendment right against self-incrimination), it could be constitutional here, too. "I'm not in favor of torture, but if you're going to have it, it should damn well have court approval," Dershowitz says.

7   Not surprisingly, judges and lawyers in both Israel and the United States don't agree. They prefer looking the other way to giving even mild torture techniques the patina of legality. This leaves them in a strange moral position. The torture they can't see (or that occurs after deportation) is harder on the person they claim to be concerned about—the detainee—but easier on their consciences. Out of sight, out of mind.

8   Short of physical torture, there's always sodium pentothal ("truth serum"). The FBI is eager to try it, and deserves the chance. Unfortunately, truth serum, first used on spies in World War II, makes suspects gabby but not necessarily truthful. The same goes for even the harshest torture. When the subject breaks, he often lies. Prisoners "have only one objective—to end the pain," says retired Col. Kenneth Allard, who was trained in interrogation. "It's a huge limitation."

9   Some torture clearly works. Jordan broke the most notorious terrorist of the 1980s, Abu Nidal, by threatening his family. Philippine police reportedly helped crack the 1993 World Trade Center bombings (plus a plot to crash 11 U.S. airliners and kill the pope) by convincing a suspect that they were about to turn him over to the Israelis. Then there's painful Islamic justice, which has the added benefit of greater acceptance among Muslims.

10   We can't legalize physical torture; it's contrary to American values. But even as we continue to speak out against human-rights abuses around the world, we need to keep an open mind about certain measures to fight terrorism, like court-sanctioned psychological interrogation. And we'll have to think about transferring some suspects to our less squeamish allies, even if that's hypocritical. Nobody said this was going to be pretty.

The My Lai Massacre:
A Military Crime of Obedience
Herbert C. Kelman and V. Lee Hamilton

This article details one of the worse atrocities committed by the U.S. military: the My Lai Massacre. Why were hundreds of innocents slaughtered in a single incident during the Vietnam conflict? What prompted such behavior? The authors explain how the massacre erupted and explore the role of conformity in this tragedy. In particular, they examine the power of conformity to compel people to act against their own beliefs and moral code.

1   March 16, 1968, was a busy day in U.S. history. Stateside, Robert F. Kennedy announced his presidential candidacy, challenging a sitting president from his own party—in part out of opposition to an undeclared and disastrous war. In Vietnam, the war continued. In many ways, March 16 may have been a typical day in that war. We will probably never know. But we do know that on that day a typical company went on a mission—which may or may not have been typical—to a village called Son (or Song) My. Most of what is remembered from that mission occurred in the subhamlet known to Americans as My Lai 4.

2   The My Lai massacre was investigated and charges were brought in 1969 and 1970. Trials and disciplinary actions lasted into 1971. Entire books have been written about the army's year-long cover-up of the massacre (for example, Hersh, 1972), and the cover-up was a major focus of the army's own investigation of the incident. Our central concern here is the massacre itself—a crime of obedience—and public reactions to such crimes, rather than the lengths to which many went to deny the event. Therefore this account concentrates on one day: March 16, 1968.[1]

3   Many verbal testimonials to the horrors that occurred at My Lai were available. More unusual was the fact that an army photographer, Ronald Haeberle, was assigned the task of documenting the anticipated military engagement at My Lai—and documented a massacre instead. Later, as the story of the massacre emerged, his photographs were widely distributed and seared the public conscience. What might have been dismissed as unreal or exaggerated was depicted in photographs of demonstrable authenticity. The dominant image appeared on the cover of *Life*: piles of bodies jumbled together in a ditch along a trail—the dead all apparently unarmed. All were Oriental, and all appeared to be children, women, or old men. Clearly there had been a mass execution, one whose image would not quickly fade.

4   So many bodies (over twenty in the cover photo alone) are hard to imagine as the handiwork of one killer. These were not. They were the product of what we call a crime of obedience. Crimes of obedience begin with orders. But orders are often vague and rarely survive with any clarity the transition from one authority down a chain of subordinates to the ultimate actors. The operation at Son My was no exception.

5   "Charlie" Company, Company C, under Lt. Col. Frank Barker's command, arrived in Vietnam in December of 1967. As the army's investigative unit, directed by Lt. Gen. William R. Peers, characterized the personnel, they "contained no significant deviation from the average" for the time. Seymour S. Hersh (1970) described the "average" more explicitly: "Most of the men in Charlie Company had volunteered for the draft, only a few had gone to college for even one year. Nearly half were black, with a few Mexican-Americans. Most were eighteen to twenty-two years old. The favorite reading matter of Charlie Company, like that of other line infantry units in Vietnam, was comic books" (p. 18). The action at My Lai, like that throughout Vietnam, was fought by a cross-section of those Americans who either believed in the war or lacked the social resources to avoid participating in it. Charlie Company was indeed average for that time, that place, and that war.

6   Two key figures in Charlie Company were more unusual. The company's commander, Capt. Ernest Medina, was an upwardly mobile Mexican-American who wanted to make the army his career, although he feared that he might never advance beyond captain because of his lack of formal education. His eagerness had earned him a nickname among his men: "Mad Dog Medina." One of his admirers was the platoon leader Second Lt. William L. Calley, Jr., an undistinguished, five-foot-three-inch junior-college dropout who had failed four of the seven courses in which he had enrolled his first year. Many viewed him as one of those "instant officers" made possible only by the army's then-desperate need for manpower. Whatever the cause, he was an insecure leader whose frequent claim was "I'm the boss." His nickname among some of the troops was "Surfside 5 1/2," a reference to the swashbuckling heroes of a popular television show, "Surfside 6."

7   The Son My operation was planned by Lieutenant Colonel Barker and his staff as a search-and-destroy mission with the objective of rooting out the Forty-eighth Viet Cong Battalion from their base area of Son My village. Apparently no written orders were ever issued. Barker's superior, Col. Oran Henderson, arrived at the staging point the day before. Among the issues he reviewed with the assembled officers were some of the weaknesses of prior operations by their units, including their failure to be appropriately aggressive in pursuit of the enemy. Later briefings by Lieutenant Colonel Barker and his staff asserted that no one except Viet Cong was expected to be in the village after 7 A.M. on the following day. The "innocent" would all be at the market. Those present at the briefings gave conflicting accounts of Barker's exact orders, but he conveyed at least a strong suggestion that the Son My area was to be obliterated. As the army's inquiry reported: "While

there is some conflict in the testimony as to whether LTC Barker ordered the destruction of houses, dwellings, livestock, and other foodstuffs in the Song My area, the preponderance of the evidence indicates that such destruction was implied if not specifically directed, by his orders of 15 March" (Peers Report, in Goldstein et al., 1976, p. 94).

8   Evidence that Barker ordered the killing of civilians is even more murky. What does seem clear, however, is that—having asserted that civilians would be away at the market—he did not specify what was to be done with any who might nevertheless be found on the scene. The Peers Report therefore considered it "reasonable to conclude that LTC Barker's minimal or nonexistent instructions concerning the handling of noncombatants created the potential for grave misunderstandings as to his intentions and for interpretation of his orders as authority to fire, without restriction, on all persons found in target area" (Goldstein et al., 1976, p. 95). Since Barker was killed in action in June 1968, his own formal version of the truth was never available.

9   Charlie Company's Captain Medina was briefed for the operation by Barker and his staff. He then transmitted the already vague orders to his own men. Charlie Company was spoiling for a fight, having been totally frustrated during its months in Vietnam—first by waiting for battles that never came, then by incompetent forays led by inexperienced commanders, and finally by mines and booby traps. In fact, the emotion-laden funeral of a sergeant killed by a booby trap was held on March 15, the day before My Lai. Captain Medina gave the orders for the next day's action at the close of that funeral. Many were in a mood for revenge.

10   It is again unclear what was ordered. Although all participants were still alive by the time of the trials for the massacre, they were either on trial or probably felt under threat of trial. Memories are often flawed and self-serving at such times. It is apparent that Medina relayed to the men at least some of Barker's general message—to expect Viet Cong resistance, to burn, and to kill livestock. It is not clear that he ordered the slaughter of the inhabitants, but some of the men who heard him thought he had. One of those who claimed to have heard such orders was Lt. William Calley.

11   As March 16 dawned, much was expected of the operation by those who had set it into motion. Therefore a full complement of "brass" was present in helicopters overhead, including Barker, Colonel Henderson, and their superior, Major General Koster (who went on to become commandant of West Point before the story of My Lai broke). On the ground, the troops were to carry with them one reporter and one photographer to immortalize the anticipated battle.

12   The action for Company C began at 7:30 as their first wave of helicopters touched down near the subhamlet of My Lai 4. By 7:47 all of Company C was present and set to fight. But instead of the Viet Cong Forty-eighth Battalion, My Lai was filled with the old men, women, and children who were supposed to have gone to market. By this time, in their version of the

war, and with whatever orders they thought they had heard, the men from Company C were nevertheless ready to find Viet Cong everywhere. By nightfall, the official tally was 128 VC killed and three weapons captured, although later unofficial body counts ran as high as 500. The operation at Son My was over. And by nightfall, as Hersh reported: "the Viet Cong were back in My Lai 4, helping the survivors bury the dead. It took five days. Most of the funeral speeches were made by the Communist guerrillas. Nguyen Bat was not a Communist at the time of the massacre, but the incident changed his mind. 'After the shooting,' he said, 'all the villagers became Communists'" (1970, p. 74). To this day, the memory of the massacre is kept alive by markers and plaques designating the spots where groups of villagers were killed, by a large statue, and by the My Lai Museum, established in 1975 (Williams, 1985).

13   But what could have happened to leave American troops reporting a victory over Viet Cong when in fact they had killed hundreds of noncombatants? It is not hard to explain the report of victory; that is the essence of a cover-up. It is harder to understand how the killings came to be committed in the first place, making a cover-up necessary.

Mass Executions and the Defense of Superior Orders

14 Some of the atrocities on March 16, 1968, were evidently unofficial, spontaneous acts: rapes, tortures, killings. For example, Hersh (1970) describes Charlie Company's Second Platoon as entering "My Lai 4 with guns blazing" (p. 50); more graphically, Lieutenant "Brooks and his men in the second platoon to the north had begun to systematically ransack the hamlet and slaughter the people, kill the livestock, and destroy the crops. Men poured rifle and machine-gun fire into huts without knowing—or seemingly caring—who was inside" (pp. 49–50). . . .

15   But a substantial amount of the killing was organized and traceable to one authority: the First Platoon's Lt. William Calley. Calley was originally charged with 109 killings, almost all of them mass executions at the trail and other locations. He stood trial for 102 of these killings, was convicted of 22 in 1971, and at first received a life sentence. Though others—both superior and subordinate to Calley—were brought to trial, he was the only one convicted for the My Lai crimes. Thus, the only actions of My Lai for which anyone was ever convicted were mass executions, ordered and committed. We suspect that there are commonsense reasons why this one type of killing was singled out. In the midst of rapidly moving events with people running about, an execution of stationary targets is literally a still life that stands out and whose participants are clearly visible. It can be proven that specific people committed specific deeds. An execution, in contrast to the shooting of someone on the run, is also more likely to meet the legal definition of an act resulting from intent—with malice aforethought. Moreover, American military law specifically forbids the killing of unarmed civilians or military prisoners, as does the Geneva Convention

between nations. Thus common sense, legal standards, and explicit doctrine all made such actions the likeliest target for prosecution.

16   When Lieutenant Calley was charged under military law it was for violation of the Uniform Code of Military justice (UMCI) Article 118 (murder). This article is similar to civilian codes in that it provides for conviction if an accused:

> without justification or excuse, unlawfully kills a human being, when he—
>
> 1. has a premeditated design to kill;
>
> 2. intends to kill or inflict great bodily harm;
>
> 3. is engaged in an act which is inherently dangerous to others and evinces a wanton disregard of human life, or
>
> 4. is engaged in the perpetration or attempted perpetration of burglary, sodomy, rape, robbery, or aggravated arson. (Goldstein et al., 1976, p. 507)

For a soldier, one legal justification for killing is warfare; but warfare is subject to many legal limits and restrictions, including, of course, the inadmissibility of killing unarmed noncombatants or prisoners whom one has disarmed. The pictures of the trail victims at My Lai certainly portrayed one or the other of these. Such an action would be illegal under military law; ordering another to commit such an action would be illegal; and following such an order would be illegal.

17   But following an order may provide a second and pivotal justification for an act that would be murder when committed by a civilian. . . . American military law assumes that the subordinate is inclined to follow orders, as that is the normal obligation of the role. Hence, legally, obedient subordinates are protected from unreasonable expectations regarding their capacity to evaluate those orders:

> An order requiring the performance of a military duty may be inferred to be legal. An act performed manifestly beyond the scope of authority, or pursuant to an order that a man of ordinary sense and understanding would know to be illegal, or in a wanton manner in the discharge of a lawful duty, is not excusable. (Par. 216, Subpar. *d*, Manual for Courts Martial, United States, 1969 Rev.)

Thus what *may* be excusable is the good-faith carrying out of an order, as long as that order appears to the ordinary soldier to be a legal one. In military law, invoking superior orders moves the question from one of the action's consequences—the body count—to one of evaluating the actor's motives and good sense.

18   In sum, if anyone is to be brought to justice for a massacre, common sense and legal codes decree that the most appropriate targets are those who make themselves executioners. This is the kind of target the government selected in prosecuting Lieutenant Calley with the greatest fervor. And in a military context, the most promising way in which one can redefine one's undeniable deeds into acceptability is to invoke superior orders. This is what Calley did in attempting to avoid conviction. . . .

· · ·

19   The core of Lieutenant Calley's defense was superior orders. What this meant to him—in contrast to what it meant to the judge and jury—can be gleaned from his responses to a series of questions from his defense attorney, George Latimer, in which Calley sketched out his understanding of the laws of war and the actions that constitute doing one's duty within those laws:

> LATIMER: Did you receive any training . . . which had to do with the obedience to orders?
>
> CALLEY: Yes, sir.
>
> LATIMER: . . . what were you informed [were] the principles involved in that field?
>
> CALLEY: That all orders were to be assumed legal, that the soldier's job was to carry out any order given him to the best of his ability.
>
> LATIMER: . . . what might occur if you disobeyed an order by a senior officer?
>
> CALLEY: You could be court-martialed for refusing an order and refusing an order in the face of the enemy, you could be sent to death, sir.
>
> LATIMER: [I am asking] whether you were required in any way, shape or form to make a determination of the legality or illegality of an order?
>
> CALLEY: No, sir. I was never told that I had the choice, sir.
>
> LATIMER: If you had a doubt about the order, what were you supposed to do?
>
> CALLEY: . . . I was supposed to carry the order out and then come back and make my complaint. (Hammer, 1971, pp. 240–41)

20   Lieutenant Calley steadfastly maintained that his actions within My Lai had constituted, in his mind, carrying out orders from Captain Medina. Both his own actions and the orders he gave to others (such as the instruction to Meadlo to "waste 'em") were entirely in response to superior orders. He

denied any intent to kill individuals and any but the most passing awareness of distinctions among the individuals: "I was ordered to go in there and destroy the enemy. That was my job on that day. That was the mission I was given. I did not sit down and think in terms of men, women, and children. They were all classified the same, and that was the classification that we dealt with, just as enemy soldiers." When Latimer asked if in his own opinion Calley had acted "rightly and according to your understanding of your directions and orders," Calley replied, "I felt then and I still do that I acted as I was directed, and I carried out the orders that I was given, and I do not feel wrong in doing so, sir" (Hammer, 1971, p. 257).

21   His court-martial did not accept Calley's defense of superior orders and clearly did not share his interpretation of his duty. The jury evidently reasoned that, even if there had been orders to destroy everything in sight and to "waste the Vietnamese," any reasonable person would have realized that such orders were illegal and should have refused to carry them out. . . .

. . .

22   Lieutenant Calley was initially sentenced to life imprisonment. That sentence was reduced: first to twenty years, eventually to ten (the latter by Secretary of Defense Callaway in 1974).[2] Calley served three years before being released on bond. The time was spent under house arrest in his apartment, where he was able to receive visits from his girlfriend. He was granted parole on September 10, 1975.

Sanctioned Massacres

23 The slaughter at My Lai is an instance of a class of violent acts that can be described as sanctioned massacres (Kelman, 1973): acts of indiscriminate, ruthless, and often systematic mass violence, carried out by military or paramilitary personnel while engaged in officially sanctioned campaigns, the victims of which are defenseless and unresisting civilians, including old men, women, and children. Sanctioned massacres have occurred throughout history. Within American history, My Lai had its precursors in the Philippine war around the turn of the century (Schirmer, 1971) and in the massacres of American Indians. Elsewhere in the world, one recalls the Nazis' "final solution" for European Jews, the massacres and deportations of Armenians by Turks, the liquidation of the kulaks and the great purges in the Soviet Union, and more recently the massacres in Indonesia and Bangladesh, in Biafra and Burundi, in South Africa and Mozambique, in Cambodia and Afghanistan, in Syria and Lebanon. Sanctioned massacres may vary on a number of dimensions. For present purposes, however, we want to focus on features they share. Two of these are the *context* and the *target* of the violence.

24   Sanctioned massacres tend to occur in the context of an overall policy that is explicitly or implicitly genocidal: designed to destroy all or part

of a category of people defined in ethnic, national, racial, religious, or other terms. Such a policy may be deliberately aimed at the systematic extermination of a population group as an end in itself, as was the case with the Holocaust during World War II. In the Nazis' "final solution" for European Jewry, a policy aimed at exterminating millions of people was consciously articulated and executed (see Levinson, 1973), and the extermination was accomplished on a mass-production basis through the literal establishment of a well-organized, efficient death industry. Alternatively, such a policy may be aimed at an objective other than extermination—such as the pacification of the rural population of South Vietnam, as was the case in U.S. policy for Indochina—but may include the deliberate decimation of large segments of a population as an acceptable means to that end. . . .

25   A second feature of sanctioned massacres is that their targets have not themselves threatened or engaged in hostile actions toward the perpetrators of the violence. The victims of this class of violence are often defenseless civilians, including old men, women, and children. By all accounts, at least after the first moments at My Lai, the victims there fit this description, although in guerrilla warfare there always remains some ambiguity about the distinction between armed soldiers and unarmed civilians. As has often been noted, U.S. troops in Vietnam had to face the possibility that a woman or even a child might be concealing a hand grenade under clothing.

26   There are, of course, historical and situational reasons particular groups become victims of sanctioned massacres, but these do not include their own immediate harmfulness or violence toward the attackers. Rather, their selection as targets for massacre at a particular time can ultimately be traced to their relationship to the pursuit of larger policies. Their elimination may be seen as a useful tool or their continued existence as an irritating obstacle in the execution of policy.

27   The genocidal or near-genocidal context of this class of violence and the fact that it is directed at a target that—at least from an observer's perspective—did not provoke the violence through its own actions has some definite implications for the psychological environment within which sanctioned massacres occur. It is an environment almost totally devoid of the conditions that usually provide at least some degree of moral justification for violence. Neither the reason for the violence nor its purpose is of the kind that is normally considered justifiable. Although people may disagree about the precise point at which they would draw the line between justifiable and unjustifiable violence, most would agree that violence in self-defense or in response to oppression and other forms of strong provocation is at least within the realm of moral discourse. In contrast, the violence of sanctioned massacres falls outside that realm.

28   In searching for a psychological explanation for mass violence under these conditions, one's first inclination is to look for forces that might

impel people toward such murderous acts. Can we identify, in massacre situations, psychological forces so powerful that they outweigh the moral restraints that would normally inhibit unjustifiable violence?

. . .

29   In sum, the occurrence of sanctioned massacres cannot be adequately explained by the existence of psychological forces—whether these be characterological dispositions to engage in murderous violence or profound hostility against the target—so powerful that they must find expression in violent acts unhampered by moral restraints. Instead, the major instigators for this class of violence derive from the policy process. The question that really calls for psychological analysis is why so many people are willing to formulate, participate in, and condone policies that call for the mass killings of defenseless civilians. Thus it is more instructive to look not at the motives for violence but at the conditions under which the usual moral inhibitions against violence become weakened. Three social processes that tend to create such conditions can be identified: authorization, routinization, and dehumanization. Through authorization, the situation becomes so defined that the individual is absolved of the responsibility to make personal moral choices. Through routinization, the action becomes so organized that there is no opportunity for raising moral questions. Through dehumanization, the actors' attitudes toward the target and toward themselves become so structured that it is neither necessary nor possible for them to view the relationship in moral terms.

Authorization

30 Sanctioned massacres by definition occur in the context of an authority situation, a situation in which, at least for many of the participants, the moral principles that generally govern human relationships do not apply. Thus, when acts of violence are explicitly ordered, implicitly encouraged, tacitly approved, or at least permitted by legitimate authorities, people's readiness to commit or condone them is enhanced. That such acts are authorized seems to carry automatic justification for them. Behaviorally, authorization obviates the necessity of making judgments or choices. Not only do normal moral principles become inoperative, but—particularly when the actions are explicitly ordered—a different kind of morality, linked to the duty to obey superior orders, tends to take over.

31   In an authority situation, individuals characteristically feel obligated to obey the orders of the authorities, whether or not these correspond with their personal preferences. They see themselves as having no choice as long as they accept the legitimacy of the orders and of the authorities who give them. Individuals differ considerably in the degree to which—and the conditions under which—they are prepared to challenge the legitimacy of an order on the grounds that the order itself is illegal, or that those giving it have overstepped their authority, or that it stems from a policy that violates

fundamental societal values. Regardless of such individual differences, however, the basic structure of a situation of legitimate authority requires subordinates to respond in terms of their role obligations rather than their personal preferences; they can openly disobey only by challenging the legitimacy of the authority. Often people obey without question even though the behavior they engage in may entail great personal sacrifice or great harm to others.

32   An important corollary of the basic structure of the authority situation is that actors often do not see themselves as personally responsible for the consequences of their actions. Again, there are individual differences, depending on actors' capacity and readiness to evaluate the legitimacy of orders received. Insofar as they see themselves as having had no choice in their actions, however, they do not feel personally responsible for them. They were not personal agents, but merely extensions of the authority. Thus, when their actions cause harm to others, they can feel relatively free of guilt. A similar mechanism operates when a person engages in antisocial behavior that was not ordered by the authorities but was tacitly encouraged and approved by them—even if only by making it clear that such behavior will not be punished. In this situation, behavior that was formerly illegitimate is legitimized by the authorities' acquiescence.

33   In the My Lai massacre, it is likely that the structure of the authority situation contributed to the massive violence in both ways—that is, by conveying the message that acts of violence against Vietnamese villagers were *required,* as well as the message that such acts, even if not ordered, were *permitted* by the authorities in charge. The actions at My Lai represented, at least in some respects, responses to explicit or implicit orders. . . .

. . .

Routinization

34 Authorization processes create a situation in which people become involved in an action without considering its implications and without really making a decision. Once they have taken the initial step, they are in a new psychological and social situation in which the pressures to continue are powerful. As Lewin (1947) has pointed out, many forces that might originally have kept people out of a situation reverse direction once they have made a commitment (once they have gone through the "gate region") and now serve to keep them in the situation. For example, concern about the criminal nature of an action, which might originally have inhibited a person from becoming involved, may now lead to deeper involvement in efforts to justify the action and to avoid negative consequences.

35   Despite these forces, however, given the nature of the actions involved in sanctioned massacres, one might still expect moral scruples to intervene; but the likelihood of moral resistance is greatly reduced by transforming

the action into routine, mechanical, highly programmed operations. Routinization fulfills two functions. First, it reduces the necessity of making decisions, thus minimizing the occasions in which moral questions may arise. Second, it makes it easier to avoid the implications of the action, since the actor focuses on the details of the job rather than on its meaning. The latter effect is more readily achieved among those who participate in sanctioned massacres from a distance—from their desks or even from the cockpits of their bombers.

. . .

Dehumanization

36 Authorization processes override standard moral considerations; routinization processes reduce the likelihood that such considerations will arise. Still, the inhibitions against murdering one's fellow human beings are generally so strong that the victims must also be stripped of their human status if they are to be subjected to systematic killing. Insofar as they are dehumanized, the usual principles of morality no longer apply to them.

37   Sanctioned massacres become possible to the extent that the victims are deprived in the perpetrators' eyes of the two qualities essential to being perceived as fully human and included in the moral compact that governs human relationships: *identity*—standing as independent, distinctive individuals, capable of making choices and entitled to live their own lives— and *community*—fellow membership in an interconnected network of individuals who care for each other and respect each other's individuality and rights (Kelman, 1973; see also Bakan, 1966, for a related distinction between "agency" and "communion"). Thus, when a group of people is defined entirely in terms of a category to which they belong, and when this category is excluded from the human family, moral restraints against killing them are more readily overcome.

38   Dehumanization of the enemy is a common phenomenon in any war situation. Sanctioned massacres, however, presuppose a more extreme degree of dehumanization, insofar as the killing is not in direct response to the target's threats or provocations. It is not what they have done that marks such victims for death but who they are—the category to which they happen to belong. They are the victims of policies that regard their systematic destruction as a desirable end or an acceptable means. Such extreme dehumanization becomes possible when the target group can readily be identified as a separate category of people who have historically been stigmatized and excluded by the victimizers; often the victims belong to a distinct racial, religious, ethnic, or political group regarded as inferior or sinister. The traditions, the habits, the images, and the vocabularies for dehumanizing such groups are already well established and can be drawn upon when the groups are selected for massacre. Labels help deprive the victims of identity and community, as in the epithet "gooks" that was commonly used to refer to Vietnamese and other Indochinese peoples.

39   The dynamics of the massacre process itself further increase the participants' tendency to dehumanize their victims. Those who participate as part of the bureaucratic apparatus increasingly come to see their victims as bodies to be counted and entered into their reports, as faceless figures that will determine their productivity rates and promotions. Those who participate in the massacre directly—in the field, as it were—are reinforced in their perception of the victims as less than human by observing their very victimization. The only way they can justify what is being done to these people—both by others and by themselves—and the only way they can extract some degree of meaning out of the absurd events in which they find themselves participating (see Lifton, 1971, 1973) is by coming to believe that the victims are subhuman and deserve to be rooted out. And thus the process of dehumanization feeds on itself.

Endnotes

1. In reconstructing the events of that day, we consulted Hammer (1970), in addition to the sources cited in the text. Schell (1968) provided information on the region around My Lai. Concerning Vietnam and peasant rebellions, we consulted FitzGerald (1972), Paige (1975), Popkin (1979), and Wolf (1969).

2. The involvement of President Nixon in the case may have had something to do with these steadily lower sentences. Immediately after the Calley conviction, Nixon issued two presidential edicts. The president first announced that Calley was to stay under house arrest until appeals were settled, rather than in the stockade. The subsequent announcement was that President Nixon would personally review the case. These edicts received wide popular support. The latter announcement in particular brought sharp criticism from Prosecutor Daniel and others, on grounds that Nixon was interfering inappropriately with the process of justice in the case. Nevertheless, the president's interest and intention to review the case could have colored the subsequent appeals process or the actions of the Secretary of Defense. By the time of Secretary Callaway's action, of course, the President was himself fighting to avoid impeachment.

Opinions and Social Pressure
Solomon E. Asch

In the early 1950s, Solomon Asch (1907–1996), a social psychologist at Rutgers University, conducted a series of simple but ingenious experiments on the influence of group pressure upon the individual. Essentially, he discovered, individuals can be influenced by groups to deny the evidence of their own senses. Together with the Milgram experiments of the next decade (see the selections that follow here), these studies provide powerful evidence of the degree to which individuals can surrender their own judgment to others, even when those others are clearly in the wrong. The results of these experiments have implications far beyond the laboratory: They can explain a good deal of the normal human behavior we see every day—at school, at work, at home.

1 In what follows I shall describe some experiments in an investigation of the effects of group pressure which was carried out recently with the help of a number of my associates. The tests not only demonstrate the operations of group pressure upon individuals but also illustrate a new kind of attack on the problem and some of the more subtle questions that it raises.

2 A group of seven to nine young men, all college students, are assembled in a classroom for a "psychological experiment" in visual judgment. The experimenter informs them that they will be comparing the lengths of lines. He shows two large white cards [see Figure 1]. On one is a single vertical black line—the standard whose length is to be matched. On the other card are three vertical lines of various lengths. The subjects are to choose the one that is of the same length as the line on the other card. One of the three actually is of the same length; the other two are substantially different, the difference ranging from three quarters of an inch to an inch and three quarters.

3 The experiment opens uneventfully. The subjects announce their answers in the order in which they have been seated in the room, and on the first round every person chooses the same matching line. Then a second set of cards is exposed; again the group is unanimous. The members appear ready to endure politely another boring experiment. On the third trial there is an unexpected disturbance. One person near the end of the group disagrees with all the others in his selection of the matching line. He looks surprised, indeed incredulous, about the disagreement. On the following trial he disagrees again, while the others remain unanimous in their choice. The dissenter becomes more and more worried and hesitant as the disagreement continues in succeeding trials; he may pause before announcing his answer and speak in a low voice, or he may smile in an embarrassed way.

4 What the dissenter does not know is that all the other members of the group were instructed by the experimenter beforehand to give incorrect answers in unanimity at certain points. The single individual who is not a party to this prearrangement is the focal subject of our experiment. He is placed in a position in which, while he is actually giving the correct

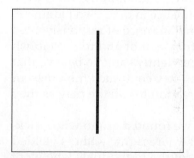 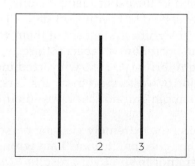

FIGURE 1 Subjects were shown two cards. One bore a standard line. The other bore three lines, one of which was the same length as the standard. The subjects were asked to choose this line.

answers, he finds himself unexpectedly in a minority of one, opposed by a unanimous and arbitrary majority with respect to a clear and simple fact. Upon him we have brought to bear two opposed forces: the evidence of his senses and the unanimous opinion of a group of his peers. Also, he must declare his judgments in public, before a majority which has also stated its position publicly.

5   The instructed majority occasionally reports correctly in order to reduce the possibility that the naive subject will suspect collusion against him. (In only a few cases did the subject actually show suspicion; when this happened, the experiment was stopped and the results were not counted.) There are 18 trials in each series, and on 12 of these the majority responds erroneously.

6   How do people respond to group pressure in this situation? I shall report first the statistical results of a series in which a total of 123 subjects from three institutions of higher learning (not including my own Swarthmore College) were placed in the minority situation described above.

7   Two alternatives were open to the subject: he could act independently, repudiating the majority, or he could go along with the majority, repudiating the evidence of his senses. Of the 123 put to the test, a considerable percentage yielded to the majority. Whereas in ordinary circumstances individuals matching the lines will make mistakes less than 1 per cent of the time, under group pressure the minority subjects swung to acceptance of the misleading majority's wrong judgments in 36.8 per cent of the selections.

8   Of course individuals differed in response. At one extreme, about one quarter of the subjects were completely independent and never agreed with the erroneous judgments of the majority. At the other extreme, some individuals went with the majority nearly all the time. The performances of individuals in this experiment tend to be highly consistent. Those who strike out on the path of independence do not, as a rule, succumb to the majority even over an extended series of trials, while those who choose the path of compliance are unable to free themselves as the ordeal is prolonged.

9   The reasons for the startling individual differences have not yet been investigated in detail. At this point we can only report some tentative generalizations from talks with the subjects, each of whom was interviewed at the end of the experiment. Among the independent individuals were many who held fast because of staunch confidence in their own judgment. The most significant fact about them was not absence of responsiveness to the majority but a capacity to recover from doubt and to reestablish their equilibrium. Others who acted independently came to believe that the majority was correct in its answers, but they continued their dissent on the simple ground that it was their obligation to call the play as they saw it.

10   Among the extremely yielding persons we found a group who quickly reached the conclusion: "I am wrong, they are right." Others yielded in order "not to spoil your results." Many of the individuals who went along suspected that the majority were "sheep" following the first responder, or that the majority were victims of an optical illusion; never-

theless, these suspicions failed to free them at the moment of decision. More disquieting were the reactions of subjects who construed their difference from the majority as a sign of some general deficiency in themselves, which at all costs they must hide. On this basis they desperately tried to merge with the majority, not realizing the longer-range consequences to themselves. All the yielding subjects underestimated the frequency with which they conformed.

11 Which aspect of the influence of a majority is more important—the size of the majority or its unanimity? The experiment was modified to examine this question. In one series the size of the opposition was varied from one to 15 persons. The results showed a clear trend. When a subject was confronted with only a single individual who contradicted his answers, he was swayed little: he continued to answer independently and correctly in nearly all trials. When the opposition was increased to two, the pressure became substantial: minority subjects now accepted the wrong answer 13.6 per cent of the time. Under the pressure of a majority of three, the subjects' errors jumped to 31.8 per cent. But further increases in the size of the majority apparently did not increase the weight of the pressure substantially. Clearly the size of the opposition is important only up to a point.

12 Disturbance of the majority's unanimity had a striking effect. In this experiment the subject was given the support of a truthful partner—either another individual who did not know of the prearranged agreement among the rest of the group, or a person who was instructed to give correct answers throughout.

13 The presence of a supporting partner depleted the majority of much of its power. Its pressure on the dissenting individual was reduced to one fourth: that is, subjects answered incorrectly only one fourth as often as under the pressure of a unanimous majority. The weakest persons did not yield as readily. Most interesting were the reactions to the partner. Generally the feeling toward him was one of warmth and closeness; he was credited with inspiring confidence. However, the subjects repudiated the suggestion that the partner decided them to be independent.

14 Was the partner's effect a consequence of his dissent, or was it related to his accuracy? We now introduced into the experimental group a person who was instructed to dissent from the majority but also to disagree with the subject. In some experiments the majority was always to choose the worst of the comparison lines and the instructed dissenter to pick the line that was closer to the length of the standard one; in others the majority was consistently intermediate and the dissenter most in error. In this manner we were able to study the relative influence of "compromising" and "extremist" dissenters.

15 Again the results are clear. When a moderate dissenter is present the effect of the majority on the subject decreases by approximately one third, and extremes of yielding disappear. Moreover, most of the errors the subjects do make are moderate, rather than flagrant. In short, the dissenter largely controls the choice of errors. To this extent the subjects broke away from the majority even while bending to it.

16   On the other hand, when the dissenter always chose the line that was more flagrantly different from the standard, the results were of quite a different kind. The extremist dissenter produced a remarkable freeing of the subjects; their errors dropped to only 9 percent. Furthermore, all the errors were of the moderate variety. We were able to conclude that dissents *per se* increased independence and moderated the errors that occurred, and that the direction of dissent exerted consistent effects.

17   In all the foregoing experiments each subject was observed only in a single setting. We now turned to studying the effects upon a given individual of a change in the situation to which he was exposed. The first experiment examined the consequences of losing or gaining a partner. The instructed partner began by answering correctly on the first six trials. With his support the subject usually resisted pressure from the majority: 18 of 27 subjects were completely independent. But after six trials the partner joined the majority. As soon as he did so, there was an abrupt rise in the subjects' errors. Their submission to the majority was just about as frequent as when the minority subject was opposed by a unanimous majority throughout.

18   It was surprising to find that the experience of having had a partner and of having braved the majority opposition with him had failed to strengthen the individuals' independence. Questioning at the conclusion of the experiment suggested that we had overlooked an important circumstance; namely, the strong specific effect of "desertion" by the partner to the other side. We therefore changed the conditions so that the partner would simply leave the group at the proper point. (To allay suspicion it was announced in advance that he had an appointment with the dean.) In this form of the experiment, the partner's effect outlasted his presence. The errors increased after his departure, but less markedly than after a partner switched to the majority.

19   In a variant of this procedure the trials began with the majority unanimously giving correct answers. Then they gradually broke away until on the sixth trial the naive subject was alone and the group unanimously against him. As long as the subject had anyone on his side, he was almost invariably independent, but as soon as he found himself alone, the tendency to conform to the majority rose abruptly.

20   As might be expected, an individual's resistance to group pressure in these experiments depends to a considerable degree on how wrong the majority was. We varied the discrepancy between the standard line and the other lines systematically, with the hope of reaching a point where the error of the majority would be so glaring that every subject would repudiate it and choose independently. In this we regretfully did not succeed. Even when the difference between the lines was seven inches, there were still some who yielded to the error of the majority.

21   The study provides clear answers to a few relatively simple questions, and it raises many others that await investigation. We would like to know the degree of consistency of persons in situations which differ in content

and structure. If consistency of independence or conformity in behavior is shown to be a fact, how is it functionally related to qualities of character and personality? In what ways is independence related to sociological or cultural conditions? Are leaders more independent than other people, or are they adept at following their followers? These and many other questions may perhaps be answerable by investigations of the type described here.

22   Life in society requires consensus as an indispensable condition. But consensus, to be productive, requires that each individual contribute independently out of his experience and insight. When consensus comes under the dominance of conformity, the social process is polluted and the individual at the same time surrenders the powers on which his functioning as a feeling and thinking being depends. That we have found the tendency to conformity in our society so strong that reasonably intelligent and well-meaning young people are willing to call white black is a matter of concern. It raises questions about our ways of education and about the values that guide our conduct.

23   Yet anyone inclined to draw too pessimistic conclusions from this report would do well to remind himself that the capacities for independence are not to be underestimated. He may also draw some consolation from a further observation: those who participated in this challenging experiment agreed nearly without exception that independence was preferable to conformity.

The Power of Situations
Lee Ross and Richard E. Nisbett

Erich Fromm conceives of obedience and disobedience as products of one's character or of one's moral choices. In the selection that follows, Lee Ross and Richard E. Nisbett present findings from experiments in social psychology that suggest that situations, rather than some essential personal quality or the dictates of one's conscience, tend to determine behavior. From this vantage point, a "helpful" person may not be consistently helpful nor a "kind" person consistently kind. In each new situation, subtle and profound social cues influence our ultimate behavior—which is why, as we all know, people behave inconsistently. According to philosopher Gilbert Harman, "It seems that ordinary attributions of character traits to people are often deeply misguided, and it may even be the case that there is no such thing as character, no ordinary character traits of the sort people think there are, none of the usual moral virtues and vices." Harmon reached this radical notion after reading accounts of the same experiments in social psychology that you are about to read in this chapter. You may not draw the same conclusions, but Ross and Nisbett, Milgram, Asch, Lessing, and the account of the mock-prison experiment will almost certainly convince you that the situation in which we act can powerfully influence our behavior—including our choice to obey or disobey a questionable order.

Lee Ross is a professor of psychology at Stanford University. Richard E. Nisbett is professor of psychology at the University of Michigan. This selection is excerpted from their text The Person and the Situation: Perspectives of Social Psychology *(1991).*

1   Undergraduates taking their first course in social psychology generally are in search of an interesting and enjoyable experience, and they rarely are disappointed. They find out many fascinating things about human behavior, some of which validate common sense and some of which contradict it. The inherent interest value of the material, amounting to high-level gossip about people and social situations, usually ensures that the students are satisfied consumers.

2   The experience of serious graduate students, who, over the course of four or five years, are immersed in the problems and the orientation of the field, is rather different. For them, the experience is an intellectually wrenching one. Their most basic assumptions about the nature and the causes of human behavior, and about the very predictability of the social world, are challenged. At the end of the process, their views of human behavior and society will differ profoundly from the views held by most other people in their culture. Some of their new insights and beliefs will be held rather tentatively and applied inconsistently to the social events that unfold around them. Others will be held with great conviction, and will be applied confidently. But ironically, even the new insights that they are most confident about will tend to have the effect of making them less certain than their peers about predicting social behavior and making inferences about particular individuals or groups. Social psychology rivals philosophy in its ability to teach people that they do not truly understand the nature of the world. This book is about that hard-won ignorance and what it tells us about the human condition.

. . .

3   Consider the following scenario: While walking briskly to a meeting some distance across a college campus, John comes across a man slumped in a doorway, asking him for help. Will John offer it, or will he continue on his way? Before answering such a question, most people would want to know more about John. Is he someone known to be callous and unfeeling, or is he renowned for his kindness and concern? Is he a stalwart member of the Campus Outreach Organization, or a mainstay of the Conservative Coalition Against Welfare Abuse? In short, what kind of person is John and how has he behaved when his altruism has been tested in the past? Only with such information in hand, most people would agree, could one make a sensible and confident prediction.

4   In fact, however, nothing one is likely to know or learn about John would be of much use in helping predict John's behavior in the situation we've described. In particular, the type of information about personality that most laypeople would want to have before making a prediction would prove to be of relatively little value. A half century of research has taught

us that in this situation, and in most other novel situations, one cannot predict with any accuracy how particular people will respond. At least one cannot do so using information about an individual's personal dispositions or even about that individual's past behavior.

. . .

5   While knowledge about John is of surprisingly little value in predicting whether he will help the person slumped in the doorway, details concerning the specifics of the situation would be invaluable. For example, what was the appearance of the person in the doorway? Was he clearly ill, or might he have been a drunk or, even worse, a nodding dope addict? Did his clothing make him look respectably middle class or decently working class, or did he look like a homeless derelict?

6   Such considerations are fairly obvious once they are mentioned, and the layperson, upon reflection, will generally concede their importance. But few laypeople would concede, much less anticipate, the relevance of some other, subtler, contextual details that empirical research has shown to be important factors influencing bystander intervention. Darley and Batson (1973) actually confronted people with a version of the situation we've described and found what some of these factors are. Their subjects were students in a religious seminary who were on their way to deliver a practice sermon. If the subjects were in a hurry (because they thought they were late to give a practice sermon), only about 10 percent helped. By contrast, if they were not in a hurry (because they had plenty of time before giving their sermon), about 63 percent of them helped.

7   Social psychology has by now amassed a vast store of such empirical parables. The tradition here is simple. Pick a generic situation; then identify and manipulate a situational or contextual variable that intuition or past research leads you to believe will make a difference (ideally, a variable whose impact you think most laypeople, or even most of your peers, somehow fail to appreciate), and see what happens. Sometimes, of course, you will be wrong and your manipulation won't "work." But often the situational variable makes quite a bit of difference. Occasionally, in fact, it makes nearly all the difference, and information about traits and individual differences that other people thought all-important proves all but trivial. If so, you have contributed a situationist classic destined to become part of our field's intellectual legacy. Such empirical parables are important because they illustrate the degree to which ordinary men and women are apt to be mistaken about the power of the situation—the power of particular situational features, and the power of situations in general.

8   People's inflated belief in the importance of personality traits and dispositions, together with their failure to recognize the importance of situational factors in affecting behavior, has been termed the "fundamental attribution error" (Ross, 1977; Nisbett & Ross, 1980; see also Jones, 1979; Gilbert & Jones, 1986). Together with many other social psychologists, we have directed our attention to documenting this . . . error and attempting to track down its origins.

References

Darley, J. M., & Batson, C. D. (1973). From Jerusalem to Jericho: A study of situational and dispositional variables in helping behavior. *Journal of Personality and Social Psychology, 27,* 100–119.

Gilbert, D. T., & Jones, E. E. (1986). Perceiver-induced constraints: Interpretation of self-generated reality. *Journal of Personality and Social Psychology, 50,* 269–280.

Jones, E. E. (1979). The rocky road from acts to dispositions. *American Psychologist, 34,* 107–117.

Nisbett, R. E., & Ross, L. (1980). *Human inference: Strategies and shortcomings of social judgment.* Englewood Cliffs, NJ: Prentice-Hall.

Ross, L. (1977). The intuitive psychologist and his shortcomings. In L. Berkowitz (Ed.), *Advances in experimental social psychology* (Vol. 10). New York: Academic.

Weight Debate

3

**Prevalence of Obesity Among U.S. Adults,
by Characteristics and by State**
Centers for Disease Control and Prevention

The Centers for Disease Control and Prevention (CDC) published a report entitled "U.S. Obesity Trends in Adults from 1991–2001," from which a broad conclusion emerged: "The prevalence of obesity among U.S. adults increased to 20.9 percent in 2001, a 5.6 percent increase in 1 year and a 74 percent increase since 1991." On its Web site, the CDC describes itself as "the lead federal agency for protecting the health and safety of people—at home and abroad, providing credible information to enhance health decisions, and promoting health through strong partnerships." As such, the CDC is charged with devising and implementing strategies for preventing disease. The first stage in developing a strategy, of course, is to understand the extent of a problem, which the CDC attempted to do with its study. Note that Dr. Jeffrey Koplan, lead author of the JAMA editorial immediately preceding these tables, was a former director of the CDC. The two tables below are from the 2002 study. To see complete data, go to the CDC Web site at <http://www.cdc.gov/nccdphp/dnpa/obesity/>.

Prevalence of Obesity Among U.S. Adults, by Characteristics

1   In 2000, the prevalence of obesity among U.S. adults was 19.8 percent, which reflects a 61 percent increase since 1991.

2   In 2000, 38.8 million American adults met the classification of obesity, defined as having a body mass index, BMI score of 30 or more.

3   Between 2000 and 2001 obesity prevalence climbed from 19.8 percent of American adults to 20.9 percent of American adults.

4   Currently, more than 44 million Americans are considered obese by BMI index; that is, have a Body Mass Index (Kg/m^2) greater than or equal to 30. This reflects an increase of 74 percent since 1991.

5   This table reflects the percentages of individuals who are obese within specific categories such as, gender, age, race, education, and smoking status.

Prevalence of Obesity Among U.S. Adults, by State

6   [There is an] obesity epidemic within the U.S. . . . [In] 1991, only 4 of 45 participating states had obesity prevalence rates of 15 to 19 percent and none had prevalence greater than 20 percent.

7   By the year 2000, all of the 50 states except Colorado had prevalences of 15 percent or greater, with 22 of the 50 states having obesity prevalence as high as 20 percent or greater.

TABLE 1   1991–2001 Prevalence of Obesity Among U.S. Adults, by Characteristics

Characteristics	Percent Obese BRFSS Data by Year:[*]					
	1991	1995	1998	1999	2000	2001
Total	12.0	15.3	17.9	18.9	19.8	20.9
Gender						
Men	11.7	15.6	17.7	19.1	20.2	21.0
Women	12.2	15.0	18.1	18.6	19.4	20.8
Age groups						
18–29	7.1	10.1	12.1	12.1	13.5	14.0
30–39	11.3	14.4	16.9	18.6	20.2	20.5
40–49	15.8	17.9	21.2	22.4	22.9	24.7
50–59	16.1	21.6	23.8	24.2	25.6	26.1
60–69	14.7	19.4	21.3	22.3	22.9	25.3
<70	11.4	12.1	14.6	16.1	15.5	17.1
Race, ethnicity						
White, non Hispanic	11.3	14.5	16.6	17.7	18.5	19.6
Black, non Hispanic	19.3	22.6	26.9	27.3	29.3	31.1
Hispanic	11.6	16.8	20.8	21.5	23.4	23.7
Other	7.3	9.6	11.9	12.4	12.0	15.7
Educational Level						
Less than High School	16.5	20.1	24.1	25.3	26.1	27.4
High school degree	13.3	16.7	19.4	20.6	21.7	23.2
Some college	10.7	15.1	17.8	18.1	19.5	21.0
College or above	8.0	11.0	13.1	14.3	15.2	15.7
Smoking status						
Never smoked	12.0	15.2	17.9	19.0	19.9	20.9
Ex-smoker	14.0	17.9	20.9	21.5	22.7	23.9
Current smoker	9.9	12.3	14.8	15.7	16.3	17.8

[*] Behavioral Risk Factor Surveillance System.

8   In 2001, 20 states had obesity prevalence of 15–19 percent; 29 states had prevalences of 20–24 percent; and one state reported a prevalence more than 25 percent. The prevalence of obesity among U.S. adults increased to 20.9 percent in 2001, a 5.6 percent increase in 1 year and a 74 percent increase since 1991.

References

Mokdad AH, Serdula M, Dietz W, et al. The spread of the obesity epidemic in the United States, 1991–1998. *JAMA* 1999;282:1519–1522.

Mokdad AH, Serdula M, Dietz W, et al. The continuing obesity epidemic in the United States. *JAMA* 2000;284:1650–1651.

Mokdad AH, Bowman BA, Ford ES, et al. The continuing epidemics of obesity and diabetes in the United States. *JAMA* 2001;286(10):1195–1200.

Mokdad AH, Bowman BA, Ford ES, et al. Prevalence of obesity, diabetes, and obesity related health risk factors, 2001. *JAMA* 2003:289;76–79.

TABLE 2 Obesity Prevalence Among U.S. Adults by State. BRFSS Data by Year[*]

State Obesity	1991	1995	1998	1999	2000	2001
Alabama	13.2	18.3	20.7	21.8	23.5	23.4
Alaska	13.1	19.2	20.7	19.2	20.5	21.0
Arizona	11.0	12.8	12.7	11.6	18.8	17.9
Arkansas	12.7	17.3	19.2	21.9	22.6	21.7
California	10.0	14.4	16.8	19.6	19.2	20.9
Colorado	8.4	10.00	14.0	14.3	13.8	14.4
Connecticut	10.9	11.9	14.7	14.5	16.9	17.3
Delaware	14.9	16.2	16.6	17.1	16.2	20.0
District of Columbia	15.2	n/a	19.9	17.9	21.2	19.9
Florida	10.1	16.5	17.4	17.9	18.1	18.4
Georgia	9.2	12.6	18.7	20.7	20.9	22.1
Hawaii	10.4	10.4	15.3	15.3	15.1	17.6
Idaho	11.7	13.8	16.0	19.5	18.4	20.0
Illinois	12.7	16.4	17.9	20.2	20.9	20.5
Indiana	14.8	19.6	19.5	19.4	21.3	24.0
Iowa	14.4	17.2	19.3	20.9	20.8	21.8
Kansas	n/a	15.8	17.3	18.5	20.1	21.0
Kentucky	12.7	16.6	19.9	21.1	22.3	24.2
Louisiana	15.7	17.4	21.3	21.5	22.8	23.3
Maine	12.1	13.7	17.0	18.9	19.7	19.0
Maryland	11.2	15.8	19.8	17.6	19.5	19.8
Massachusetts	8.8	11.1	13.8	14.3	16.4	16.1
Michigan	15.2	17.7	20.7	22.1	21.8	24.4
Minnesota	10.6	15.0	15.7	15.0	16.8	19.2
Mississippi	15.7	18.6	22.0	22.8	24.3	25.9
Missouri	12.0	18.0	19.8	20.8	21.6	22.5
Montana	9.5	12.6	1.7	14.7	15.2	18.2
Nebraska	12.5	15.7	17.5	20.2	20.6	20.1
Nevada	n/a	13.3	13.4	15.3	17.2	19.1
New Hampshire	10.4	14.7	14.7	13.8	17.1	19.0
New Jersey	9.7	14.2	15.2	16.8	17.6	19.0
New Mexico	7.8	12.7	14.7	17.3	17.8	18.8
New York	12.8	13.3	15.9	16.9	17.2	19.7
North Carolina	13.0	16.5	19.0	21.0	21.3	22.4
North Dakota	12.9	15.6	18.7	21.2	19.8	19.9
Ohio	14.9	17.2	19.5	19.8	21.0	21.8
Oklahoma	11.9	13.0	18.7	20.2	19.0	22.1
Oregon	11.2	14.7	17.8	19.6	21.0	20.7
Pennsylvania	14.4	16.1	19.0	19.0	20.7	21.4
Rhode Island	9.1	12.9	16.2	16.01	16.8	17.3
South Carolina	13.8	16.1	20.2	20.2	21.5	21.7
South Dakota	12.8	13.6	15.4	19.0	19.2	20.6
Tennessee	12.1	18.0	18.5	20.1	22.7	22.6
Texas	12.7	15.0	19.9	21.1	22.7	23.8
Utah	9.7	12.6	15.3	16.3	18.5	18.4
Vermont	10.0	14.2	14.4	17.2	17.7	17.1
Virginia	10.1	15.2	18.2	18.6	17.5	20.0
Washington	9.9	13.5	17.6	17.7	18.5	18.9
West Virginia	15.2	17.8	22.9	23.9	22.8	24.6
Wisconsin	12.7	15.3	17.9	19.3	19.4	21.9
Wyoming	n/a	13.9	14.5	16.4	17.6	19.2

[*]Behavioral Risk Factor Surveillance System.

Rethinking Weight
Amanda Spake

*One sure sign that the obesity epidemic has caught the nation's attention is the increased
number of articles devoted to the subject in the popular press. The following selection
appeared as a cover story in the 9 February 2004 edition of* U.S. News and World Report.
*Amanda Spake is a senior writer for the magazine and has served both as a contributor
to* Salon.com *and as an editor to the* Washington Post *magazine and* Mother Jones. *In this
piece, Spake directs our attention to a central debate among obesity researchers: whether
or not to classify obesity as a disease (just as alcoholism is classified as a disease). The
ultimate positions of the government and insurance companies in this debate will determine for tens of millions the levels of support they will receive in fighting to achieve a
healthy weight.*

1   Maria Pfisterer has never in her life been skinny. The Arlington, Texas,
mother of three was at her slimmest at age 18, when she married Fred, an
Air Force sergeant. But she was plump, not seriously fat. She first became
seriously overweight at age 21, when she gained about 70 pounds during
her first pregnancy. By the time she delivered her daughter Jordan, now 14,
she was carrying over 200 pounds on her 5-foot, 2-inch frame.

2   Over the past 14 years, Pfisterer has tried every weight-loss strategy
imaginable: She has taken the (now banned) appetite-suppressing drug
combo fen-phen (she lost 60 pounds only to regain it during her second
pregnancy). She went on a doctor-prescribed and -supervised low-calorie
diet (she lost 10 pounds but regained it). She has been enrolled in Jenny
Craig, Weight Watchers, Curves, and a variety of quick-weight-loss fads. All
resulted in a little lost and more regained. She has taken antidepressants,
reputed to have weight loss as a side effect. They didn't for her. She would
love to get into one of those intensive medical weight-loss programs, but
she can't afford the $4,000-plus price tag. So she does what she can. "If I lose
weight, it seems like I always go back up to that same 197 to 202 range," she
says. "I just don't know how to keep it off."

3   Pfisterer isn't alone. A majority of Americans—now 64 percent—are
overweight or obese and struggling to conquer their expanding waistlines
before their fat overtakes their health and makes them sick or kills them.
At the heart of this obesity epidemic is a debate over whether obesity is a
biological "disease" and should be treated like any other life-threatening
illness—cancer, heart disease—or whether it is simply a risk factor for
those killers. The stakes are high because the answer may determine who
gets treated for obesity, what treatments are available, who pays for treatment, and, ultimately, who stays healthy.

4   New understandings of the biology of obesity are driving the debate. "I
think there's enough data now relating to mechanisms of food intake regulation that suggest obesity is a biologically determined process," says Xavier
Pi-Sunyer, director of the Obesity Research Center at St. Luke's-Roosevelt
Hospital in New York City. And many national and international health

organizations—from the National Institutes of Health (NIH) to the World Health Organization—agree. The WHO has listed obesity as a disease in its International Classification of Diseases since 1979. In fact, the organization recently called on member states to adopt programs to encourage a reduction of fat and sugar in the global diet. The recommendation did not sit well with the U.S. food industry or with some within the Bush administration, who still maintain the obesity epidemic can be reversed by individuals taking more personal responsibility and making better lifestyle choices. Many health insurers agree. "For a wide number of people in this country the question is: How do you motivate people to make changes in diet and increase physical activity?" says Susan Pisano of the Health Insurance Association of America.

5   The reason governments, insurance companies, and others still take such positions, says Pi-Sunyer, is that "they are worried they will have to reimburse doctors and patients for treatment. And now, you have such a huge number of people needing treatment." On any given day, about 29 percent of men and 44 percent of women are trying to lose weight, and presumably a large percentage of those would love to be offered medically supervised treatment if it were covered in their health insurance plan.

6   Instead, they pay out of pocket for a $33 billion commercial diet industry—and keep getting fatter. The number of people who are severely obese—that is, those with a body mass index of 40 or above or who are more than 100 pounds overweight—is growing two times as fast as is obesity generally. From 1986 to 2000, the prevalence of Americans reporting a BMI of 40 or above quadrupled, from about 1 in 200 adults to 1 in 50. People who are severely obese generally have more weight-related illnesses and require more expensive treatments than do those who are merely "too fat."

7   **Fat's High Price** A new study by RTI International and the Centers for Disease Control and Prevention, published this month in the journal *Obesity Research,* shows that the nation is spending about $75 billion a year on weight-related disease. Type II diabetes, heart disease, hypertension, high cholesterol, gallbladder disease, osteoarthritis merely top the list. Almost 80 percent of obese adults have one of these conditions, and nearly 40 percent have two or more.

8   Healthcare costs for illnesses resulting from obesity now exceed those related to both smoking and problem drinking. About 325,000 deaths a year are attributed to obesity. The trend lines are only expected to get worse, since childhood obesity is also increasing rapidly.

9   Researchers are encouraged by the stance taken by the WHO and NIH, as well as the American Medical Association, the National Academy of Sciences, and the CDC. Says Yale psychologist Kelly Brownell: "The ramifications could be enormous—for opening up better treatments, and to some extent for social attitudes toward people with this problem. When alcoholism was declared a disease, it changed attitudes and reduced the stigma of blame."

10   And to be sure, there is no shortage of stigma and blame when it comes to obesity. Weight discrimination dates back to the early Christian church, which included "gluttony" as one of the seven deadly sins. Obesity was viewed as the outward manifestation of the "sin" of overindulgence. Most overweight adults have suffered ridicule, self-consciousness, or depression, particularly if they were obese as children or adolescents. Severely obese patients frequently report workplace discrimination. One woman told researchers: "They put my desk in the back office where no one could see me."

11   Prejudice against the obese stems from the widely held belief that getting fat—and certainly staying fat—results from a failure of willpower, a condition that could be remedied if obese people simply made a personal choice to eat less. But to most obesity experts this notion of personal choice is downright nutty. "Who would choose to be obese?" asks Rudolph Leibel, a Columbia University geneticist and a noted obesity researcher. "Telling someone they've decided to become obese is like saying, 'You've decided to give yourself a brain tumor.'"

12   Increasingly, researchers are demonstrating that obesity is controlled by a powerful biological system of hormones, proteins, neurotransmitters, and genes that regulate fat storage and body weight and tell the brain when, what, and how much to eat. "This is not debatable," says Louis Aronne, director of the Comprehensive Weight Control Program at New York-Presbyterian Hospital and president-elect of the North American Association for the Study of Obesity.* "Once people gain weight, then these biological mechanisms, which we're beginning to understand, develop to prevent people from losing weight. It's not someone fighting 'willpower.' The body resists weight loss."

13   This wonder of natural chemical engineering evolved over centuries to protect humans against famine and assure reproduction of the species. "The idea that nature would leave this system to a matter of 'choice' is naive," says Arthur Frank, director of George Washington University's Weight Management Program. "Eating is largely driven by signals from fat tissue, from the gastrointestinal tract, the liver. All those organs are sending information to the brain to eat or not to eat. So, saying to an obese person who wants to lose weight, 'All you have to do is eat less,' is like saying to a person suffering from asthma, 'All you have to do is breathe better.' "

14   When Maria Pfisterer looks at her family, she sees her future—and it is frightening. Her father, a diabetic with congestive heart failure and hypertension, weighs nearly 400 pounds, and at age 60 he can scarcely move. Her older sister is also obese and suffers from hypertension. Both Maria and her sister worry they will eventually develop diabetes like their dad.

15   "My daughter Jordan is very heavy. She's struggling already with weight, and if she gets any more sedentary, I worry what will happen to her,"

---

* *The North American Association for the Study of Obesity* is later referred to by its acronym *NAASO*. See the organization's Web site at <http://www.naaso.org/>.

says Pfisterer. "I'm trying to teach her to eat better and keep active. She's into dance, but she'll say, 'I'm the fattest kid there.' It breaks my heart."

16   Pfisterer herself says she does not eat a lot and is always on the go. "I don't eat half gallons of ice cream or bags of chips. But if I lose a little, I regain. I think genetics have a lot to do with it."

17 **Studies of Twins** Leibel, director of the division of molecular genetics at Columbia University College of Physicians and Surgeons, has spent a career documenting what Pfisterer knows intuitively. He says, "I believe there are strong genetic factors that determine susceptibility to obesity." Obesity does not result from a single gene, he explains, but rather a variety of genes that interact with environmental influences to increase one's chance of becoming obese. In studies of adult twins, who share many or all of the same genes, BMI,* body composition, and other measures of fatness appear to be 20 to 70 percent inherited.

18   Still, biology is not destiny. Overweight results from one thing: eating more food than one burns in physical activity. Genes simply facilitate becoming fat. "I think the primary problem is on the food intake side," Leibel adds. "There are multiple genes involved in that intake process, and there is good reason to believe that nature and evolution have selected for ingestion of large amounts of food."

19   But even when limitless food is available, not everyone gets fat. In a series of studies of adult twins in Quebec who ate a high-calorie diet designed to produce weight gain, results between sets of twins were vastly different. Some twin pairs gained three times as much weight and fat as others. "We know there are genetic factors," says Jules Hirsch, professor emeritus at Rockefeller University, "but obesity may be a multistep process." Hirsch says an overabundance of fat cells leading to obesity may be the result of gene-environmental interactions that occur in infancy or in utero, leading to vastly different responses to food in adulthood. The story of the offspring of women who survived the Dutch winter famine of 1944–45 may be a case in point. Babies born to women who suffered severe undernutrition early in their pregnancies tended to have more fat and become obese more readily as adults. But the offspring of women who were undernourished late in pregnancy tended to be leaner and have less fat as adults. Clearly, says Hirsch, there is a great deal more to learn about how obesity develops.

20   Even scientists who basically accept that obesity is a sophisticated biological problem feel that treatment has to consider the powerful roles of social organization and psychology. Take the case of the bottomless soup bowls.

21   University of Illinois nutrition and marketing professor Brian Wansink sat student volunteers in front of bowls of tomato soup in his lab and told

---

BMI, or Body Mass Index, is a ratio of weight in relation to height and one measure of fatness.

them they were involved in a "taste test." Some of the students' bowls were normal. The others had bowls that automatically refilled from a hidden tube in the bottom. The students with the bottomless bowls ate an average of about 40 percent more soup before their brain told them they were full. "Biology has made us efficient at storing fat," says Wansink. "But obesity is not just biology; it's psychology. We're not good at tracking how much we eat. So we use cues—we eat until the plate is empty, or the soup is gone, or the TV show is over."

22   Indeed, research shows that people eat more in groups and with friends than they do when dining alone. Simply eating with one other person increases the average amount eaten at meals by 44 percent. Meals eaten with large groups of friends tend to be longer in duration and are as much as 75 percent bigger that those eaten alone. Eating with someone, suggests John DeCastro, the author of these studies, probably leads to relaxation and a "disinhibition of restraint."

23   Viewing obesity principally as a biological disease worries Wansink because he fears it will remove personal control and shift blame to someone else. But doctors who treat overweight patients say that thinking of obesity as a disease would simply make more treatment available. Most obesity programs rely on personal responsibility to put into action behavioral techniques designed to achieve greater control over biology. "Most of our treatment is still based on modifying choice," says GWU's Frank. "But underneath it all you've got to recognize why it is so difficult to eat less and lose weight. It doesn't make it easier, but it takes it out of the world of willful misconduct."

24 **Frauds** The biggest dilemma overweight people face is the world of largely mediocre, misleading, useless, or downright dangerous devices, diet programs, supplements, and drugs promoted to reduce fat. "The treatment of obesity is littered with a history of abuses," says NAASO's Aronne. "Every infomercial out there about weight is damaging people because it's giving them an unrealistic view of what can be done." Most university- and hospital-based weight-loss programs produce a 10 percent loss of body weight in six months. This is more than enough to reduce the incidence of Type II diabetes by 58 percent and lower blood pressure in borderline hypertensives. But it is not enough to make a fat person as thin as a Hollywood celebrity. Coverage of obesity by health insurers might bring science and sanity to the chaos of weight loss, where, as Aronne puts it, "ethical treatments are competing in an unethical marketplace."

25   But clinicians acknowledge that weight-loss successes are modest. "To be frank, a lot of the treatment has not been very effective," says Pi-Sunyer. He points out that there are currently two drugs approved for long-term treatment of obesity, sibutramine and orlistat. Their effect is modest, and their cost is high, about $100 a month. "So for people to pay that amount, they would like to see more impressive results." Two drugs approved for treating epilepsy, topiramate and zonisamide, are being tested to treat obesity,

but the jury is still out on them. "So that's an out for the insurers," says Pi-Sunyer. They can say, 'Unless you have a treatment that takes weight off and keeps it off, then why pay for it?' It would be a much stronger argument if we had a more proven treatment."

26   What's standing in the way? Basically funding for research. The American Obesity Association reports that NIH funding for research on obesity is less than one sixth that spent on AIDS. "Given the nature of the problem and the side effects," says Pi-Sunyer, "we're spending a pittance."

27   The health insurance industry argues that obesity treatments can't be covered because there is no evidence of effectiveness. Critics counter that the same argument could apply to a lot of complicated diseases. "We don't have a good way of treating Alzheimer's disease," says GWU's Frank, "and we don't have a particularly good way of treating AIDS either. We have a health insurance system based on illness, not treatment effectiveness. Why should obesity be the one disease that's subjected to this cost-effectiveness standard?"

28   About half of the $75 billion yearly price tag for obesity is covered by taxpayers in Medicare and Medicaid funds. These government health plans are debating right now whether the plans should cover obesity treatment. Currently, only in cases of severe obesity will government and some private insurers reimburse doctors for surgery to reduce girth.

29   But not always. Samantha Moore, a 26-year-old Maine woman who weighs nearly 400 pounds, was recently turned down a third time for gastric bypass surgery. Even though she has been dieting all her life, her insurer denied surgery because she has not made enough "medically supervised" attempts at weight loss. Does the insurer pay for medically supervised weight loss? "No," says Moore. "It's shocking to me that the insurance company keeps saying, essentially, 'You're not sick enough to get this surgery.' I think they're putting off a decision because if I wait much longer, I'll be too sick to get the surgery."

30 **Fat or Fit?** Not all scientists agree that labeling obesity "a disease" will improve the situation for people like Pfisterer or Moore. Stephen Ball, an exercise physiologist at the University of Missouri, says, "If we call obesity a disease, then anything that reduces one's fatness or lowers BMI would be a successful treatment, such as liposuction or a very low-calorie diet, where we know these are not healthy. By the same token, if you don't lose weight with an exercise program but your blood glucose becomes normal, cholesterol improves, then that could be considered a failure, because it didn't reduce weight. Fitness is a more important indicator of health outcomes than fatness."

31   Indeed, Steven Blair at the Cooper Institute in Dallas has shown that cardiovascular fitness as measured on a treadmill test is a better predictor of mortality and illness than BMI. "I'm convinced . . . that people who are active or fit but in a high BMI group have lower death rates from all causes—cancer, heart disease, diabetes—than the sedentary and unfit in the normal or lean BMI category. Even among women in our study with

BMIs of 37, 20 percent did well enough on the treadmill test to be considered fit. We're obsessed with weight, but where has that gotten us?"

32   Ultimately, if better and more accessible treatments are not offered to obese Americans, the cost not only of obesity but of treatment and health insurance will escalate. The number of people undergoing surgery doubled from 2001 to 2003, in part because people are becoming more obese but also because many want medical help with weight loss and can't find any other treatment health insurers will cover.

33   Frustrated with her options and limited ability to pay for treatment, about six months ago Maria Pfisterer began to explore the possibility of gastric bypass surgery. She is not 100 pounds overweight, and her BMI is not over 40—generally the criteria physicians use for evaluating candidates who would benefit from surgery. Gastric bypass surgery is an irreversible procedure in which the size of the stomach is reduced and the small intestine is bypassed to produce rapid weight loss in people whose fat is putting their lives in danger. Recovery is long, complication rates are high, side effects are bothersome, and it's major surgery—people die from it. But Pfisterer learned through obesity-help.com, a Web site offering advice to the obese, that her insurer might pay for surgery, given her family history.

34   "For people like me, who are considered on the low end for surgery, there are other options that might be better," she says. "But I can't take advantage of them unless health insurance starts to pay for them."

Too Much of a Good Thing
Greg Critser

In an op-ed essay for the Los Angeles Times *(22 July 2001), Greg Critser argues that, faced with a rising obesity epidemic, we should stigmatize overeating. Critser is careful to distinguish between stigmatizing the person and the act, but he makes no apologies for urging that we teach children that "[e]ating too much food is a bad thing." Critser has written a book on the obesity epidemic:* Supersize *(Houghton Mifflin, 2002).*

1   Sometime over the next month or so, United Nations health and nutrition experts will convene in New York to begin discussing what many consider to be the pivotal medical issue of our day: obesity and its impact on children. For the U.N., traditionally concerned with starvation and malnutrition, it is a historic first, following up on an alarm it sounded about obese adults in 1999. "Obesity," the U.N. proclaimed, "is the dominant unmet global health issue, with Westernized countries topping the list."

2   Solid epidemiological data drives the effort. In Canada, Great Britain, Japan, Australia—even coastal China and Southeast Asia—the rate of childhood obesity has been soaring for more than a decade. Closer to

home, at least 25% of all Americans under age nineteen are overweight or obese, a figure that has doubled over the last 30 years and a figure that moved the surgeon general to declare childhood obesity an epidemic. The cost in health care dollars to treat obesity's medical consequences—from diabetes to coronary heart disease to a variety of crippling bone conditions— will eventually make the battle against HIV/AIDS seem inexpensive. Yet in the U.S., the most important foot soldiers against obesity are increasingly paralyzed by years of media-induced food hysteria, over-generalized and outdated nutritional wisdom, and, truth be told, an unwillingness to set firm and sometimes unpopular food parameters. That infantry is the much-strained American family and its increasingly harried commandant, *Parentis americanus.* What it needs to promulgate is dietary restraint, something our ancestors knew simply as avoiding gluttony.

3   This is not to say that parents should be blamed for the nation's growing dietary permissiveness. They are wary of confronting their children's eating habits for a reason: For years, conventional wisdom held that food should never become a dinner table battleground. "Pressure causes tension," write Harvey and Marilyn Diamond, authors of the classic *Fit for Life,* which has sold more than 3 million copies. "Where food is concerned, tension is always to be avoided." The operative notion is that a child restrained from overeating will either rebel by secretly gorging when away from the table or, worse, will suffer such a loss of self-esteem that a lifetime of disastrous eating behavior will follow.

4   Of course, no one should be stigmatized for being overweight. But stigmatizing the unhealthful behaviors that cause obesity would conform with what we know about effective health messages. In both the campaign against unsafe sex and the campaign against smoking, stigmatizing such behaviors proved highly effective in reducing risk and harm. It's true, smokers—and homosexuals—may have experienced a modicum of stereotyping in the short run, but such is the price of every public health advance: short-term pain for long-term gain.

5   Another inhibition to imposing dietary restraint is the belief, promoted in handbook after handbook of parental advice, that "kids know when they are full." But perhaps not. In fact, new research suggests just the opposite: Kids don't know when they are full.

6   In a recent study, Pennsylvania State University nutritional scholar Barbara Rolls and her associates examined the eating habits of two groups of kids, one of three-year-olds, another of five-year-olds. The children were presented with a series of plates of macaroni and cheese. The first plate was a normal serving built around baseline nutritional needs; the second was slightly larger; the third was what might be called "supersized."

7   What the researchers found is that the younger children consistently ate the same baseline amount, leaving more food on the plates with larger servings. The 5-year-olds, though, altered their eating behavior dramatically depending on the amount they were served, devouring whatever was on the plate. Something had happened. The mere presence of an oversized portion had induced exaggerated eating. The authors concluded that

"these early years may provide a unique opportunity for interventions that reduce the risk of developing overweight." Those interventions "should include clear information on appropriate portion sizes for children."

8   Theorizing aside, our disinclination to restrain eating flies in the face of overwhelming evidence that, of all age groups, children seem to be the ones who respond most positively to dietary advice. In four randomized studies of obese 6- to 12-year-olds, those who were offered frequent, simple behavioral advice were substantially less overweight 10 years later than kids who did not get the advice. In fact, 30% of those studied were no longer obese at all.

9   The case for early intervention has been further buttressed by new studies on another age-old medical injunction: never put a kid on a diet. (The concern was that under-nutrition could lead to stunted growth.) But as the authors of a study of 1,062 kids under age three concluded in the journal *Pediatrics,* "a supervised, low-saturated-fat and low-cholesterol diet has no influence on growth during the first three years of life." Overweight kids who were put on such a diet ended up with better, more moderate eating habits.

10   Changing the eating habits of children, though, is antithetical to some notions many parents hold dear. And to some it seems a relic of an earlier, more religious era of moral certainties when gluttony was vilified as one of the seven deadly sins. Many boomer parents believe, as one parent and nutritionist said at a recent summit on childhood obesity, that "kids have the right to make bad nutrition decisions." That may be true. But ours is a world where at least a billion dollars a year is spent by just one fast-food chain to convince families to visit a crazy-looking clown with his own playground and purchase a thousand supersize calories for a mere $2.50. McDonald's official line today is that three meals a week at its restaurants are perfectly acceptable for an average kid. That's three meals a week of grease, refined flour, and a jumbo shot of sugar.

11   Given today's bounty of cheap and unhealthful food alternatives, and given the inconvenience that goes with making good nutritional choices, one might wonder if a campaign against over-consumption, a campaign advocating restraint, could work. On this point, we might take a cue from the French. In the early 20th century France, in response to its first experiences with widespread child obesity, launched the puericulture movement, which focused on excessive weight gain in early childhood and adolescence. Its prescription: All meals should be adult-supervised; all portions should be moderate, with "seconds" a rare treat. All but an occasional small snack were forbidden. As its historian Peter N. Stearns writes in *Fat History,* puericulture's message was simple: Eating too much food is a bad thing.

12   Therein lies at least part of the explanation for the legendary leanness of the French: They were taught in childhood not to overeat. And it didn't seem to do much harm to their self-esteem.

Fat and Happy: In Defense of Fat Acceptance
Mary Ray Worley

Mary Ray Worley is a member of NAAFA, the National Association to Advance Fat Acceptance. Hers is the only first-person account you will read in this chapter of the social and psychological pressures that fat people can experience. She does much to elucidate anti-fat stereotypes and, through her spirited writing, does much to dispel them. As you read, you might bear in mind the contrasts between Worley's position on obesity and that of Greg Critser, who argues that we should stigmatize the act of overeating.

1   If you've grown up in twentieth-century American society, you probably believe that being fat is a serious personal, social, and medical liability. Many Americans would rather die or cut off a limb than be fat, many believe that fatness is a serious health risk, and many are convinced that it is a simple matter to reduce one's body size and are so offended by body fat that they believe it is acceptable to shun fat people and make them the butt of cruel jokes. Those who are fat quickly learn to be deeply ashamed of their bodies and spend their lives trying to become what they are not and hide what cannot be hidden. Our society believes that thinness signals self-discipline and self-respect, whereas fatness signals self-contempt and lack of resolve. We're so accustomed to this way of thinking that many of us have never considered that there might be an alternative.

2   Nevertheless, a growing number of people believe it's possible to be happy with your body even if it happens to be fat. In August 2000 I attended the annual convention of the National Association to Advance Fat Acceptance (NAAFA) in San Diego, and it was like visiting another planet altogether. I hadn't realized how deeply my body shame affected my life until I spent a glorious week without it. I'll never be the same again.

3   The first time I had that "different planet" feeling was at the pool party on the first night of the convention. Here were all these fat people in stylish swimsuits and cover-ups, and whereas on my home planet a fat person was expected to feel apologetic and embarrassed about her body—especially in a swimsuit—here were a hundred or so fat people who were enjoying being in their bodies without a shred of self-consciousness. They were having so much fun it was infectious. I felt light-headed and giddy. I kept noticing how great everyone looked. They were confident and radiant and happy—and all sizes of fat. Definitely not my planet.

4   One of the features of NAAFA's conventions is that they invite vendors who sell stylish large-size clothing. So whereas on my home planet, you're lucky if you can find a swimsuit that fits at all, on this planet you have choices and can find a swimsuit that's made from beautiful fabric and looks absolutely smashing on you. Where I come from, you're grateful if you can find clothes that you can actually get on, and forget finding clothes that really fit you. But on this planet there were play clothes, dress-up

clothes, you name it. Choices galore. Beautiful fabrics with an elegant drape and a certain panache. I'd never before had so many choices. The clothes I tried on (and bought) not only fit me but looked terrific. As the week wore on and everyone had visited the vendors' booths, we all looked snazzier and snazzier, and the ones who had been to past conventions looked snazzy from the get-go.

5   The next night at the talent show those of us who didn't get a part in the high school musical because we were too fat had a chance to play the lead for five minutes. (I sang a snappy little number by Stephen Sondheim called "The Ladies Who Lunch," from *Company*, and hammed it up big time. I had a blast!) Top billing was given to a troupe of belly dancers called the Fatimas. Now, I had read about this attraction in the literature I received about the convention, and I have to admit that I thought it would be some kind of a spoof or a joke. I just couldn't conceive of a group of fat women doing serious belly dancing, but it was no joke. These women were indeed serious—and excellent—belly dancers. They wore the full belly-dancing regalia—that is, gauze and bangles and beads and not much else. When they first looped and bobbed their way out into the middle of the room, I think my chin must have dropped through the floor. They were exquisitely beautiful and voluptuous and graceful and serene. I thought that anyone, no matter how acculturated to my home planet, would have to be just about dead not to recognize how beautiful they were. And they were all so different from each other. We are accustomed to seeing mostly thin bodies that look more or less the same, but these bodies showed an amazing degree of delightful diversity. Body fat does not distribute itself on every fat person in the same way, so there's lots of variety. Plus they weren't all young. A couple of them had to have been past fifty, and they were so beautiful. And exotic, and mesmerizing. I had always assumed that as a fat woman I could never do that, and especially not as a fat woman past fifty. Wrong, wrong, wrong. I felt a jolt as my old assumptions were jettisoned out into space. Bag that old paradigm. This one is definitely a lot more fun.

6   One of the featured speakers at the convention was Dr. Diane Budd, who spoke about the medical and scientific communities' take on fatness. Although the data gathered for most current studies indicate that body size is primarily determined by one's genetic makeup, most researchers conclude—in spite of their own findings—that fat individuals should try to lose weight anyway. There are no data that indicate (a) that such efforts are likely to be effective (in fact, more than 90 percent of those who lose weight gain it back), (b) that a person's overall health would be improved by losing weight, or (c) that the effort to lose weight won't in fact turn out to have lasting harmful effects on one's appetite, metabolism, and self-esteem. Our assumptions about the desirability of thinness are so deeply ingrained that scientists find it next to impossible to align their recommendations with their findings; apparently they cannot bring themselves to say that since body size is largely a result of one's genetic makeup it's best to get on with the business of learning to live in the body you have, whatever its size.

7   Moreover, none of the studies take into account the physical implications of the social ostracism and body hate that are a regular part of most fat people's lives. Fat people are often taunted in public and are pressured by family members to lose weight. Complete strangers feel they are not out of line to criticize the contents of a fat person's grocery cart, and family members may evaluate everything a fat person puts on her plate. Fat people need to be active and strong enough to carry their body weight comfortably, but they may feel ill at ease exercising in public because of unkind stares and comments. They may feel that they can't wear shorts or sleeveless t-shirts or swimsuits for fear of offending the delicate sensibilities of others and inviting rude comments, and so they will be too hot and too embarrassed and will give up on regular exercise because they don't have the support they need to continue. Now *that* is a health risk.

8   Moreover, fat people are often reluctant to seek medical attention because health professionals are among the most prejudiced people around. Regardless of the ailment you are seeking treatment for, if you are fat, your doctor may put you on a diet before she treats your cough, and attribute whatever complaint you have to your weight. Pressures like these must certainly contribute to the shortening of many fat people's lives, quite apart from any physical risk resulting from a preponderance of body fat.

9   The upshot is that it's very likely that the health risks of being fat have been highly overestimated. In combination with other risk factors, being fat may occasionally contribute to compromised health, but not nearly to the degree that many people think. When a fat person goes to a weight-loss clinic, the goal is usually to lose weight as quickly as possible, as though to snatch the poor fat soul out of the jaws of imminent death. And often the harsh methods used to effect that weight loss are in and of themselves much more harmful than being fat is. In fact, it is my understanding that statistically a person is much less likely to regain weight that is lost very slowly. So what's the big rush? The big rush is that we hate fat and want to put as much distance between ourselves and it as quickly as possible. Quick and dramatic weight loss sells; slow and gradual weight loss does not. There's nothing compassionate, rational, or scientific about it. We just hate fat.

10   Many fat people have made numerous efforts and spent thousands of dollars throughout their lives to lose weight and each time regained the lost pounds plus a few more. Have this happen to you enough times and you will be apprehensive at the prospect of losing weight for fear of gaining back more than you lose. On my own account, there's no way I want to diet again, because it will just make me fatter in the long run. Help like that I don't need, and I sure as spitfire don't need to pay through the nose for it.

11   After years and years of dieting it slowly dawned on me that my body rebelled when I tried to restrict my food intake. All those years I figured that it was me who was failing, and then I began to realize that it was the method that was failing. I began to wonder whether the problem itself was being incorrectly defined. I began raising new questions just about the time that researchers were discovering that, rather than being a simple intake-outtake equation, body weight resulted from a complex interplay of set

point (the body's tendency to stay within a certain narrow weight range), appetite and satiety cues, metabolism, and genes. Moreover, our bodies are designed to protect us from starvation and have some powerful defenses against it. They react to dieting just as they do to starving. They don't know there is a McDonald's around every corner. For all they know, we're still living in the Ice Age, when the next meal may be hours or days or miles away. So when we decrease the amount of food we eat, our bodies slow the metabolic rate to fend off possible starvation. It's a great system, really. In my case I'm convinced that as determined as I have been to become thin, my body has always been more determined to save me from starvation. My body is more stubborn than I am. Amazing.

12   So I stopped dieting and began to make peace with food and with my body. I slowly stopped being afraid of food. In 1999 I became a vegetarian, and somehow that change—and the culture that seems to go with it—put food in a new light for me. Food was no longer the enemy; it was a gift and a source of joy. I began to slow down and relish my meals, to enjoy food and be grateful for all the ways that it nourishes me.

13   Over the last fifteen years or so I've made many attempts to become more active on a regular basis with varying degrees of success. I often would go swimming three or four times a week for two, three, or four months followed by a hiatus of several weeks or months. About two years ago, I realized that I always felt better when I was being active. So why the long hiatuses? Because I was exercising in hopes of losing weight. After months of dogged discipline with what I considered to be meager results at best, I would naturally become discouraged and stop. Within a few weeks I would stop feeling the surge of energy and well-being that comes with regular exercise.

14   So what would happen if I just exercised because I felt better when I did? How about moving just for the fun of it? So I gave up the notion of losing weight and consequently gave up feeling hopeless, and as a result the hiatuses have become fewer and shorter in duration. I began to vary my workouts more, so that I got less bored and enjoyed myself more. Who knew that moving, even in a large body, could be this much fun? I'd never allowed myself to have this kind of fun in my body before.

15   I discovered to my delight that the more physically competent I became, the better I felt about my body. My husband, Tom, and I go for long hikes in the woods, and some of those hikes have been challenging for me—not too challenging, but just enough. Two years ago we visited Yosemite National Park, and we hiked partway up to the top of Vernal Fall. It was a demanding hike, and pretty much everybody was huffing and puffing. We made it up to the bridge that's just shy of halfway to the top. It was good to know when to stop, but it rankled me that I didn't have the energy or stamina to make it all the way. So I decided that next time I will. Next spring we're planning another trip to Yosemite, and I'm going to make it to the top of Vernal Fall. I don't care how long it takes me or how much I have to huff and puff. My only stipulation is that I have to be strong enough to have fun doing it. I don't want it to be a torture session.

16   I've been training with that goal in mind for months now. Instead of avoiding stairs, I look for them. I'm no longer ashamed of huffing and puffing—I'm proud. I'm pushing myself just enough so that I'm becoming stronger and have more endurance all the time. This summer I discovered that I can hike all day long. What a thrill! In July, Tom and I hiked in Copper Falls State Park from 12 noon until 8 P.M. (we stopped to rest three times). And in August I traipsed around the San Diego Wild Animal Park from 9 A.M. until 8 P.M. (again with three rests). How wonderful to have a body that will carry me through an entire day of fun! I never realized before what a miracle my body is, its glorious ability to build muscle and save me from starvation. I'm only beginning to discover what a marvelous gift it is.

17   After years of fighting our set points, our metabolism, our genes, and our hunger, after decades of being ashamed, hating our bodies, and trying to manipulate them into being something they're not, after spending mountains of money and energy trying to conform to someone else's ideal, it isn't surprising that some of us question whether this is the best way to for us to live. A few of us brave adventurers have found another way, and it involves much less agony, costs much less money, and is much more fun.

18   We're not giving up, and we're not letting ourselves go. Rather we're forging a new relationship with our bodies, one that doesn't involve self-loathing, one that appreciates the miraculous bodies we have, one that brings joy. There's plenty of room on this new planet, and here you needn't apologize for your size. You're entitled to the space you take up. You can find clothes that show off the gorgeous person you are, you can play and dance without self-consciousness, you can be proud of yourself and never dread unwanted attention, you can be a brave pioneer and a friend to those who have suffered on planets less kind and less joyous than this one.

Too "Close to the Bone": The Historical Context for Women's Obsession with Slenderness
Roberta Seid

Roberta Seid critiques our culture's "religion" of thinness and explains how Americans have come to be adherents of this religion, as well of the psychological and even spiritual costs of adherence. You will find in Seid's essay an excellent example of how scholarship—historical and cultural scholarship, in this case—can shine a light on complex problems, helping us to view them in entirely new ways. When she wrote this piece in 1994, Seid was a lecturer in the Program for the Study of Women and Men in Society at the University of Southern California, Los Angeles.

1   Why have Americans, particularly American women, become fatphobic? Why and how have they come to behave as though the shape of their lives depends on the shape of their bodies? Why have they clung to these beliefs

despite the toll they take on private lives, and especially despite their most extreme and dangerous manifestation, eating disorders? This chapter addresses these questions by placing the phenomenon in a broad historical context, with particular focus on fashion and the unique and dangerous twist it has taken in our era.

2   Although current explanations for our thinness mania are valuable, they often leave many questions unanswered. Feminists have often blamed fashion for oppressing and subordinating women, but fashion has rarely had the destructive effects we see today. Moreover, the fashion for thinness, which has prevailed only for the past 40 years or so, requires explanation itself. The eating disorders literature, often focused on individual psychopathology, has found neither a consistent etiological profile nor a universally accepted explanation for why eating disorders have swelled into a social disease. Nor does it explain why millions of women without clinical eating disorders mimic the behavior and mind set of affected women. Finally, a much weaker body of literature attributes the phenomenon to the mass media's influence. Although the media's power to shape our perceptions cannot be underestimated, this explanation also begs the question. Why would the media necessarily promote slenderness?

3   A more comprehensive explanation emerges when we stand back and, employing a broad historical perspective, look at the underlying cultural beliefs that affect both genders. Our culture is swept up in a web of peculiar and distorted beliefs about beauty, health, virtue, eating, and appetite. We have elevated the pursuit of a lean, fat-free body into a new religion. It has a creed: "I eat right, watch my weight, and exercise." Indeed, anorexia nervosa could be called the paradigm of our age, for our creed encourages us all to adopt the behavior and attitudes of the anorexic. The difference is one of degree, not of kind. Like any religion worthy of the name, ours also has its damnation. Failure to follow the creed—and the corporeal stigmata of that failure, fatness and flabbiness—produce a hell on earth. The fat and flabby are damned to failure, regardless of professional and personal successes. Our religion also has its rewards, its salvation. In following the creed, one is guaranteed beauty, energy, health, and a long successful life. Followers are even promised self-transformation: The "thin person within," waiting to burst through the fat, is somehow a more exciting, sexy, competent, successful self. Virtue can be quantified by the numbers on the scale, the lean-to-fat ratio, clothing size, and body measurements. And, in a curious inversion of capitalist values, less is always better.

Body Ideals Before the 20th Century

4   The creed of thinness is composed of prejudices, and they have a history. A cursory review of Western civilization's aesthetic and health ideals indicates the novelty and arbitrariness of current beliefs. The female body has not altered for thousands of years; the range of body types in the past does not differ from the range we know today. What has changed is the body type (or types) regarded as ideal, as well as the effort put into meeting this ideal and the methods used to do so. Although styles of dress have tended to change at an ever-quickening tempo since the 12th century, body ideals have

changed slowly. By looking at the visual evidence provided by paintings of dressed people and of the nude, we can see that never before have men or women desired a body so "close to the bone."

5   There have been, of course, other periods when slenderness was admired. During the 15th century, paintings of long-limbed ladies reverberated with the vaulting reaches of Gothic cathedrals. Sixteenth-century Mannerists in northern Europe painted elongated nudes, such as the nymphs in Cranach the Elder's *The Judgment of Paris*. More recently, the Romantic vogue for slenderness in the 1830s–1850s encouraged young ladies to strive for the tiny waist favored by fashion—an effort later immortalized in *Gone with the Wind* when Scarlett O'Hara's stays are tightened to achieve a 17-inch waist.*

6   Nonetheless, it would be misleading to assume that these eras resembled our own. Gothic and Mannerist nudes had not a bone or muscle showing; they were sweetly and fully fleshed. Women of the Romantic period may have wanted tiny waists, but they also wanted their shoulders, arms, calves, and bosoms ample, indicating an "amorous plenitude."** Indeed, thinness was considered ugly, a woman's misfortune. The French epicure J. A. Brillat-Savarin defined thinness as those of his epoch typically did—as "the condition of the individual whose muscular flesh, not being filled with fat, reveals the forms and angles of the bony structure." Thinness in women was, he observed, "a terrible misfortune. . . . The most painstaking toilette, the sublimest costume, cannot hide certain absences, or disguise certain angles."† Nor did the Romantic lady equate slenderness with health and energy as we do today; health was not part of her aesthetic ideal. Rather, slenderness signified delicacy and fragility, the qualities she sought.

7   Just a century ago, body ideals and ideas were the reverse of our own, underscoring the fact that there was no folk wisdom about the value of slenderness that science has recently confirmed. Indeed, the female ideal was Junoesque: tall, full-busted, full-figured, mature. Dimpled flesh—what we today shudderingly call "cellulite"—was considered desirable. Sinewy, "close to the bone" women "no bigger than a whipping post" suffered disdain, not those with amply fleshed curves properly distributed and disciplined only by the corset.‡ The undergarment industry even came to the aid of the slighted thin woman with inflatable rubber garments (replete with

---

* For a fuller discussion of past body ideals, see Roberta P. Seid, *Never Too Thin: Why Women Are at War with Their Bodies* (New York: Prentice-Hall Press, 1989), 37–81. The best sources for a general overview are Francois Boucher, *20,000 Years of Fashion: The History of Costume and Personal Adornment,* expanded edition (New York: Harry N. Abrams, 1987) and Kenneth Clark, *The Nude: A Study in Ideal Form* (Princeton, NJ: Princeton University Press, 1956).

** See the excellent discussion of this ideal in Valerie Steele, *Fashion and Eroticism: Ideals of Feminine Beauty from the Victorian Era to the Jazz Age* (New York: Oxford University Press, 1985), 108–110.

† Jean Anthelme Brillat-Savarin, *The Physiology of Taste or Meditations on Transcendental Gastronomy* (New York: Doubleday, 1926 [orig. 1826]), 172, 187.

‡ Steele, 1985, 218–223; Hillel Schwartz, *Never Satisfied: A Cultural History of Diets, Fantasies, and Fat* (New York: Free Press, 1986), Illustration 5 (1857 cartoon from *Harper's Weekly*).

dimples) for her back, calves, shoulders, and hips. They may have provided meager comfort, for they could deflate at unexpected moments.*

8   Fat was seen as a "silken layer" that graced the frames of elegant ladies. It was regarded as "stored-up force," equated with reserves of energy and strength. Plumpness was deemed a sign of emotional well-being; it was identified with a good temperament, with a clean conscience, with temperate and disciplined habits, and above all with good health. Today, of course, we have totally inverted these associations.**

9   In the mid-19th century, the prolific writer Catherine Beecher described healthy weight. If you felt heavy and got on the scale (a rare experience in the 19th century), and weighed either heavy or light, you were in bad health. But if you felt light and weighed heavy, then you were in excellent health; weighing heavy was good. More importantly, Beecher distinguished between feelings and actual weight—a distinction lost to many today, who determine how they feel by the numbers on the scale.†

Development of the Obsession with Thinness

10   The transformation of these values began at about the turn of the present century, when slenderness came into fashion. This occurred for a variety of reasons, among them the modernist aesthetic with its idealization of speed and motion, and its penchant for stripping things down to their essential forms. (Some called it the revenge of the thin who for so long had been slighted.) But "slim" is a relative term, and the women who boasted the new form would by contemporary standards be called overweight. In addition, in the first half of this century, the belief that plumpness signaled robust health remained strong.

11   The culture of slimming as we know it is really a post–World War II phenomenon.‡ Fashion continued to value a slender (if curving) form, and the health industry, finally convinced by insurance companies, launched massive campaigns to persuade Americans to lose weight. Key ideas that would take full force in subsequent decades began to emerge. Chief among these was "fatphobia," the conviction that animal fat of any kind— on the body, in the blood, on the plate—was dangerous. The perception developed that Americans were too fat and getting fatter; that they ate too much, ate the wrong foods, and were sedentary and therefore flabby. Americans' self-perception shifted to that of a diseased, unhealthy group,

---

* David Kunzle, "The Corset as Erotic Alchemy: From Rococo Galanterie to Montaut's Physiologies," in Thomas Hess and Linda Nochlin, eds., *Art News Annual,* vol. 38, *Woman as Sex Object: Erotic Art, 1730–1970* (1972); Steele, 1985, 128, 221.

** Seid, 1989, 70–80.

† Beecher's standards are quoted by Harvey Green, *Fit for America: Health–Fitness–Sport and American Society* (New York: Pantheon Books, 1986), 64.

‡ For a fuller discussion with citations of sources, see Seid, 1989, Chapters 12 and 13.

even though they enjoyed the best health and greatest longevity ever known in American society. These pronouncements did not abate, even though average life expectancy continued to improve. Most important was the growing fear that Americans were getting physically and *morally* soft. For at the heart of all the campaign literature was a moral concern about how Americans would react to postwar plenty and leisure—how they would handle modernization.

12   In subsequent decades, these ideas intensified. Weight loss techniques began to be seen as life-prolonging in and of themselves. The fitness ethic emerged from these beliefs and fueled obsession with exercise. But the new emphasis on fitness was just a variation on the theme of slenderness. The ideal remained a fat-free body. The "health food" craze played on the same dynamic, growing out of and then later helping to fuel and dignify diet obsessions. In addition, the standards of slenderness grew more extreme, both in charts of ideal weight and in fashion. The famous 1960s model Twiggy, at 5 feet 7 inches and 98 pounds, represented the boundary beyond which no ambulatory person could go; however, her image became one that women thereafter aspired to meet. Female beauty had come to be represented by a gawky, bare-boned adolescent. Simultaneously, definitions of "overweight" and "obesity" began to include normal-sized Americans.

13   More compelling, however, were the principles underlying fatphobia, which turned it into a national obsession. The health industry embraced the questionable concept of "ideal weight"—the idea that the weight associated with optimum health and longevity could be determined by height. It was then decreed that everyone of the same height and bone structure should meet this ideal. But this injunction assumed that body weight and the ratios of fat to lean tissue were direct functions of exercise and eating habits. The obvious corollary was that everybody should reduce to ideal weight and that everybody could easily do so—if they exerted enough willpower. In short, these decrees blamed the victim: if you were fat, it was your fault. This is the most powerful and pernicious aspect of fatphobia; indeed, in modern America, being fat is as shameful as being dirty. We seem to believe that slenderness is as attainable as cleanliness, and as crucial to respectable grooming. We can easily embrace these ideas because they fit so well with America's self-help-oriented, democratic ideology. We can all be body aristocrats, we believe, if we just try hard enough. This set of beliefs fuels prejudices against fat and has allowed the thinness mania to spiral into a religion.

14   More and more evidence is emerging that discredits this whole ideology and shows that its premises are empirically flawed. The thinner are not necessarily healthier, nor are they more fit. Our fundamental beliefs—that people of the same height should have the same weight, and that people can exercise absolute control over their body weights—are also flawed. Numerous studies demonstrate that the majority of the "fat" cannot slim down permanently. The problem is not their lack of willpower, but the unreasonable expectation placed on them to weigh

a certain amount. Animal breeders have long known that nature did not intend everyone to be the same size, but modern science seems to have temporarily forgotten.

15   Sadly, efforts to squeeze into the ideal size are often useless and destructive—not only because they can exacerbate the problem they are designed to cure, but because they trigger psychological, physiological, and behavioral consequences, including binge eating, food obsessions, and, in susceptible individuals, eating disorders. Even worse, dieters pay a price in sense of well-being, in health, and in the ability to lead rich and productive lives. The contemporary and historical literature on famine describes ennui, tension, irritability, preoccupation with food, loss of libido, and lassitude created by diets equivalent to those advised for weight loss. The United Nations World Health Organization has established a daily intake of 1000 calories as the border of semistarvation; modern diets often recommend less. The famine literature attributes these symptoms to hunger and undernourishment; the literature on overweight attributes them to lack of willpower or to psychopathology.

16   Laboring under perverse notions about food and appetite, we believe that permanent dieting and chronic hunger are healthy and energy-giving; we are convinced that food does not nourish, but rather kills. If we find ourselves eating with unbridled appetite, we believe that there is either something wrong with us or with the food itself, which must be "addictive." In truth, the well-nourished, not the undernourished, grow strong, healthy, and productive. Poor appetite is a sign of the depressed and the ill; indeed, women are often grateful for an illness—it makes dieting easier.

17   It is hard to resist the parallel between Victorian attributes toward sex and modern attitudes toward food. In the 19th century, the control of sexual instincts was the acme of virtue; sexual behavior was the yardstick of goodness. Today, eating habits and body weights have become the yardsticks of virtue, and food rules have become as dour and inhibitory as the sex rules of the 19th century. Perhaps cultures require some kind of instinctual control to feel that they qualify as "civilized."

Why Women More Than Men?

18   Given that this belief system pervades our culture, why does it affect women so much more than men? Why do more women than men suffer from eating disorders, obesity, and distorted body image? Why are women, not men, at war with their bodies? There are many reasons, some more obvious than others.

19   One reason is biological. Standards for males simply are not as extreme or as inimical to normal masculine body builds as are women's standards. Indeed, our female ideal violates the anthropomorphic reality of the average female body. The ideal female weight, represented by actresses, models, and Miss Americas, has progressively decreased to that of the thinnest 5–10% of American women. Consequently, 90–95% of American

women feel that they don't "measure up."* Societies have never been kind
to deviants, but in America a statistical deviation has been normalized,
leading millions of women to believe that they are abnormal.

20   In addition, the taut, lean, muscled body—the "fit" form so many strive
to achieve—is more like the body of a male than of a female. The goal is
to suppress female secondary sexual characteristics, from dimpled flesh to
plumpness in thighs, behinds, hips, and bosom. Women consequently are
pitted in a war against their own biologies to meet the standard.

21   It is not just biology that confounds women. They strive to meet this
unreasonable standard because it has become a moral imperative in our
society, and because, despite a quarter-century of feminism, the quest for
physical beauty remains deeply powerful. On even a practical level,
women's self-image, their social and economic success, and even their survival can still be determined largely by their beauty and by the men it
allows them to attract, while for men these are based largely on how they
act and what they accomplish. Looks simply are of secondary importance
for male success.

22   But the impulse toward beauty runs much deeper than the desire for
social acceptance and success. Beauty and fashion are intertwined, and
women try to meet unreasonable weight standards also because fashion—
our system of dress—requires them to do so. Though many have castigated fashion as a shallow and frivolous vanity, it is propelled by
profound impulses, which it shares with all dress systems. Dress and
adornment are basic to all human cultures. Even the most primitive
tribes find ways to decorate the body. The overwhelming importance
of dress is underscored by the fact that from the moment we slip out of
the womb to the moment of our deaths, we alter our natural appearance.
How we choose to dress is a complex cultural phenomenon. Clothing
and adornment are simultaneously a material object, a social signal, a
ritual, and a form of art. Every facet of a society—from its economic base

---

* Although exact figures on this subject remain elusive, many sources confirm this general trend. This
percentage was suggested by Rita Freedman, *Beauty Bound* (Lexington, Mass.: Lexington Books,
1986), 149, but it is corroborated by other sources. I studied statistics of Miss America contenders with
data for the earlier periods from Frank Deford, *There She Is: The Life and Times of Miss America* (New
York: Viking Press, 1971), 313–316, and from Miss America Pageant Yearbooks, 1972–1983, and
found a dramatic slenderizing trend. For more details, see Seid, 1989, Chapter 10. For a study of a similar development in the *Playboy* centerfolds, whose average weights dropped from 11% below the
national average in 1970 to 17% below it in 1978, see Paul E. Garfinkel and David M. Garner, *Anorexia
Nervosa: A Multidimensional Perspective* (New York: Brunner/Mazel, 1982), 108–109, and D. M.
Garner, P. E. Garfinkel, D. Schwartz, and M. Thompson, "Cultural Expectations of Thinness in Women,"
Psychological Reports 47 (1980): 483–491. On the rise of an emaciated ideal in the ballet subculture,
see L. M. Vincent, *Competing with the Sylph* (New York: Andrews & McMeel, 1979). Jennifer Brenner,
professor of psychology at Brandeis University, and Dr. Joseph Cunningham recently reported the results
of their study comparing the weights of New York fashion models and Brandeis students. "Female
models are 9 percent taller and 16 percent thinner than average women," Brenner reported in an
article by Lena Williams, "Girl's Self-Image Is Mother of the Woman," *New York Times* (National Edition),
February 6, 1992, A1, A12.

to its social structure, from its values about human beings and their bodies to its loftiest spiritual and aesthetic ideals—influences the forms and rules of dress. Each culture sets up its own rules, and in following them, people defer to and perpetuate fundamental social values and norms.

23   In obeying fashion's dictates, we are bowing to powerful constraints about self-presentation and about how others should interpret our attitudes, behavior, and identity. The enormous time and energy women (and men) devote to it is simply another of civilization's many demands and, possibly, pleasures. For in dressing, in following fashion, we are engaged in a game, a plastic art, a process whereby we partially create ourselves. We are involved in social and private play of the profoundest type—trying to transcend our uncivilized, animal state, to make ourselves human. Friedrich Nietzsche, in *The Birth of Tragedy*, argued that "We derive such dignity as we possess from our status as art works." Fun, fantasy, humor, artistic creativity, and our deepest aspirations exist in the dress constraints of everyday life.*

24   Fashion, the dress system of the West, has, however, taken a rather peculiar twist in recent decades—one that helps explain our body obsessions. Fashionable beauty is no longer about the clothes covering the body, but about the naked body itself. This has not been true before in the history of fashion. Fashion is, as we have seen, a plastic art. Although it would be foolhardy to describe the past as Edenic, it nonetheless is true that fashion has traditionally been a handmaiden to beauty. It allowed people to approach the reigning ideal by manipulating cosmetics and clothing—that is, by manipulating what they put *on* themselves, not what they *were* underneath those clothes, stays, girdles, and so forth.

25   By the late 20th century, however, women's bodies, which heretofore had never been exposed to the public eye, virtually became wholly exposed. With the introduction of the miniskirt and teeny tops, women's legs, thighs, and upper bodies were suddenly revealed, bereft of the aid of body-shaping undergarments. The fitness craze and the growing liberalization in censorship and in acceptable norms of nudity intensified the trend.

26   By the 1980s, even fashion magazines showed naked or leotarded bodies more than they showed clothing. The undressed body—the bare bones of being, celebrated as liberating and "natural"—had become the focus of fashion. No longer did a woman have the luxury of manipulating only what was outside her body, the "not me"; now she had to manipulate her self, the once private stretches of the body.

27   This new, "natural" look could not really be liberating, because fashion is antithetical (almost by definition) to nature, so stringent standards began being set for the now-exposed form. Suddenly, the average American

---

* Nietzsche's statement is quoted in Steele, 1985, 245. For a fuller theoretical discussion and bibliography on the role of dress and adornment in human culture, see Roberta P. Seid, *The Dissolution of Traditional Rural Culture in Nineteenth-Century France: A Study of the Bethmale Costume* (New York: Garland Press, 1987), 1–45.

woman became aware of flaws she never knew existed; pronouncements were made about how every private crevice of her anatomy was to look. Women consequently ran smack into a dilemma between the naked and the nude.

28   The art historian Sir Kenneth Clark argued that the nude is a form of art; the naked is merely the human body undressed, replete with all its flaws and blemishes. The naked becomes the nude through art, with the artist transforming that humble and flawed form into an ideal of beauty.* Yet today, bombarded by verbal and visual commercial images of the nude, women have been seduced into believing that they should—and could, with enough effort—have one of those perfect bodies. They expect the image reflected in their mirrors to look like the nude. It almost never does. And so they renew their battle against their recalcitrant bodies.

29   Changes in the structure of fashion contributed further to the battle: No authorities put brakes on the urge to meet the slender ideal. This, too, was new in fashion's history. Although there has always been considerable harmony among standards of feminine beauty, health, and the gestalt of an era, excesses of fashion were heretofore severely criticized by social authorities, including doctors, teachers, and clergy, parents, and, since the 19th century, feminists. The clergy and moralists, in particular, stressed that there were values more important than outward appearance; that the soul and one's deeds mattered, not fashion standards; that, in the words of the old adage, "Pretty is as pretty does." In the late 20th century—at least until alarm about eating disorders spread—all these authorities, especially physicians, seemed to agree that one could never be too thin. This unholy alliance between societal and fashion authorities allowed the vogue for thinness to go to extremes.

30   Even contemporary feminists have been slow to resist the slenderness fashion. They were initially seduced, perhaps, by its underlying message that biology is not destiny. Even more, the rhetoric of the slenderness ideal—that health is beauty and beauty health, and both are fit and thin—may have persuaded them. They applauded the fact that physical strength and health were now feminine ideals. It took a while for them to realize that what was sought, what had become ideal, was merely the *appearance* of health and vigor—and that dangerous means were being used to achieve it.

31   Despite the historical uniqueness of these developments, some rather cruel historical consistencies remain. More stringent bodily controls are still required of the female than of the male. Animal-like functions, such as belching, nose wiping, urinating, sweating, scratching, spitting, masturbating, farting, and even body odor, remain less permissible for women than for men. In the male subculture, unlike female subcultures, there is an acceptance of and a certain humor about these behaviors, which sometimes become the subject of good-natured contests. Men simply are permitted to be more comfortable about natural functions and

---

*Clark, 1956, 3–9.

to exhibit them to a greater extent in public. They do not compromise masculinity; rather, they often confirm it. Women, on the other hand, compromise their femininity if they do not control these behaviors. The same discrepancy applies to diet and body size: Women are expected to manage these even more stringently than men. Similarly, as long as control of appetite and body weight is regarded as virtuous, women must exercise this control more than men. Once again, women are expected to be the custodians and embodiments of virtue for the culture.

Thinness and Our Cultural and Spiritual Values

32 What remains puzzling about this unique fashion for bare-boned skinniness is what it suggests about our aesthetic ideals—and, even more importantly, about our values, our gestalt. If we step back a moment and look at our ideal of beauty from a more distant perspective (perhaps that of a future historian or anthropologist), we can perhaps see how peculiar it is that we celebrate the living version of Giacometti sculptures, anorexics with barbells.

33   Future historians might conjecture that Americans had fallen in love with death, or at least with mortification of the flesh. They might speculate that terror of nuclear destruction had made fashion play with cadavers and turn them into images of beauty. Or they might argue that we had been so influenced by modern art, Bauhaus aesthetics, and contemporary steel architecture that our ideal human body also had come to consist only of the scaffolding that held it up and of the machinery that made it move. Or they might suggest that we had come to see technology, not human beings, as the prime force in history, and so had chosen to resemble our conquerors.

34   Alternatively, they might argue that our fascination with the unconscious, and our new awareness that scientific reality was concealed from us—that the universe was made up of particles we could not see and governed by laws that defied the logic of our senses—led us to strip the outer body of any meaning or significance and of any possible beauty. Or, more simply, they might conjecture that in an era of population density, it was more practical and economical to have skinny people. Thin people would need less room, so more of them could be squeezed into the spaces on mass transit and into workplaces, and they could live in smaller houses. It certainly also might be interpreted as democratic. No one had the right to take up more space than another or to command respect through the imposing grandeur of body size.

35   They might also conjecture that late 20th-century America had so confused its image of women that what looked female could no longer be considered beautiful. Even more, they might contend that we had dehumanized, not just masculinized, the human form. We had reduced it to its smallest, least imposing form. They might argue that we had come to idealize technology, and also (befitting our secular age) to distinguish humans from other animals and the civilized from the uncivilized not by the presence of consciousness, a soul, and a conscience, but by the suppression of

animal fat. They might even suggest that we had become so terrified of what made us human—especially our passions and our vulnerability—that we didn't want our bodies to betray any softness, curves, or idiosyncracies. Or they might think that we had suppressed tender flesh because we no longer saw human beings as sources of comfort and nurture.

36   From a purely aesthetic perspective, our fat-free beauties might come out no better. Indeed, even unprejudiced present-day observers may be taken aback. Faces are gaunt and angular; necks are steeples of bones. Unfleshed arms and legs, full of sharp angles, look gangly and disproportionately long. Indeed, dieted women look as though the life and color have been sucked out of them. Nor, for all the paeans to strength, do these scrawny, narrow women look strong or stable, or as if they have a stature to be reckoned with. Indeed, the lean body looks as repressed and controlled as the spirit that must have gotten it that way.

37   It is odd, too, that we have developed an erotic ideal that suppresses flesh and minimizes sexual characteristics. There is little to linger over, to explore, to discover. When the body has been efficiently reduced to a flat surface, it offers no softness, no warmth, no tenderness, no mysteries—qualities once integral to images of sexuality. Our erotic ideal has become as hard and unyielding, perhaps, as the love relationships that dominate social life.

38   In criticizing our new religion, I am not suggesting that we gorge wantonly or that we ignore our health and our physical appearance. This would be a surrender to the treacherous polarities that dominate our thinking: Our choices seem to be thinness or fatness, gluttony or starvation, vigorous exercise or lethargy, ascetic rituals or self-indulgence, youthfulness or old age, beauty or ugliness. I am suggesting that we recultivate our tastes and find a saner middle ground where our bodies can round out with more life, flesh, and health; where we can relish the fruits of our prosperity without self-punishment; and where we understand that the nourishment that is one of life's greatest pleasures is also one of its most basic necessities.

39   It would be a tragedy, after 25 years of the women's movement, if women did not rebel against this "religion" that threatens to sabotage their hard-won victories. Is the "liberated woman," supposedly at ease in the boardroom, really consumed with self-loathing and obsessed with tallying calories, exercise, and the vital statistics of the body (weight, muscle-to-fat ratio, inches of breast, hip, and thigh)? Never measuring quite right, she may be as victimized by biology as her predecessors.

40   I am not suggesting, as many past and present feminists have, that we do away with beauty and fashion standards altogether. It would be a bleak world if we did not celebrate beauty and if we did not encourage the imagination and play involved in bedecking ourselves and molding our own images. The impulses toward adornment and self-beautification run deep in human culture and are connected to its noblest aspirations. Nor am I suggesting that fashion standards of the past were always benign. Each era has exacted its own price for beauty, though our era is unique in producing a standard based exclusively on the bare bones of being, which can be disastrous for human health, happiness, and productivity.

41   But I am urging that we dismantle this new religion, because it is misguided and destructive. It does not provide reasonable guidelines by which to live. Our bodies, our fitness, and our food should not be our paramount concerns. They have nothing to do with ethics, or relationships, or community responsibilities, or with the soul. They have nothing to say about the purpose of life, except that we should survive as well and as long and as beautifully as we can. They give us no purpose beyond ourselves. This is a religion appropriate only for a people whose ideals do not extend beyond their physical existence, and whose vision of the future and of the past is strangely empty. Surely Americans can produce a worthier creed.

42   In making the denial of hunger and its physical manifestations, thinness, into a primary virtue, our "religion" is unique among the major world religions. Although there is a long history of fasting for spiritual cleansing or purity, no religion has set it up as a virtue; indeed, most have condemned it. Buddha rejected fasting because he did not find it a way to enlightenment. Judaism prescribes only a few fast days a year. Otherwise, it proscribes such deprivation: According to the Talmud, people must be well nourished so they can do what is important in life—follow God's commandments and perform *mitzvot* (good deeds). The early fathers of the Christian Church, too, condemned fasting, and the Church exacted higher penances for the sin of not eating than it did for the sin of gluttony. The Muslims, even during their great fast of Ramadan, do not abstain from food. They are merely proscribed from eating during certain hours, and the other hours are given to feasting. In these religions, food has not been seen as a temptation put in humanity's path, but as vital for people to carry out their larger spiritual tasks.

43   It is one thing to follow a rigid dietary code and rituals of behavior in accordance with the laws of a God or gods we worship. The faithful are trying to fulfill God's or the gods' commandments, not only for their own salvation, but also to hasten the arrival of a more perfect world. It is quite another thing to follow rigid dietary and behavior codes only to improve our physical selves. Such actions are not part of a larger system of morals. They have no vision of a higher good or of a better future that their rituals might help create. This is a solipsistic religion in the narrowest and strictest sense, in that it is only about the bare bones of being. If avoiding fatness and possible disease is the main preoccupation of our lives, then what are we living for?

44   Our new religion bankrupts us. Historically unprecedented numbers of us are healthy—able to enjoy sex without fear of unwanted pregnancy, to go through childbirth without the once omnipresent threat of death, to treat once-fatal infectious diseases easily, and to alleviate the minor aches and pains that caused discomfort to our forebears (from toothaches to earaches to headaches to skin eruptions to upset stomachs). Advances in technology, medicine, and food production, wrought by painstaking human efforts, have given us a well-being virtually unknown in previous centuries. We should be grateful, but instead we hate our bodies because they bulge here or are flabby there or fail to respond to our most rigorous diets. Surely this is the worst form of

hubris—to despise our bodies because they are not perfect. Our new religion neither puts checks on this kind of vanity nor underscores how trivial is the accomplishment of weight loss and of physical perfection. Instead, it seduces us into believing that this quest is the worthiest of human goals.

45   We must abandon our new religion because it trivializes human life itself. We must restore a humanistic vision in which self-improvement means cultivating the mind and enlarging the soul; developing generosity, humor, dignity, and humility; living more graciously with biology, aging, and death; living with our limitations. We need a concept of self-improvement that reminds us to learn from the past, to build on it, and to bequeath wisdom to future generations. We stand poised between a past for which we have lost respect and a future we must now struggle to envision.

Fat and Happy?
Hillel Schwartz

"Fat and Happy?" forms the final chapter of historian Hillel Schwartz's book-length study of dieting, Never Satisfied *(Free Press, 1986). Like Seid, who critiques what she terms a "religion" of thinness, Schwartz critiques what he calls a "despotism of slenderness." The selection has a satiric feel to it, but underlying all satire—this included—are points seriously made. Indeed, much of the logic presented here you will find shared by other writers, such as Seid and Worley. In the two sections of the chapter reproduced here, Schwartz presents a "Vindication of Fat" and an image of "The Fat Society: A Utopia."*

Recently there has been a growing protest against the despotism of slenderness, and a scientific debate over the dangers of a moderate fatness. Underlying the protest and the debate is a utopian vision of a Fat Society where neither overweight nor obesity stands in the way of social freedom or personal happiness.

The Vindication of Fat

1   Fatness is fine.

2   If fat people are unhappy people, blame not their fat but their fellow citizens who bill them as clowns, clodhoppers, cannibals, or criminals; who spread such commercial rumors as "To be fat is the end of life"; who sport bumper stickers on their vans, "No fat chicks"; who print posters which read, "It's in to be thin. It's out to be stout."* Blame the kindergarten teachers, the coaches, the friends and physicians who goad fat people into a

* Marvin Grosswirth, *Fat Pride* (NY, 1971) 161, D-Zerta ad, and American Physical Fitness Research Institute poster, "Fit to Quote" (Santa Monica, Calif., 1969).

maze of diets from which they may never return. Dieting makes everything worse, for the chances are high that fat people will fail. They will be saddened and frustrated by their failures, and they will come to agree with everyone else that they are failures in all of life. Because they have failed they are fat, and because they are fat they fail.

3   It is the taking off and the putting on of weight that endangers the body. Not the fat or the pounds but the dieting itself, the frustration, and the constant hunger. No one has been able to prove that fatness *per se* cuts life short. If left alone, 99 percent of human beings will reach a plateau weight, a set point at which their metabolisms will be satisfied and their bodies healthy. It is the dieting, the anxiety, and the perpetual scrimmaging with food that lead to illness. "What causes the most damage is not the actual weight itself, but the fear of weight." People who drive their weights down and up through a series of diets are those most likely to become fatter and unhappier than before, for they upset the natural equilibrium of their bodies. In self-defense, their bodies stockpile fat whenever and wherever possible, hedging as they may against the next (self-imposed) privation. Meanwhile hearts suffer through cycles of feast and famine, strained at each new feast, shocked at each new famine. "To fat, to starve—/Perchance to die of it! Ah, there's the rub." Pokeberry, dinitrophenol, rainbow pills, liquid protein—there is no end to death by dieting.*

4   And still the dieting goes on, as fat people are compromised and persecuted. Like other minorities, fat people are treated like children, given silly nicknames, considered socially and sexually immature. The "Diet Conscience," an electronic guardian, sneers when the refrigerator door

---

* Louis I. Dublin believed that he had demonstrated that weight-reducing decreased mortality: "Overweight shortens life," *MLIC* 32 (Oct 1951) 1–4, and idem, "Relation of obesity to longevity," *NEJM* 248 (1953) 971–74. But see Public Health Service, *Obesity and Health* (Washington, D.C., 1966) 59; George V. Mann, "Obesity, the national spook," *AJPH* 61 (1971) 1491–98; idem, "Influence of obesity on health," *NEJM* 291 (1974) 178–85, 226–32; and William Bennett and Joel Gurin, *The Dieter's Dilemma* (NY, 1982) 134–35.

On the absence of a causal relationship between fatness or overweight and increased mortality, see Ancel Keys et al., "Coronary heart disease: overweight and obesity as risk factors," *AIM* 77 (1972) 15–27; Tavia Gordon and William B. Kannel, "Obesity and cardiovascular disease: the Framingham study," *Clinics in Endocrinology and Metabolism* 5 (1976) 367–75; Susan C. Wooley et al., "Obesity and women—I. A closer look at the facts," *Women's Studies Int Q* 2 (1979) 74; Reubin Andres, "Effect of obesity on total mortality," *IJO* 4 (1980) 381–86; Kelly D. Brownell, "Obesity," *J of Consulting and Clinical Psych* 50 (1982) 820; and Carol Sternhill, "We'll always be fat, but fat can be fit," *Ms.* (May 1985) 142. On the dangers of a weight-loss/weight-gain cycle, see Vinne Young, *It's Fun to Be Fat* (NY, 1953) 10, 26 and quote on 23; Nick Lyons, *Locked Jaws* (NY, 1979) 13 quote; and Sharon G. Patton, "Why dieting can make you fat," *New Woman* (Aug 1984) 34.

On deaths from dieting, see Roland C. Curtin, "The heart and its danger in the treatment of obesity," *J of Balneology and Climatology* 12 (1908) 223 on pokeberry; Chapter Seven on dinitrophenol and amphetamines; House of Representatives Subcommittee on Health and the Environment, *Hearing ... on the Most Popular Diet in America Today, Liquid Protein, Dec 28, 1977* (Washington, D.C., 1978) 3–7; Centers for Disease Control, "Follow-up on deaths associated with liquid protein diets," *Morbidity and Mortality Weekly Report* 27 (1978) 223–24; Harold E. Sours et al., "Sudden death associated with very low calorie weight reduction regimens," *AJCN* 34 (1981) 453–61, and see also 1639–40, 2855–57.

is opened, "Are you eating again? Shame on you! No wonder you look the way you do! Ha! Ha! Ha! You'll be sorry, fatty. Do yourself a favor; *shut the door!*"*

5   Like other minorities, fat people are seen as throwbacks to a more primitive time. Neanderthals in museum dioramas are squat and fat; cannibals stirring pots are fat; Oriental despots are fat; harems are full of slothful fat women and supervised by fat eunuchs. The modern world is passing them by. Fat people are stuck in the past, so much so that modern businessmen and scientists prefer an employee who has been in jail or in a mental ward to one who is fat. Criminality and insanity seem less intransigent, less rooted, than obesity.**

6   If fat people are not such atavisms, why do they do so poorly in school and in business? The same vicious circle surrounding other minorities surrounds fat people, who have more difficulty getting into the best colleges and who are not promoted as quickly as their leaner rivals. How they look is more important than how well they do their jobs. The New York City Traffic Department in 1965 dismissed six meter maids for being overweight; National Airlines fired a stewardess for being 4 lbs overweight. As of 1982 only Michigan had a law specifically banning discrimination on account of weight. In 1980 a *New Yorker* cartoon depicted a judge sentencing a defendant: "It is the Court's opinion that, although innocent, you are dangerously overweight." This comedy had already been played out in Miami, where a woman being sentenced for a misdemeanor assault explained that at 315 lbs she was too heavy to work. The judge gave her three years' probation on the condition that she lose 65 lbs at 3 lbs per week; if she went off her diet, she would go to prison.[†]

7   Physicians are equally unsympathetic. They find fat patients distasteful. Fat people seem more difficult to examine, less likely to cooperate. Fat people are waddling reminders of the failure of medicine to come up with a safe, workable program for long-term weight reduction, just as poor people and homeless people are stark reminders of the failure of the

---

* Ann M. Lingg, "A plump girl talks back," *Amer Mercury* 78 (March 1954) 30, an early reference to minority status; Lew Louderback, "More people should be fat," *SEP* 240 (Nov 4, 1967) 10; Grosswirth, *Fat Pride*, 40; and Mildred Klingman, *Secret Lives of Fat People* (Boston, 1981) 72 on Diet Conscience. See also Lisa Schoenfielder and Barb Wieser, eds., *Shadow on a Tightrope: Writings by Women on Fat Oppression* (Iowa City, Ia., 1983).

** Robert J. Homant and Daniel B. Kennedy, "Attitudes toward ex-offenders: a comparison of social stigmas," *J of Criminal Justice* 10 (1982) 383–91.

† Peter L. Benson et al., "Social costs of obesity," *Social Behavior and Personality* 8 (1980) 91–96 on colleges; Llewellyn Louderback, *Fat Power* (NY, 1970) 47, 52, 53, 55; Chris Chase, *The Great American Waistline* (NY, 1981) 196 on stewardesses; *New Yorker* (Sept 29, 1980) 49; and "Better than prison," *Time* 97 (June 7, 1971) 39. Concerning weight discrimination at law, see David H. Tucker for the Maryland Commission on Human Relations, *Report on the Study of Weight and Size Discrimination*, typescript (Baltimore, 1980); Jane O. Baker, "The Rehabilitation Act of 1973: protection for victims of weight discrimination?" *UCLA Law R* 29 (April 1982) 947–71; David Berreby, "Is being fat a handicap? Courts differ," *National Law J* 4 (Aug 30, 1982) 3:1; Lynne Reaves, "Fat folks' rights: weight bias issues emerging," *Amer Bar Assoc J* 69 (1983) 878; and Lauren R. Reskin, "Employers must give obese job applicants a fat chance," *Amer Bar Assoc J* 71 (Sept 1985) 104.

economic system. Like politicians, physicians blame the victims. It is not the doctor's fault if fat people are weak, dishonest, lazy, and childish. All one can do with such people is to threaten them with disease and death, play on their fears. "If, knowing these dangers—as you now do—you continue to overeat, it must be obvious that you are acting in a childish fashion. You are immature. This *alone* will prove to you that you are acting *like a child* if you continue to be fat. Now it is up to you. . . . Be childish and die, or grow up and live!"*

8   Yet nearly half of all dieters get their dieting information from such patronizing doctors, doctors who until recently have had no specific training in nutrition. In 1970, three-quarters of doctors surveyed found obesity and overweight to be very frequent among their patients, yet few have pursued the study of obesity (bariatrics) in order to improve their courses of treatment. Nor have they been in particularly good shape themselves; the Scarsdale diet doctor Herman Tarnower was 15 lbs overweight according to his own charts. Physicians are no better than gamblers playing "statistical roulette with the lives of fat people," prescribing diet pills that affect blood pressure and kidneys, dictating diets that are subtle forms of sadism, calling for a "grim, dour self-punishment. If we submit we become miserable, if not actually neurotic."**

9   And then? "Then you are told that your frustrations, your worries, your inhibitions, and your insecurities turn into fat." Tranquilizers will not work; they make you fatter. You need psychological help. A woman in the 1950s was given the name of a psychiatrist because she was fat. She wrote to Dear Abby, "Now Abby, I am not *crazy,* I am just a little overweight. Have you ever heard of anything so insulting?" Abby thought a psychiatrist might do her a world of good, but Abby had no statistics to support such a claim, and there are none now. Psychiatrists are as inept with fat people as they are, still, with the schizophrenics whom they often use as a model for the obese. Perhaps because they are so inept, they demand much more of their fat patients. "Goddammit!" cried one fat woman at her psychiatrist, "You call *me* insatiable; you're the one who's never satisfied."†

---

* George L. Maddox et al., "Overweight as a problem of medical management in a public outpatient clinic," *AJMS* 252 (Oct 1966) 394–402; Hilde Bruch, *The Importance of Overweight* (NY, 1957) 318–24; Howard D. Kurland, "Obesity: an unfashionable problem," *Psychiatric Opinion* 7,6 (1970) 20–24; and Alfred J. Cantor, *How to Lose Weight the Doctor's Way* (NY, 1959) quote on 40.

** Ruth Adams, *Did You Ever See a Fat Squirrel?* (Emmaus, Pa., 1972) 197; Tillie Lewis Tasti Diet ad in *Supermarket News* (March 29, 1976) on "Where Do Diet Food Customers Get Their Information?"; Louis Harris and Associates, *Harris Survey Yearbook* (NY, 1971) 203, 213; Diana Trilling, *Mrs. Harris: The Death of the Scarsdale Diet Doctor* (NY, 1981) 85 and cf. Peter Wyden and Barbara Wyden, *How the Doctors Diet* (NY, 1968); interview with Dr. Frederick J. Stare, Sept 27, 1984, concerning physician education in nutrition; and Martin Lederman, *The Slim Gourmet* (NY, 1955) quote on 8.

† Vinne Young, "Don't get ill getting thin," *Science Digest* 36 (Aug 1954) 1 (quote); Abigail van Buren (= Pauline Phillips), *Dear Abby* (Englewood Cliffs, N.J., 1958) 121; Walter W. Hamburger, "Psychology of dietary change," *AJPH* 48 (1958) 1342–48; Robert M. Lindner, *The Fifty-Minute Hour* (NY, 1955) 133 (quote); Albert J. Stunkard and A. J. Rush, "Dieting and depression reexamined," *AIM* 81 (1974) 526–33; and Colleen S. W. Rand, "Treatment of obese patients in psychoanalysis," *Psychiatric Clinics of North Amer* 1 (1978) 661–72.

10   Society itself will not be satisfied until all fat people are gone. Aldebaran, a member of the Los Angeles Fat Underground, wrote an open letter to a doctor in 1977: "You see fat as suicide, I see weight-loss as murder—genocide, to be precise—the systematic murder of a biological minority by organized medicine." But not just by organized medicine. By society as a whole. In the United States, a fat person's prior identification is with fatness; as a status, fatness comes before religion, race, sexual preference, income, gender. Only in a society intent on doing away with fat people could fatness become so distinct and so negative a stigma. George Nathan Blomberg, fat hero of the 1978 novel by Mark Dintenfass, *The Case Against Org,* becomes defiant in the face of such genocide: "Listen, one must choose to be obese: it is an act of courage." Near the end he knows, "There is no skinny guy inside me struggling to get out. I am Org forever." And on the last page he imagines "I and the world and a chocolate cherry all melting together, becoming one and everything."*

The Fat Society: A Utopia

11 If the tables could be turned, if this were a fat society, a society that admired and rewarded fatness—a society that has never existed in this country for both sexes at the same time—things would be very much different and very much better. It would be like Servia, Indiana, in 1899, "A Town of Fat People," population 206, temperate, quiet, and affluent. Or like Roseto, Pennsylvania, in the 1960s, population 1,700, nearly all of the residents obese and hardly a heart murmur among them.**

12   In a fat society, dinners would be scrumptious, sociable, and warm. No Mixed Gelatinoids as hors d'oeuvres, no Strained Nitrogen Gumbo for the soup, no Grilled Proteids with Globulin Patties for the entrée, no Compôte of Assorted Vitamins for dessert. There would be 101 Things To Do With Cottage Cheese—use it as a facial, take it out on a leash for a walk, build a snowman—but no one would have to eat it.†

13   In a fat society, children would be fed and fed well when hungry. When they were fed, they would be satisfied, because there would be no snares laid around food. Feeding would be calm and loving, always sufficient, never forced. Children as they grew into adolescence would acquire no eating disorders, since fat people and thin people would be on equal terms and there would be none of that anxious dieting which so often starts off the career of an anorectic or bulimic. No one would be obsessed with food

---

* Aldebaran, "Fat liberation—a luxury?" *State and Mind* 5 (June–July 1977) 34; Stuart Byron, "The unmaking of a fattie," *Village Voice* (Dec 17, 1970) 10; and Mark Dintenfass, *The Case Against Org* (Boston, 1978) 5, 189, 246, quoted with permission from Little, Brown & Co.

** *NYDT* (Sept 3, 1899) illus, supp. 20:3; Louderback, *Fat Power,* 167.

† Irvin S. Cobb, *At His Best* (Garden City, N.Y., 1929) 244 on gelatinoids, and Totie Fields, *I Think I'll Start on Monday: The Official 8 1/2 Oz Mashed Potato Diet* (NY, 1972) 32 on cottage cheese. On conviviality and its suppression by dieters, see James A. Pike and Howard A. Johnson, *Man in the Middle* (Greenwich, Conn., 1956) 53; Robert Waithman, "Plea to the joyless eaters," *NYT Mag* (Feb 12, 1956) 19, 62; and Jean Kerr, *Please Don't Eat the Daisies* (NY, 1957) 172.

because all people would have the opportunity to be powerful and expressive beyond the dining table.*

14   In a fat society, fat people would dress expressively. Their fashions would no longer be called "oversize" or "halfsize," and they would have the same choice of fabrics and designs as everyone else. Not just pantyhose but all clothes would be "Just my Size." Full-size models would be featured in the salons of *haute couture;* full-size fiberglass mannequins would pose with others in the most elite shop-windows. Fat people would no longer need to buy their clothes at specialty shops like The Forgotten Woman and Catherine Stout, or discreetly through the mails from Lane Bryant, Roaman's, and King-Size. A fat woman could wear dramatic colors and horizontal stripes when the fancy struck; a fat man could indulge a secret desire to wear a large-checked light gray suit.**

15   A fat society would be forthright about the body beneath the clothes. It would be relaxed about bodily functions, assured about sensuality, confident with sexuality. Compulsive weighing would disappear; no longer would the scale (always described as a male) lord it over anyone's body. The prudery of weight-watching, the overzealous guardianship of the body, would vanish. Beauty and sexuality would be independent of pounds and of calipers. The fat person would be a "strikingly *unavoidable* creature," and neither the fat man nor the fat woman would be typed as nonsexual or sexually corrupt. "I am touchable," fat people would say to themselves, and they would think of their pounds as "voluptuous planes." Like Sarah Fay Cohen Campbell in the novel *Fat People* (1982), they would accept their bodies as loving instruments and learn to play them in an open tuning.†

16   Women in particular would wear their weight with new conviction. They would affirm their physiological gifts, their genetic and cultural tendencies to put on flesh, their extra layering of body fat. Fat women would not live in the future conditional, suspended between what they are and who they will be when they are finally thin. Fat women would not have to invent fantasy selves a quarter their bulk and four times as lovely. "I've earned my

---

* Cf. Margaret Atwood, *Lady Oracle* (NY, 1976) esp. 74, 321; Susan C. Wooley and Orland W. Wooley, "Should obesity be treated at all?" in *Eating and Its Disorders,* eds. A. J. Stunkard and E. Stellar (NY, 1984) 185–92.

** Margaret Dana, *Behind the Label* (Boston, 1938) 117–20; Marya Mannes, "Juno in limbo: the trauma of size 16," *Harper's Mag* (July 1964) 37–40; Grosswirth, *Fat Pride,* 69; Susie Orbach, *Fat Is a Feminist Issue* (NY, 1979) 90–91; Jean DuCoffe and Sherry Suib Cohen, *Making It Big* (NY, 1980) 12, 22, 25–31; Evelyn Roaman and Dee Ratterree, *The Evelyn Roaman Book: An Expert Shows You How Heavy Can Be Happy* (NY, 1980); Dale Godey, *Your Guide to Dressing Thin* (NY, 1981) 12–27; Ann Harper and Glenn Lewis, *The Big Beauty Book* (NY, 1982) 104; and William Johnston, "The fun of being a fat man," *Amer Mag* 94 (July 1922) 54–55.

† Lila Austin, "I'm fat, and I like it!" *GH* III (Sept 1940) 48; Nora S. Kinzer, *Put Down and Ripped Off* (NY, 1977) 34, 49–50; Marcia Millman, *Such a Pretty Face: Being Fat in America* (NY, 1980) 106, 162–63; Harper and Lewis, *Big Beauty Book,* quote on 3; DuCoffe and Cohen, *Making It Big,* 258 (quote), 260–63; David Newman and Robert Benton, "Fat power," *Esquire* 66 (Dec 1966) 212–15 on visual grandeur of fat men; Carol S. Smith, *Fat People* (NY, 1978); and see "Fatso" film (20th-Century Fox, 1980).

wrinkles and padding," women would say with Ruthanne Olds. "They represent a lot of rewarding life experience." So everyone would at last welcome back the Earth Mother, the Venus of Willendorf, the female colossus, the grand diva, "La Stupenda," and divinity would once more be nurturant rather than vindictive.*

17   A fat society would be a comforting society, less harried, more caring. It would favor the gourmet over the glutton, slow food over fast food, matriarchy and communal affection over patriarchy and self-hate, eroticism over pornography, philanthropy and art over greed and blind technology. It would mean therefore an end to narcotics and narcissism. In a fat society, there would be no "flight from feelings," no need to resort to a form of privacy that kills as it protects. No one would have such stingy personal boundaries that the self would seem always under siege. Mirrors would neither frighten nor enchant. There would be more to the person than a mercurial reflection from shopwindows. "Sizing up" a person would be a wonderfully complex experience; tape measures and scales would have nothing to do with it.†

18   A fat society would be less harshly competitive, less devouring. People could be assertive without seeming aggressive or threatening. There would be no cannibalism, no fear of swallowing or being swallowed up. Accepting one's own bulk, one need not consume others or gnaw at one's self. Dieting is cannibalism. Dieters eat off their own bodies: "You start to get thin when you begin to *live on your own fat.*" Dieters are encouraged to be cannibals: "If your body-republic doesn't get enough food to support all the citizens, some will die and be cannibalized to feed the others. . . . In this body-politic of cell-citizens, you can fool all of the people all of the time, and if you want to *get* thin and *stay* thin, that's what you must do." Dieters have no recourse but to be cannibals: "To reduce weight, an obese person must burn his own body fat. It's as simple as that. He must eat himself up! A bit cannibalistic? I'm afraid so. But it's the only way to lose weight." That legendary diet drug which was nothing but a live tapeworm was the folkloric representation of such cannibalism. In a fat society, no one would be eaten up from within and no one would be eaten alive. Fat people, weighted, solid, would not fear the desires of others or their own desires. If fat people now lie or steal or hide, that is because they are always trying to save

---

* Charlotte C. Rowett, "Success, avoirdupois, and clothes," *Woman Beautiful* 4 (June 1910) 40–41; DuCoffe and Cohen, *Making It Big,* 334; Anne Scott Beller, *Fat and Thin* (NY, 1977) esp. ch. 7; Kim Chernin, *The Obsession: Reflections on the Tyranny of Slenderness* (NY, 1981) esp. 133, 139; Jean Stafford, "The echo and the nemesis," *Children Are Bored on Sunday* (NY, 1953) 10–39, a fantasy self; Ruthanne Olds, *Big and Beautiful: Overcoming Fat Phobia* (Washington, D.C., 1982) 13; Stella J. Reichman, *Great Big Beautiful Doll* (NY, 1977) 26–28; and Marion Woodman, *The Owl Was a Baker's Daughter* (Toronto, 1980) 10, 18.

† See Donald B. Meyer, *The Positive Thinkers* (Garden City, N.Y., 1965) 120 on the "flight from feelings"; Véronique Nahoum, "La belle femme ou le stade du miroir en histoire," *Communications* 31 (1979) 22–32 on mirrors; and Susan Griffin, *Pornography and Silence* (NY, 1981) esp. 60–62.

face ("such a pretty face") and disguise their needs. They must act sur-
reptitiously, with the night and the bathroom as their refuge. In a fat
society, no one would be forced to such humiliating secrecy. All hunger
would be honest hunger.*

The Man Who Couldn't Stop Eating
Atul Gawande

*Atul Gawande tells the story of Vincent Caselli, who underwent a gastric bypass to lose
weight by surgically reducing the size of his stomach, thus making him physically unable to
eat and absorb the nutrients from more than an ounce of food at a sitting. The statistics on
the gastric-bypass procedure, the last resort of people who cannot shed weight in other
ways, confirm the sharp rise of obesity in this country. According to the American Society
for Bariatric Surgery, in 1992 surgeons performed 16,200 of the procedures. In 2002, the
number jumped to 63,100 and one year later to 103,200. Gawande, who assisted on the
surgery, calls this "among the strangest operations surgeons perform" in that it "is intended
to control a person's will—to manipulate his innards so that he does not overeat." Those
who, like Caselli, are morbidly obese and whose weight profoundly reduces their quality
of life are turning to the gastric bypass more frequently. Gawande, a surgical resident and
also a staff writer for the* New Yorker, *uses the story of Caselli to "contemplate the human
appetite." As such, he provides a fitting and compelling end to the selections in this chapter on obesity. The essay appeared originally in the 9 July 2001 issue of the* New Yorker.
Gawande is the author of Complications: A Surgeon's Notes on an Imperfect Science
(Picador, 2002).

1   At 7:30 A.M. on September 13, 1999, an anesthesiologist and two orderlies
rolled our patient, whom I will call Vincent Caselli, into the operating room,
where his attending surgeon and I awaited him. Caselli was a short man
of middle age—five feet seven, fifty-four years old. The son of Italian immigrants, he had worked as a heavy-machine operator and road-construction
contractor. (He and his men had paved a rotary in my own neighborhood.)
He had been married for thirty-five years; he and his wife had three girls,
all grown now. And he weighed four hundred and twenty-eight pounds.
Housebound, his health failing, he no longer had anything resembling a
normal life. And so, although he was afraid of surgery, he had come for a
Roux-en-Y gastric-bypass operation. It is the most drastic treatment we
have for obesity. It is also among the strangest operations surgeons perform.

---

* Nina W. Putnam, *Tomorrow We Diet* (NY, 1922) 89; Phillip W. Haberman, Jr., "How to diet if you
have no character at all," *Vogue* 135 (June 1960) 148; and Thyra S. Winslow, *Think Yourself Thin*
(NY, 1951) 113. On tapeworms, Ronald L. Baker, *Hoosier Folk Legends* (Bloomington, Ind., 1982)
226, and Jane Fonda, *Workout Book* (NY, 1981) 10.

It removes no disease, repairs no defect or injury. It is an operation that is intended to control a person's will—to manipulate his innards so that he does not overeat—and it is soaring in popularity. Some forty-five thousand patients underwent obesity surgery in 1999, and the number is expected to double by 2003.

2   For the very obese, general anesthesia alone is a dangerous undertaking; major abdominal surgery can easily become a disaster. Obesity substantially increases the risk of respiratory failure, heart attacks, wound infections, hernias—almost every complication possible, including death. Nevertheless, Dr. Sheldon Randall, the attending surgeon, was relaxed, having done more than a thousand of these operations. I, the assisting resident, remained anxious. Watching Caselli struggle to shift himself from the stretcher onto the operating table and then stop halfway to catch his breath, I was afraid that he would fall in between. Once he was on the table, his haunches rolled off the sides, and I double-checked the padding that protected him from the table's sharp edges. He was naked except for his "universal"–size johnny, which covered him like a napkin, and a nurse put a blanket over his lower body for the sake of modesty. When we tried to lay him down, he lost his breath and started to turn blue, and the anesthesiologist had to put him to sleep sitting up. Only with the breathing tube and a mechanical ventilator in place were we able to lay him flat.

3   He was a mountain on the table. I am six feet two, but even with the table as low as it goes I had to stand on a step stool; Dr. Randall stood on two stools stacked together. He nodded to me, and I cut down the middle of our patient's belly, through skin and then dense inches of glistening yellow fat, and we opened the abdomen. Inside, his liver was streaked with fat, too, and his bowel was covered by a thick apron of it, but his stomach looked ordinary—a smooth, grayish-pink bag the size of two fists. We put metal retractors in place to hold the wound open and keep the liver and the slithering loops of bowel out of the way. Working elbow deep, we stapled his stomach down to the size of an ounce. Before the operation, it could accommodate a quart of food and drink; now it would hold no more than a shot glass. We then sewed the opening of this little pouch to a portion of bowel two feet past his duodenum—past the initial portion of the small bowel, where bile and pancreatic juices break food down. This was the bypass part of the operation, and it meant that what food the stomach could accommodate would be less readily absorbed.

4   The operation took us a little over two hours. Caselli was stable throughout, but his recovery was difficult. Patients are usually ready to go home three days after surgery; it was two days before Caselli even knew where he was. His kidneys failed for twenty-four hours, and fluid built up in his lungs. He became delirious, seeing things on the walls, pulling off his oxygen mask, his chest leads for the monitors, even yanking out the I.V. We were worried, and his wife and daughters were terrified, but gradually he pulled through.

5   By the third day after surgery, he was well enough to take sips of clear liquids (water, apple juice, ginger ale), up to one ounce every four hours.

On my afternoon rounds, I asked him how he'd done. "O.K.," he said. We began giving him four-ounce servings of Carnation Instant Breakfast for protein and modest calories. He could finish only half, and that took him an hour. It filled him up and, when it did, he felt a sharp, unpleasant pain. This was to be expected, Dr. Randall told him. It would be a few days before he was ready for solid food. But he was doing well. He no longer needed I. V. fluids. And, after he'd had a short stay in a rehabilitation facility, we sent him home.

6   A couple of weeks later, I asked Dr. Randall how Caselli was getting on. "Just fine," the surgeon said. Although I had done a few of these cases with him, I had not seen how the patients progressed afterward. Would he really lose all that weight? I asked. And how much could he eat? Randall suggested that I see Caselli for myself. So one day that October, I gave him a call, and he invited me to stop by.

7   Vincent Caselli and his wife live in an unassuming saltbox house not far outside Boston. To get there, I took Route 1, past four Dunkin' Donuts, four pizzerias, three steak houses, two McDonald's, two Ground Rounds, a Taco Bell, a Friendly's, and an International House of Pancakes. (A familiar road-side vista, but that day it seemed a sad tour of our self-destructiveness.) I rang the doorbell, and a long minute passed. I heard a slow footfall coming toward the door, and Caselli, visibly winded, opened it. But he smiled broadly when he saw me and gave my hand a warm squeeze. He led me—his hand on table, wall, doorjamb for support—to a seat at a breakfast table in his flowered-wallpaper kitchen.

8   I asked him how things were going. "Real good," he said. He had no more pain from the operation, the incision had healed, and, though it had been only three weeks, he'd already lost forty pounds. But, at three hundred and ninety, and still stretching his size-64 slacks and size-XXXXXXL T-shirts (the largest he could find at the local big-and-tall store), he did not yet feel different. Sitting, he had to keep his legs apart to let his abdomen sag between them, and the weight of his body on the wooden chair forced him to shift every minute or two because his buttocks would fall asleep. Sweat rimmed the folds of his forehead and made his thin salt-and-pepper hair stick to his pate. His brown eyes were rheumy, above dark bags. He breathed with a disconcerting wheeze.

9   We talked about his arrival home from the hospital. The first solid food he had tried was a spoonful of scrambled eggs. Just that much, he said, made him so full it hurt, "like something was ripping," and he threw it up. He was afraid that nothing solid would ever go down. But he gradually found that he could tolerate small amounts of soft foods—mashed potatoes, macaroni, even chicken if it was finely chopped and moist. Breads and dry meats, he found, got "stuck," and he'd have to put a finger down his throat and make himself vomit.

10   Caselli's battle with obesity, he explained, began in his late twenties. "I always had some weight on me," he said—he was two hundred pounds at nineteen, when he married Teresa (as I'll call her), and a decade later he reached three hundred. He would diet and lose seventy-five pounds, then

put a hundred back on. By 1985, he weighed four hundred pounds. On one diet, he got down to a hundred and ninety, but he gained it all back. "I must have gained and lost a thousand pounds," he told me. He developed high blood pressure, high cholesterol, and diabetes. His knees and his back ached all the time, and he had limited mobility. He used to get season tickets to Boston Bruins games, and go out regularly to the track at Seekonk every summer to see the auto racing. Years ago, he drove in races himself. Now he could barely walk to his pickup truck. He hadn't been on an airplane since 1983, and it had been two years since he had been to the second floor of his own house, because he couldn't negotiate the stairs. "Teresa bought a computer a year ago for her office upstairs, and I've never seen it," he told me. He had to move out of their bedroom, upstairs, to a small room off the kitchen. Unable to lie down, he had slept in a recliner ever since. Even so, he could doze only in snatches, because of sleep apnea, which is a common syndrome among the obese and is thought to be related to excessive fat in the tongue and in the soft tissues of the upper airway. Every thirty minutes, his breathing would stop, and he'd wake up asphyxiating. He was perpetually exhausted.

11   There were other troubles, too, the kind that few people speak about. Good hygiene, he said, was nearly impossible. He could no longer stand up to urinate, and after moving his bowels he often had to shower in order to get clean. Skin folds would become chafed and red, and sometimes develop boils and infections. And, he reported, "Sex life is nonexistent. I have real hopes for it." For him, though, the worst part was his diminishing ability to earn a livelihood.

12   Vincent Caselli's father had come to Boston from Italy in 1914 to work in construction, and he soon established his own firm. In 1979, Vincent went into business for himself. He was skilled at operating heavy equipment—his specialty was running a Gradall, a thirty-ton, three-hundred-thousand-dollar hydraulic excavator—and he employed a team of men year-round to build roads and sidewalks. Eventually, he owned his own Gradall, a ten-wheel Mack dump truck, a backhoe, and a fleet of pickup trucks. But in the past three years he had become too big to operate the Gradall or keep up with the daily maintenance of the equipment. He had to run the business from his house, and pay others to do the heavy work; he enlisted a nephew to help manage the men and the contracts. Expenses rose, and since he could no longer go around to city halls himself, he found contracts harder to get. If Teresa hadn't had a job—she is the business manager for an assisted-living facility in Boston—they would have gone bankrupt.

13   Teresa, a freckled redhead, had been pushing him for a long time to diet and exercise. He, too, wanted desperately to lose weight, but the task of controlling himself, day to day, meal to meal, seemed beyond him. "I'm a man of habits," he told me. "I'm very prone to habits." And eating, he said, was his worst habit. But, then, eating is everyone's habit. What was different about *his* habit? I asked. Well, the portions he took were too big, and he could never leave a crumb on his plate. If there was pasta left in the pot, he'd eat that, too. But why, I wanted to know. Was it that he just loved

food? He pondered this question for a moment. It wasn't love, he decided. "Eating felt good instantaneously," he said, "but it only felt good instantaneously." Was it excessive hunger that drove him? "I was never hungry," he said.

14   As far as I could tell, Caselli ate for the same reasons that everyone eats: because food tasted good, because it was seven o'clock and time for dinner, because a nice meal had been set out on the table. And he stopped eating for the same reason everyone stops: because he was full and eating was no longer pleasurable. The main difference seemed to be that it took an unusual quantity of food to make him full. (He could eat a large pizza as if it were a canapé.) To lose weight, he faced the same difficult task that every dieter faces—to stop eating before he felt full, while the food still tasted good, and to exercise. These were things that he could do for a little while, and, with some reminding and coaching, for perhaps a bit longer, but they were not, he had found, things that he could do for long. "I am not strong," he said.

15   In the spring of 1999, Caselli developed serious infections in both legs: as his weight increased, and varicosities appeared, the skin thinned and broke down, producing open, purulent ulcers. Despite fevers and searing pain, it was only after persistent coaxing from his wife that he finally agreed to see his doctor. The doctor diagnosed a serious case of cellulitis, and he spent a week in the hospital receiving intravenous antibiotics.

16   At the hospital, he was given an ultrasound scan to check whether blood clots had formed in the deep veins of his legs. A radiologist came to give him the results. Caselli recounted the conversation to me. "He says, 'You don't have blood clots, and I'm really surprised. A guy like you, in the situation you're in, the odds are you're gonna have blood clots. That tells me you're a pretty healthy guy'"—but only, he went on, if Caselli did something about his weight. A little later, the infectious-disease specialist came by to inspect his wounds. "I'm going to tell you something," Caselli recalls the man saying. "I've been reading your whole file—where you were, what you were, how you were. You take that weight off—and I'm not telling you this to bust your ass—you take that weight off and you're a very healthy guy. Your heart is good. Your lungs are good. You're strong."

17   "I took that seriously," Caselli said. "You know, there are two different doctors telling me this. They don't know me other than what they're reading from their records. They had no reason to tell me this. But they knew the weight was a problem. And if I could get it down somewhere near reality . . ."

18   When he got home, he remained sick in bed for another two weeks. Meanwhile, his business collapsed. Contracts stopped coming in entirely, and he knew that when his men finished the existing jobs he would have to let them go. Months before, his internist had suggested that he consider surgery and he had dismissed the notion. But he didn't now. He went to see Dr. Randall, who spoke with him frankly about the risks involved. There was a one-in-two-hundred chance of death and a one-in-ten chance of a significant complication, such as bleeding, infection, gastric ulceration,

blood clots, or leakage into the abdomen. The doctor also told him that it would change how he ate forever. Unable to work, humiliated, ill, and in pain, Vincent Caselli decided that surgery was his only hope.

19   It is hard to contemplate the human appetite without wondering if we have any say over our lives at all. We believe in will—in the notion that we have a choice over such simple matters as whether to sit still or stand up, to talk or not talk, to have a slice of pie or not. Yet very few people, whether heavy or slim, can voluntarily reduce their weight for long. The history of weight-loss treatment is one of nearly unremitting failure. Whatever the regimen—liquid diets, high-protein diets, or grapefruit diets, the Zone, Atkins, or Dean Ornish diet—people lose weight quite readily, but they do not keep it off. A 1993 National Institutes of Health expert panel reviewed decades of diet studies and found that between ninety and ninety-five per cent of people regained one-third to two-thirds of any weight lost within a year—and all of it within five years. Doctors have wired patients' jaws closed, inflated plastic balloons inside their stomachs, performed massive excisions of body fat, prescribed amphetamines and large amounts of thyroid hormone, even performed neurosurgery to destroy the hunger centers in the brain's hypothalamus—and still people do not keep the weight off. Jaw wiring, for example, can produce substantial weight loss, and patients who ask for the procedure are highly motivated; yet some still take in enough liquid calories through their closed jaws to gain weight, and the others regain it once the wires are removed. We are a species that has evolved to survive starvation, not to resist abundance.

20   Children are the surprising exception to this history of failure. Nobody would argue that children have more self-control than adults; yet in four randomized studies of obese children between the ages of six and twelve, those who received simple behavioral teaching (weekly lessons for eight to twelve weeks, followed by monthly meetings for up to a year) ended up markedly less over-weight ten years later than those who didn't; thirty per-cent were no longer obese. Apparently, children's appetites are malleable. Those of adults are not.

21   There are at least two ways that humans can eat more than they ought to at a sitting. One is by eating slowly but steadily for far too long. This is what people with Prader-Willi syndrome do. Afflicted with a rare inherited dysfunction of the hypothalamus, they are incapable of experiencing satiety. And though they eat only half as quickly as most people, they do not stop. Unless their access to food is strictly controlled (some will eat garbage or pet food if they find nothing else), they become mortally obese.

22   The more common pattern, however, relies on rapid intake. Human beings are subject to what scientists call a "fat paradox." When food enters your stomach and duodenum (the upper portion of the small intestine), it triggers stretch receptors, protein receptors, and fat receptors that signal the hypothalamus to induce satiety. Nothing stimulates the reaction more quickly than fat. Even a small amount, once it reaches the duodenum, will cause a person to stop eating. Still we eat too much fat.

How can this be? It turns out that foods can trigger receptors in the mouth which get the hypothalamus to *accelerate* our intake—and, again, the most potent stimulant is fat. A little bit on the tongue, and the receptors push us to eat fast, before the gut signals shut us down. The tastier the food, the faster we eat—a phenomenon called "the appetizer effect." (This is accomplished, in case you were wondering, not by chewing faster but by chewing less. French researchers have discovered that, in order to eat more and eat it faster, people shorten their "chewing time"—they take fewer "chews per standard food unit" before swallowing. In other words, we gulp.)

23   Apparently, how heavy one becomes is determined, in part, by how the hypothalamus and the brain stem adjudicate the conflicting signals from the mouth and the gut. Some people feel full quite early in a meal; others, like Vincent Caselli, experience the appetizer effect for much longer. In the past several years, much has been discovered about the mechanisms of this control. We now know, for instance, that hormones, like leptin and neuropeptide Y, rise and fall with fat levels and adjust the appetite accordingly. But our knowledge of these mechanisms is still crude at best.

24   Consider a 1998 report concerning two men, "BR" and "RH," who suffered from profound amnesia. Like the protagonist in the movie *Memento,* they could carry on a coherent conversation with you, but, once they had been distracted, they recalled nothing from as recently as a minute before, not even that they were talking to you. (BR had had a bout of viral encephalitis; RH had had a severe seizure disorder for twenty years.) Paul Rozin, a professor of psychology at the University of Pennsylvania, thought of using them in an experiment that would explore the relationship between memory and eating. On three consecutive days, he and his team brought each subject his typical lunch (BR got meat loaf, barley soup, tomatoes, potatoes, beans, bread, butter, peaches, and tea; RH got veal parmigiana with pasta, string beans, juice, and apple crumb cake). Each day, BR ate all his lunch, and RH could not quite finish. Their plates were then taken away. Ten to thirty minutes later, the researchers would reappear with the same meal. "Here's lunch," they would announce. The men ate just as much as before. Another ten to thirty minutes later, the researchers again appeared with the same meal. "Here's lunch," they would say, and again the men would eat. On a couple of occasions, the researchers even offered RH a fourth lunch. Only then did he decline, saying that his "stomach was a little tight." Stomach stretch receptors weren't completely ineffectual. Yet, in the absence of a memory of having eaten, social context alone—someone walking in with lunch—was enough to re-create appetite.

25   You can imagine forces in the brain vying to make you feel hungry or full. You have mouth receptors, smell receptors, visions of tiramisu pushing one way and gut receptors another. You have leptins and neuropeptides saying you have either too much fat stored or too little. And you have your own social and personal sense of whether eating more is a good idea. If one mechanism is thrown out of whack, there's trouble.

26   Given the complexity of appetite and our imperfect understanding of it, we shouldn't be surprised that appetite-altering drugs have had only meager success in making people eat less. (The drug combination of fenfluramine and phentermine, or "fen-phen," had the most success, but it was linked to heart-valve abnormalities and was withdrawn from the market.) University researchers and pharmaceutical companies are searching intensively for a drug that will effectively treat serious obesity. So far, no such drug exists. Nonetheless, one treatment has been found to be effective, and, oddly enough, it turns out to be an operation.

27   At my hospital, there is a recovery-room nurse who is forty-eight years old and just over five feet tall, with boyish sandy hair and an almost athletic physique. Over coffee one day at the hospital café, not long after my visit with Vincent Caselli, she revealed that she once weighed more than two hundred and fifty pounds. Carla (as I'll call her) explained that she had had gastric-bypass surgery some fifteen years ago.

28   She had been obese since she was five years old. She started going on diets and taking diet pills—laxatives, diuretics, amphetamines—in junior high school. "It was never a problem losing weight," she said. "It was a problem keeping it off." She remembers how upset she was when, on a trip with friends to Disneyland, she found that she couldn't fit through the entrance turnstile. At the age of thirty-three, she reached two hundred and sixty-five pounds. One day, accompanying her partner, a physician, to a New Orleans medical convention, she found that she was too short of breath to walk down Bourbon Street. For the first time, she said, "I became fearful for my life—not just the quality of it but the longevity of it."

29   This was 1985. Doctors were experimenting with radical obesity surgery, but there was dwindling enthusiasm for it. Two operations had held considerable promise. One, known as jejunoileal bypass—in which nearly all the small intestine was bypassed, so that only a minimum amount of food could be absorbed—was killing people. The other, stomach stapling, was proving not to be very effective over time; people tended to adapt to the tiny stomach, eating densely caloric foods more and more frequently.

30   Working in the hospital, however, Carla heard encouraging reports about the gastric-bypass operation—stomach stapling plus a rerouting of the intestine so that food bypassed only the duodenum. She knew that the data about its success was still sketchy, that other operations had failed, but in May of 1986, after a year of thinking about it, she had the surgery.

31   "For the first time in my life, I experienced fullness," she told me. Six months after the operation, she was down to a hundred and eighty-five pounds. Six months after that, she weighed a hundred and thirty pounds. She lost so much weight that she had to have surgery to remove the aprons of skin that hung from her belly and thighs down to her knees. She was unrecognizable to anyone who had known her before, and even to herself. "I went to bars to see if I could get picked up—and I did," she said. "I always said no," she quickly added, laughing. "But I did it anyway."

32   The changes weren't just physical, though. She said she felt a profound and unfamiliar sense of will power. She no longer *had* to eat anything:

"Whenever I eat, somewhere in the course of that time I end up asking myself, 'Is this good for you? Are you going to put on weight if you eat too much of this?' And I can just stop." She knew, intellectually, that the surgery was why she no longer ate as much as she used to. Yet she felt as if she were choosing not to do it.

33   Studies report this to be a typical experience of a successful gastric-bypass patient. "I do get hungry, but I tend to think about it more," another woman who had had the operation told me, and she described an internal dialogue very much like Carla's: "I ask myself, 'Do I really need this?' I watch myself." For many, this feeling of control extends beyond eating. They become more confident, even assertive—sometimes to the point of conflict. Divorce rates, for example, have been found to increase significantly after the surgery. Indeed, a few months after her operation, Carla and her partner broke up.

34   Carla's dramatic weight loss has proved to be no aberration. Published case series now show that most patients undergoing gastric bypass lose at least two-thirds of their excess weight (generally more than a hundred pounds) within a year. They keep it off, too: ten-year follow-up studies find an average regain of only ten to twenty pounds. And the health benefits are striking: patients are less likely to have heart failure, asthma, or arthritis; eighty percent of those with diabetes are completely cured of it.

35   I stopped in to see Vincent Caselli one morning in January of 2000, about four months after his operation. He didn't quite spring to the door, but he wasn't winded this time. The bags under his eyes had shrunk. His face was more defined. Although his midriff was vast, it seemed smaller, less of a sack.

36   He told me that he weighed three hundred and forty-eight pounds—still far too much for a man who was only five feet seven inches tall, but ninety pounds less than he weighed on the operating table. And it had already made a difference in his life. Back in October, he told me, he missed his youngest daughter's wedding because he couldn't manage the walking required to get to the church. But by December he had lost enough weight to resume going to his East Dedham garage every morning. "Yesterday, I unloaded three tires off the truck," he said. "For me to do that three months ago? There's no way." He had climbed the stairs of his house for the first time since 1997. "One day around Christmastime, I say to myself, 'Let me try this. I gotta try this.' I went very slow, one foot at a time." The second floor was nearly unrecognizable to him. The bathroom had been renovated since he last saw it, and Teresa had, naturally, taken over the bedroom, including the closets. He would move back up eventually, he said, though it might be a while. He still had to sleep sitting up in a recliner, but he was sleeping in four-hour stretches now—"Thank God," he said. His diabetes was gone. And although he was still unable to stand up longer than twenty minutes, his leg ulcers were gone, too. He lifted his pants legs to show me. I noticed that he was wearing regular Red Wing work boots—in the past, he had to cut slits along the sides of his shoes in order to fit into them.

37   "I've got to lose at least another hundred pounds," he said. He wanted to be able to work, pick up his grandchildren, buy clothes off the rack at Filenes, go places without having to ask himself, "Are there stairs? Will I fit in the seats? Will I run out of breath?" He was still eating like a bird. The previous day, he'd had nothing all morning, a morsel of chicken with some cooked carrots and a small roast potato for lunch, and for dinner one fried shrimp, one teriyaki chicken strip, and two forkfuls of chicken-and-vegetable lo mein from a Chinese restaurant. He was starting up the business again, and, he told me, he'd gone out for a business lunch one day recently. It was at a new restaurant in Hyde Park—"beautiful"—and he couldn't help ordering a giant burger and a plate of fries. Just two bites into the burger, though, he had to stop. "One of the fellas says to me, 'Is that all you're going to eat?' And I say, 'I can't eat any more.' 'Really?' I say, 'Yeah, I can't eat any more. That's the truth.'"

38   I noticed, however, that the way he spoke about eating was not the way Carla had spoken. He did not speak of stopping because he wanted to. He spoke of stopping because he had to. You want to eat more, he explained, but "you start to get that feeling in your insides that one more bite is going to push you over the top." Still, he often took that bite. Overcome by waves of nausea, pain, and bloating—the so-called dumping syndrome—he'd have to vomit. If there were a way to eat more, he would. This scared him, he admitted. "It's not right," he said.

39   Three months later, in April, Caselli invited me and my son to stop by his garage in East Dedham. My son was four years old and, as Vince remembered my once saying, fascinated with all things mechanical. The garage was huge, cavernous, with a two-story rollup door and metal walls painted yellow. There, in the shadows, was Vince's beloved Gradall, a handsome tank of a machine, as wide as a county road, painted yield-sign yellow, with shiny black tires that came up to my chest and his company name emblazoned in curlicue script along its flanks. On the chassis, six feet off the ground, was a glass-enclosed control cab and a thirty-foot telescoping boom, mounted on a three-hundred-and-sixty-degree swivel. Vince and a friend of his, a fellow heavy-equipment contractor I'll call Danny, were sitting on metal folding chairs in a sliver of sunlight, puffing fat Honduran cigars, silently enjoying the day. They both rose to greet us. Vince introduced me as "one of the doctors who did my stomach operation."

40   I let my son go off to explore the equipment and asked Vince how his business was going. Not well, he said. Except for a few jobs in late winter plowing snow for the city in his pickup truck, he had brought in no income since the previous August. He'd had to sell two of his three pickup trucks, his Mack dump truck, and most of the small equipment for road building. Danny came to his defense. "Well, he's been out of action," he said. "And you see we're just coming into the summer season. It's a seasonal business." But we all knew that wasn't the issue.

41   Vince told me that he weighed about three hundred and twenty pounds. This was about thirty pounds less than when I had last seen him, and he was proud of that. "He don't eat," Danny said. "He eats half of what I eat."

But Vince was still unable to climb up into the Gradall and operate it. And he was beginning to wonder whether that would ever change. The rate of weight loss was slowing down, and he noticed that he was able to eat more. Before, he could eat only a couple of bites of a burger, but now he could sometimes eat half of one. And he still found himself eating more than he could handle. "Last week, Danny and this other fellow, we had to do some business," he said. "We had Chinese food. Lots of days, I don't eat the right stuff—I try to do what I can do, but I ate a little bit too much. I had to bring Danny back to Boston College, and before I left the parking lot there I just couldn't take it anymore. I had to vomit.

42   "I'm finding that I'm getting back into that pattern where I've always got to eat," he went on. His gut still stopped him, but he was worried. What if one day it didn't? He had heard about people whose staples gave way, returning their stomach to its original size, or who managed to put the weight back on in some other way.

43   I tried to reassure him. I told him what I knew Dr. Randall had already told him during a recent appointment: that a small increase in the capacity of his stomach pouch was to be expected, and that what he was experiencing seemed normal. But could something worse happen? I didn't want to say.

44   Among the gastric-bypass patients I had talked with was a man whose story remains a warning and a mystery to me. He was forty-two years old, married, and had two daughters, both of whom were single mothers with babies and still lived at home, and he had been the senior computer-systems manager for a large local company. At the age of thirty-eight, he had had to retire and go on disability because his weight—which had been above three hundred pounds since high school—had increased to more than four hundred and fifty pounds and was causing unmanageable back pain. He was soon confined to his home. He could not walk half a block. He could stand for only brief periods. He went out, on average, once a week, usually for medical appointments. In December, 1998, he had a gastric bypass. By June of the following year, he had lost a hundred pounds.

45   Then, as he put it, "I started eating again." Pizzas. Boxes of sugar cookies. Packages of doughnuts. He found it hard to say how, exactly. His stomach was still tiny and admitted only a small amount of food at a time, and he experienced the severe nausea and pain that gastric-bypass patients get whenever they eat sweet or rich things. Yet his drive was stronger than ever. "I'd eat right through pain—even to the point of throwing up," he told me. "If I threw up, it was just room for more. I would eat straight through the day." He did not pass a waking hour without eating something. "I'd just shut the bedroom door. The kids would be screaming. The babes would be crying. My wife would be at work. And I would be eating." His weight returned to four hundred and fifty pounds, and then more. The surgery had failed. And his life had been shrunk to the needs of pure appetite.

46   He is among the five to twenty percent of patients—the published reports conflict on the exact number—who regain weight despite gastric-bypass surgery. (When we spoke, he had recently submitted to another, more radical gastric bypass, in the desperate hope that something would work.) In these failures, one begins to grasp the power that one is up against. An operation that makes overeating both extremely difficult and extremely unpleasant—which, for more than eighty percent of patients, is finally sufficient to cause appetite to surrender and be transformed—can sometimes be defeated after all. Studies have yet to uncover a single consistent risk factor for this outcome. It could, apparently, happen to anyone.

47   It was a long time before I saw Vince Caselli again. Earlier this year, I called him to ask about getting together, and he suggested that we go out to see a Boston Bruins game. A few days later, he picked me up at the hospital in his rumbling Dodge Ram. For the first time, he looked almost small in the outsized truck. He was down to about two hundred and fifty pounds. "I'm still no Gregory Peck," he said, but he was now one of the crowd—chubby, in an ordinary way. The rolls beneath his chin were gone. His face had a shape. His middle no longer rested between his legs. And, almost a year and a half after the surgery, he was still losing weight. At the FleetCenter, where the Bruins play, he walked up the escalator without getting winded. Our tickets were taken at the gate—the Bruins were playing the Pittsburgh Penguins—and we walked through the turnstiles. Suddenly, he stopped and said, "Look at that. I went right through, no problem. I never would have made it through there before." It was the first time he'd gone to an event like this in years.

48   We took our seats about two dozen rows up from the ice, and he laughed a little about how easily he fit. The seats were as tight as coach class, but he was quite comfortable. (I, with my long legs, was the one who had trouble finding room.) Vince was right at home here. He had been a hockey fan his whole life, and could supply me with all the details: the Penguins' goalie Garth Snow was a local boy from Wrentham and a friend of one of Vince's cousins; Joe Thornton and Jason Allison were the Bruins' best forwards, but neither could hold a candle to the Penguins' Mario Lemieux. There were nearly twenty thousand people at the game, but within ten minutes Vince had found a friend from his barbershop sitting just a few rows away.

49   The Bruins won, and we left cheered and buzzing. Afterward, we went out to dinner at a grill near the hospital. Vince told me that his business was finally up and running. He could operate the Gradall without difficulty, and he'd had full-time Gradall work for the past three months. He was even thinking of buying a new model. At home, he had moved back upstairs. He and Teresa had taken a vacation in the Adirondacks; they were going out evenings, and visiting their grandchildren.

50   I asked him what had changed since I saw him the previous spring. He could not say precisely, but he gave me an example. "I used to love Italian cookies, and I still do," he said. A year ago, he would have eaten to the

point of nausea. "But now they're, I don't know, they're too sweet. I eat one now, and after one or two bites I just don't want it." It was the same with pasta, which had always been a problem for him. "Now I can have a bite and I'm satisfied."

51   Partly, it appeared that his taste in food had changed. He pointed to the nachos and buffalo wings and hamburgers on the menu, and said that, to his surprise, he no longer felt like eating any of them. "It seems like I lean toward protein and vegetables nowadays," he said, and he ordered a chicken Caesar salad. But he also no longer felt the need to stuff himself. "I used to be real reluctant to push food away," he told me. "Now it's just—it's different." But when did this happen? And how? He shook his head. "I wish I could pinpoint it for you," he said. He paused to consider. "As a human, you adjust to conditions. You don't think you are. But you are."

52   These days, it isn't the failure of obesity surgery that is prompting concerns but its success. Physicians have gone from scorning it to encouraging, sometimes imploring, their most severely overweight patients to undergo a gastric-bypass operation. That's not a small group. More than five million adult Americans meet the strict definition of morbid obesity. (Their "body mass index"—that is, their weight in kilograms divided by the square of their height in metres—is forty or more, which for an average man is roughly a hundred pounds or more overweight.) Ten million more weigh just under the mark but may nevertheless have obesity-related health problems that are serious enough to warrant the surgery. There are ten times as many candidates for obesity surgery right now as there are for heart-bypass surgery in a year. So many patients are seeking the procedure that established surgeons cannot keep up. The American Society of Bariatric Surgery has only five hundred members nationwide who perform gastric-bypass operations, and their waiting lists are typically months long. Hence the too familiar troubles associated with new and lucrative surgical techniques (the fee can be as much as twenty thousand dollars): newcomers are stampeding to the field, including many who have proper training but have not yet mastered the procedure, and others who have no training at all. Complicating matters further, individual surgeons are promoting a slew of variations on the standard operation which haven't been fully researched—the "duodenal switch," the "long limb" bypass, the laparoscopic bypass. And a few surgeons are pursuing new populations, such as adolescents and people who are only moderately obese.

53   Perhaps what's most unsettling about the soaring popularity of gastric-bypass surgery, however, is simply the world that surrounds it. Ours is a culture in which fatness is seen as tantamount to failure, and get-thin-quick promises—whatever the risks—can have an irresistible allure. Doctors may recommend the operation out of concern for their patients' health, but the stigma of obesity is clearly what drives many patients to the operating room. "How can you let yourself look like that?" is society's sneering,

unspoken question, and often its spoken one as well. Women suffer even more than men from the social sanction, and it's no accident that seven times as many women as men have had the operation. (Women are only an eighth more likely to be obese.)

54   Indeed, deciding *not* to undergo the surgery, if you qualify, is at risk of being considered the unreasonable thing to do. A three-hundred-and-fifty-pound woman who did not want the operation told me of doctors browbeating her for her choice. And I have learned of at least one patient with heart disease being refused treatment by a doctor unless she had a gastric bypass. If you don't have the surgery, you will die, some doctors tell their patients. But we actually do not know this. Despite the striking improvements in weight and health, studies have not yet proved a corresponding reduction in mortality.

55   There are legitimate grounds for being wary of the procedure. As Paul Ernsberger, an obesity researcher at Case Western Reserve University, pointed out to me, many patients undergoing gastric bypass are in their twenties and thirties. "But is this really going to be effective and worthwhile over a forty-year span?" he asked. "No one can say." He was concerned about the possible long-term effects of nutritional deficiencies (for which patients are instructed to take a daily multivitamin). And he was concerned about evidence from rats that raises the possibility of an increased risk of bowel cancer.

56   We want progress in medicine to be clear and unequivocal, but of course it rarely is. Every new treatment has gaping unknowns—for both patients and society—and it can be hard to decide what to do about them. Perhaps a simpler, less radical operation will prove effective for obesity. Perhaps the long-sought satiety pill will be found. Nevertheless, the gastric bypass is the one thing we have now that works. Not all the questions have been answered, but there are more than a decade of studies behind it. And so we forge ahead. Hospitals everywhere are constructing obesity-surgery centers, ordering reinforced operating tables, training surgeons and staff. At the same time, everyone expects that, one day, something new and better will be discovered that will make what we're now doing obsolete.

57   Across from me, in our booth at the grill, Vince Caselli pushed his chicken Caesar salad aside only half eaten. "No taste for it," he said, and he told me he was grateful for that. The operation, he said, had given him his life back. But, after one more round of drinks, it was clear that he still felt uneasy.

58   "I had a serious problem and I had to take serious measures," he said. "I think I had the best technology that is available at this point. But I do get concerned: Is this going to last my whole life? Someday, am I going to be right back to square one—or worse?" He fell silent for a moment, gazing into his glass. "Well, that's the cards that God gave me. I can't worry about stuff I can't control."

**Thinking Sociologically about Sources
of Obesity in the United States**
Robert L. Peralta

*We live in a society obsessed with thinness—though one that also differentially applies this
concern (e.g., it's more important for women than for men to be slender). Ours is a society
in which individual blame is also readily assigned—in other words, it's the fault of fat people
that they are fat. Peralta's article calls this conventional wisdom into question, providing a
sociological perspective on sources of obesity.*

As medicine increasingly targets and identifies obesity as a disease, it
is important for social and behavioral scientists to participate in the identification of obesity origins which exist outside of the immediate individual in question. While scholars in the medical arena often focus on
proximate factors contributing to ill-health, distal factors can be critical
sources of public health problems such as obesity. This paper will highlight important distal factors found to be associated with obesity.
Empirical studies reveal the allocation of resources and goods such as
fresh fruits, vegetables, low fat-high protein foods, exercise opportunity,
and education on nutrition, health, and diet are not equally distributed.
Moreover, cultural attitudes toward thinness, health, and beauty are not
universal but subject to cultural and ethnic interpretation. The unequal
and often distinctly different distribution of goods, services, and knowledge has been directly linked to obesity disparity rates by race, social
class, and gender. Policy recommendations and suggestions for future
research conclude the paper.

1   A central lesson derived from sociological research and analysis is social
problems are rarely, if ever, equally distributed within a given society. Rates
of illness and disease often vary by race, social class, gender, sexual orientation, education level, and social psychological factors such as conformity
pressure. Obesity, a condition recently claimed by the medical community
as a "disease," is no different in its tendency to vary by the aforementioned
variables. Medical researchers tend to place emphasis on proximate factors
on illness such as "overeating" or genetic susceptibility instead of distal factors such as the density of fast-food outlets in a given neighborhood touched
by racism and socioeconomic marginalization. This essay will provide a brief
overview of some of the relevant distal factors associated with obesity and
call attention to the need for delineating social origins of obesity and edu-
cating scholars about these important sources of obesity.

2   The social origins of obesity discussed in this piece will include an examination of how unequal distribution of goods and resources affect obesity rates.
The goods and resources referenced include: (1) the geographic availability,

Reprinted from *Gender Issues* 21:3 by permission.

prevalence and cost of nutritious foods and unhealthy fast-food options; (2) time, facilities, and equipment for exercise; and (3) the availability and level of education regarding nutrition and exercise. First, a brief overview of the epidemiology of obesity in the United States will be presented. Conformity to definitions of health and beauty as well as rebellious attitudes against "thinness" as the ideal will be discussed. In addition, isolation and segregation from cultural messages regarding health and beauty will be explored as a source of obesity disparity by race and ethnicity.

Increasing Rates of Obesity—An Epidemiological Overview

3   Disparities in obesity by race and ethnicity are a reflection of how allocation of resources and cultural norms regarding weight and health influence different groups physically (i.e., weight) and psychologically (i.e., body image and social definitions of beauty). The focus on proximate risk factors, potentially controllable at the individual level, resonate with the value and belief system of Western culture that emphasize both the ability of the individual to control his or her personal fate and the importance of doing so (Becker, 1993). Sociologists orient themselves differently from individual-level explanations and seek to understand the social conditions that protect against or accelerate and exacerbate risk. As risk behaviors and their resulting consequences become increasingly claimed by medicine, it is important for social scientists to revisit and reaffirm the social origins of public health concerns such as obesity for effective prevention and intervention (Link and Phelan, 1995).

4   Obesity is defined as an excessively high amount of body fat or adipose tissue in relation to lean body mass. Obesity is currently on the rise in the United States; about 31 percent of U.S. adults are now obese, which is twice the rate of twenty years ago. Many more Americans are expected to be clinically defined as obese soon, as 64.5 percent of Americans are currently considered "overweight" (being overweight is defined by the National Institutes of Health as 21 percent lighter than obese (Fontaine et al., 2003).

5   Table 1 displays an epidemiological portrait of overweight and obesity in America for men and women of different ethnic and racial identities. The table shows obesity and overweight prevalence rates vary by gender: men are more likely to be overweight and women are more likely to be obese. African American women have the highest rates of obesity (55.4 percent), while white males are the least likely to be obese (27.4 percent).

6   Experts agree overeating, especially the over-consumption of high fat and high sugar foods, is an important factor contributing to the rising rates of obesity (Frazao, 1999). The emphasis on the individualistic behavior of "overeating" is a good place to begin a critique of person-level approaches to the phenomenon of obesity and its increased incidence in the United States. While overeating certainly is a source of obesity, the sociocultural context in which overeating takes place must be acknowledged. Social surveys suggest the majority of citizens understand obesity to be a fundamental question of "individual responsibility." On its own, stance is not useful in examining,

Table 1   Overweight and Obesity among Persons 20–74 According to Sex, Race, and Hispanic Origin: United States, 1999–2000.*

	Percent of Population (standard error) Overweight[1]	Obesity[2]
Both Sexes[3]	64.5(1.5)	30.9(1.6)
Male	67.0(1.5)	27.7(1.7)
Female	62.0(2.0)	34.0(2.0)
Mexican Male[4]	74.4(2.8)	29.4(2.5)
Mexican Female	71.8(2.5)	40.1(3.8)
White Male	67.3(2.0)	27.4(1.9)
White Female	57.2(2.7)	30.4(2.3)
Black Male	60.3(2.3)	28.9(2.4)
Black Female	77.7(1.9)	50.4(2.8)

*Sources: Centers for Disease Control and Prevention, National Center for Health Statistics, National Health and Nutrition Examination Survey, Hispanic Health and Nutrition Survey, and National Health Examination Survey. Data are based on measured height and weight of a sample of the civilian noninstitutionalized population.
1 Body mass index (BMI) greater than or equal to 25.
2 Body mass index (BMI) greater than or equal to 30.
3 Excludes pregnant women.
4 Persons of Mexican origin may be of any race.

preventing, and treating the problem of obesity. Examining social variables related to overeating is not to "blame society" but to provide a more holistic and accurate understanding of obesity as a public health problem.

7   Previous research reveals education is correlated with obesity. Being obese is less prevalent and perhaps more stigmatized among the well educated, especially well-educated women. Among those who do not have a high school degree, 32 percent were obese. Among those with at least a high school degree, 23 percent were obese. Finally, among those with a college degree or more, only 18 percent were obese (Ross, 1994). Especially for women, socioeconomic status has been found to be highly correlated with obesity in a negative direction. Sobal and Stunkard (1989) found in a review of 141 studies that women's education was negatively correlated with obesity in 93 percent of studies conducted in the United States. A complete and accurate explanation for the growing problem of obesity is needed if there is to be any hope of confronting the problem effectively.

Social Origins of Obesity

8   Social conditions are factors involving a person's relationship to other people. Ranging from relationships with intimates (micro-level) to positions occupied within the social and economic structures of U.S. society (macro-level). In addition to factors such as race, gender, and socioeconomic status, stressful life events of a social nature need to be included in

the definition of "social conditions." Variables such as violent victimization, job-loss, as well as stress-process variables like social support, fall
within the realm of social conditions (Link and Phelan, 1995).

9   While overeating is an important and obvious factor contributing to
obesity, the results of research reveals a dramatic increase in marketed
portion sizes over time (ranging from candy bars to restaurant meals)
and sheds light on the context in which eating takes place (Spake, 2002;
Winslow and Landers, 2002). Moreover, per capita availability of foods
high in fat and sugar has increased by at least 20 percent since 1977
(Drewnowski, 2003). The results of this research become all the more
interesting when juxtaposed with research suggesting individuals unwit-
tingly consume more food when presented with larger portions in comparison to those presented with smaller food portions (Gossnell et al.,
2001). To suggest individuals are choosing to eat larger amounts of food
of their own free will is not entirely accurate. These two social structural mechanisms work in conjunction with individual decisions to eat, creating an ideal—and perhaps unconscious—condition for overweight and
obesity to proliferate.

10   The social patterning of disease has a relatively long history of empirical research. Most obvious is the often strong association between health
and socioeconomic status. Lower SES is associated with lower life
expectancy and higher overall mortality rates (Pappas et al., 1993; Adler
et al., 1994). Of note, research strongly suggests the social patterning of
disease is not a case of social selection but of social causation, especially
for specific diseases (Dohrenwend et al., 1992). For example, Catalano and
colleagues (1993) related job layoffs to the emergence or reemergence of
alcohol abuse, and Lin and Ensel (1989) and Ensel and Lin (1991) showed
that stressful circumstances predicted subsequent illness including obesity
and mental illness using longitudinal designs. Overall, this body of literature suggests the common mechanisms underlying some aspects of disease including obesity are social in origin.

11   Thus, it is important to ask what it is about an individual's life circumstances that shapes their exposure to risk factors such as poor diet and sedentary lifestyle. Research on social inequality suggests people of higher SES are
more favorably situated to know about the risks and to have the resources
to allow them to engage in protective efforts to avoid them. Declines in coronary heart disease, for example, have been greatest among people of higher
socioeconomic status. Beaglehole (1990) explains higher SES individuals
have been better-informed and more able to implement changes in health
behaviors like smoking, exercise, and diet. The result has been a widening in
the gap for rates of heart disease between the rich and the poor (Link and
Phelan, 1995).

Resource Allocation: Results of Unequal Resource Distribution

12 Why would SES be associated with obesity? The link between SES and obesity is centered on access to resources that can be used to avoid obesity or
to minimize the consequences of obesity once it occurs. Money, knowledge,

power, prestige, and interpersonal resources related to social networks and social support comprise important social resources. Race, ethnicity, and gender are closely tied to resources like money, power, prestige, and social connectedness. In 2002, 12.1 percent of the U.S. population was living in poverty. This statistic was higher for African Americans and Hispanics, at 24.1 percent and 21.8 percent, respectively (U.S. Census, 2002). The situation for African American females is worse, with a higher percentage living below the poverty line in comparison to their male counterparts.

13   The causes and consequences of diseases such as obesity are dynamic and continually transforming. The resources described above are portable from situation to situation and are thus effective at preventing or reducing the consequences of disease. As new sources of obesity emerge (such as the proliferation of fast food, foods with high concentrations of trans-fatty acids, and sugar laden products) those with the fewest resources are among the last to realize the health hazards associated with these convenience foods (Link and Phelan, 1995). An evaluation of health habits among a sample of urban teenagers, for example, found African American females to practice the poorest health habits, with the highest intakes of foods high in saturated fat, cholesterol, salt, and simple sugars compared with same-age white, Hispanic, and Asian American females (Fardy et al., 2000). The link between money, knowledge, power, prestige, and interpersonal resources are structured differently for different groups. The health disparities mentioned here are manifestations of this.

14   Drewnowski (2003) has gone as far as to say "obesity in the U.S. and similar societies may be a socioeconomic, as opposed to a medical, problem that is related to diet structure and costs." Drewnowski (2003) reports foods contributing to obesity are chosen in part because of their convenience, high palatability, and low energy cost of added sugars and fats. For low-income families, obtaining sufficient dietary energy at the lowest possible cost is the overwhelming concern. Food Stamp Program participants reported food price was the most important consideration in making food choices and the overriding concern when choosing and preparing food was to ensure no one would "feel hungry" after a meal (Basiotis, 1998).

15   Language barriers, low socioeconomic status, low education, and low nutrition knowledge place the Latino population at an increased level of health risk. Indeed, Boulanger and colleagues (2002) support previous research (Harnack et al., 1992), which identified a link between education level, the number of children living in a household, and nutrition knowledge. To make healthy eating decisions, individuals need to be informed. Clearly, differences exist in access to quality education by race and ethnicity thus affecting obesity rates. Studies in California and elsewhere have documented a pattern in which low-income neighborhoods have higher concentrations of fast-food restaurants and convenience stores which tend to sell high-fat, non-nutritious foods, and fewer grocery stores and farmers markets which sell lower-fat foods, fruits, and vegetables (Alaimo et al., 2001).

16   Aside from diet habits, exercise habits are deserving of mention. Well established that recent trends reveal the well-educated exercise more than

the poorly educated, men exercise more than women and men are more likely to exercise more strenuously than women (Ross, 1994). These differences are commonly explained by accessibility obstacles to gyms and recreation centers due to geographic placement, economic deterrents to membership, and gender norms which determine if and how men and women should exercise. Also relevant is time for exercise when many low-income heads of families are strained for time due to labor and child-care demands. These factors correspond with the obesity trends reported in Table One above.

Social-Psychological Origins: Deviance, Gender, Race, and SES

17 Obesity is an interesting sociological issue because it is considered by most both a physical characteristic, like deafness and genetically-based deformities, and a form of behavioral deviance, like drug addiction and homosexuality. Unlike the physically disabled, the obese are held responsible for their condition. Obesity itself is looked upon with antipathy because most Americans consider it unsightly and unaesthetic. Obesity is also considered a manifestation of a weak, self-indulgent, or lazy individual. Research suggests, however, if the condition is "medical" in nature and cannot easily be controlled, individuals are less likely to be held responsible, thus reducing stigma. If the condition is not due to a medical predisposition to obesity, however, the likelihood of an obese individual being stigmatized increases because it is felt this person is personally responsible for his or her own deviance (DeJong, 1980).[1]

18   How might the powerful forces of conformity contribute to obesity? According to the reflected self-appraisal perspective, we view ourselves through others. Opinions are reflected back to us in words or actions of acceptance or rejection, esteem or disrespect, liking or hate (Cooley, 1964). The stigma of obesity and the need to conform to thinness has created a multi-billion dollar industry selling diet books, exercise programs, and equipment, diet pills, liposuction, and mechanical devices for reducing weight (Goode, 2004; Falk, 2001; Sobal, 1984). Individuals who internalize the stigma will either blame themselves for their obesity or become depressed while others will turn to diet and exercise to conform to general health and beauty standards. Others reject the stigma of being obese by organizing formal and informal groups that project pride in being overweight and fight discrimination on the basis of one's weight. Regardless, research suggests obese people are more likely to diet and to experience worse physical health, both of which are associated with depression (Ross, 1994). Moreover, dieting to lose weight as an attempt to fit appearance norms is more distressing than being overweight or obese per se (Ross, 1994).

19   With increasing rates of overweight and obese Americans, one would assume the stigma associated with being obese would diminish—yet this has not occurred. Ross (1994) suggests, however, being overweight (as opposed to being obese) is not stigmatized as commonly believed perhaps due to its prevalence (Ross, 1994). Paradoxically, the social stigma attached to obesity remains high (Sobal, 1984). Standards of beauty are in part to

blame for the current state of affairs. For women, the standard of beauty has become much thinner; for men, beauty has become defined as lean yet muscular. Both ideals become increasingly out of reach as the rates of obesity in America climb for both women and men. Ross (1994) reports an "emphasis on health rather than appearance, would likely discourage dieting and distress over being fat, and encourage exercise . . . women's health would be improved by exercising more and dieting less."

20   For all Americans, and especially women, being obese is a source of body dissatisfaction, rejection, and humiliation (Sobal and Mauerer, 1999). The degree of body dissatisfaction and marginalization, however, varies by race and ethnicity (this is yet another example of how obesity and the reaction it evokes vary by social categories). What is universal is that women of all backgrounds endure the brunt of obesity-based social stigma because women are more likely to be objectified (Schur, 1984; Sobal and Stunkard, 1989). In a survey of 33,000 readers of *Glamour* magazine placed in the August 1983 issue, 75 percent said that they were "too fat," even though only one quarter were overweight, according to standards set by the Metropolitan Life Insurance Company's 1959 height-weight tables. What is more surprising, 45 percent of underweight women felt that they were too fat. In addition, most obese individuals and especially women tend to internalize their stigma, believing the condemnation they experience is deserved (Cahnman, 1968). Recent literature reports similar self-image body distortion (see Monteath and McCabe, 1997). Sanderson and colleagues (2002), for example, report undergraduate female participants believed, compared to themselves, other women are thinner, want to be thinner, exercise more frequently and for more aesthetic reasons (e.g., weight loss, attractiveness), and are more aware of and influenced by the thinness norm. Moreover, upper-class women showed more evidence of perceiving a discrepancy on behavioral norms such as eating and exercising behaviors. It has yet to be determined whether this internalization is due to the intense preoccupation with the self and individual responsibility discussed earlier. Perhaps if the obese and others understood the social conditions that contribute to and reinforce obesity in the United States, internalization of stigma wouldn't be so widespread and motivation for change would be more possible.

21   As displayed in Table 1, African Americans and Mexican Americans are disproportionately overweight and obese compared to white Americans, especially among these women of color. Within a highly segregated country such as the United States, many argue cultural norms play a role in insulating African Americans from dominant cultural messages regarding the relationship between health, wellness, thinness and beauty. To be obese in communities segregated from white America is to have fewer direct encounters with the stigma surrounding obesity (Ingrassia, 1995; Parker et al., 1995).

22   In addition, racial differences in attitudes toward weight are substantial. Black teenage girls and women regard being overweight as more acceptable for themselves and others than is true of white girls and women

(Milkie, 1999). Evidence suggests African Americans have been relatively immune to the allure of thinness a highly valued characteristic among white men and women. In a study of junior high school and high school girls, 90 percent of white teens expressed dissatisfaction with their weight while 70 percent of their African American counterparts said they were satisfied with their weight (Ingrassia, 1995). Nearly two thirds of black teenagers said it is better to be a little overweight than a little underweight. Substantially overweight black teenagers described themselves as "happy" with their weight. Finally, black girls recognize black teenagers are not attracted to thinness. Social conditions such as those colored by racial segregation contribute to disparities in obesity by race in the United States (Parker et al., 1995). Individual-level explanations for obesity, such as lack of exercise and over eating, fall short of explaining critical differences.

Conclusion/Policy Recommendations

23 My purpose is to highlight the research advancing our understanding of social conditions contributing to obesity and to underscore the importance of continued research in this direction. As social scientists, it is critical to be closely involved in the study of public health problems that have become medicalized. Obesity is not a primarily medical problem and should not be addressed solely by medical approaches. If the medical community assumes exclusive expertise in obesity research, the examination of proximate conditions may overshadow the importance of distal determinants thus debilitating our effectiveness at treatment and prevention. Individualistic approaches to this health problem are doomed to failure unless the social contexts in which eating and exercising behaviors take place are taken into account.

24   If one wishes to address the fundamental social causes of obesity, interventions must address inequality in the resources that fundamental causes entail. Many believe this is impractical because social inequality is so firmly entrenched in society. There are, however, many policies that have a direct bearing on the effects of social inequality. These policies have an effect on the extent to which people from different social circumstances have access to health-related resources. Policies which involve social and racial integration, the minimum wage, equality in access to quality education and child care, access to exercise programs and equipment, parenting leave, funding for physical education in schools, equitable tax policies, affordable nutritious foods, and other initiatives of this type produce social change.

25   Understanding the social-psychological origins of obesity in the United States is important as well. Differentiating between "deliberate" behavior and the possession of a physical trait are cultural and constructed phenomenon. Negative attitudes toward the obese stem from the assumption that they are fat because they are gluttonous and self-indulgent—they are lazy and they eat too much; most people believe that the obese "could control their weight if they really wanted to" (Katz, 1981). These social-psychological orientations have an impact on how the social problem is

understood by the obese and the physically fit alike these assumptions distorts the overall approach to the public health problem.

26   Social class and race further complicate the social mechanisms influencing obesity rates. The stigma associated with obesity varies by social class as well as race. For developed countries like the United States, obesity is more prevalent among the poor. For poorer countries, it is the wealthy that tend to be overweight or obese. Thus those who are poor and heavy in the United States bear a double burden of stigma. Could this double burden increase or decrease the probability of improving health by reducing risky weight levels? To my knowledge, there is very little research on this question.

27   Where race is concerned, research suggests black self-acceptance among obese girls and women are distinct from white patterns of self-disparagement. This is demonstrative of how social factors impact individual behaviors. We know empirically the stigma of obesity among African Americans is significantly less relevant and more subdued than it is among whites. Thus, obesity is far less deviant in black versus white communities. However, as previously mentioned, the causes and consequences of disease are continually shifting. Recent research suggests that "thin is beautiful" mantra is penetrating communities of color.

28   Future social and behavioral research in this area needs to contextualize risk factors associated with obesity. To contextualize risk factors is to attempt to understand how people come to be exposed to individually based risk factors such as poor diet and lack of exercise so that effective interventions can be designed. Next, researchers need to recognize some social conditions can be fundamental causes of disease. Fundamental causes can include access to resources that help individuals avoid diseases and their negative consequences altogether. For example, there are powerful social, cultural, and economic factors shaping the diet of poor people in the United States. Consequently, providing information about healthy diet to poor people and exhorting them to follow nutritional guidelines is unlikely to have much impact, given their need for convenient, affordable foods. Without an understanding of the context that leads to risk, the responsibility for reducing risk rests solely with the individual. Adopting a comprehensive understanding of obesity in the United States will position us to further improve the health of the nation.

Endnote

1. It is yet unknown what the implications are for this variation in the social allocation of marginalized status. Are obese individuals likely to be successful in reducing his or her weight if their condition is understood as a medical condition or would an obese person be successful at losing weight in response to the social stigma associated with obesity stemming from non-medical reasons? This is an important research question that needs to be addressed.

References

Adler, N. E., Boyce, T., Chesney, M. A., Cohen, S., Folkman, S., Kahn, R. L., & S. Leonard Syme. 1994. "Socioeconomic Status and Health: The Challenge of the Gradient." *American Psychologist,* 49: 15–24.

Alaimo, K., Olson, C. M., Frongillo Jr., E. A., & Ronette, R. B. 2001. "Food Insufficiency, Family Income, and Health in U.S. Preschool and School Aged Children." *American Journal of Public Health,* 91(5): 781–86.

Basiotis, P. P., Kramer-LeBlanck, C.S., & Kennedy, E. T. 1998. "Maintaining Nutrition Security and Diet Quality: The Role of the Food Stamp Program and WIC." *Family Economic Nutrition Review,* 11: 4–16.

Beaglehole, R. 1990. "International Trends in Coronary Heart Disease Mortality, Morbidity, and Risk Factors." *Epidemiologic Reviews,* 12: 1–16.

Becker, M. H. 1993. "A Medical Sociologist Looks at Health Promotion." *Journal of Health and Social Behavior,* 34: 1–16.

Cahnman, W. J. 1968. "The Stigma of Obesity." *Sociological Quarterly,* 9: 283–99.

Cooley, C. H. 1964. *Human Nature and the Social Order,* New York, NY: Schocken Books.

DeJong, W. 1980. "The Stigma of Obesity: The Consequences of Naïve Assumptions Concerning the Causes of Physical Deviance." *Journal of Health and Social Behavior,* 21(1): 75–87.

Dohrenwend, B. P., Levav, I., Shrout, P., Schwartz, S., Naveh, G., Link, B., Skodal, A., & Stueve, A. 1992. "Socioeconomic Status and Psychiatric Disorders: The Causation Selection Issue." *Science,* 255: 946–51.

Drewnowski, A. 2003. "Fat and Sugar: An Economic Analysis." *The Journal of Nutrition,* 133(3): 838s-840s.

Fontaine, K. R., Redden, D.T., Wang, C., Westfall, A.O., & Allison, D. B. 2003. "Years of Life Lost Due to Obesity." *Journal of the American Medical Association,* 289(2): 187–93.

Frazoa, E. (Ed.). 1999. *America's Eating Habits: Changes and Consequences.* USDA/ERS Ari. Info. Bull. 750.

Falk, G. 2001. *Stigma: How We Treat Outsiders.* Amherst, N.Y.: Prometheus Books.

Fardy, P. S., Azzollini, A., Magel, J. R., White, R. E. C., Schmitz, M.K., Agin, D., Clark, L. T., Bayne-Smith, M., Kohn, S., & Terverk, L. 2000. "Gender and Ethnic Differences in Health Behaviors and Risk Factors for Coronary Disease among Urban Teenagers: The Path Program." *The Journal of Gender-Specific Medicine,* 3(2): 59–68.

Goode, E. 2004. "The Stigma of Obesity." In *Readings in Deviant Behavior.* Edited by Alex Thio and Thomas C. Calhoun 3rd ed. Boston, MA: Allyn and Bacon.

Gosnell, B. A., Mitchell, J. E., Lancaster, K. L., Burgard, M. A., Wonderlich, S. A., & Crosby, R. D. 2001. "Food Presentation and Energy Intake in a Feeding Laboratory Study of Subjects with Binge Eating Disorder." *International Journal of Eating Disorders,* 30(4): 441–46.

Harnack, L, Block, G., Subar, A., & Lane, S. 1998. "Cancer Prevention-Related Nutrition Knowledge. Beliefs and Attitudes of U.S. Adults: NHIS Cancer Epidemiology Supplement." *Journal of Nutrition Education,* 30: 121–38.

Ingrassia, M. 1995. "The Body of the Beholder." *Newsweek* April 24: 66–67.

Katz, I. 1981. *Stigma: A Social Psychological Analysis.* Hillside, NJ: Lawrence Erlbaum.

Link, B. G. & Phelan, J. 1995. "Social Conditions as Fundamental causes of Disease." *Journal of Health and Social Behavior* Extra Issue: 80–94.

Louderback, L. 1970. *Fat Power: What Ever You Weigh Is Right.* New York: Hawthorne Books.

McKernan, P., Perez-Escamilla, R., Himmelgreen, D., Segura-Millan, S., & Haldeman, L. 2002. "Determinants of Nutrition Knowledge among Low Income Latino *Caretakers in Hartford, Conn.*" Journal of the American Dietetic Association, 102(7):978–82.

Milkie, M. A. 1999. "Social Comparisons, Reflected Appraisals, and Mass Media: The Impact of Pervasive Beauty Images on Black and White Girls' Self Concepts." *Social Psychology Quarterly,* 62: 190–210.

Monteath, S. A. & McCABE, M. P. 1997. "The Influence of Societal Factors on Female Body Image." *Journal of Social Psychology,* 137: 708–27.

Pappas, G., Queen, S., Hadden, W., & Fisher, G. 1993. "The Increasing Disparity in Mortality between Socioeconomic Groups in the United States." *The New England Journal of Medicine,* 329: 103–109.

Parker, S. et al. 1995, "Body Image and Weight Concerns among African American and White Adolescent Females: Differences Make a Difference." *Human Organization,* 54: 103–14.

Ross, C.E. 1994. "Overweight and Depression." *Journal of Health and Social Behavior,* 35: 63–78.

Sanderson, C. A., Darley, J. M., & Messinger, C. S. 2002. ' "I'm Not as Thin as You Think I Am': The Development and Consequences of Feeling Discrepant from the Thinness Norm." *Personality and Social Psychology Bulletin,* 28: 172–83.

Schur, E. M. 1984. *Labeling Women Deviant: Gender, Stigma, and Social Control.* New York, NY: McGraw-Hill.

Sobal, J. 1984. "Group Dieting, the Stigma of Obesity, and Overweight Adolescents." *Marriage and Family Review,* 7: 9–20.

Sobal, J. & Stunkard, A. J. 1989. "Socioeconomic Status and Obesity: A Review of the Literature." *Psychological Bulletin,* 195: 260–75.

Spake, Amanda. 2002. "A Fat Nation." *U.S. News and World Report* August 19: pp 40–47.

U.S. Census Bureau. *Number in Poverty and Poverty Rate by Race and Hispanic Origin: 2001 and 2002.* Available at http://www.census.gov. Accessed May 21, 2004.

Winslow, R. & Landers, P. 2002. "Obesity: A World Wide Woe." *Wall Street Journal,* July l: pp. B1, B4.

Green Power

4

1   We begin our exploration of Green Power by inviting you to virtually attend a lively presentation at M.I.T. by New York Times columnist Thomas Friedman. Then go online to read a provocative discussion, by scientists Robert H. Socolow and Stephen W. Pacala, about the kind of massively scaled energy projects that will be required to reduce planet-wide CO_2 emissions in meaningful ways.

2   Thomas Friedman, foreign affairs columnist for the *Times*, has won three Pulitzer Prizes for his books, which include *From Beirut to Jerusalem* (1989), *The Lexus and the Olive Tree* (1999), and *The World Is Flat* (2005). (We offer an excerpt from *The World Is Flat* in Chapter 9, "The Changing Landscape of Work in the Twenty-First Century.") In his M.I.T., talk Friedman discusses issues covered in his more recent book *Hot, Flat, and Crowded: Why We Need a Green Revolution—And How It Can Renew America* (2008).

> Go to: YouTube.com
> *Search terms: "thomas friedman mit green energy"*

3   Using less restrictive search terms (e.g., "thomas friedman green energy"), you can find clips of Friedman in many other academic venues and in TV interviews. Look, especially, for an interview with Friedman by Fareed Zakaria. In *Hot, Flat, and Crowded*, Friedman discusses the startling findings of Socolow and Pacala concerning just how much hard work will be required to truly accomplish a "green revolution"—and not just a "green party." In their September 2006 *Scientific American* article, Socolow and Pacala introduce the concept of "wedges"—each wedge of the circle representing an activity that reduces the world's carbon levels by 25 billion tons over the next 50 years. A workable carbon strategy, according to Socolow and Pacala, requires the implementation of seven such wedges. Socolow and Pacala head the Carbon Migration Initiative at Princeton University. Socolow is a professor of mechanical engineering. Pacala is a professor of ecology.

> Go to: Google or Bing
> *Search terms: "a plan to keep carbon in check"*

**National Security Consequences
of U.S. Oil Dependence**
Report of an Independent Task Force

The following selection is excerpted from the "Overview and Introduction" of a Task Force report issued in October 2006 by the Council on Foreign Relations. The Task Force chairs were John Deutch (who served as deputy s1ecretary of defense from 1994 to 1995 and as director of the Central Intelligence Agency from 1995 to 1996) and James Schlesinger (secretary of defense from 1973 to 1975 and America's first secretary of energy under President Carter). The blue-ribbon group included twenty-four other members.

1   The lack of sustained attention to energy issues is undercutting U.S. foreign policy and U.S. national security. Major energy suppliers—from Russia to Iran to Venezuela—have been increasingly able and willing to use their energy resources to pursue their strategic and political objectives. Major energy consumers—notably the United States, but other countries as well—are finding that their growing dependence on imported energy increases their strategic vulnerability and constrains their ability to pursue a broad range of foreign policy and national security objectives. Dependence also puts the United States into increasing competition with other importing countries, notably with today's rapidly growing emerging economies of China and India. At best, these trends will challenge U.S. foreign policy; at worst, they will seriously strain relations between the United States and these countries.

2   This report focuses on the foreign policy issues that arise from dependence on energy traded in world markets and outlines a strategy for response. And because U.S. reliance on the global market for oil, much of which comes from politically unstable parts of the world, is greater than for any other primary energy source, this report is mainly about oil. To a lesser degree it also addresses natural gas.

3   Put simply, the reliable and affordable supply of energy—"energy security"— is an increasingly prominent feature of the international political landscape and bears on the effectiveness of U.S. foreign policy. At the same time, however, the United States has largely continued to treat "energy policy" as something that is separate and distinct—substantively and organizationally—from "foreign policy." This must change. The United States needs not merely to coordinate but to integrate energy issues with its foreign policy.

4   The challenge over the next several decades is to manage the consequences of unavoidable dependence on oil and gas that is traded in world markets and to begin the transition to an economy that relies less on petroleum. The longer the delay, the greater will be the subsequent trauma. For the United States, with 4.6 percent of the world's population using 25 percent of the world's oil, the transition could be especially disruptive.

5   During the next twenty years (and quite probably beyond), it is infeasible to eliminate the nation's dependence on foreign energy sources. The
voices that espouse "energy independence" are doing the nation a disservice by focusing on a goal that is unachievable over the foreseeable future
and that encourages the adoption of inefficient and counterproductive
policies. Indeed, during the next two decades, it is unlikely that the United
States will be able to make a sharp reduction in its dependence on imports,
which currently stand at 60 percent of consumption. The central task for
the next two decades must be to manage the consequences of dependence
on oil, not to pretend the United States can eliminate it.

6   A popular response to the steep rise in energy prices in recent years is
the false expectation that policies to lower imports will automatically lead
to a decline in prices. The public's continuing expectation of the availability of cheap energy alternatives will almost surely be disappointed. While
oil prices may retreat from their current high levels, one should not expect
the price of oil to return, on a sustained basis, to the low levels seen in the
late 1990s. In fact, if more costly domestic supply is used to substitute for
imported oil, then prices will not moderate. Yet the public's elected representatives have allowed this myth to survive, as they advocate policies that
futilely attempt to reduce import dependence quickly while simultaneously lowering prices. Leaders of both political parties, especially when
seeking public office, seem unable to resist announcing unrealistic goals
that are transparent efforts to gain popularity rather than inform the public
of the challenges the United States must overcome. Moreover, the political
system of the United States has so far proved unable to sustain the policies
that would be needed to manage dependence on imported fuels. As history since 1973 shows, the call for policy action recedes as prices abate.

7   These problems rooted in the dependence on oil are neither new nor
unique to the United States. Other major world economies that rely on
imported oil—from Western Europe to Japan, and now China and India—
face similar concerns. All are having difficulties in meeting the challenges
of managing demand for oil. But these countries do not share the foreign
policy responsibilities of the United States. And the United States, insuffi-
ciently aware of its vulnerability, has not been as attentive as the other large
industrialized countries in implementing policies to slow the rising
demand for oil. Yet even if the United States were self-sufficient in oil (a
condition the Task Force considers wholly infeasible in the foreseeable
future), U.S. foreign policy would remain constrained as long as U.S. allies
and partners remained dependent on imports because of their mutual
interdependence. Thus, while reducing U.S. oil imports is desirable, the
underlying problem is the high and growing demand for oil worldwide.

8   The growing worldwide demand for oil in the coming decades will
magnify the problems that are already evident in the functioning of the
world oil market. During that period, the availability of low-cost oil
resources is expected to decline; production and transportation costs
are likely to rise. As more hydrocarbon resources in more remote areas
are tapped, the world economy will become even more dependent on

elaborate and vulnerable infrastructures to bring oil and gas to the markets where they are used.

9 For the last three decades, the United States has correctly followed a policy strategy that, in large measure, has stressed the importance of markets. Energy markets, however, do not operate in an economically perfect and transparent manner. For example, the Organization of Petroleum Exporting Countries (OPEC), quite notably, seeks to act as a cartel. Most oil and gas resources are controlled by state-run companies, some of which enter into supply contracts with consumer countries that are accompanied by political arrangements that distort the proper functioning of the market. These agreements, such as those spearheaded by the Chinese government in oil-rich countries across Africa and elsewhere, reflect many intentions, including the desire to "lock up" particular supplies for the Chinese market. Some of the state companies that control these resources are inefficient, which imposes further costs on the world market. And some governments use the revenues from hydrocarbon sales for political purposes that harm U.S. interests. Because of these realities, an active public policy is needed to correct these market failures that harm U.S. economic and national security. The market will not automatically deliver the best outcome.

· · ·

10 [W]hile the United States has limited leverage to achieve its energy security objectives through foreign policy actions, it has considerable ability to manage its energy future through the adoption of domestic policies that complement both a short- and long-term international strategy.

11 The Task Force is unanimous in recommending the adoption of incentives to slow and eventually reverse the growth in consumption of petroleum products, especially transportation fuels such as motor gasoline. However, the Task Force did not agree about the particular options that would best achieve this objective. The Task Force considered three measures:

- A tax on gasoline (with the tax revenue recycled into the economy with a fraction possibly earmarked for specific purposes such as financing of energy technology research and development [R&D]);
- Stricter and broader mandated Corporate Average Fuel Economy standards, known as CAFE standards; and
- The use of tradable gasoline permits that would cap the total level of gasoline consumed in the economy.

12 Used singly or in combination, these measures would not only encourage higher-efficiency vehicles (although these will take time to find their way into the fleet), but also encourage the introduction of alternative fuels, as well as promote changes in behavior such as the greater use of public transportation. While there are other domestic policies that could be adopted to limit demand for fuels, no strategy will be effective without higher prices for transportation fuels or regulatory incentives to use more efficient vehicles. . . .

13   At the same time that the United States promotes measures to reduce oil demand, it should also be prepared to open some new areas for exploration and production of oil and gas, for example, in Alaska, along the East and West coasts, and in the Gulf of Mexico. In addition to modestly increasing supply, encouraging domestic production is a valuable, if not essential, element for increasing the credibility of U.S. efforts to persuade other nations to expand their exploration and production activities.

14   Ultimately, technology will be vital to reducing the dependence on oil and gas, and to making a transition away from petroleum fuels. These benefits of improved technology will come in the future only if investments are made today in research, development, and demonstration (RD&D).

15   The Task Force notes that higher energy prices are unleashing remarkable forces for innovation in this country. Entrepreneurs are seeking new ideas for products and services, such as batteries, fuel cells, and biofuels. Private equity capital is seeking opportunities to invest in new energy technologies. Large corporations are investing in RD&D in all aspects of energy production and use. These activities will undoubtedly result in a steady improvement in the ability of the U.S. economy to meet energy needs.

16   The U.S. government has an important role in supporting this innovation in the private sector, especially for technologies that require significant development efforts to demonstrate commercial potential. The Task Force recommends that the federal government offer greatly expanded incentives and investments aimed at both short- and long-term results to address a wide range of technologies that includes higher-efficiency vehicles, substitutes for oil in transportation (such as biomass and electricity), techniques to enhance production from existing oil wells, and technologies that increase the energy efficiency of industrial processes that use oil and gas. Government spending is appropriate in this context because the market alone does not make as much effort as is warranted by national security and environmental considerations. . . .

The Dangerous Delusions of Energy Independence
Robert Bryce

In the following selection, Robert Bryce argues that it is neither possible nor desirable for the United States to become independent of foreign energy supplies. Those who advocate such independence, he claims, are "woefully ignorant about the fundamentals of energy and the energy business." Bryce's provocative conclusion flies in the face of often unexamined assumptions held by many politicians, as well as environmentalists.

Robert Bryce, a fellow at the Institute for Energy Research and a managing editor of the Energy Tribune, *has written about energy for more than two decades. His articles have appeared in such publications as the* Atlantic Monthly, *the* Guardian, *and the* Nation. *His books include* Cronies: Oil, the Bushes, and the Rise of Texas, America's Superstate *(2004) and* Power Hungry: The Myths of Green Energy and the Real Fuels of the Future *(2010). This selection is excerpted from the introduction ("The Persistent Delusion") to his book* Gusher of Lies: The Dangerous Delusions of "Energy Independence" *(2008).*

1   Americans love independence.

2   Whether it's financial independence, political independence, the Declaration of Independence, or grilling hotdogs on Independence Day, America's self-image is inextricably bound to the concepts of freedom and autonomy. The promises laid out by the Declaration—life, liberty, and the pursuit of happiness—are the shared faith and birthright of all Americans.

3   Alas, the Founding Fathers didn't write much about gasoline.

4   Nevertheless, over the past 30 years or so—and particularly over the past 3 or 4 years—American politicians have been talking as though Thomas Jefferson himself warned about the dangers of imported crude oil. Every U.S. president since Richard Nixon has extolled the need for energy independence. In 1974, Nixon promised it could be achieved within 6 years.[1] In 1975, Gerald Ford promised it in 10.[2] In 1977, Jimmy Carter warned Americans that the world's supply of oil would begin running out within a decade or so and that the energy crisis that was then facing America was "the moral equivalent of war."[3]

5   The phrase "energy independence" has become a prized bit of meaningful-sounding rhetoric that can be tossed out by candidates and political operatives eager to appeal to the broadest cross section of voters. When the U.S. achieves energy independence, goes the reasoning, America will be a self-sufficient Valhalla, with lots of good-paying manufacturing jobs that will come from producing new energy technologies. Farmers will grow fat, rich, and happy by growing acre upon acre of corn and other plants that can be turned into billions of gallons of oil-replacing ethanol. When America arrives at the promised land of milk, honey, and supercheap motor fuel, then U.S. soldiers will never again need visit the Persian Gulf, except, perhaps, on vacation. With energy independence, America can finally dictate terms to those rascally Arab sheikhs from troublesome countries. Energy independence will mean a thriving economy, a positive balance of trade, and a stronger, better America.

6   The appeal of this vision of energy autarky has grown dramatically since the terrorist attacks of September 11. That can be seen through an analysis of news stories that contain the phrase "energy independence." In 2000, the Factiva news database had just 449 stories containing that phrase. In 2001, there were 1,118 stories. By 2006, that number had soared to 8,069.

7   The surging interest in energy independence can be explained, at least in part, by the fact that in the post–September 11 world, many Americans have been hypnotized by the conflation of two issues: oil and terrorism. America was attacked, goes this line of reasoning, because it

has too high a profile in the parts of the world where oil and Islamic extremism are abundant. And buying oil from the countries of the Persian Gulf stuffs petrodollars straight into the pockets of terrorists like Mohammad Atta and the 18 other hijackers who committed mass murder on September 11.

8   Americans have, it appears, swallowed the notion that all foreign oil—and thus, presumably, all foreign energy—is bad. Foreign energy is a danger to the economy, a danger to America's national security, a major source of funding for terrorism, and, well, just not very patriotic. Given these many assumptions, the common wisdom is to seek the balm of energy independence. And that balm is being peddled by the Right, the Left, the Greens, Big Agriculture, Big Labor, Republicans, Democrats, senators, members of the House, [former president] George W. Bush, the opinion page of the *New York Times,* and the neoconservatives. About the only faction that dismisses the concept is Big Oil. But then few people are listening to Big Oil these days.

9   Environmental groups like Greenpeace and Worldwatch Institute continually tout energy independence.[4] The idea has long been a main talking point of Amory Lovins, the high priest of the energy-efficiency movement and the CEO of the Rocky Mountain Institute.[5] One group, the Apollo Alliance, which represents labor unions, environmentalists, and other left-leaning groups, says that one of its primary goals is "to achieve sustainable American energy independence within a decade."[6]

10   Al Gore's 2006 documentary about global warming, *An Inconvenient Truth,* implies that America's dependence on foreign oil is a factor in global warming.[7] The film, which won two Academy Awards (for best documentary feature and best original song), contends that foreign oil should be replaced with domestically produced ethanol and that this replacement will reduce greenhouse gases.[8] (In October 2007, Gore was awarded the Nobel Peace Prize.)

11   The leading Democratic candidates for the White House in 2008 have made energy independence a prominent element of their stump speeches. [Former] Illinois senator Barack Obama has declared that "now is the time for serious leadership to get us started down the path of energy independence."[9] In January 2007, in the video that she posted on her Website that kicked off her presidential campaign, New York senator Hillary Clinton said she wants to make America "energy independent and free of foreign oil."[10]

12   The Republicans are on board, too. In January 2007, shortly before Bush's State of the Union speech, one White House adviser declared that the president would soon deliver "headlines above the fold that will knock your socks off in terms of our commitment to energy independence."[11] In February 2007, Arizona senator and presidential candidate John McCain told voters in Iowa, "We need energy independence. We need it for a whole variety of reasons."[12] In March 2007, former New York mayor Rudolph Giuliani insisted that the federal government "must treat energy independence as a matter of national security." He went on, saying that "we've been talking about energy independence for over 30 years and

it's been, well, really, too much talk and virtually no action. . . . I'm impatient and I'm single-minded about my goals, and we will achieve energy independence."[13]

. . .

13   Polls show that an overwhelming majority of Americans are worried about foreign oil. A March 2007 survey by Yale University's Center for Environmental Law and Policy found that 93 percent of respondents said imported oil is a serious problem and 70 percent said it was "very" serious.[14] That finding was confirmed by an April 2007 poll by Zogby International, which found that 74 percent of Americans believe that cutting oil imports should be a high priority for the federal government. And a majority of those surveyed said that they support expanding the domestic production of alternative fuels.[15]

14   The energy independence rhetoric has become so extreme that some politicians are even claiming that lightbulbs will help achieve the goal. In early 2007, U.S. Representative Jane Harman, a California Democrat, introduced a bill that would essentially outlaw incandescent bulbs by requiring all bulbs in the U.S. to be as efficient as compact fluorescent bulbs. Writing about her proposal in the *Huffington Post*, Harman declared that such bulbs could "help transform America into an energy efficient and energy independent nation."[16]

15   While Harman may not be the brightest bulb in the chandelier, there's no question that the concept of energy independence resonates with American voters and explains why a large percentage of the American populace believes that energy independence is not only doable but desirable.

16   But here's the problem: It's not and it isn't.

17   Energy independence is hogwash. From nearly any standpoint—economic, military, political, or environmental—energy independence makes no sense. Worse yet, the inane obsession with the idea of energy independence is preventing the U.S. from having an honest and effective discussion about the energy challenges it now faces.

18   [Let's] acknowledge, and deal with, the difference between rhetoric and reality. The reality is that the world—and the energy business in particular—is becoming ever more interdependent. And this interdependence will likely only accelerate in the years to come as new supplies of fossil fuel become more difficult to find and more expensive to produce. While alternative and renewable forms of energy will make minor contributions to America's overall energy mix, they cannot provide enough new supplies to supplant the new global energy paradigm, one in which every type of fossil fuel—crude oil, natural gas, diesel fuel, gasoline, coal, and uranium—gets traded and shipped in an ever more sophisticated global market.

19   Regardless of the ongoing fears about oil shortages, global warming, conflict in the Persian Gulf, and terrorism, the plain, unavoidable truth is that the U.S., along with nearly every other country on the planet, is mar-

ried to fossil fuels. And that fact will not change in the foreseeable future, meaning the next 30 to 50 years. That means that the U.S. and the other countries of the world will continue to need oil and gas from the Persian Gulf and other regions. Given those facts, the U.S. needs to accept the reality of *energy interdependence*.

20   The integration and interdependence of the $5-trillion-per-year global energy business can be seen by looking at Saudi Arabia, the biggest oil producer on the planet.[17] In 2005, the Saudis *imported* 83,000 barrels of gasoline and other refined oil products per day.[18] It can also be seen by looking at Iran, which imports 40 percent of its gasoline needs. Iran also imports large quantities of natural gas from Turkmenistan.[19] If the Saudis, with their 260 billion barrels of oil reserves, and the Iranians, with their 132 billion barrels of oil and 970 trillion cubic feet of natural gas reserves, can't be energy independent, why should the U.S. even try?[20]

21   An October 2006 report by the Council on Foreign Relations put it succinctly: "The voices that espouse 'energy independence' are doing the nation a disservice by focusing on a goal that is unachievable over the foreseeable future and that encourages the adoption of inefficient and counterproductive policies."[21]

22   America's future when it comes to energy—as well as its future in politics, trade, and the environment—lies in accepting the reality of an increasingly interdependent world. Obtaining the energy that the U.S. will need in future decades requires American politicians, diplomats, and business people to be actively engaged with the energy-producing countries of the world, particularly the Arab and Islamic producers. Obtaining the country's future energy supplies means that the U.S. must embrace the global market while acknowledging the practical limits on the ability of wind power and solar power to displace large amounts of the electricity that's now generated by fossil fuels and nuclear reactors.

23   The rhetoric about the need for energy independence continues largely because the American public is woefully ignorant about the fundamentals of energy and the energy business.[22] It appears that voters respond to the phrase, in part, because it has become a type of code that stands for foreign policy isolationism—the idea being that if only the U.S. didn't buy oil from the Arab and Islamic countries, then all would be better. The rhetoric of energy independence provides political cover for protectionist trade policies, which have inevitably led to ever larger subsidies for politically connected domestic energy producers, the corn ethanol industry being the most obvious example.

24   But going it alone with regard to energy will not provide energy security or any other type of security. Energy independence, at its root, means protectionism and isolationism, both of which are in direct opposition to America's long-term interests in the Persian Gulf and globally.

25   Once you move past the hype and the overblown rhetoric, there's little or no justification for the push to make America energy independent. And that's the purpose of this book: to debunk the concept of energy independence and show that none of the alternative or renewable energy sources

now being hyped—corn ethanol, cellulosic ethanol, wind power, solar power, coal-to-liquids, and so on—will free America from imported fuels. America's appetite is simply too large and the global market is too sophisticated and too integrated for the U.S. to secede.

26   Indeed, America is getting much of the energy it needs because it can rely on the strength of an ever-more-resilient global energy market. In 2005, the U.S. bought crude oil from 41 different countries, jet fuel from 26 countries, and gasoline from 46.[23] In 2006, it imported coal from 11 different countries and natural gas from 6 others.[24] American consumers in some border states rely on electricity imported from Mexico and Canada.[25] Tens of millions of Americans get electricity from nuclear power reactors that are fueled by foreign uranium. In 2006, the U.S. imported the radioactive element from 8 different countries.[26]

27   Yes, America does import a lot of energy. But here's an undeniable truth: It's going to continue doing so for decades to come. Iowa farmers can turn all of their corn into ethanol, Texas and the Dakotas can cover themselves in windmills, and Montana can try to convert all of its coal into motor fuel, but none of those efforts will be enough. America needs energy, and lots of it. And the only way to get that energy is by relying on the vibrant global trade in energy commodities so that each player in that market can provide the goods and services that it is best capable of producing.

Endnotes

1. Richard Nixon, State of the Union address, January 30, 1974. Available: http://www.thisnation.com/library/sotu/1974rn.html.

2. Gerald Ford, State of the Union address, January 15, 1975. Available: http://www.ford.utexas.edu/LIBRARY/SPEECHES/750028.htm.

3. Jimmy Carter, televised speech on energy policy, April 18, 1977. Available: http://www.pbs.org/wgbh/amex/carter/filmmore/ps_energy.html.

4. Greenpeace is perhaps the most insistent of the environmental groups regarding energy independence. This 2004 statement is fairly representative: http://www .greenpeace.org/international/campaigns/no-war/war-on-iraq/it-s-about-oil. For Worldwatch, see its press release after George W. Bush's 2007 State of the Union speech, which talks about "increased energy independence." Available: http://www.worldwatch.org/node/4873.

5. See any number of presentations by Lovins on energy independence. One sample: his presentation before the U.S. Senate Committee on Energy and Natural Resources on March 7, 2006. Available: http://energy.senate.gov/public/index .cfm?FuseAction=Hearings.Testimony&Hearing_ID=1534&Witness_ID=4345. Or see *Winning the Energy Endgame*, by Lovins et al., 228, discussing the final push toward "total energy independence" and the move to the hydrogen economy.

6. National Apollo Alliance Steering Committee statement. Available: http://www .apolloalliance.org/about_the_alliance/who_we_are/steeringcommittee.cfm.

7. At approximately 1:32 into the movie, in a section that discusses what individuals can do to counter global warming, a text message comes onto the screen: "Reduce our dependence on foreign oil, help farmers grow alcohol fuels."

8. AMPAS data. Available: http://www.oscars.org/79academyawards/nomswins.html.

9. Barack Obama, "Energy Security Is National Security," Remarks of Senator Barack Obama to the Governor's Ethanol Coalition, February 28, 2006. Available: http://obama.senate.gov/speech/060228-energy_security_is_national_security/index.html.

10. Original video at www.votehillary.org. See also, http://www.washingtonpost.com/wp-dyn/content/article/2007/01/20/AR2007012000426.html.

11. *New York Times*, "Energy Time: It's Not about Something for Everyone," January 16, 2007.

12. Shailagh Murray, "Ethanol Undergoes Evolution as Political Issue," *Washington Post*, March 13, 2007, A06. Available: http://www.washingtonpost.com/wp-dyn/content/article/2007/03/12/AR2007031201722_pf.html.

13. Richard Perez-Pena, "Giuliani Focuses on Energy," *The Caucus: Political Blogging from the New York Times*, March 14, 2007. Available: http://thecaucus.blogs.nytimes.com/2007/03/14/giuliani-focuses-on-energy.

14. Yale Center for Environmental Law and Policy, 2007 Environment survey. Available: http://www.yale.edu/envirocenter/YaleEnvironmentalPoll2007Keyfindings.pdf.

15. UPI, "Americans Want Energy Action, Poll Says," April 17, 2007. Available: http://www.upi.com/Energy/Briefing/2007/04/17/americans_want_energy_action_poll_says.

16. Jane Harman, "A Bright Idea for America's Energy Future," *Huffington Post*, March 15, 2007. Available: http://www.huffingtonpost.com/rep-jane-harman/a-bright-idea-for-america_b_43519.html.

17. http://www.infoplease.com/ipa/A0922041.html.

18. Organization of Arab Petroleum Exporting Countries (OPEC), *Annual Statistical Report 2006*, 75. Available: http://www.oapecorg.org/images/A%20S%20R%202006.pdf.

19. Nazila Fathi and Jad Mouawad, "Unrest Grows amid Gas Rationing in Iran," *New York Times*, June 29, 2007. According to this story, Iran imports gasoline from 16 countries. Iran has been importing natural gas from Turkmenistan since the late 1990s. In 2008, those imports will likely be about 1.3 billion cubic feet of natural gas per day. The fuel will be used to meet demand in northern Iran. For more, see, David Wood, Saeid Mokhatab, and Michael J. Economides, "Iran Stuck in Neutral," *Energy Tribune*, December 2006, 19.

20. EIA oil reserve data for Saudi Arabia available: http://www.eia.doe.gov/emeu/cabs/saudi.html. EIA oil reserve data for Iran available: http://www.eia.doe.gov/emeu/cabs/Iran/Oil.html. EIA natural gas data for Iran available: http://www.eia.goe.gov/emeu/cabs/Iran/NaturalGas.html.

21. Council on Foreign Relations, "National Security Consequences of U.S. Oil Dependency," October 2006, 4. Available: http://www.cfr.org/content/publications/attachments/EnergyTFR.pdf.

22. A June 2007 survey done by Harris Interactive for the American Petroleum Institute found that only 9 percent of the respondents named Canada as America's biggest supplier of oil for the year 2006. For more on this, see Robert Rapier, "America's Energy IQ," R-Squared Energy Blog, June 29, 2007. Available: http://i-r-squared.blogspot.com/2007/06/americas-energy-iq.html#links. For the results of the entire survey, see: http://www.energytomorrow.org/energy_issues/energy_iq/energy_iq_survey.html.

23. EIA crude import data available: http://tonto.eia.doe.gov/dnav/pet/pet_move_impcus_a2_nus_epc0_im0_mbbl_a.htm. EIA data for jet fuel available: http://tonto

.eia.doe.gov/dnav/pet/pet_move_impcus_a2_nus_EPJK_im0_mbbl_a.htm. EIA data for finished motor gasoline available: http://tonto.eia.doe.gov/dnav/pet/pet_move_impcus_a2_nus_epm0f_im0_mbbl_a.htm.

24. EIA coal data available: http://www.eia.doe.gov/cneaf/coal/quarterly/html/t18p01p1.html. For gas imports, EIA data available: http://tonto.eia.doe.gov/dnav/ng/ng_move_impc_sl_a.htm.

25. EIA data available: http://www.eia.doe.gov/cneaf/electricity/epa/epat6p3.html.

26. Information from 2006, EIA data available: http://www.eia.doe.gov/cneaf/nuclear/umar/table3.html.

A DEBATE ON THE FUTURE OF NUCLEAR POWER, POST-FUKUSHIMA

On March 11, 2011, a magnitude 9.0 earthquake off the northeastern coast of Japan, followed by a massive tsunami that flooded the Tohoku region, caused extensive damage to the Fukushima Daiichi power plant, a complex of six nuclear reactors operated by the Tokyo Electric Power Company. In the days that followed, three of the reactors experienced a nuclear meltdown when power failures caused the cooling-water levels in the nuclear core to drop, exposing and overheating the uranium fuel rods (see diagram, p. 252). A series of hydrogen explosions and the release of radioactive cesium into the atmosphere hampered plant workers from shutting down the reactors and controlling the damage. Residents within a 20 km. (12 mile) radius were evacuated, and the government subsequently banned the sale of food grown in the region. The plant's reactors would not be stabilized until mid-December, at which time 160,000 residents were still displaced.

Fukushima was the worst nuclear disaster since 1986, when the Chernobyl nuclear power reactor in the Ukraine suffered a meltdown, eventually exposing over half a million cleanup workers to toxic levels of radioactivity and releasing lesser levels of contamination over much of the western USSR and Europe. Hundreds of miles around Chernobyl remain uninhabitable today. The Fukushima accident renewed the long-dormant debate over the safety of nuclear power, just at the time when this technology was increasingly being viewed as a financially viable and relatively green alternative to the burning of coal as a source of electricity.

That debate is represented in the following four brief selections, originally published as op-eds in American newspapers soon after the disaster occurred. In "The Future of Nukes, and Japan," published on 16 March, 2011, *Wall Street Journal* columnist Holman W. Jenkins asserts that the impact of the nuclear accident at Fukushima was ultimately minimal but fears that "antinuclear panic" will forestall the further development of nuclear power in this country. Eugene Robinson, writing on 15 March 2011 for the *Washington Post*, argues in "Japan's Nuclear Crisis Might Not Be Its Last" that the kind of disaster that struck Japan could also strike the United States. In his 23 April 2011 op-ed for the *Wall Street Journal*, William Tucker reminds us that all fuel sources (even ones considered "green") have their costs and drawbacks. Finally, in an op-ed published on 15 March 2011, *Washington Post* commentator Anne Applebaum wonders: "If the Japanese Can't Build a Safe Reactor, Who Can?"

HOW A NUCLEAR REACTOR WORKS

All power plants convert a source of energy or fuel into electricity. Most large plants do that by heating water to create steam, which turns a turbine that drives an electric generator. Inside the generator, a large electromagnet spins within a coil of wire, producing electricity.

A fossil plant burns coal or oil to make the heat that creates the steam. Nuclear power plants . . . make the steam from heat that is created when atoms split apart—called fission.

The fuel for nuclear power plants is uranium, which is made into pellets and sealed inside long metal tubes, called fuel rods. The rods are located in the reactor vessel.

The fission process takes place when the nucleus of a uranium atom is split when struck by a neutron. The "fissioning" of the nucleus releases two or three new neutrons and energy in the form of heat. The released neutrons then repeat the process, releasing more neutrons and producing more nuclear energy. The repeating of the process is called a chain reaction and creates the heat needed to turn water into steam.

In a pressurized water reactor . . . water is pumped through the reactor core and heated by the fission process. The water is kept under high pressure inside the reactor so it does not boil.

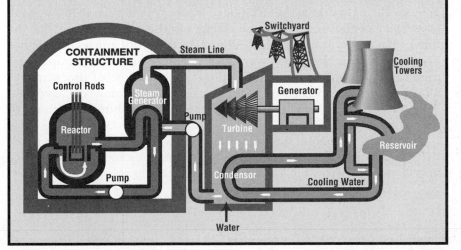

The heated water from the reactor passes through tubes inside four steam generators, where the heat is transferred to water flowing around the tubes. The water boils and turns to steam.

The steam is piped to the turbines. The force of the expanding steam drives the turbines, which spin a magnet in coil of wire—the generator—to produce electricity.

After passing through the turbines, the steam is converted back to water by circulating it around tubes carrying cooling water in the condenser. The condensed steam—now water—is returned to the steam generators to repeat the cycle.

The cooling water from the condenser is sprayed into the air inside the cooling tower and falls about 60 feet, which cools it before it is continuously recycled to condense more steam. Water in the vapor rising from the cooling tower is replenished to the condenser cooling system using [pumped-in water, generally from a nearby river].

The three water systems at [a nuclear power plant] are separate from each other, and the radioactive water is not permitted to mix with other nonradioactive water systems.

Adapted from "How Sequoyah Works," Tennessee Valley Authority, http://www.tva.gov/power/nuclear/sequoyah_howworks.htm.

The Future of Nukes, and of Japan
Holman W. Jenkins, Jr.

1 You can't beat for drama the struggle of Japanese operators to manage the emergency cool-down of nuclear reactors in the tsunami zone. For the things that matter most, though—life and safety—the nuclear battle has been a sideshow. Hundreds were feared dead when entire trains went missing. Whole villages were wiped out with the loss of thousands of inhabitants. So far one worker at one nuclear plant is known to have died in a hydrogen explosion and several others have exhibited symptoms of radiation poisoning.

2 As for environmental degradation, video testifies to the brown murk that the tsunami waters became when they crossed into land. An infinity of contaminants—sewage, fuels, lubricants, cleaning solvents—have been

scattered across the Earth and into aquifers. Radiation releases, meanwhile, haven't been a serious threat to anyone but the plant's brave workers.

3   Just under a decade ago, when Americans were worried about the vulnerability of nuclear plants to deliberate terrorist destruction, Nuclear Regulatory Commission Chairman Nils Diaz gave a notable speech: "In general, I do not believe nuclear power is being portrayed in a balanced manner. . . . This is probably the fault of all of us who know better since there have been strong currents for not mentioning consequences [of nuclear accidents] out loud."

4   He proceeded to lay out the consequences of Chernobyl, a uniquely bad nuclear accident, in which a graphite core reactor burned in the open air for more than a week. Along with 59 firemen and workers who lost their lives, the failure to evacuate or take other precautionary steps led to 1,800 thyroid cancer cases among children, though fewer than a dozen deaths. "Leukemia has been expected to be among the early primary latent health effects seen among those exposed to significant amounts of radiation," Mr. Diaz continued, "yet excess cases of leukemia that can be attributed to Chernobyl have not been detected."

5   Do not pretty up what Mr. Diaz was saying. He was not offering risk-free energy. Now think about Japan. It suffered its worst earthquake in perhaps 1,100 years, followed by a direct-hit tsunami on two nuclear plants. Plenty of other industrial systems on which the Japanese rely—transportation, energy, water, food, medical, public safety—were overwhelmed and failed. A mostly contained meltdown of one or more reactors would not be the worst event of the month.

6   Note, as a matter of realism, we say "mostly contained." In a full or partial meltdown, you don't really know what you will get unless you know the condition of the containment structure and, even more, what's going on inside it, especially in terms of fluids and gases that might have to be vented. Complicating matters in Japan's case is also the failed cooling of spent fuel, yesterday contributing to a burst of emissions that alarmed but didn't threaten the wider public. Tokyo Electric has an almighty mess to clean up, but even in circumstances compounded by a region-wide natural disaster a Chernobyl-scale release seems likely to be avoided—in which case this year's deaths from nuclear power will be less than those from coal-mining accidents.

7   So here's a question: The world has gas and coal with which to produce electricity. Nuclear is a hot-house plant, requiring lots of government support. Environmental groups, with their perhaps unmerited moral authority, have insisted for years that curbing carbon is the greatest human challenge, and those groups that haven't opted for escapism, insisting wind and solar somehow can make up the difference, have quietly recognized that the only alternative to fossil energy is nuclear.

8   Where will these groups be in the morning? China and India, two fast-growing producers of greenhouse gases, have dozens of nuclear plants planned or under construction. India being a democracy, that country is

particularly ripe to be turned off course by political reaction to Japan. If they believe their climate rhetoric, will environmentalists speak up in favor of nuclear realism or will they succumb to the fund-raising and media lure of antinuclear panic?

9   We suspect we already know the answer. In the unlikely event the world was ever going to make a concerted dent in CO_2 output, nuclear was the key. Let's just guess this possibility is now gone, for better or worse.

No Fail-Safe Option
Eugene Robinson

1 Nuclear power was beginning to look like a panacea—a way to lessen our dependence on oil, make our energy supply more self-sufficient and significantly mitigate global warming, all at the same time. Now it looks more like a bargain with the devil.

2   I wish this were not so. In recent years, some of the nation's most respected environmentalists—including Stewart Brand, founder of the Whole Earth Catalog—have come to champion nuclear power. But as Japanese engineers struggle frantically to keep calamity from escalating into catastrophe, we cannot ignore the fact that nuclear fission is an inherently and uniquely toxic technology.

3   The cascading sequence of system failures, partial meltdowns and hydrogen explosions at the Fukushima Daiichi nuclear power plant was touched off by a once-in-a-lifetime event: the most powerful earthquake in Japan's recorded history, which triggered a tsunami of unimaginable destructive force. It is also true that the Fukushima reactors are of an older design, and that it is possible to engineer nuclear plants that would never suffer similar breakdowns.

4   But it is also true that there is no such thing as a fail-safe system. Stuff happens.

5   The Earth is alive with tectonic movement, volcanism, violent weather. We try to predict these phenomena, but our best calculations are probabilistic and thus imprecise. We have computers that are as close to infallible as we can imagine, but the data they produce must ultimately be interpreted by human intelligence. When a crisis does occur, experts must

make quick decisions under enormous pressure; usually they're right, sometimes they're wrong.

6   The problem with nuclear fission is that the stakes are unimaginably high. We can engineer nuclear power plants so that the chance of a Chernobyl-style disaster is almost nil. But we can't eliminate it completely—nor can we envision every other kind of potential disaster. And where fission reactors are concerned, the worst-case scenario is so dreadful as to be unthinkable.

7   Engineers at the Fukushima plant are struggling to avert a wholesale release of deadly radiation, which is the inherent risk of any fission reactor. In the Chernobyl incident, a cloud of radioactive smoke and steam spread contamination across hundreds of square miles; even after 25 years, a 20-mile radius around the ruined plant remains off-limits and uninhabitable. Studies have estimated that the release of radioactivity from Chernobyl has caused at least 6,000 excess cases of thyroid cancer, and scientists expect more cancers to develop in the years to come.

8   It seems unlikely that the Fukushima crisis will turn into another Chernobyl, if only because there is a good chance that prevailing winds would blow any radioactive cloud out to sea. Japanese authorities seem to be making all the right decisions. Yet even in a nation with safety standards and technological acumen that are second to none, look at what they're up against—and how little margin for error they have to work with.

9   At first, the focus was on the Unit 1 reactor and the struggle to keep the nuclear fuel rods immersed in water—which is necessary, at all times, to avoid a full meltdown and a catastrophic release of radiation. Pumping sea water into the reactor vessel seemed to stabilize the situation, despite a hydrogen explosion—indicating a partial meltdown—that blew the roof off the reactor's outer containment building.

10   But then, attention shifted to Unit 3, which may have had a worse partial meltdown; it, too, experienced a hydrogen explosion. Officials said they believed they were stabilizing that reactor but acknowledged that it was hard to be sure. Meanwhile, what could be the most crucial failure of all was happening in Unit 2, which suffered an explosion Tuesday after its fuel rods were twice fully exposed. Scientists had no immediate way of knowing how much of that reactor's fuel had melted—or what the consequences might be.

11   The best-case scenario is that Japanese engineers will eventually get the plant under control. Then, I suppose, it will be possible to conclude that the system worked. As President Obama and Congress move forward with a new generation of nuclear plants, designs will be vetted and perhaps altered. We will be confident that we have taken the lessons of Fukushima into account.

12   And we will be fooling ourselves, because the one inescapable lesson of Fukushima is that improbable does not mean impossible. Unlikely failures can combine to bring any nuclear fission reactor to the brink of disaster. It can happen here.

**Why I Still Support Nuclear Power,
Even After Fukushima**
William Tucker

1   It's not easy being a supporter of nuclear energy these days. The events in Japan have confirmed many of the critics' worst predictions. We are way past Three Mile Island. It is not quite Chernobyl, but the possibilities of widespread radioactive contamination remain real.

2   Still, other energy technologies are not without risk. In 1944 a natural gas explosion in Cleveland leveled an entire neighborhood and killed 130 people. Yet we still pipe gas right into our homes. Coal mining killed 100,000 workers in the 20th century, and still kills an average of six a day in China, but we haven't given up coal. A hydroelectric dam collapsed in Japan during the earthquake, wiping away 1,800 homes and killing an undetermined number of people, yet nobody has paid much attention.

3   But talk about the risks of other energy sources really doesn't cut to the issue. The obvious question people are asking is, "Why do we have to mess with this nuclear stuff in the first place? Why do we have to risk these horrible accidents when other better technologies are available?" The answer is that there are no better alternatives available. If we are going to maintain our standard of living—or anything approximating it—without overwhelming the earth with pollution, we are going to have to master nuclear technology.

4   Consider: Uranium fuel rods sit in a reactor core for five years. During that time six ounces of their weight—six ounces!—will be completely transformed into energy. But the energy produced by that transformation will be enough to power a city the size of San Francisco for five years.

5   A coal plant must be fed by a 100-car freight train arriving every 30 hours. A nuclear reactor is refueled by a fleet of six trucks arriving once every two years. There are 283 coal mines in West Virginia and 449 in Kentucky. There are only 45 uranium mines in the entire world. Russia is offering to supply uranium to most of the developing world with the output from one mine. That is why the environmental impact of nuclear is infinitely smaller.

6   What about natural gas? Huge reservoirs of shale gas have been unlocked by hydrofracking. But "fracking" has been able to proceed so rapidly only because it has been exempted from federal regulations governing air and water pollution. Now that concern has arisen about damaged aquifers, natural gas production may slow as well.

7   So what about hydro, wind and solar? These energy sources will not bring about utopia. The only reason we don't object to the environmental effects of these renewables is because we haven't yet encountered them.

8   The amount of energy that can be derived from harnessing wind or water is about 15 orders of magnitude less than what can be derived from uranium. Thus a hydroelectric dam such as Hoover must back up a 250-square-mile reservoir (Lake Mead) in order to generate the same electricity produced by a reactor on one square mile.

9   Windmills require even more space, since air is less dense than water. Replacing just one of the two 1,000-megawatt reactors at Indian Point in Westchester County, N.Y., would require lining the Hudson River from New York to Albany with 45-story windmills one-quarter mile apart—and then they would generate electricity only about one-third of the time, when the wind is blowing.

10   Solar collectors must be built to the same scale. It would take 20 square miles of highly polished mirrors or photovoltaic cells to equal the output of one nuclear reactor—and then only when the sun shines. Such facilities may one day provide supplementary power or peaking output during hot summer afternoons, but they will never be able to supply the uninterrupted flow of electricity required by an industrial society.

11   It will be impossible to meet the consumer demands of a contemporary society without a reliable source of energy like nuclear. Other countries have already acknowledged this. There are 65 reactors under construction around the world (far safer and more advanced than the 30-year-old technology at Fukushima Daiichi), but none in the U.S.

12   The Russians' sale of uranium to the world comes with an offer to take back the "nuclear waste" and reprocess it into more fuel, at a profit. The Chinese have commercialized their first Integral Fast Breeder, a reactor that can burn any kind of "waste" and promises unlimited quantities of cheap energy.

13   We have become the world's predominant industrial power because our forebears were willing to take the risks and make the sacrifices necessary to develop new technologies—the steam engine, coal mining, electricity, automobiles, airplanes, electronics, space travel. If we are not willing to take this next set of risks, others will. Then the torch will be passed to another generation that is not our own and our children and grandchildren will live with the consequences.

If the Japanese Can't Build a Safe Nuclear Reactor, Who Can?
Anne Applebaum

1   In the aftermath of a disaster, the strengths of any society become immediately visible. The cohesiveness, resilience, technological brilliance and extraordinary competence of the Japanese are on full display. One report from Rikuzentakata—a town of 25,000, annihilated by the tsunami that followed Friday's massive earthquake—describes volunteer firefighters

working to clear rubble and search for survivors; troops and police efficiently directing traffic and supplies; survivors are not only "calm and pragmatic" but also coping "with politeness and sometimes amazingly good cheer."

2   Thanks to these strengths, Japan will eventually recover. But at least one Japanese nuclear power complex will not. As I write, three reactors at the Fukushima Daiichi nuclear power station appear to have lost their cooling capacity. Engineers are flooding the plant with seawater—effectively destroying it—and then letting off radioactive steam. There have been two explosions. The situation may worsen in the coming hours.

3   Yet Japan's nuclear power stations were designed with the same care and precision as everything else in the country. More to the point, as the only country in the world to have experienced true nuclear catastrophe, Japan had an incentive to build well, as well as the capability, laws and regulations to do so. Which leads to an unavoidable question: If the competent and technologically brilliant Japanese can't build a completely safe reactor, who can?

4   It can—and will—be argued that the Japanese situation is extraordinary. Few countries are as vulnerable to natural catastrophe as Japan, and the scale of this earthquake is unprecedented. But there are other kinds of extraordinary situations and unprecedented circumstances. In an attempt to counter the latest worst-possible scenarios, a Franco-German company began constructing a super-safe, "next-generation" nuclear reactor in Finland several years ago. The plant was designed to withstand the impact of an airplane—a post-Sept. 11 concern—and includes a chamber allegedly able to contain a core meltdown. But it was also meant to cost $4 billion and to be completed in 2009. Instead, after numerous setbacks, it is still unfinished—and may now cost $6 billion or more.

5   Ironically, the Finnish plant was meant to launch the renaissance of the nuclear power industry in Europe—an industry that has, of late, enjoyed a renaissance around the world, thanks almost entirely to fears of climate change. Nuclear plants emit no carbon. As a result, nuclear plants, after a long, post-Chernobyl lull, have became fashionable again. Some 62 nuclear reactors are under construction at the moment, according to the World Nuclear Association; a further 158 are being planned and 324 others have been proposed.

6   Increasingly, nuclear power is also promoted because it safe. Which it is—except, of course, when it is not. Chances of a major disaster are tiny, one in a hundred million. But in the event of a statistically improbable major disaster, the damage could include, say, the destruction of a city or the poisoning of a country. The cost of such a potential catastrophe is partly reflected in the price of plant construction, and it partly explains the cost overruns in Finland: Nobody can risk the tiniest flaw in the concrete or the most minimal reduction in the quality of the steel.

7   But as we are about to learn in Japan, the true costs of nuclear power are never reflected even in the very high price of plant construction. Inevitably, the enormous costs of nuclear waste disposal fall to taxpayers, not the

7   Excluding large hydroelectric operations, less than 12% of the state's electricity came from renewable sources in 2007, according to the commission. Solar ranked last, supplying just 0.2% of California's needs. Rooftop photovoltaic panels are unaffordable or impractical for most Californians even with generous state incentives.

8   Enter Big Solar.

9   Proponents say utility-scale solar is a way to get lots of clean megawatts online quickly, efficiently and at lower costs. Solar thermal plants such as Ausra's are essentially giant boilers made of glass and steel. They use the sun's heat to create steam to power turbines that generate electricity.

10   Costing about 18 cents a kilowatt-hour at present, solar thermal power is roughly 40% cheaper than that generated by the silicon-based panels that sit on the roofs of homes and businesses, according to a June report by Clean Edge Inc. and the Co-op American Foundation. Analysts say improved technology and economies of scale should help lower the cost of solar thermal to about 5 cents a kilowatt-hour by 2025. That would put it on par with coal, the cheap but carbon-spewing fuel that generates about half the nation's electricity.

11   Size matters, said Sun Microsystems Inc. co-founder-turned-venture-capitalist Vinod Khosla, whose Khosla Ventures has invested more than $30 million in Ausra. A square patch of desert about 92 miles long on each

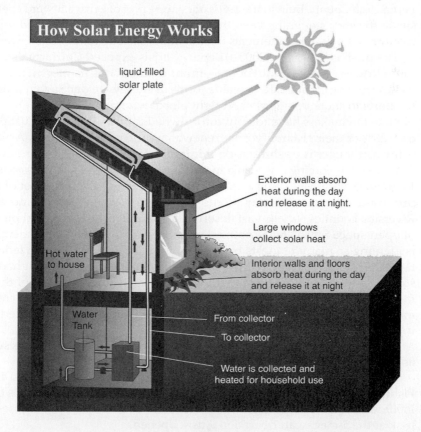

side blanketed with Ausra's technology could generate enough electricity to meet the entire nation's demand, company executives say. "Utility-scale solar is probably the only way to achieve real scale . . . and reduce our carbon emissions" significantly, Khosla said.

12   Critics fear that massive solar farms would create as many environmental problems as they purport to solve. This new-age electricity still requires old-fashioned power towers and high-voltage lines to get it to people's homes. A proposed 150-mile transmission line known as the Sunrise Powerlink that would carry renewable power from Imperial County to San Diego has run into stiff resistance from grass-roots groups and environmentalists.

13   Solar plants require staggering amounts of land, which could threaten fragile ecosystems and mar the stark beauty of America's deserts. And in contrast to rooftop panels, which enable homeowners to pursue energy independence, these centralized facilities keep consumers tethered to utility companies.

14   "They are trying to perpetuate the old Big Energy paradigm into the renewable-energy era," said Sheila Bowers, a Santa Monica attorney and environmental activist. "They have a monopoly agenda."

15   California already has the largest operating collection of solar thermal facilities in the world: nine plants totaling just over 350 megawatts in San Bernardino County. Built in the 1980s, they were part of a drive toward energy self-sufficiency stemming from the '70s oil shocks. The boom ended when California dropped requirements forcing utilities to buy renewable power.

16   The push is back. The 2000–01 energy crisis exposed California's continued dependence on outsiders—more than 30% of its electricity still comes from out of state. Renewable forms of energy are once again central to efforts to shore up supply and fight global warming.

17   State lawmakers have told investor-owned utilities that they must procure 20% of their electricity from renewable sources by 2010; Gov. Arnold Schwarzenegger is pushing for a minimum of 33% by 2020. A landmark 2006 state law forcing California to reduce its greenhouse gas emissions to 1990 levels within 12 years also is boosting green generation. Most of the proposed utility-scale solar plants are slated for San Bernardino and Riverside counties, whose vast deserts offer abundant sunshine and plenty of open space for the behemoths. The U.S. Bureau of Land Management is juggling so many requests from companies looking to build on federal land—79 at last count, covering more than 690,000 acres—that it had to stop accepting applications for a few weeks last summer. Many of these facilities may never get built. Environmentalists are mobilizing. U.S. credit markets are in a deep freeze. Oil and natural gas prices are falling, reducing some of the urgency to go green.

18   Still, the obstacles haven't clouded the ambitions of solar start-ups such as Ausra.

19   "Our investors perceive there is a huge opportunity here," said Bob Fishman, Ausra's president and chief executive. A group of dignitaries that included Schwarzenegger gathered near here in October to get a close-up look at the 5-megawatt operation Ausra opened.

20   The company uses a technology known as a compact linear Fresnel reflector. Acres of mirrors are anchored to metal frames and held roughly 6 feet off the ground in parallel rows. Controlled by computers, these panels make hundreds of barely perceptible movements throughout the day, tracking the sun's path across the sky.

21   The mirrors catch the sun's rays and reflect them onto a cluster of water pipes overhead. The intense heat—it can reach 750 degrees—generates pressurized steam inside the pipes. That steam is then fed into a turbine whose spinning generates electricity.

22   "It's like when you were a kid and you used a magnifying glass to fry a bug" on a sunny day, said Dave DeGraaf, vice president of product development. "We're focusing all that energy."

23   Despite its mammoth size, this pilot plant generates a modest amount of electricity, enough to power just 3,500 homes when the sun is shining. Ausra is thinking much bigger.

24   It has set up a manufacturing facility in Nevada that will supply a 177-megawatt solar plant planned for a site near Carrizo Plain National Monument in eastern San Luis Obispo County.

25   The facility's mirrors will occupy a full square mile of terrain. The project is still in the permitting process. Ausra has never tried something on this scale. But Pacific Gas & Electric is confident enough that is has agreed to buy the power from Carrizo to help it meet its green energy needs.

26   Other companies looking to shine in California with utility-scale plants include Solel Inc., whose proposed 553-megawatt project in the Mojave Desert would span nine square miles; BrightSource Energy Inc. of Oakland; SunPower Corp. of San Jose; OptiSolar Inc. of Hayward, Calif.; Stirling Energy Systems Inc. of Phoenix; and FPL Energy of Juno Beach, Fla.

27   "Climate change is the greatest challenge that mankind has ever faced," said Peter Darbee, president and chief executive of Pacific Gas & Electric and head of its parent, San Francisco-based PG&E Corp. "It's imperative to seek out the most cost-effective solutions."

Here Comes the Sun
Paul Krugman

1   For decades the story of technology has been dominated, in the popular mind and to a large extent in reality, by computing and the things you can do with it. Moore's Law—in which the price of computing power falls

roughly 50 percent every 18 months—has powered an ever-expanding range of applications, from faxes to Facebook.

2   Our mastery of the material world, on the other hand, has advanced much more slowly. The sources of energy, the way we move stuff around, are much the same as they were a generation ago.

3   But that may be about to change. We are, or at least we should be, on the cusp of an energy transformation, driven by the rapidly falling cost of solar power. That's right, solar power.

4   If that surprises you, if you still think of solar power as some kind of hippie fantasy, blame our fossilized political system, in which fossil fuel producers have both powerful political allies and a powerful propaganda machine that denigrates alternatives.

5   Speaking of propaganda: Before I get to solar, let's talk briefly about hydraulic fracturing, aka fracking.

6   Fracking—injecting high-pressure fluid into rocks deep underground, inducing the release of fossil fuels—is an impressive technology. But it's also a technology that imposes large costs on the public. We know that it produces toxic (and radioactive) wastewater that contaminates drinking water; there is reason to suspect, despite industry denials, that it also contaminates groundwater; and the heavy trucking required for fracking inflicts major damage on roads.

7   Economics 101 tells us that an industry imposing large costs on third parties should be required to "internalize" those costs—that is, to pay for the damage it inflicts, treating that damage as a cost of production. Fracking might still be worth doing given those costs. But no industry should be held harmless from its impacts on the environment and the nation's infrastructure.

8   Yet what the industry and its defenders demand is, of course, precisely that it be let off the hook for the damage it causes. Why? Because we need that energy! For example, the industry-backed organization *energyfromshale.org* declares that "there are only two sides in the debate: those who want our oil and natural resources developed in a safe and responsible way; and those who don't want our oil and natural gas resources developed at all."

9   So it's worth pointing out that special treatment for fracking makes a mockery of free-market principles. Pro-fracking politicians claim to be against subsidies, yet letting an industry impose costs without paying compensation is in effect a huge subsidy. They say they oppose having the government "pick winners," yet they demand special treatment for this industry precisely because they claim it will be a winner.

10   And now for something completely different: the success story you haven't heard about.

11   These days, mention solar power and you'll probably hear cries of "Solyndra!" Republicans have tried to make the failed solar panel company both a symbol of government waste—although claims of a major scandal are nonsense—and a stick with which to beat renewable energy.

12   But Solyndra's failure was actually caused by technological success: the price of solar panels is dropping fast, and Solyndra couldn't keep up with the competition. In fact, progress in solar panels has been so dramatic and sustained that, as a blog post at *Scientific American* put it, "there's now frequent talk of a 'Moore's law' in solar energy," with prices adjusted for inflation falling around 7 percent a year.

13   This has already led to rapid growth in solar installations, but even more change may be just around the corner. If the downward trend continues— and if anything it seems to be accelerating—we're just a few years from the point at which electricity from solar panels becomes cheaper than electricity generated by burning coal.

14   And if we priced coal-fired power right, taking into account the huge health and other costs it imposes, it's likely that we would already have passed that tipping point.

15   But will our political system delay the energy transformation now within reach?

16   Let's face it: a large part of our political class, including essentially the entire G.O.P., is deeply invested in an energy sector dominated by fossil fuels, and actively hostile to alternatives. This political class will do everything it can to ensure subsidies for the extraction and use of fossil fuels, directly with taxpayers' money and indirectly by letting the industry off the hook for environmental costs, while ridiculing technologies like solar.

17   So what you need to know is that nothing you hear from these people is true. Fracking is not a dream come true; solar is now cost-effective. Here comes the sun, if we're willing to let it in.

Solar Is Getting Cheaper, but How Far Can It Go?
Brad Plumer

1   The usual take on solar power is that it's a niche energy source, too pricey and erratic to meet more than a sliver of our electricity needs. Bill Gates has mocked solar as "cute." But, as Paul Krugman reminds us today, that's changing far more quickly than people realize. "In fact," Krugman writes, "progress in solar panels has been so dramatic and sustained that, as a blog post at *Scientific American* put it, 'there's now frequent talk of a Moore's law in solar energy,' with prices adjusted for inflation falling around 7 percent a year."

2   A couple of things are driving the drop in costs. Solar-panel technology is getting more efficient, true, but that's just part of the tale. China is also heavily subsidizing its domestic industry, driving a 40 percent plunge in prices over the past year (and bulldozing a few U.S. companies into

bankruptcy). But it's not all about over-production from China, either. Solar companies are figuring out how to set up systems cheaply: installation and other non-module costs in the United States dropped 17 percent in 2010.

3   One big point to add to Krugman's column is that solar is *already* being deployed on a large scale. Tom Dinwoodie, chief technical officer at SunPower, notes that the industry has been growing at a 65 percent annual rate in the past five years. In 2010, some 17 gigawatts of solar power were manufactured, shipped and installed—the equivalent of 17 large nuclear power plants. So just how far can solar go?

4   One key question is whether solar can reach "grid parity"—the point at which it can compete with fossil fuels without subsidies. As Shayle Kann explains at Greentech Media, this could happen in two ways. One, solar would become attractive to utilities even after accounting for the fact that the sun doesn't always shine. At some point, for example, power companies may decide to rely on solar for hot, electricity-gobbling afternoons instead of relying on dirty natural-gas peaking plants. Alternatively, solar could reach the point at which huge numbers of retail consumers see big savings on their energy bills from installing rooftop solar.

5   It's hard to know when, exactly, grid parity will arrive. Kees van der Leun, of the energy consulting firm Ecofys, predicts that solar could be competitive with fossil fuels by 2018 or so. On the other hand, as Tyler Cowen notes, energy markets don't appear to be betting on this development. If it does happen at some point, though, a steep plunge in solar costs could be incredibly transformative. The International Energy Agency projects that solar could provide more than half of the world's energy needs by 2060 if costs fell to $100 per megawatt hour—around 50 cents per watt installed. (At the moment, solar panels are gunning for the $1-per-watt threshold.)

6   A lot depends on government policy. The progress being made by the U.S. solar industry will likely slow at the end of this year if a federal grant program that makes a production tax credit more accessible is allowed to expire. A price on carbon would also make a big difference in giving solar a leg up against fossil fuels, which currently offload some of their total cost into the atmosphere. And the Energy Department is pushing research into energy storage and other technologies—check out the Optical Cavity Furnace—to bring prices down. So there are a lot of variables here. But at this point, it's safe to say that solar has moved squarely out of "cute" territory.

WIND POWER

As one heads southwest toward San Francisco on Route 580 in northern California, approaching the barren hills of the Altamont Pass between Livermore and Tracy, an eerie sight gradually reveals itself. Lining the hillsides and hilltops on both sides of the highway, numerous columns of wind turbines stand sentry as if waiting to attack the vehicles passing below. The Livermore wind farm was one of the first in the world and is still one of the largest, consisting of over 4,900 medium-size wind turbines that generate 576 megawatts (thousand watts) of electricity per year. There are hundreds of wind farms around the world. China's turbines annually generate more than 44 gigawatts (thousand megawatts) of the world's total estimated consumption of more than 1,700 gigawatts—1.7 terawatts—of electricity. The United States' wind farms generate 40 gigawatts, followed by Germany (27 gigawatts), Spain (20), and India (13). Collectively, the world's wind farms create 194 gigawatts. Denmark (treated in Kolbert, below), at 3.7 gigawatts, generates almost 20% of its energy from wind power.

Many of the advantages and disadvantages of solar power also apply to wind power. Both are clean, renewable sources of energy. Neither needs to be laboriously and dangerously extracted from the earth. The raw materials are free. But so far, neither solar nor wind power can generate electricity on anything approaching the scale of fossil fuels or nuclear power. Both solar and wind are intermittent energy sources: Just as the sun doesn't always shine, the wind doesn't always blow. When the sun and the wind stop, backup power must be provided by fossil fuels, unless the energy has been stored. So far, however, large-scale energy storage from these sources is not viable. Additionally, wind farms, even more than industrial solar arrays, require vast amounts of acreage. Besides being unsightly (to some), wind turbines kill bats and birds (including eagles). Environmentalists worry about them damaging fragile ecosystems. Others oppose them on both aesthetic and economic grounds. In the acerbic opinion of British broadcaster Eric Robson, "It's surely self-evident that wind farms are an economic and technological nonsense, sustainable only if the government stuffs their owners' mouths with money, but slack-brained environmentalists hail them as the answer to all our prayers."*

Two perspectives on wind power are presented in the following selections. In "The Island in the Wind," excerpted from a longer article in the *New Yorker,* Elizabeth Kolbert describes in vivid imagery "an unlikely social movement": how the people of the Danish island of Samsø got all their homes and farms to run on electricity generated entirely by wind power. Kolbert is a journalist who specializes in environmental issues. She wrote for the *New York Times* from 1984 to 1999 and has been a staff reporter for *The New Yorker* since 1999. She is the author of *Field Notes from a Catastrophe: Man and Nature and Climate Change* (2006). In "Wind Power Puffery," H. Sterling Burnett discusses the limitations and drawbacks of wind power. Burnett is a senior fellow with the National Center for Policy Analysis. In 2000 he served as a member of the Environment and Natural Resources Task Force in the Texas Comptroller's e-Texas commission. His articles and opinion pieces have been published in *Environmental Ethics, International Studies in Philosophy, USA Today,* the *Los Angeles Daily News, Rocky Mountain News,* and the *Seattle Times.* This piece appeared in the *Washington Times* on 4 February 2004.

---

*Eric Robson, *Outside Broadcaster*, Frances Lincoln Ltd, 2007: p. 177.

The Island in the Wind
Elizabeth Kolbert

1   Jørgen Tranberg is a farmer who lives on the Danish island of Samsø. He is a beefy man with a mop of brown hair and an unpredictable sense of humor. When I arrived at his house, one gray morning this spring, he was sitting in his kitchen, smoking a cigarette and watching grainy images on a black-and-white TV. The images turned out to be closed-circuit shots from his barn. One of his cows, he told me, was about to give birth, and he was keeping an eye on her. We talked for a few minutes, and then, laughing, he asked me if I wanted to climb his wind turbine. I was pretty sure I didn't, but I said yes anyway.

2   We got into Tranberg's car and bounced along a rutted dirt road. The turbine loomed up in front of us. When we reached it, Tranberg stubbed out his cigarette and opened a small door in the base of the tower. Inside were eight ladders, each about twenty feet tall, attached one above the other. We started up, and were soon huffing. Above the last ladder, there was a trapdoor, which led to a sort of engine room. We scrambled into it, at which point we were standing on top of the generator. Tranberg pressed a button, and the roof slid open to reveal the gray sky and a patchwork of green and brown fields stretching toward the sea. He pressed another button. The rotors, which he had switched off during our climb, started to turn, at first sluggishly and then much more rapidly. It felt as if we were about to take off. I'd like to say the feeling was exhilarating; in fact, I found it sickening. Tranberg looked at me and started to laugh.

3   Samsø, which is roughly the size of Nantucket, sits in what's known as the Kattegat, an arm of the North Sea. The island is bulgy in the south and narrows to a bladelike point in the north, so that on a map it looks a bit like a woman's torso and a bit like a meat cleaver. It has twenty-two villages that hug the narrow streets; out back are fields where farmers grow potatoes and wheat and strawberries. Thanks to Denmark's peculiar geography, Samsø is smack in the center of the country and, at the same time, in the middle of nowhere.

4   For the past decade or so, Samsø has been the site of an unlikely social movement. When it began, in the late nineteen-nineties, the island's forty-three hundred inhabitants had what might be described as a conventional attitude toward energy: as long as it continued to arrive, they weren't much interested in it. Most Samsingers heated their houses with oil, which was brought in on tankers. They used electricity imported from the mainland via cable, much of which was generated by burning coal. As a result, each Samsinger put into the atmosphere, on average, nearly eleven tons of carbon dioxide annually.

5   Then, quite deliberately, the residents of the island set about changing this. They formed energy coöperatives and organized seminars on wind

Catching the wind

Alternative energy sources are getting a new look as demand for fossil fuels increases worldwide, and as technical innovations help reduce the costs of alternatives. California produces more wind-generated electricity than any state except Texas and Iowa. A look at wind farms:

Wind turbine

These modern windmills catch the wind by either turning into or away from air currents that blow from 8 to 65 mph.

Rotor

130 feet

Rotors move to increase efficiency.

Enclosure

Generator

WIND DIRECTION

Enclosure rotates so rotor blades face into or away from the wind.

Cables carry electric flow down the tower.

230 feet

Tower

The step-up transformer allows the electricity to be transferred to the power grid.

Human figure to scale

How it works

Wind moves a propeller, which turns shafts to work a generator.

❶ Anemometer, which gauges wind speed and direction, sends the information to the controller.

Anemometer

Rotor

Gearbox

Low-speed shaft

Enclosure

High-speed shaft

Brake

Controller

Generator

Yaw bearings

Yaw motor

Tower

❷ The controller directs the yaw motor to turn the rotor to face toward or away from the wind.

❸ A gearbox converts the slow rotations of one shaft into fast rotations of a second shaft.

❹ The high-speed shaft drives a generator that converts mechanical energy to electricity.

Upside, downside

Wind power producers get tax credits and state incentives, and don't have to worry about fuel price increases, pollution production or long construction delays. Some drawbacks:

- Sites with consistent high wind are limited.
- Turbines are loud.
- Blades are a danger to birds.
- Older turbines are less cost-effective.
- Views are affected.
- Installation can be costly.

Shrinking bottom line

The Electric Power Research Institute estimates that the cost of producing wind power has dropped fourfold since 1980.

Sources: California Energy Commission, National Wind Technology Center, U.S. Department of Energy's Energy Information Administration, National Renewable Energy Laboratory

DOUG STEVENS Los Angeles Times

power. They removed their furnaces and replaced them with heat pumps. By 2001, fossil-fuel use on Samsø had been cut in half. By 2003, instead of importing electricity, the island was exporting it, and by 2005 it was producing from renewable sources more energy than it was using.

6   The residents of Samsø that I spoke to were clearly proud of their accomplishment. All the same, they insisted on their ordinariness. They were, they noted, not wealthy, nor were they especially well educated or idealistic. They weren't even terribly adventuresome. "We are a conservative farming community" is how one Samsinger put it. "We are only normal people," Tranberg told me. "We are not some special people."

7   This year, the world is expected to burn through some thirty-one billion barrels of oil, six billion tons of coal, and a hundred trillion cubic feet of natural gas. The combustion of these fossil fuels will produce, in aggregate, some four hundred quadrillion B.T.U.s of energy. It will also yield around thirty billion tons of carbon dioxide. Next year, global consumption of

fossil fuels is expected to grow by about two per cent, meaning that emissions will rise by more than half a billion tons, and the following year consumption is expected to grow by yet another two per cent.

8   When carbon dioxide is released into the air, about a third ends up, in relatively short order, in the oceans. (CO_2 dissolves in water to form a weak acid; this is the cause of the phenomenon known as "ocean acidification.") A quarter is absorbed by terrestrial ecosystems—no one is quite sure exactly how or where—and the rest remains in the atmosphere. If current trends in emissions continue, then sometime within the next four or five decades the chemistry of the oceans will have been altered to such a degree that many marine organisms—including reef-building corals—will be pushed toward extinction. Meanwhile, atmospheric CO_2 levels are projected to reach five hundred and fifty parts per million—twice pre-industrial levels—virtually guaranteeing an eventual global temperature increase of three or more degrees. The consequences of this warming are difficult to predict in detail, but even broad, conservative estimates are terrifying: at least fifteen and possibly as many as thirty per cent of the planet's plant and animal species will be threatened; sea levels will rise by several feet; yields of crops like wheat and corn will decline significantly in a number of areas where they are now grown as staples; regions that depend on glacial runoff or seasonal snowmelt—currently home to more than a billion people—will face severe water shortages; and what now counts as a hundred-year drought will occur in some parts of the world as frequently as once a decade.

9   Today, with CO_2 levels at three hundred and eighty-five parts per million, the disruptive impacts of climate change are already apparent. The Arctic ice cap, which has shrunk by half since the nineteen-fifties, is melting at an annual rate of twenty-four thousand square miles, meaning that an expanse of ice the size of West Virginia is disappearing each year. Over the past ten years, forests covering a hundred and fifty million acres in the United States and Canada have died from warming-related beetle infestations. It is believed that rising temperatures are contributing to the growing number of international refugees—"Climate change is today one of the main drivers of forced displacement," the United Nations' high commissioner for refugees, António Guterres, said recently—and to armed conflict: some experts see a link between the fighting in Darfur, which has claimed as many as three hundred thousand lives, and changes in rainfall patterns in equatorial Africa.

10   "If we keep going down this path, the Darfur crisis will be only one crisis among dozens of other," President Nicolas Sarkozy, of France, told a meeting of world leaders in April. The Secretary-General of the United Nations, Ban Ki-moon, has called climate change "the defining challenge of our age."

11   In the context of this challenge, Samsø's accomplishments could be seen as trivial. Certainly, in numerical terms they don't amount to much: all the island's avoided emissions of the past ten years are overwhelmed by the CO_2 that a single coal-fired power plant will emit in the next three weeks, and China is building new coal-fired plants at the rate of roughly four a

month. But it is also in this context that the island's efforts are most significant. Samsø transformed its energy systems in a single decade. Its experience suggests how the carbon problem, as huge as it is, could be dealt with, if we were willing to try.

12   Samsø set out to reinvent itself thanks to a series of decisions that it had relatively little to do with. The first was made by the Danish Ministry of Environment and Energy in 1997. The ministry, looking for ways to promote innovation, decided to sponsor a renewable-energy contest. In order to enter, a community had to submit a plan showing how it could wean itself off fossil fuels. An engineer who didn't actually live on Samsø thought the island would make a good candidate. In consultation with Samsø's mayor, he drew up a plan and submitted it. When it was announced that Samsø had won, the general reaction among residents was puzzlement. "I had to listen twice before I believed it," one farmer told me.

13   The brief surge of interest that followed the announcement soon dissipated. Besides its designation as Denmark's "renewable-energy island," Samsø received basically nothing—no prize money or special tax breaks, or even government assistance. One of the few people on the island to think the project was worth pursuing was Søren Hermansen.

14   Hermansen, who is now forty-nine, is a trim man with close-cropped hair, ruddy cheeks, and dark-blue eyes. He was born on Samsø and, save for a few stints away, to travel and go to university, has lived there his entire life. His father was a farmer who grew, among other things, beets and parsley. Hermansen, too, tried his hand at farming—he took over the family's hundred acres when his father retired—but he discovered he wasn't suited to it. "I like to talk, and vegetables don't respond," he told me. He leased his fields to a neighbor and got a job teaching environmental studies at a local boarding school. Hermansen found the renewable-energy-island concept intriguing. When some federal money was found to fund a single staff position, he became the project's first employee.

15   For months, which stretched into years, not much happened. "There was this conservative hesitating, waiting for the neighbor to do the move," Hermansen recalled. "I know the community and I know this is what usually happens." Rather than working against the islanders' tendency to look to one another, Hermansen tried to work with it.

16   "One reason to live here can be social relations," he said. "This renewable-energy project could be a new kind of social relation, and we used that." Whenever there was a meeting to discuss a local issue—any local issue—Hermansen attended and made his pitch. He asked Samsingers to think about what it would be like to work together on something they could all be proud of. Occasionally, he brought free beer along to the discussions. Meanwhile, he began trying to enlist the support of the island's opinion leaders. "This is where the hard work starts, convincing the first movers to be active," he said. Eventually, much as Hermansen had hoped, the social dynamic that had stalled the project began to work in its favor. As more people got involved, that prompted others to do so. After a while, enough Samsingers were participating that participation became the norm.

17   "People on Samsø started thinking about energy," Ingvar Jørgensen, a farmer who heats his house with solar hot water and a straw-burning furnace, told me. "It became a kind of sport."

18   "It's exciting to be a part of this," Brian Kjæ, an electrician who installed a small-scale turbine in his back yard, said. Kjæ's turbine, which is seventy-two feet tall generates more current than his family of three can use, and also more than the power lines leading away from his house can handle, so he uses the excess to heat water, which he stores in a tank that he rigged up in his garage. He told me that one day he would like to use the leftover electricity to produce hydrogen, which could potentially run a fuel-cell car.

19   "Søren, he has talked again and again, and slowly it's spread to a lot of people," he said.

20   Since becoming the "renewable energy island," Samsø has increasingly found itself an object of study. Researchers often travel great distances to get there, a fact that is not without its own irony. The day after I arrived, from New York via Copenhagen, a group of professors from the University of Toyama, in Japan, came to look around. They had arranged a tour with Hermansen, and he invited me to tag along. We headed off to meet the group in his electric Citroën, which is painted blue with white puffy clouds on the doors. It was a drizzly day, and when we got to the dock the water was choppy. Hermansen commiserated with the Japanese, who had just disembarked from the swaying ferry; then we all boarded a bus.

21   Our first stop was a hillside with a panoramic view of the island. Several wind turbines exactly like the one I had climbed with Tranberg were whooshing nearby. In the wet and the gray, they were the only things stirring. Off in the distance, the silent fields gave way to the Kattegat, where another group of turbines could be seen, arranged in a soldierly line in the water.

22   All told, Samsø has eleven large land-based turbines. (It has about a dozen additional micro-turbines.) This is a lot of turbines for a relatively small number of people, and the ratio is critical to Samsø's success, as is the fact that the wind off the Kattegat blows pretty much continuously; flags on Samsø, I noticed, do not wave—they stick straight out, as in children's drawings. Hermansen told us that the land-based turbines are a hundred and fifty feet tall, with rotors that are eighty feet long. Together, they produce some twenty-six million kilowatt-hours a year, which is just about enough to meet all the island's demands for electricity. (This is true in an arithmetic sense; as a practical matter, Samsø's production of electricity and its needs fluctuate, so that sometimes it is feeding power into the grid and sometimes it is drawing power from it.) The offshore turbines, meanwhile, are even taller—a hundred and ninety-five feet high, with rotors that extend a hundred and twenty feet. A single offshore turbine generates roughly eight million kilowatt-hours of electricity a year, which, at Danish rates of energy use, is enough to satisfy the needs of some two thousand homes. The offshore turbines—there are ten of them—were erected to compensate for Samsø's continuing use of fossil fuels in its cars, trucks, and ferries. Their combined output, of around eighty million kilowatt-hours a

year, provides the energy equivalent of all the gasoline and diesel oil consumed on the island, and then some; in aggregate, Samsø generates about
ten per cent more power than it consumes.

23   "When we started, in 1997, nobody expected this to happen,"
Hermansen told the group. "When we talked to local people, they said,
Yes, come on, maybe in your dreams." Each land-based turbine cost the
equivalent of eight hundred and fifty thousand dollars. Each offshore turbine cost around three million dollars. Some of Samsø's turbines were
erected by a single investor, like Tranberg; others were purchased collectively. At least four hundred and fifty island residents own shares in the
onshore turbines, and a roughly equal number own shares in those offshore. Shareholders, who also include many nonresidents, receive annual
dividend checks based on the prevailing price of electricity and how much
their turbine has generated.

24   "If I'm reduced to being a customer, then if I like something I buy it, and
if I don't like it I don't buy it," Hermansen said. "But I don't care about the
production. We care about the production, because we own the wind turbines. Every time they turn around, it means money in the bank. And,
being part of it, we also feel responsible." Thanks to a policy put in place
by Denmark's government in the late nineteen-nineties, utilities are
required to offer ten-year fixed-rate contracts for wind power that they can
sell to customers elsewhere. Under the terms of these contracts, a turbine
should—barring mishap—repay a shareholder's -initial investment in
about eight years.

25   From the hillside, we headed to the town of Ballen. There we stopped at
a red shed-shaped building made out of corrugated metal. Inside, enormous
bales of straw were stacked against the walls. Hermansen explained that the
building was a district heating plant that had been designed to run on biomass. The bales, each representing the equivalent of fifty gallons of oil,
would be fed into a furnace, where water would be heated to a hundred and
fifty-eight degrees. This hot water would then be piped underground to two
hundred and sixty houses in Ballen and in the neighboring town of Brundby.
In this way, the energy of the straw burned at the plant would be transferred
to the homes, where it could be used to provide heat and hot water.

26   Samsø has two other district heating plants that burn straw—one in
Tranebjerg, the other in Onsbjerg—and also a district plant, in Nordby, that
burns wood chips. When we visited the Nordby plant, later that afternoon,
it was filled with what looked like mulch. (The place smelled like a potting
shed.) Out back was a field covered in rows of solar panels, which provide
additional hot water when the sun is shining. Between the rows, sheep with
long black faces were munching on the grass. The Japanese researchers
pulled out their cameras as the sheep snuffled toward them, expectantly.

27   Of course, burning straw or wood, like burning fossil fuels, produces
CO_2. The key distinction is that while fossil fuels release carbon that otherwise would have remained sequestered, biomass releases carbon that
would have entered the atmosphere anyway, through decomposition. As
long as biomass regrows, the CO_2 released in its combustion should be

reabsorbed, meaning that the cycle is—or at least can be—carbon neutral. The wood chips used in the Nordby plant come from fallen trees that previously would have been left to rot. The straw for the Ballen-Brundby plant comes mainly from wheat stalks that would previously have been burned in the fields. Together, the biomass heating plants prevent the release of some twenty-seven hundred tons of carbon dioxide a year.

28   In addition to biomass, Samsø is experimenting on a modest scale with biofuels: a handful of farmers have converted their cars and tractors to run on canola oil. We stopped to visit one such farmer, who grows his own seeds, presses his own oil, and feeds the leftover mash to his cows. The farmer couldn't be located, so Hermansen started up the press himself. He stuck a finger under the spout, then popped it into his mouth. "The oil is very good," he announced. "You can use it in your car, and you can use it on your salad."

29   After the tour, I went back with Hermansen to his office, in a building known as the Energiakademi. The academy, which looks like a Bauhaus interpretation of a barn, is covered with photovoltaic cells and insulated with shredded newspapers. It is supposed to serve as a sort of interpretive center, though when I visited, the place was so new that the rooms were mostly empty. Some high-school students were kneeling on the floor, trying to put together a miniature turbine.

30   I asked Hermansen whether there were any projects that hadn't worked out. He listed several, including a plan to use natural gas produced from cow manure and an experiment with electric cars that failed when one of the demonstration vehicles spent most of the year in the shop. The biggest disappointment, though, had to do with consumption.

31   "We made several programs for energy savings," he told me. "But people are acting—what do you call it?—irresponsibly. They behave like monkeys." For example, families that insulated their homes better also tended to heat more rooms, "so we ended up with zero." Essentially, he said, energy use on the island has remained constant for the past decade.

32   I asked why he thought the renewable-energy-island effort had got as far as it did. He said he wasn't sure, because different people had had different motives for participating. "From the very egoistic to the more overall perspective, I think we had all kinds of reasons."

33   Finally, I asked what he thought other communities might take from Samsø's experience.

34   "We always hear that we should think globally and act locally," he said. "I understand what that means—I think we as a nation should be part of the global consciousness. But each individual cannot be part of that. So 'Think locally, act locally' is the key message for us."

35   "There's this wish for showcases," he added. "When we are selected to be the showcase for Denmark, I feel ashamed that Denmark doesn't produce anything bigger than that. But I feel proud because we are the showcase. So I did my job, and my colleagues did their job, and so did the people of Samsø."

Wind Power Puffery
H. Sterling Burnett

1 Whenever there is a discussion of energy policy, many environmentalists and their political allies tout wind power as an alternative to burning fossil fuels. Even if electricity from wind power is more expensive than conventional fuel sources, and it is, wind advocates argue its environmental benefits are worth it. In particular, proponents claim increased reliance on wind power would reduce air pollution and greenhouse gas emissions.

2 But is this assertion correct? No, the truth is wind power's environmental benefits are usually overstated, while its significant environmental harms are often ignored.

3 Close inspection of wind power finds the promised air pollution improvements do not materialize. There are several reasons, the principal one being that wind farms generate power only when the wind blows within a certain range of speed. When there is too little wind, wind towers don't generate power. Conversely, when the wind is too strong, they must be shut off for fear of being blown down.

4 Due to this fundamental limitation, wind farms need conventional power plants to supplement the power they supply and to replace a wind farm's expected supply to the grid when the towers are not turning. After all, the power grid requires a regulated constant flow of energy to function properly.

5 Yet bringing a conventional power plant on line to supply power is not as simple as turning on a switch. Most "redundant" fossil fuel power stations must run, even if at reduced levels, continuously. When these factors are combined with the emissions of pollutants and CO_2 caused by the manufacture and maintenance of wind towers and their associated infrastructure, very little of the air quality improvements actually result from expansion of wind power.

6 There are other problems. A recent report from Great Britain—where wind power is growing even faster than in the U.S.—says that as wind farms grow, wind power is increasingly unpopular. Why? Wind farms are noisy, land-intensive and unsightly. The industry has tricked its way into unspoiled countryside in "green" disguise by portraying wind farms as "parks." In reality, wind farms are more similar to highways, industrial buildings, railways and industrial farms. This wouldn't be a major consideration if it weren't that, because of the prevailing wind currents, the most favorable locations for wind farms usually are areas with particularly spectacular views in relatively wild places.

7 Worse, wind farms produce only a fraction of the energy of a conventional power plant but require hundreds of times the acreage. For instance, two of the biggest wind "farms" in Europe have 159 turbines and cover thousands of acres between them. But together they take a year to produce less than four days' output from a single 2,000-megawatt conventional

power station—which takes up 100 times fewer acres. And in the U.S., a proposed wind farm off the coast of Massachusetts would produce only 450 megawatts of power but require 130 towers and more than 24 square miles of ocean.

8   Perhaps the most well-publicized harmful environmental impact of wind power relates to its effect on birds and bats. For efficiency, wind farms must be located where the wind blows fairly constantly. Unfortunately, such locations are prime travel routes for migratory birds, including protected species like Bald and Golden Eagles. This motivated the Sierra Club to label wind towers "the Cuisinarts of the air."

9   Indeed, scientists estimate as many as 44,000 birds have been killed over the past 20 years by wind turbines in the Altamont Pass, east of San Francisco. The victims include kestrels, red-tailed hawks and golden eagles—an average of 50 golden eagles are killed each year.

10   These problems are exacerbated, explains one study, as "Wind farms have been documented to act as both bait and executioner—rodents taking shelter at the base of turbines multiply with the protection from raptors, while in turn their greater numbers attract more raptors to the farm."

11   Deaths are not limited to the United States or to birds. For example, at Tarif, Spain, thousands of birds from more than 13 species protected under European Union law have been killed by the site's 269 wind turbines. During last fall's migration, at least 400 bats, including red bats, eastern pipistrelles, hoary bats and possible endangered Indiana bats, were killed at a 44-turbine wind farm in West Virginia.

12   As a result of these problems and others, lawsuits are either pending or being considered to prevent expansion of wind farms in West Virginia and California and to prevent the construction of offshore wind farms in a number of New England states.

13   Indeed, the Audubon society has called for a moratorium on new wind development in bird-sensitive areas—which, because of the climatic conditions needed for wind farms, includes the vast majority of the suitable sites for proposed construction.

14   Wind power is expensive, doesn't deliver the environmental benefits it promises and has substantial environmental costs. In short, wind power is no bargain. Accordingly, it doesn't merit continued government promotion or funding.

ELECTRIC CARS

In 2006, American moviegoers lined up to see a fascinating murder mystery, *Who Killed the Electric Car?* The producers of this award-winning documentary pointed an accusatory finger at the vehicle's manufacturer, General Motors, which produced and leased thousands of the popular cars—the EV1 (for "electric vehicle 1")—between 1996 and 1999, only to repossess and crush the entire fleet when the vehicles proved unprofitable.*

Electric cars, which release no carbon emissions into the atmosphere, are environmentally appealing. Thus far, however, they remain a niche product because they're expensive, even when subsidized by the government, largely owing to their costly battery packs. Sales have also suffered because of so-called "range anxiety"—the fear among drivers that they would run out of electricity before reaching their destination and become stranded. The Chevy Volt, which went into production in 2010, runs only 35 miles on its battery pack before its backup gasoline engine kicks in; the all-electric Nissan Leaf runs 75 miles. Such ranges are adequate for most trips, but far less than what American consumers have come to expect. For these reasons, all-electric cars (as opposed to hybrids such as the Toyota Prius) cannot yet compete on a large scale with vehicles running on conventional internal combustion engines.

But battery technology is improving and, with it, the promise of practical, reasonably priced electric cars. To proponents of green power, the appeal of electric vehicles is obvious: By replacing gasoline with electric power, we can drastically reduce air pollution and CO_2 emissions from the exhaust pipes of millions of vehicles around the world. We also reduce our dependence upon oil and its politically unstable sources of supply. So electric cars—present from the dawn of the automobile era—may in fact be the wave of the future.

The following selections offer two current perspectives on the prospects for electric cars. The first is by Daniel Yergin, considered one of the world's most authoritative voices on energy issues. Yergin's earlier book *The Prize: The Epic Quest for Oil, Money, and Power* (1992), won the Pulitzer Prize for non-fiction and was later made into a PBS documentary mini-series. In the selection below, "The Great Electric Car Experiment," excerpted from his recent book *The Quest: Energy, Security, and the Remaking of the Modern World* (2011), Yergin discusses the technology of electric vehicles and the "race to reshape transportation." Then, somewhat dampening Yergin's enthusiasm, Joseph B. White explains "Why the Gasoline Engine Isn't Going Away Any Time Soon."

White reports on automobile and energy-related stories for the *Wall Street Journal*, where the article below first appeared on September 15, 2008.

---

*Ironically, when GM itself was dying several years later, and declared bankruptcy, it placed significant hopes for its renewal on its development of another electric vehicle, the Chevrolet Volt, which went on sale in 2010. After the federal government assumed a major financial stake in the company, GM subsequently became profitable again, though not because of the Volt, the sales of which were unimpressive. (During its first year, fewer than 7,000 Volts were sold, despite GM's initial forecast of 10,000.)

| The Great Electric Car Experiment |
| *Daniel Yergin* |

The Race Resumes

1   Oil had held its seemingly impregnable position as king of the realm of transportation for almost a century. By the beginning of the twenty-first century, however, people were beginning to question how long oil would—or should—hold on to its crown. Yet as late as 2007 in the debate over the future of automotive transportation, the electric car was only a peripheral topic. Biofuels were the focus.

2   Within a few years, however, the electric car would move onto center stage. It could, said its proponents, break the grip of oil on transportation, allowing motorists to unplug from turbulence in the oil-exporting world and high prices at the pump. It could help reduce pollution and offset the carbon emissions that precipitate climate change. And it could provide a powerful answer to the great puzzle of how the world can accommodate the move from one billion cars to two billion. The electric car is powered by electricity that can be generated from any number of different sources, none of which need be oil. Perhaps more than any other technology, the electric car represents a stark alternative road to the future for the global energy system.

3   The electric vision rapidly became so compelling that expectations for electric cars far exceed the actual impact such cars might have on the world's auto-fleet in terms of numbers, at least in the next decade or two. Yet their presence in the fleet, even if small, will change attitudes about both oil and autos far ahead of the numerical impact. In decades further out, the effect could be much larger. There are, however, two big questions: Can they deliver the performance that is promised at a cost that is acceptable? And will consumers choose to make them a mainstream purchase as opposed to a niche product?

4   In the meantime, very big bets are now being placed on the renewed race—between the battery and the internal combustion engine, between electricity and oil—that was supposedly decided a century ago. The outcome will have enormous significance in terms of both economics and geopolitics.

5   The conviction is also growing that electric vehicles could constitute a great "new industry," the epitome of cleantech, and the means to leapfrog to leadership in the global auto industry. This is a big opportunity for companies, entrepreneurs, and investors. But it is seen as much more than an opportunity in the marketplace. A French government minister has declared that "the battle of the electric car" has begun. "Electric vehicles are the future and the driver of the Industrial Revolution," said one of Europe's economic leaders. By 2010 the Obama administration had provided $5 billion in grants and loan guarantees to battery makers, entrepreneurs, major auto companies, and equipment suppliers to jump-start

the electric car and build out the infrastructure systems that would support it. "Here in the United States," Obama announced, "we've created an entire new industry."[1]

6   This, indeed, is a game of nations. For countries like China and Korea, it is the opportunity to take a dominant position in a critical growth sector. Conversely, success in electric transportation may be required if the traditional leading countries in automobiles—the United States, Japan, and Germany—are to maintain their positions. If batteries are to be the "new oil," then the winners in battery know-how and production can capture a decisive new role in the world economy—and the rewards that will go with that.

. . .

The Return of the EV

7 With the opening of the new century, several factors started to converge to give new life to the electric vehicle.

8   Environmental pollution from auto exhausts has created anguish and been a major topic of public policy in the United States. In the decades since, other urban areas, from Mexico City to Beijing, have come to suffer under similar affliction and have also sought to find relief from air pollution. Moreover, now there was something new: concern about climate change. Although transportation on a global basis is responsible for about 17 percent of CO_2 emissions, the absolute volume of emissions is large and could get much larger. Rising oil prices also renewed interest. The electric car held out the prospect of insulating consumers from high prices, and blunting the impact of oil price shocks.

9   One other development built support. The introduction of hybrids had a major impact on the psychology of motorists. Hybrids served as a kind of mental bridge to electric cars by creating public acceptance of battery-driven vehicles and what they could mean: a much larger role for electricity in transportation.

10   This convergence propelled the electric car out of the automotive museum and back onto the street. Today, in contrast to a century ago, there are two primary types of electrically powered vehicles. One is a direct lineal descendant of the sort that Thomas Edison sought to get out on the road, a pure battery-operated electric vehicle: the EV. It operates only on electricity and is charged from an electric socket. But now there is a variant, the plug-in hybrid electric vehicle, the PHEV. It is an immediate descendant of the hybrid but is much more of an electric vehicle than the Prius-type hybrid, It is "plugged in" to its primary fuel source: electricity. However, after the plug-in hybrid runs for some distance on electricity and the battery runs down, a combustion engine takes over, either recharging the battery or directly providing power to propel the car, or both.

11   Research and experimentation with plug-in hybrids had been going on for decades, but hardly anyone paid notice. That changed in 2007 when GM unveiled its PHEV Chevy Volt as a sporty concept car at the Detroit

Auto Show. Its public debut got so much attention and created such a clamor that GM decided to actually push the Volt into production. Within 12 months the model would come to symbolize the shift in focus from biofuels to EVs.

12   By the time of the 2008 presidential campaign, "Detroit's plug-in electric car, the Chevrolet Volt," said one political observer, had become "a must-have prop for U.S. presidential candidates." Despite GM's crushing economic problems, candidates Barack Obama and John McCain could not get close enough to the vehicle. McCain proudly announced that "the eyes of the world are now on the Volt." For his part, Barack Obama promised during the campaign to have a million such plug-in hybrids and electric cars on the road by 2015.[2]

. . .

The Road Map

13 The core of electric vehicles is the battery. The move toward electric cars would require a major technological advance in batteries. The basic lead-acid battery goes back to the second half of the nineteenth century. Other types of batteries were introduced subsequently, but the lead-acid battery remained the mainstay of the auto industry.

14   However, in the 1970s and 1980s, researchers, beginning in an Exxon laboratory, were figuring out how lithium, the lightest of metals, could provide the basis for a new rechargeable battery. The oil crises of the 1970s and the fear of a lasting shortage of petroleum had sparked interest in reviving the electric car. In 1976, Congress approved funding for "Electric and Hybrid" research. That same year, Forbes reported that "the electric car's rebirth is as sure as the need to end our dependence on imported oil." A number of automobile companies were working on electric vehicles. In 1979, in the middle of the Iranian oil crisis, Fortune announced, "Here Come the Electrics." But then the price of oil went down, it turned out that the world was amply supplied with petroleum, and the interest in electric cars once again faded away.

15   But the work on lithium batteries could be put to very good use for another big need. In 1991, Sony took the lead and introduced lithium-ion batteries in consumer electronics. These smaller, more efficient batteries enabled laptop computers to run faster and longer on a single charge. And lithium batteries were decisively important for something else. They made it possible to shrink the size of cell phones enormously, and thus powered the cell phone revolution. In theory, the greater density of lithium batteries, combined with their lower costs, could make them a more viable and competitive battery for EVs—better than both the nickel-metal-hydride batteries used in the first hybrids and the lead-acid battery that is customary today in automobiles. But that was all in theory. No one had yet road-tested the idea.[3]

. . .

Taking a Leaf

16 Today all the major automakers are moving, with varying degrees of conviction, toward an electric-car offering. Certainly all car companies would be more than happy to find some way to blunt their vulnerability to high oil prices. But among the major international companies, none has been more fervent about the electric car than the Nissan-Renault alliance. And no one more outspoken than its joint CEO, Carlos Ghosn.

17   Ghosn is about as international as an executive of a global company can be. Raised in both Lebanon and Brazil and educated further in France, he ran Michelin Tires in the United States, and then became a senior executive at Renault. After Renault formed an alliance with Japan's Nissan, Ghosn set out to rescue Nissan, which was teetering on collapse with $20 billion of debt. He became famous for bringing Nissan back from the brink and ended up as the CEO of both companies.

18   Toyota has its hybrid, Prius. Honda is the "engine company," focused on the superior characteristics of a more-efficient internal combustion engine. By contrast, going "all-electric" gives Nissan a distinctive leadership. The opportunity emerged by accident out of the company's financial wreck.

19   When Ghosn arrived at Nissan in Japan in 1999, he slashed costs almost everywhere. But something about the battery program gave him pause. "Nissan had been working on the electric battery for 18 years," said Ghosn. "I was really struck by those engineers when I met with them. They thought that an electric car could be feasible and affordable. I had no clue, but I was very impressed by their passion." Despite Nissan's perilous financial condition, that was one cut he did not make. "Sometimes you only connect the dots afterward," he added.

20   By 2002 Nissan had what it considered a breakthrough in lithium-ion technology. "After 2003, Nissan was out of turn-around," said Ghosn. "But I was very surprised by the amount of criticism that we were getting for not having a hybrid. I asked myself why there was so much passion about this. I realized how strong were the public's concerns around the environment. At the same time, the price of oil was going up. Also, very strong environmental regulations were coming out of California. We couldn't fulfill them without some kind of new technology. We needed to think out of the box. We needed to jump-start the electric. That was the only solution. You can't go from 850 million to 2 billion cars without an environmental car." Nissan had what its engineers believed was the technology. Ghosn gave the go-ahead to go all-out for a new all-electric car.

21   The reaction within the company was diverse. Some were puzzled. Why, they asked, didn't Nissan try instead to build a competitive hybrid? Others were enthusiastic that the company was trying to take leadership in a new technology.

22   While Nissan would also develop its own hybrids, Ghosn looked at it only as a bridge technology. "If you have an efficient battery for a hybrid, why not go all the way and go for electric cars?" he said. "It has the most zero emissions of anything."

23   And so if Nissan was going to spend several billion dollars to develop a new car, it would be for an all-electric car. "No tailpipe," said Ghosn. Not a drop of gasoline. And it was not going to just be a car for the motor show. It was going to be an affordable car for the mass market." In the autumn of 2010, Nissan went to market with the Leaf—which stands for Leading, Environmentally friendly, Affordable, Family car. It rolled into showrooms with a 600-pound pack of lithium-ion batteries and promised an average driving range of around 90 to 100 miles and a top speed of 90 miles per hour. Nissan is targeting that 10 percent of its sales in 2020 will be EVs. "The only thing that is missing is real scale, and to achieve that, we have to cut costs of the battery," said Ghosn.

24   "The race to zero emissions has begun," he declared. For him, it was truly the world according to CARB. "This is not a bet," he said. "The only question about zero emissions is, When? Do we do it do now or in five years? Our competitors may see it differently." But Nissan believes "it is now."[4]

Charge It

25 For most of the previous two decades, the center of the advanced battery world has been in Asia, in Japan, and in South Korean. While the United States was pushing ahead, the Japanese and South Korean companies have redoubled their own efforts. After all, it was a Korean company, LG Chem, that made the Chevy Volt battery cells. In response to America's new politics of electric cars, it hastened to open a plant in Michigan.

26   Backed by strong government incentives, the U.S. industry is expanding rapidly. The Obama administration projects America to host 40 percent of the world's advanced automotive battery manufacturing capacity by 2015, as opposed to 2 percent when Obama took office.[5]

27   But the battery is only half of the equation; the other is charging—getting electricity into the car reliably and with speed and convenience. Japanese companies have formed an industrial consortium whose name is a pun on "Won't you at least have some tea?" The idea is that charging time needs to be speeded up and that it should take no more time than having a cup of tea. Currently, a Chevy Volt requires four to ten hours to recharge—and that would be quite a number of cups of tea. But various researchers are trying to find the pathway that would reduce charging to something less than the time required to drink a hot cup of tea; that is, the time it takes to fill up with gasoline.

Where Will the Electricity Come from?

28 The current general theory of electric cars is that they would recharge overnight, when demand is at its lowest. This would create a new market for electric power companies and, at the same time, balance out the load. And it would be a very big market. Charging a car overnight would take about

as much electricity as would be used by two houses over twenty-four hours. In other words, were EVs to become ubiquitous, electric power companies would be virtually doubling their residential load without the need to build much more capacity.

29   Over the last few years, a compelling new vision has taken shape: Wind and solar will generate the new supplies of electricity. That electricity will then be wheeled long-distance over a much-expanded and modernized transmission system. And then, when it gets to dense urban areas, the electricity will be managed by a smart grid that will move it through the distribution system, into the household or the charging station, and finally it will be fed into the battery of an electric car. Some even take the vision further and imagine that cars will act as storage systems, "roving" batteries, which, when idle, will feed electricity back into the grid.

30   But that is quite different from the electric system that exists today in which renewables provide less than 2 percent of the power. Lee Schipper, a professor at Stanford University, argues that many EVs will become what he dubs EEVs—"emissions elsewhere vehicles." That is, the emissions and greenhouse gases associated with transportation will not come out of the tailpipe of the car but potentially from the smokestack of a coal-fired power plant that generates the electricity that is fed into the EV. So one also has to take into account how the power is generated. Is it uranium or coal or wind? Or something else? Will it be natural gas, with about half the CO_2 emissions of coal and now a much more abundant fuel because of the breakthrough on shale gas worldwide? This last prospect also provides an alternative to burning natural gas in engines as a mass-market fuel. Natural gas would in effect become a motor fuel, but indirectly, by generating more of the electricity that ends up in the battery of an electric car[6]

31   How fast can an electric-vehicle future happen? On a global basis, estimates for new-car sales in 2030 of EVs and PHEVs, depending upon the scenario, range between 10 percent and 32 percent of total annual sales. Under the most optimistic of the scenarios, the penetration of such vehicles (in other words, the total number of EVs and PHEVs in the global fleet) would be 14 percent.[7]

32   The policies of governments will be one of the critical determinants in the actual outcome. For it is such policies—regulations, incentives, and subsidies—that today are promoting the development of the electric car and on which the current economics depend. Innovation could change that calculus and drive down costs, just as Henry Ford did with the Model T. That is one of the primary arguments for the policies and incentives and subsidies: they are meant to stimulate greater scale and significant cost-cutting innovation. One critical question, therefore, is how stable will be those policies that are now aimed at making electricity the mainstay of the auto fleet? After all, energy policies have shown the recurrent characteristic of being "pendulumatic," moving in one direction and then another, and then back again.

"Thermal Runaway"?

33 EVs are already in production and in the marketplace. But as a product for a mass market, it remains a great experiment with big hurdles still to be surmounted.

34   Batteries still need to be smaller, weigh less, charge more quickly, and be able to last much longer on a single charge. They also need to prove that they can be long lived, despite the continuing charging and discharging. It will have to be demonstrated that problems like "thermal runaway"—destructive overheating—do not occur. In addition to propelling the vehicle, batteries also need sufficient capacity to power all the other accoutrements that drivers expect, from power steering and air-conditioning to the traveling entertainment center. And the cost needs to come down substantially—unless governments are willing and capable of providing continuing subsidies on a very large scale.[8]

35   Batteries are now a focus of intense and well-funded research around the world, aimed at addressing these questions. The entire effort is also very competitive—indeed, a global "battery race." At the same time, there is a global debate as to where the "learning curve" battery technology is and how fast it can come down.

36   Infrastructure is the second challenge. Today's automobile system could not operate without the dense network of gasoline stations built up over so many decades. A large fleet of electric cars will need a similar network of charging stations. One car in a neighborhood can be easily accommodated with an extension cord. But what happens to the transformers in the power system when everybody on the block, and on the next block, and on the next three blocks decides to recharge at the same time?[9]

37   Moreover, it is necessary to get beyond the "hand raisers"—those who put their names in the order book prior to the release of a model—and the

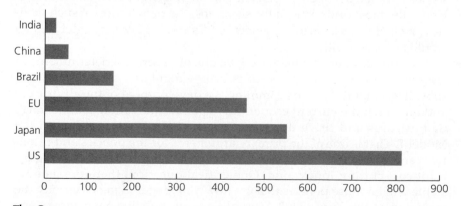

The Gap
Cars per 1,000 population in 2010
Source: IHS Global Insight

early adopters. In the 1990s General Motors "subsidized the hell out of the EV1," said former GM CEO Rick Wagher. "But if customers don't want to buy, it's hard to do." The EV has to attract a large population of drivers. To that end, charging stations need to be built and powered around urban areas and into the countryside to ensure convenience and reliability—and to ensure that people don't get stranded.[10]

38   Government can implement only so many regulations, incentives, and subsidies. Buyers have to find the price, functionality, performance, and reliability that they want. That will take time to demonstrate. Specifically, what is called range anxiety—the fear of being stranded with a rundown battery—will be a major factor in what consumers actually do.

39   Perhaps the answer to consumer needs will be to parse those needs—different cars for different purposes. People may use a small urban electric runabout for local needs and commuting—a sort of modern version of the Detroit Electrics and Baker Runabouts of the early twentieth century—and drive a bigger oil-fueled or hybrid car for longer trips or weekend getaways. At the same time, as when any kind of new product is introduced, there is always the risk of the unexpected in terms of operations or performance that could negatively affect public acceptance of EVs as a category.

40   Finally, there is the matter of power supply. It is generally assumed that sufficient unused electric power–generating capacity, especially at night, is available to accommodate a large fleet of electric cars. That may well be the case, but major growth in electric cars would be a very major new draw on the electric-power industry. What happens if people don't charge their EVs at night? What happens if instead large numbers of people decide to recharge during peak demand? How will the system cope?

. . .

The Cars of the Future

41 Electric cars, hybrids, biofuels, natural gas vehicles, more efficient internal combustion engines, fuel cells at some later date—the race to reshape transportation and for "the car of the future" is once again on. Or, perhaps, it will be plural—"the cars of the future." In the last race, a century ago, the internal combustion engine won hands down—on the basis of cost, convenience, performance, and range. But this time there may not be a single winner but rather different vehicles for different purposes.

42   One way or the other, oil's almost total domination over transportation will either be whittled away or more drastically reduced. Cars will certainly get more efficient. It seems pretty certain that electricity will play a bigger role in transportation, either in hybrids or all-electric vehicles. Considerable effort continues to go into second-generation biofuels. Regardless of what powers cars, they are likely to get smaller in coming years, in part as baby boomers in the United States, Europe, and Japan retire. Moreover, surprises in the quest for a clean, secure form of transportation may well happen.

43   In shaping the future, developing countries will be critical participants in a way they have not been in the past. Emerging markets will fuel growth in the global auto market, and thus the direction of technology as well as environmental standards. China's surpassing the United States as the world's largest car market in 2009 was a landmark. As a result of this shift, the policies of governments in developing countries will have increasingly greater impact on the global auto market. Indeed, a day may well come when China, because of the dynamism of its market, becomes the defining force for the world auto industry, or when a Chinese environmental regulatory agency becomes the new CARB [California Air Resources Board] for the world.

44   The key criteria for victory, or at least a place in the winner's circle, will be the delivery of increasingly efficient cars that also meet the tests of environment, energy security, cost, and performance. The contest will require major advances in technology and multibillion-dollar investments, and it certainly will be shaped in part by the preferences of governments. In such uncertain circumstances, companies are hedging their futures by placing multiple bets to the degree that they can. "We're investing billions and billions, and basically we're going for everything—from diesel to hybrids to batteries," said Dieter Zetsche, the CEO of Daimler.

45   "We have taken the point of view that fuel efficiency is important to all customers," said Bill Ford, Ford's chairman. "But we still don't know what the winning technology will be. Any (long-term) sales projections today don't mean anything. So many different things are at play. I can't give a number. It's throwing a dart."[11]

To the Future

46 Where does this leave oil and the internal combustion engine? Probably in an assured position of dominance at least for the next two decades. But there will be much more efficient internal combustion engines. Cars based on the ICE technology can come into today's fleet quickly. And they will not require a new infrastructure system.

47   Internal combustion engines do a remarkable job of generating power in an affordable and compact package. The secret to the success of the ICE lies in the energy density of liquid fuels—simply put, oil. The small size and power output of the gasoline and diesel-fuel engines will continue to make them fierce competitors'—technologically speaking. Moreover, the scope certainly exists for improving the efficiency of cars—whether in gasoline and diesel engines themselves, or through "lightweighting" cars with new materials, and thus reducing emissions.

48   "A key question is how to halve the fuel consumption of the 2035 car fleet," observed John Heywood, professor of mechanical engineering at Massachusetts Institute of Technology and the former director of the university's Sloan Automotive Laboratory. "We can make vehicles that are

twice as good as those today," says Heywood. "But the next question is, how many? If it's only 15 percent of the fleet, it's of little impact. If it's 95 percent, it's a hell of a big thing."[12]

49   Yet one near certainty is that the transportation system of today will evolve significantly over the coming decades. Energy efficiency and lower emissions will continue to be major preoccupations. If issues of cost and complexity and scale can be conquered, the battery will begin to push aside oil as the motive force for much of the world's automotive transportation. But the internal combustion engine is unlikely to be shunted aside easily. The new contest may, for some time, be less decisive than when Henry Ford used his Model T to engineer victory for the internal combustion engine against the electric car.

50   But the race has certainly begun. The outcome will do much to define our energy world in the decades ahead in terms of where we get our energy, how we use it, and who the winners will be. But it is much too soon for anyone to take a victory lap.

Notes

1. Tiffany Groode and Levi Tillemann-Dick, "The Race to Build the Electric Car," *Wall Street Journal Special Section,* March 9, 2011; Agence France-Presse, October 1, 2009 ("battle"); Reuters, July 30, 2008 ("Industrial Revolution"); Barack Obama, speech. February 19, 2010.

2. *Bloomberg,* July 18, 2008.

3. Seth Fletcher; *Bottle Lightning: Superbatteries, Electric Cars, and the New Lithium Economy* (New York: Hill and Wang, 2011), pp. 30–35; National Research Council, *Transition to Alternative Transportation Technologies: Plug-in Hybrid Electric Vehicles* (Washington, DC: National Academies Press, 2010), p. 9.

4. Interview with Carlos Ghosn; *Fortune,* February 19, 2010 ("mermaid," "not a bet").

5. *Bloomberg,* July 15, 2010.

6. Interview with Lee Schipper ("emissions elsewhere").

7. IHS CERA, "Automotive Scenarios 2010"; Electrification Coalition, *Electrification Roadmap: Revolutionizing Transportation and Achieving Energy Security* (Washington, DC: Electrification Coalition, 2009).

8. Interview with Steve Koonin.

9. Calvin Timmerman, "Smart Grid's Future: Evaluating Policy Opportunities and Challenges after the Recovery Act." Brookings Institution, July 24, 2010.

10. Interview with Rick Wagoner.

11. Dieter Zetsche, remarks, *Wall Street Journal* Eco-Nomics Conference, March 13 2008; Bill Ford, remarks, *Wall Street Journal* Eco-Nomics Conference, March 3, 2011.

12. Interview with John Heywood.

**Why the Gasoline Engine Isn't
Going Away Any Time Soon**
Joseph B. White

1   An automotive revolution is coming—but it's traveling in the slow lane.

2   High oil prices have accomplished what years of pleas from environmentalists and energy-security hawks could not: forcing the world's major
auto makers to refocus their engineers and their capital on devising mass-
market alternatives to century-old petroleum-fueled engine technology.

3   With all the glitzy ads, media chatter and Internet buzz about plug-in
hybrids that draw power from the electric grid or cars fueled with hydrogen, it's easy to get lulled into thinking that gasoline stations soon will be
as rare as drive-in theaters. The idea that auto makers can quickly execute
a revolutionary transition from oil to electricity is now a touchstone for
both major presidential candidates.

4   That's the dream. Now the reality: This revolution will take years to pull
off—and that's assuming it isn't derailed by a return to cheap oil. Anyone
who goes to sleep today and wakes up in five years will find that most cars
for sale in the U.S. will still run on regular gas—with a few more than
today taking diesel fuel. That will likely be the case even if the latter-day
Rip Van Winkle sleeps until 2020.

Free to Drive

5   Cars aren't iPods or washing machines. They are both highly complex
machines and the enablers of a way of life that for many is synonymous
with freedom and opportunity—not just in the U.S., but increasingly in
rising nations such as China, India and Russia.

6   Engineering and tooling to produce a new vehicle takes three to five
years—and that's without adding the challenge of major new technology.
Most car buyers won't accept "beta" technology in the vehicles they and
their families depend on every day. Many senior industry executives—
including those at Japanese companies—have vivid memories of the back-
lash against the quality problems that resulted when Detroit rushed smaller
cars and new engines into the market after the gas-price shocks of the 1970s.
The lesson learned: Technological change is best done incrementally.

Integral to Modern Life

7   Technological inertia isn't the only issue. Cars powerful enough and large
enough to serve multiple functions are integral to modern life, particularly in suburban and rural areas not well served by mass transit.

8   Ditching the internal-combustion engine could mean ditching the way
of life that goes with it, and returning to an era in which more travel
revolves around train and bus schedules, and more people live in smaller
homes in dense urban neighborhoods.

9   Economic and cultural forces—high gas prices and empty-nest baby boomers bored with the suburbs—are encouraging some Americans to return to city life, but by no means all. In rising economies such as China, meanwhile, consumers are ravenous for the mobility and freedom that owning a car provides.

Desire Isn't Enough

10 That doesn't mean auto makers and their technology suppliers aren't serious about rethinking the status quo. But displacing internal-combustion engines fueled by petroleum won't be easy and it won't be cheap.

11   It also may not make sense. Over the past two decades, car makers have at times declared the dawn of the age of ethanol power, hydrogen power and electric power—only to wind up back where they started: confronting the internal-combustion engine's remarkable combination of low cost, durability and power. One effect of higher oil prices is that car makers now have strong incentives to significantly improve the technology they already know.

12   "There are a lot of improvements coming to the internal-combustion engine," says John German, manager for environmental and energy analysis at Honda Motor Co.'s U.S. unit.

13   Refinements to current gasoline motors, driven by advances in electronic controls, could result in motors that are a third to half the size and weight of current engines, allowing for lighter, more-efficient vehicles with comparable power. That, Mr. German says, "will make it harder for alternative technologies to succeed."

14   By 2020, many mainstream cars could be labeled "hybrids." But most of these hybrids will run virtually all the time on conventional fuels. The "hybrid" technology will be a relatively low-cost "micro hybrid" system that shuts the car off automatically at a stop light, and then restarts it and gives it a mild boost to accelerate.

Cheaper than Water

15 Gasoline and diesel are the world's dominant motor-vehicle fuels for good reasons. They are easily transported and easily stored. They deliver more power per gallon than ethanol or other biofuels. And until recently petroleum fuels were a bargain, particularly for consumers in the U.S. Even now, gasoline in the U.S. is cheaper by the gallon than many brands of bottled water.

16   Car makers have made significant advances in technology to use hydrogen as a fuel, either for a fuel cell that generates electricity or as a replacement for gasoline in an internal-combustion engine. But storing and delivering hydrogen remains a costly obstacle to mass marketing of such vehicles.

17   Natural gas has enjoyed a resurgence of interest in the wake of big new gas finds in the U.S., and Honda markets a natural-gas version of its Civic compact car.

18   But there are only about 1,100 natural-gas fueling stations around the country, of which just half are open to the public, according to the Web site for Natural Gas Vehicles for America, a group that represents various natural-gas utilities and technology providers.

19   Among auto-industry executives, the bet now is that the leading alternative to gasoline will be electricity. Electric cars are a concept as old as the industry itself. The big question is whether battery technology can evolve to the point where a manufacturer can build a vehicle that does what consumers want at a cost they can afford.

20   "The No. 1 obstacle is cost," says Alex Molinaroli, head of battery maker Johnson Controls Inc.'s Power Solutions unit. Johnson Controls is a leading maker of lead-acid batteries—standard in most cars today—and is working to develop advanced lithium-ion automotive batteries in a joint venture with French battery maker Saft Groupe SA.

The Costs Add Up

21 Cost is a problem not just with the advanced batteries required to power a car for a day's driving. There's also the cost of redesigning cars to be lighter and more aerodynamic so batteries to power them don't have to be huge.

22   There's the cost of scrapping old factories and the workers that go with them—a particular challenge for Detroit's Big Three auto makers, which have union agreements that make dismissing workers difficult and costly.

23   A world full of electricity-driven cars would require different refueling infrastructure but the good news is that it's already largely in place, reflecting a century of investment in the electric grid.

24   The refueling station is any electric outlet. The key will be to control recharging so it primarily happens when the grid isn't already stressed, but controllers should be able to steer recharging to off-peak hours, likely backed by discount rates for electricity.

25   Big utilities in the two most populous states, California and Texas, are adding millions of smart meters capable of verifying that recharging happens primarily in periods when other electricity use is slack. Studies show the U.S. could easily accommodate tens of millions of plug-in cars with no additional power plants. Three big utilities in California are planning to install smart meters capable of managing off-peak recharging. The estimated cost: $5 billion over the next five years.

Remembering the Past

26 Americans often reach for two analogies when confronted with a technological challenge: The Manhattan Project, which produced the first atomic bomb during World War II, and the race to put a man on the moon during the 1960s. The success of these two efforts has convinced three generations

of Americans that all-out, spare-no-expense efforts will yield a solution to any challenge.

27   This idea lives today in General Motors Corp.'s crash program to bring out the Chevrolet Volt plug-in hybrid by 2010—even though the company acknowledges the battery technology required to power the car isn't ready.

28   Even if GM succeeds in meeting its deadline for launching the Volt, the Volt won't be a big seller for years, especially if estimates that the car will be priced at $40,000 or more prove true.

29   Moon-shot efforts like the Volt get attention, but the most effective ways to use less energy may have less to do with changing technology than with changing habits.

30   A 20-mile commute in an electric car may not burn gasoline, but it could well burn coal—the fuel used to fire electric power plants in much of the U.S. The greener alternative would be to not make the drive at all, and fire up a laptop and a broadband connection instead.

31   [The following table accompanied White's article.]

The Road Ahead

32 Gasoline has powered the vast majority of the world's automobiles for the past century. But now amid rising oil prices and increasing concern about tailpipe emissions and global warming, new types of propulsion technologies are starting to emerge. Here's an overview of what's here now, and what's ahead.

Kelly McDaniel-Timon

	Pros	Cons	Vehicles	Availability/ Starting Prices
Hybrids Have a battery and electric motor to power the car at low speeds and a gas engine for accelerating and highway driving.	Increases fuel economy significantly, especially in heavy stop-and-go driving.	Price premium over standard models can be $2,500 or more for a Toyota Prius, $8,000 and up for large hybrid SUVs. Mileage improvements modest in some larger vehicles.	Toyota Prius, Ford Escape Hybrid, GMC Yukon Hybrid, Lexus LS600h, Lexus RX400h, Chrysler Aspen Hybrid, Dodge Durango Hybrid.	On the market now. Prius $23,375, Yukon $50,920, Lexus RX400h $43,480.

	Pros	Cons	Vehicles	Availability/ Starting Prices
Mild Hybrids Electric motor only assists the gasoline engine; it can't drive wheels on its own.	Cost. Generally less expensive than full hybrids.	Only modest improvement in fuel economy.	Honda Civic Hybrid, Chevrolet Malibu Hybrid, Saturn Aura Hybrid.	On the market now. Honda Civic $22,600, Chevy Malibu $24,695, Saturn Aura $24,930.
Plug-In Hybrids A full hybrid with a large battery that drivers can recharge by plugging the car into an AC outlet.	Dramatic boost in fuel economy— can go up to perhaps 120 miles on the battery alone.	The advanced batteries required are not yet available. They are also expensive and can overheat.	None on the market today. Some "hackers" can convert Priuses to plug-ins.	Many auto makers working to offer them in 2–4 years.
Flex Fuel Vehicles Have standard internal combustion engines that can run on gasoline or a mix of gasoline and ethanol.	No price premium, can be used in vehicles of all sizes. Reduces greenhouse gas emissions.	Ethanol not widely available. A gallon of ethanol has less energy than a gallon of gas, so mile per gallon is lower.	Almost all GM, Ford and Chrysler models.	On the market now.
Fuel Cell Vehicles Use hydrogen gas and a chemical process to generate electricity that powers an electric motor.	Uses no fossil fuel, hydrogen is widely available and the only tailpipe emission is water vapor.	Still in experimental stage, hydrogen not widely available as fuel, technology still far too expensive for commercial use.	Models now in tests include Honda FCX Clarity and Chevrolet Equinox among others.	Small number of Clarity and Equinox available for lease through test programs.

	Pros	Cons	Vehicles	Availability/ Starting Prices
Electric Car Powered by a long-lasting battery and electric motor. Can have a small gas engine on board to charge the battery.	Practically no emission or engine noise. Can be recharged from AC outlet.	Technology still unproven. Batteries not available.	GM working on Chevy Volt. Also start-up electric car makers Tesla, Fisker and others.	Volt due by 2011. Tesla, Fisker and others possibly sooner.
Clean Diesel New, advanced diesel engines that burn fuel more cleanly and use low-sulfur fuel.	20% to 40% more miles per gallon and more torque than gas engines, reduced greenhouse gas emissions.	More expensive than models with gas engines. Diesel fuel more expensive than gasoline. Unclear if Americans will embrace diesel.	Jeep Grand Cherokee and Volkswagen Jetta are two examples. BMW and Mercedes-Benz also offering clean diesel models.	VW Jetta diesel $21,999, Grand Cherokee $31,390.

Source: WSJ Reporting

The Cinderella Myth

5

Universality of the Folktale
Stith Thompson

Folklorists travel around the world, to cities and rural areas alike, recording the facts, traditions, and beliefs that characterize ethnic groups. Some folklorists record and compile jokes; others do the same with insults or songs. Still others, like Stith Thompson, devote their professional careers to studying tales. And, as it turns out, many aspects of stories and storytelling are worth examining. Among them: the art of narrative—how tellers captivate their audiences; the social and religious significance of tale telling; the many types of tales that are told; the many variants, worldwide, of single tales (such as "Cinderella"). In a preface to one of his own books, Thompson raises the broad questions and the underlying assumptions that govern the folklorist's study of tales. We begin this chapter with Thompson's overview to set a context for the variants of "Cinderella" that you will read.

Note the ways that Thompson's approach to fairy tales differs from yours. Whether or not you're con-scious of having an approach, you do have one: Perhaps you regard stories such as "Cinderella" as entertainment. Fine—this is a legitimate point of view, but it's only one of several ways of regarding folktales. Stith Thompson claims that there's much to learn in studying tales. He assumes, as you might not, that tales should be objects of study as well as entertainment.

Stith Thompson (1885–1976) led a distinguished life as an American educator, folklorist, editor, and author. Between 1921 and 1955, he was a professor of folklore and English, and later dean of the Graduate School and Distinguished Service Professor at Indiana University, Bloomington. Five insti-tutions have awarded Thompson honorary doctorates for his work in folklore studies. He published numerous books on the subject, including European Tales Among North American Indians *(1919),* The Types of the Folktales *(1928), and* Tales of the North American Indian *(1929). He is best known for his six-volume* Motif Index of Folk Literature *(1932–1937; 1955–1958, 2nd ed.).*

1   The teller of stories has everywhere and always found eager listeners. Whether his tale is the mere report of a recent happening, a legend of long ago, or an elab-orately contrived fiction, men and women have hung upon his words and satis-fied their yearnings for information or amusement, for incitement to heroic deeds, for religious edification, or for release from the overpowering monotony of their lives. In villages of central Africa, in outrigger boats on the Pacific, in the Australian bush, and within the shadow of Hawaiian volcanoes, tales of the pre-sent and of the mysterious past, of animals and gods and heroes, and of men and women like themselves, hold listeners in their spell or enrich the conversation of daily life. So it is also in Eskimo igloos under the light of seal-oil lamps, in the

tropical jungles of Brazil, and by the totem poles of the British Columbian coast. In Japan too, and China and India, the priest and the scholar, the peasant and the artisan all join in their love of a good story and their honor for the man who tells it well.

2   When we confine our view to our own occidental world, we see that for at least three or four thousand years, and doubtless for ages before, the art of the story-teller has been cultivated in every rank of society. Odysseus entertains the court of Alcinous with the marvels of his adventures. Centuries later we find the long-haired page reading nightly from interminable chivalric romances to entertain his lady while her lord is absent on his crusade. Medieval priests illustrate sermons by anecdotes old and new, and only sometimes edifying. The old peasant, now as always, whiles away the winter evening with tales of wonder and adventure and the marvelous workings of fate. Nurses tell children of Goldilocks or the House that Jack Built. Poets write epics and novelists novels. Even now the cinemas and theaters bring their stories directly to the ear and eye through the voices and gestures of actors. And in the smoking-rooms of sleeping cars and steamships and at the banquet table the oral anecdote flourishes in a new age.

3   In the present work we are confining our interest to a relatively narrow scope, the traditional prose tale—the story which has been handed down from generation to generation either in writing or by word of mouth. Such tales are, of course, only one of the many kinds of story material, for, in addition to them, narrative comes to us in verse as ballads and epics, and in prose as histories, novels, dramas, and short stories. We shall have little to do with the songs of bards, with the ballads of the people, or with poetic narrative in general, though stories themselves refuse to be confined exclusively to either prose or verse forms. But even with verse and all other forms of prose narrative put aside, we shall find that in treating the traditional prose tale—the folktale—our quest will be ambitious enough and will take us to all parts of the earth and to the very beginnings of history.

4   Although the term "folktale" is often used in English to refer to the "household tale" or "fairy tale" (the German *Märchen*), such as "Cinderella" or "Snow White," it is also legitimately employed in a much broader sense to include all forms of prose narrative, written or oral, which have come to be handed down through the years. In this usage the important fact is the traditional nature of the material. In contrast to the modern story writer's striving after originality of plot and treatment, the teller of a folktale is proud of his ability to hand on that which he has received. He usually desires to impress his readers or hearers with the fact that he is bringing them something that has the stamp of good authority, that the tale was heard from some great story-teller or from some aged person who remembered it from old days.

5   So it was until at least the end of the Middle Ages with writers like Chaucer, who carefully quoted authorities for their plots—and sometimes even invented originals so as to dispel the suspicion that some new and unwarranted story was being foisted on the public. Though the individual

genius of such writers appears clearly enough, they always depended on authority, not only for their basic theological opinions but also for the plots of their stories. A study of the sources of Chaucer or Boccaccio takes one directly into the stream of traditional narrative.

6   The great written collections of stories characteristic of India, the Near East, the classical world, and Medieval Europe are almost entirely traditional. They copy and recopy. A tale which gains favor in one collection is taken over into others, sometimes intact and sometimes with changes of plot or characterization. The history of such a story, passing it may be from India to Persia and Arabia and Italy and France and finally to England, copied and changed from manuscript to manuscript, is often exceedingly complex. For it goes through the hands of both skilled and bungling narrators and improves or deteriorates at nearly every retelling. However well or poorly such a story may be written down, it always attempts to preserve a tradition, an old tale with the authority of antiquity to give it interest and importance.

7   If use of the term "folktale" to include such literary narratives seems somewhat broad, it can be justified on practical grounds if on no other, for it is impossible to make a complete separation of the written and the oral traditions. Often, indeed, their interrelation is so close and so inextricable as to present one of the most baffling problems the folklore scholar encounters. They differ somewhat in their behavior, it is true, but they are alike in their disregard of originality of plot and of pride of authorship.

8   Nor is complete separation of these two kinds of narrative tradition by any means necessary for their understanding. The study of the oral tale . . . will be valid so long as we realize that stories have frequently been taken down from the lips of unlettered taletellers and have entered the great literary collections. In contrary fashion, fables of Aesop, anecdotes from Homer, and saints' legends, not to speak of fairy tales read from Perrault or Grimm, have entered the oral stream and all their association with the written or printed page has been forgotten. Frequently a story is taken from the people, recorded in a literary document, carried across continents or preserved through centuries, and then retold to a humble entertainer who adds it to his repertory.

9   It is clear then that the oral story need not always have been oral. But when it once habituates itself to being passed on by word of mouth it undergoes the same treatment as all other tales at the command of the raconteur. It becomes something to tell to an audience, or at least to a listener, not something to read. Its effects are no longer produced indirectly by association with words written or printed on a page, but directly through facial expression and gesture and repetition and recurrent patterns that generations have tested and found effective.

10   This oral art of taletelling is far older than history, and it is not bounded by one continent or one civilization. Stories may differ in subject from place to place, the conditions and purposes of taletelling may change as we move from land to land or from century to century, and yet everywhere it ministers to the same basic social and individual needs. The call

for entertainment to fill in the hours of leisure has found most peoples very limited in their resources, and except where modern urban civilization has penetrated deeply they have found the telling of stories one of the most satisfying of pastimes. Curiosity about the past has always brought eager listeners to tales of the long ago which supply the simple man with all he knows of the history of his folk. Legends grow with the telling, and often a great heroic past evolves to gratify vanity and tribal pride. Religion also has played a mighty role everywhere in the encouragement of the narrative art, for the religious mind has tried to understand beginnings and for ages has told stories of ancient days and sacred beings. Often whole cosmologies have unfolded themselves in these legends, and hierarchies of gods and heroes.

11   Worldwide also are many of the structural forms which oral narrative has assumed. The hero tale, the explanatory legend, the animal anecdote—certainly these at least are present everywhere. Other fictional patterns are limited to particular areas of culture and act by their presence or absence as an effective index of the limits of the area concerned. The study of such limitations has not proceeded far, but it constitutes an interesting problem for the student of these oral narrative forms.

12   Even more tangible evidence of the ubiquity and antiquity of the folktale is the great similarity in the content of stories of the most varied peoples. The same tale types and narrative motifs are found scattered over the world in most puzzling fashion. A recognition of these resemblances and an attempt to account for them brings the scholar closer to an understanding of the nature of human culture. He must continually ask himself, "Why do some peoples borrow tales and some lend? How does the tale serve the needs of the social group?" When he adds to his task an appreciation of the aesthetic and practical urge toward storytelling, and some knowledge of the forms and devices, stylistic and histrionic, that belong to this ancient and widely practiced art, he finds that he must bring to his work more talents than one man can easily possess. Literary critics, anthropologists, historians, psychologists, and aestheticians are all needed if we are to hope to know why folktales are made, how they are invented, what art is used in their telling, how they grow and change and occasionally die.

Walt Disney's "Cinderella"
Adapted by Campbell Grant

Walter Elias Disney (1901–1966), winner of thirty-two Academy Awards, is famous throughout the world for his cartoon animations. After achieving recognition with cartoon shorts populated by such immortals as Mickey Mouse and Donald Duck, he produced the full-length animated film version of Snow White and the Seven Dwarfs *in 1937. He followed with other animations, including* Cinderella (1950), *which he adapted from Perrault's version of the tale.* A Little Golden Book, *the text of which appears here, was then adapted by Campbell Grant from the film.*

1 Once upon a time in a far-away land lived a sweet and pretty girl named Cinderella. She made her home with her mean old stepmother and her two stepsisters, and they made her do all the work in the house.

2 Cinderella cooked and baked. She cleaned and scrubbed. She had no time left for parties and fun.

3 But one day an invitation came from the palace of the king.

4 A great ball was to be given for the prince of the land. And every young girl in the kingdom was invited.

5 "How nice!" thought Cinderella. "I am invited, too."

6 But her mean stepsisters never thought of her. They thought only of themselves, of course. They had all sorts of jobs for Cinderella to do.

7 "Wash this slip. Press this dress. Curl my hair. Find my fan."

8 They both kept shouting, as fast as they could speak.

9 "But I must get ready myself. I'm going, too," said Cinderella.

10 "You!" they hooted. "The Prince's ball for you?"

11 And they kept her busy all day long. She worked in the morning, while her stepsisters slept. She worked all afternoon, while they bathed and dressed. And in the evening she had to help them put on the finishing touches for the ball. She had not one minute to think of herself.

12 Soon the coach was ready at the door. The ugly stepsisters were powdered, pressed, and curled. But there stood Cinderella in her workaday rags.

13 "Why, Cinderella!" said the stepsisters. "You're not dressed for the ball."

14 "No," said Cinderella. "I guess I cannot go."

15 Poor Cinderella sat weeping in the garden.

16 Suddenly a little old woman with a sweet, kind face stood before her. It was her fairy godmother.

17 "Hurry, child!" she said. "You are going to the ball!"

18 Cinderella could hardly believe her eyes! The fairy godmother turned a fat pumpkin into a splendid coach.

19 Next her pet mice became horses, and her dog a fine footman. The barn horse was turned into a coachman.

20 "There, my dear," said the fairy godmother. "Now into the coach with you, and off to the ball you go."

21 "But my dress—" said Cinderella.

22 "Lovely, my dear," the fairy godmother began. Then she really looked at Cinderella's rags.

23 "Oh, good heavens," she said. "You can never go in that." She waved her magic wand.

"Salaga doola,
Menchicka boola,
Bibbidi bobbidi boo!" she said.

24   There stood Cinderella in the loveliest ball dress that ever was. And on her feet were tiny glass slippers!

25   "Oh," cried Cinderella. "How can I ever thank you?"

26   "Just have a wonderful time at the ball, my dear," said her fairy godmother. "But remember, this magic lasts only until midnight. At the stroke of midnight, the spell will be broken. And everything will be as it was before."

27   "I will remember," said Cinderella. "It is more than I ever dreamed of."

28   Then into the magic coach she stepped, and was whirled away to the ball.

29   And such a ball! The king's palace was ablaze with lights. There was music and laughter. And every lady in the land was dressed in her beautiful best.

30   But Cinderella was the loveliest of them all. The prince never left her side, all evening long. They danced every dance. They had supper side by side. And they happily smiled into each other's eyes.

31   But all at once the clock began to strike midnight, Bong Bong Bong—

32   "Oh!" cried Cinderella. "I almost forgot!"

33   And without a word, away she ran, out of the ballroom and down the palace stairs. She lost one glass slipper. But she could not stop.

34   Into her magic coach she stepped, and away it rolled. But as the clock stopped striking, the coach disappeared. And no one knew where she had gone.

35   Next morning all the kingdom was filled with the news. The Grand Duke was going from house to house, with a small glass slipper in his hand. For the prince had said he would marry no one but the girl who could wear that tiny shoe.

36   Every girl in the land tried hard to put it on. The ugly stepsisters tried hardest of all. But not a one could wear the glass shoe.

37   And where was Cinderella? Locked in her room. For the mean old stepmother was taking no chances of letting her try on the slipper. Poor Cinderella! It looked as if the Grand Duke would surely pass her by.

38   But her little friends the mice got the stepmother's key. And they pushed it under Cinderella's door. So down the long stairs she came, as the Duke was just about to leave.

39   "Please!" cried Cinderella. "Please let me try."

40   And of course the slipper fitted, since it was her very own.

41   That was all the Duke needed. Now his long search was done. And so Cinderella became the prince's bride, and lived happily ever after—and the little pet mice lived in the palace and were happy ever after, too.

Cinderella
Charles Perrault

Charles Perrault (1628–1703) was born in Paris of a prosperous family. He practiced law for a short time and then devoted his attentions to a job in government, in which capacity he was instrumental in promoting the advancement of the arts and sciences and in securing pensions for writers, both French and foreign. Perrault is best known as a writer for his Contes de ma mère l'oye (Mother Goose Tales), *a collection of fairy tales taken from popular folklore. He is widely suspected of having changed these stories in an effort to make them more acceptable to his audience—members of the French court.*

1   Once there was a nobleman who took as his second wife the proudest and haughtiest woman imaginable. She had two daughters of the same character, who took after their mother in everything. On his side, the husband had a daughter who was sweetness itself; she inherited this from her mother, who had been the most kindly of women.

2   No sooner was the wedding over than the stepmother showed her ill-nature. She could not bear the good qualities of the young girl, for they made her own daughters seem even less likable. She gave her the roughest work of the house to do. It was she who washed the dishes and the stairs, who cleaned out Madam's room and the rooms of the two Misses. She slept right at the top of the house, in an attic, on a lumpy mattress, while her sisters slept in panelled rooms where they had the most modern beds and mirrors in which they could see themselves from top to toe. The poor girl bore everything in patience and did not dare to complain to her father. He would only have scolded her, for he was entirely under his wife's thumb.

3   When she had finished her work, she used to go into the chimney-corner and sit down among the cinders, for which reason she was usually known in the house as Cinderbottom. Her younger stepsister, who was not so rude as the other, called her Cinderella. However, Cinderella, in spite of her ragged clothes, was still fifty times as beautiful as her sisters, superbly dressed though they were.

4   One day the King's son gave a ball, to which everyone of good family was invited. Our two young ladies received invitations, for they cut quite a figure in the country. So there they were, both feeling very pleased and very busy choosing the clothes and the hair-styles which would suit them best. More work for Cinderella, for it was she who ironed her sisters' underwear and goffered their linen cuffs. Their only talk was of what they would wear.

5   "I," said the elder, "shall wear my red velvet dress and my collar of English lace."

6   "I," said the younger, "shall wear just my ordinary skirt; but, to make up, I shall put on my gold-embroidered cape and my diamond clasp, which is quite out of the common."

7 The right hairdresser was sent for to supply double-frilled coifs, and patches were bought from the right patch-maker. They called Cinderella to ask her opinion, for she had excellent taste. She made useful suggestions and even offered to do their hair for them. They accepted willingly.

8 While she was doing it, they said to her:

9 "Cinderella, how would you like to go to the ball?"

10 "Oh dear, you are making fun of me. It wouldn't do for me."

11 "You are quite right. It would be a joke. People would laugh if they saw a Cinderbottom at the ball."

12 Anyone else would have done their hair in knots for them, but she had a sweet nature, and she finished it perfectly. For two days they were so excited that they ate almost nothing. They broke a good dozen laces trying to tighten their stays to make their waists slimmer, and they were never away from their mirrors.

13 At last the great day arrived. They set off, and Cinderella watched them until they were out of sight. When she could no longer see them, she began to cry. Her godmother, seeing her all in tears, asked what was the matter.

14 "If only I could . . . If only I could . . . " She was weeping so much that she could not go on.

15 Her godmother, who was a fairy, said to her: "If only you could go to the ball, is that it?"

16 "Alas, yes," Said Cinderella with a sigh.

17 "Well," said the godmother, "be a good girl and I'll get you there."

18 She took her into her room and said: "Go into the garden and get me a pumpkin."

19 Cinderella hurried out and cut the best she could find and took it to her godmother, but she could not understand how this pumpkin would get her to the ball. Her godmother hollowed it out, leaving only the rind, and then tapped it with her wand and immediately it turned into a magnificent gilded coach.

20 Then she went to look in her mouse-trap and found six mice all alive in it. She told Cinderella to raise the door of the trap a little, and as each mouse came out she gave it a tap with her wand and immediately it turned into a fine horse. That made a team of six horses, each of fine mouse-coloured grey.

21 While she was wondering how she would make a coachman, Cinderella said to her:

22 "I will go and see whether there is a rat in the rat-trap, we could make a coachman of him."

23 "You are right," said the godmother. "Run and see."

24 Cinderella brought her the rat-trap, in which there were three big rats. The fairy picked out one of them because of his splendid whiskers and, when she had touched him, he turned into a fat coachman, with the finest moustaches in the district.

25 Then she said: "Go into the garden and you will find six lizards behind the watering-can. Bring them to me."

26   As soon as Cinderella had brought them, her godmother changed them into six footmen, who got up behind the coach with their striped liveries, and stood in position there as though they had been doing it all their lives.

27   Then the fairy said to Cinderella:

28   "Well, that's to go to the ball in. Aren't you pleased?"

29   "Yes. But am I to go like this, with my ugly clothes?"

30   Her godmother simply touched her with her wand and her clothes were changed in an instant into a dress of gold and silver cloth, all sparkling with precious stones. Then she gave her a pair of glass slippers, most beautifully made.

31   So equipped, Cinderella got into the coach: but her godmother warned her above all not to be out after midnight, telling her that, if she stayed at the ball a moment later, her coach would turn back into a pumpkin, her horses into mice, her footmen into lizards, and her fine clothes would become rags again.

32   She promised her godmother that she would leave the ball before midnight without fail, and she set out, beside herself with joy.

33   The King's son, on being told that a great princess whom no one knew had arrived, ran out to welcome her. He handed her down from the coach and led her into the hall where his guests were. A sudden silence fell; the dancing stopped, the violins ceased to play, the whole company stood fascinated by the beauty of the unknown princess. Only a low murmur was heard: "Ah, how lovely she is!" The King himself, old as he was, could not take his eyes off her and kept whispering to the Queen that it was a long time since he had seen such a beautiful and charming person. All the ladies were absorbed in noting her clothes and the way her hair was dressed, so as to order the same things for themselves the next morning, provided that fine enough materials could be found, and skillful enough craftsmen.

34   The King's son placed her in the seat of honour, and later led her out to dance. She danced with such grace that she won still more admiration. An excellent supper was served, but the young Prince was too much occupied in gazing at her to eat anything. She went and sat next to her sisters and treated them with great courtesy, offering them oranges and lemons which the Prince had given her. They were astonished, for they did not recognize her.

35   While they were chatting together, Cinderella heard the clock strike a quarter to twelve. She curtsied low to the company and left as quickly as she could.

36   As soon as she reached home, she went to her godmother and, having thanked her, said that she would very much like to go again to the ball on the next night—for the Prince had begged her to come back. She was in the middle of telling her godmother about all the things that had happened, when the two sisters came knocking at the door. Cinderella went to open it.

37   "How late you are!" she said, rubbing her eyes and yawning and stretching as though she had just woken up (though since they had last seen each other she had felt very far from sleepy).

38   "If you had been at the ball," said one of the sisters, "you would not have felt like yawning. There was a beautiful princess there, really ravishingly beautiful. She was most attentive to us. She gave us oranges and lemons."

39   Cinderella could have hugged herself. She asked them the name of the princess, but they replied that no one knew her, that the King's son was much troubled about it, and that he would give anything in the world to know who she was. Cinderella smiled and said to them:

40   "So she was very beautiful? Well, well, how lucky you are! Couldn't I see her? Please, Miss Javotte, do lend me that yellow dress which you wear about the house."

41   "Really," said Miss Javotte, "what an idea! Lend one's dress like that to a filthy Cinderbottom! I should have to be out of my mind."

42   Cinderella was expecting this refusal and she was very glad when it came, for she would have been in an awkward position if her sister really had lent her her frock.

43   On the next day the two sisters went to the ball, and Cinderella too, but even more splendidly dressed than the first time. The King's son was constantly at her side and wooed her the whole evening. The young girl was enjoying herself so much that she forgot her godmother's warning. She heard the clock striking the first stroke of midnight when she thought that it was still hardly eleven. She rose and slipped away as lightly as a roe-deer. The Prince followed her, but he could not catch her up. One of her glass slippers fell off, and the Prince picked it up with great care.

44   Cinderella reached home quite out of breath, with no coach, no footmen, and wearing her old clothes. Nothing remained of all her finery, except one of her little slippers, the fellow to the one which she had dropped. The guards at the palace gate were asked if they had not seen a princess go out. They answered that they had seen no one go out except a very poorly dressed girl, who looked more like a peasant than a young lady.

45   When the two sisters returned from the ball, Cinderella asked them if they had enjoyed themselves again, and if the beautiful lady had been there. They said that she had, but that she had run away when it struck midnight, and so swiftly that she had lost one of her glass slippers, a lovely little thing. The Prince had picked it up and had done nothing but gaze at it for the rest of the ball, and undoubtedly he was very much in love with the beautiful person to whom it belonged.

46   They were right, for a few days later the King's son had it proclaimed to the sound of trumpets that he would marry the girl whose foot exactly fitted the slipper. They began by trying it on the various princesses, then on the duchesses and on all the ladies of the Court, but with no success. It was brought to the two sisters, who did everything possible to force their feet into the slipper, but they could not manage it. Cinderella, who was looking on, recognized her own slipper, and said laughing:

47   "Let me see if it would fit me!"

48   Her sisters began to laugh and mock at her. But the gentleman who was trying on the slipper looked closely at Cinderella and, seeing that she was

very beautiful, said that her request was perfectly reasonable and that he had instructions to try it on every girl. He made Cinderella sit down and, raising the slipper to her foot, he found that it slid on without difficulty and fitted like a glove.

49   Great was the amazement of the two sisters, but it became greater still when Cinderella drew from her pocket the second little slipper and put it on her other foot. Thereupon the fairy godmother came in and, touching Cinderella's clothes with her wand, made them even more magnificent than on the previous days.

50   Then the two sisters recognized her as the lovely princess whom they had met at the ball. They flung themselves at her feet and begged her forgiveness for all the unkind things which they had done to her. Cinderella raised them up and kissed them, saying that she forgave them with all her heart and asking them to love her always. She was taken to the young Prince in the fine clothes which she was wearing. He thought her more beautiful than ever and a few days later he married her. Cinderella, who was as kind as she was beautiful, invited her two sisters to live in the palace and married them, on the same day, to two great noblemen of the Court.

"Cinderella": A Story of Sibling Rivalry and Oedipal Conflicts
Bruno Bettelheim

Having read several variants of "Cinderella," you may have wondered what it is about this story that's prompted people in different parts of the world, at different times, to show interest in a child who's been debased but then rises above her misfortune. Why are people so fascinated with "Cinderella"?

Depending on the people you ask and their perspectives, you'll find this question answered in various ways. As a Freudian psychologist, Bruno Bettelheim believes that the mind is a repository of both conscious and unconscious elements. By definition, we aren't aware of what goes on in our unconscious; nonetheless, what happens there exerts a powerful influence on what we believe and on how we act. This division of the mind into conscious and unconscious parts is true for children no less than for adults. Based on these beliefs about the mind, Bettelheim analyzes "Cinderella" first by pointing to what he calls the story's essential theme: sibling rivalry, or Cinderella's mistreatment at the hands of her stepsisters. Competition among brothers and sisters presents a profound and largely unconscious problem to children, says Bettelheim. By hearing "Cinderella," a story that speaks directly to their unconscious, children are given tools that can help them resolve conflicts. Cinderella resolves her difficulties; children hearing the story can resolve theirs as well: This is the unconscious message of the tale.

To accept this argument, you'd have to agree with the author's reading of "Cinderella" and its hidden meanings; and you'd have to agree with his assumptions concerning the conscious and unconscious mind and the ways in which the unconscious will seize upon the content of a story in order to resolve conflicts. Even if you don't accept Bettelheim's analysis, his essay makes fascinating reading. First, it is internally consistent—that is, he begins with a set of principles and then builds logically upon them, as any good writer will. Second, his analysis demonstrates how a scholarly point of view—a coherent set of assumptions about the way the world (in this case, the mind) works—creates boundaries for a discussion. Change the assumptions and you'll change the analyses that follow from them.

Bettelheim's essay is long and somewhat difficult. While he uses no subheadings, he has divided his work into four sections: paragraphs 2–10 are devoted to sibling rivalry; paragraphs 11–19, to an analysis of "Cinderella's" hidden meanings; paragraphs 20–24, to the psychological makeup of children at the end of their Oedipal period; and paragraphs 25–27, to the reasons "Cinderella," in particular, appeals to children in the Oedipal period.

Bruno Bettelheim, a distinguished psychologist and educator, was born in 1903 in Vienna. He was naturalized as an American citizen in 1939 and served as a professor of psychology at Rockford College and the University of Chicago. Awarded the honor of fellow by several prestigious professional associations, Bettelheim was a prolific writer and contributed articles to numerous popular and professional publications. His list of books includes Love Is Not Enough: The Treatment of Emotionally Disturbed Children *(1950),* The Informed Heart *(1960), and* The Uses of Enchantment *(1975), from which this selection has been excerpted. Bettelheim died in 1990.*

1   By all accounts, "Cinderella" is the best-known fairy tale, and probably also the best-liked. It is quite an old story; when first written down in China during the ninth century A.D., it already had a history. The unrivaled tiny foot size as a mark of extraordinary virtue, distinction, and beauty, and the slipper made of precious material are facets which point to an Eastern, if not necessarily Chinese, origin.* The modern hearer does not connect sexual attractiveness and beauty in general with extreme smallness of the foot, as the ancient Chinese did, in accordance with their practice of binding women's feet.

2   "Cinderella," as we know it, is experienced as a story about the agonies and hopes which form the essential content of sibling rivalry; and about the degraded heroine winning out over her siblings who abused her. Long before Perrault gave "Cinderella" the form in which it is now widely known, "having to live among the ashes" was a symbol of being debased in comparison to one's siblings, irrespective of sex. In Germany, for example, there were stories in which such an ash-boy later becomes king, which parallels Cinderella's fate. "Aschenputtel" is the title of the Brothers Grimm's version of the tale. The term originally designated a lowly, dirty kitchenmaid who must tend to the fireplace ashes.

---

* Artistically made slippers of precious material were reported in Egypt from the third century on. The Roman emperor Diocletian in a decree of A.D. 301 set maximum prices for different kinds of footwear, including slippers made of fine Babylonian leather, dyed purple or scarlet, and gilded slippers for women. [Bettelheim]

3   There are many examples in the German language of how being forced to dwell among the ashes was a symbol not just of degradation, but also of sibling rivalry, and of the sibling who finally surpasses the brother or brothers who have debased him. Martin Luther in his *Table Talks* speaks about Cain as the God-forsaken evildoer who is powerful, while pious Abel is forced to be his ash-brother (*Asche-brüdel*), a mere nothing, subject to Cain; in one of Luther's sermons he says that Esau was forced into the role of Jacob's ash-brother. Cain and Abel, Jacob and Esau are Biblical examples of one brother being suppressed or destroyed by the other.

4   The fairy tale replaces sibling relations with relations between step-siblings—perhaps a device to explain and make acceptable an animosity which one wishes would not exist among true siblings. Although sibling rivalry is universal and "natural" in the sense that it is the negative consequence of being a sibling, this same relation also generates equally as much positive feeling between siblings, highlighted in fairy tales such as "Brother and Sister."

5   No other fairy tale renders so well as the "Cinderella" stories the inner experiences of the young child in the throes of sibling rivalry, when he feels hopelessly outclassed by his brothers and sisters. Cinderella is pushed down and degraded by her stepsisters; her interests are sacrificed to theirs by her (step)mother; she is expected to do the dirtiest work and although she performs it well, she receives no credit for it; only more is demanded of her. This is how the child feels when devastated by the miseries of sibling rivalry. Exaggerated though Cinderella's tribulations and degradations may seem to the adult, the child carried away by sibling rivalry feels, "That's me; that's how they mistreat me, or would want to; that's how little they think of me." And there are moments—often long time periods—when for inner reasons a child feels this way even when his position among his siblings may seem to give him no cause for it.

6   When a story corresponds to how the child feels deep down—as no realistic narrative is likely to do—it attains an emotional quality of "truth" for the child. The events of "Cinderella" offer him vivid images that give body to his overwhelming but nevertheless often vague and nondescript emotions; so these episodes seem more convincing to him than his life experiences.

7   The term "sibling rivalry" refers to a most complex constellation of feelings and their causes. With extremely rare exceptions, the emotions aroused in the person subject to sibling rivalry are far out of proportion to what his real situation with his sisters and brothers would justify, seen objectively. While all children at times suffer greatly from sibling rivalry, parents seldom sacrifice one of their children to the others, nor do they condone the other children's persecuting one of them. Difficult as objective judgments are for the young child—nearly impossible when his emotions are aroused—even he in his more rational moments "knows" that he is not treated as badly as Cinderella. But the child often feels mistreated, despite all his "knowledge" to the contrary. That is why he believes in the inherent truth of "Cinderella," and then he also comes to believe in her eventual

deliverance and victory. From her triumph he gains the exaggerated hopes for his future which he needs to counteract the extreme misery he experiences when ravaged by sibling rivalry.

8   Despite the name "sibling rivalry," this miserable passion has only incidentally to do with a child's actual brothers and sisters. The real source of it is the child's feelings about his parents. When a child's older brother or sister is more competent than he, this arouses only temporary feelings of jealousy. Another child being given special attention becomes an insult only if the child fears that, in contrast, he is thought little of by his parents, or feels rejected by them. It is because of such an anxiety that one or all of a child's sisters or brothers may become a thorn in his flesh. Fearing that in comparison to them he cannot win his parents' love and esteem is what inflames sibling rivalry. This is indicated in stories by the fact that it matters little whether the siblings actually possess greater competence. The Biblical story of Joseph tells that it is jealousy of parental affection lavished on him which accounts for the destructive behavior of his brothers. Unlike Cinderella's, Joseph's parent does not participate in degrading him, and, on the contrary, refers him to his other children. But Joseph, like Cinderella, is turned into a slave, and, like her, he miraculously escapes and ends by surpassing his siblings.

9   Telling a child who is devastated by sibling rivalry that he will grow up to do as well as his brothers and sisters offers little relief from his present feelings of dejection. Much as he would like to trust our assurances, most of the time he cannot. A child can see things only with subjective eyes, and comparing himself on this basis to his siblings, he has no confidence that he, on his own, will someday be able to fare as well as they. If he could believe more in himself, he would not feel destroyed by his siblings no matter what they might do to him, since then he could trust that time would bring about a desired reversal of fortune. But since the child cannot, on his own, look forward with confidence to some future day when things will turn out all right for him, he can gain relief only through fantasies of glory—a domination over his siblings—which he hopes will become reality through some fortunate event.

10   Whatever our position within the family, at certain times in our lives we are beset by sibling rivalry in some form or other. Even an only child feels that other children have some great advantages over him, and this makes him intensely jealous. Further, he may suffer from the anxious thought that if he did have a sibling, his parents would prefer this other child to him. "Cinderella" is a fairy tale which makes nearly as strong an appeal to boys as to girls, since children of both sexes suffer equally from sibling rivalry, and have the same desire to be rescued from their lowly position and surpass those who seem superior to them.

11   On the surface, "Cinderella" is as deceptively simple as the story of Little Red Riding Hood, with which it shares greatest popularity. "Cinderella" tells about the agonies of sibling rivalry, of wishes coming true, of the humble being elevated, of true merit being recognized even when hidden under rags, of virtue rewarded and evil punished—a

straightforward story. But under this overt content is concealed a welter of complex and largely unconscious material, which details of the story allude to just enough to set our unconscious associations going. This makes a contrast between surface simplicity and underlying complexity which arouses deep interest in the story and explains its appeal to the millions over centuries. To begin gaining an understanding of these hidden meanings, we have to penetrate behind the obvious sources of sibling rivalry discussed so far.

12   As mentioned before, if the child could only believe that it is the infirmities of his age which account for his lowly position, he would not have to suffer so wretchedly from sibling rivalry, because he could trust the future to right matters. When he thinks that his degradation is deserved, he feels his plight is utterly hopeless. Djuna Barnes's perceptive statement about fairy tales—that the child knows something about them which he cannot tell (such as that he likes the idea of Little Red Riding Hood and the wolf being in bed together)—could be extended by dividing fairy tales into two groups: one group where the child responds only unconsciously to the inherent truth of the story and thus cannot tell about it; and another large number of tales where the child preconsciously or even consciously knows what the "truth" of the story consists of and thus could tell about it, but does not want to let on that he knows. Some aspects of "Cinderella" fall into the latter category. Many children believe that Cinderella probably deserves her fate at the beginning of the story, as they feel they would, too; but they don't want anyone to know it. Despite this, she is worthy at the end to be exalted, as the child hopes he will be too, irrespective of his earlier shortcomings.

13   Every child believes at some period of his life—and this is not only at rare moments—that because of his secret wishes, if not also his clandestine actions, he deserves to be degraded, banned from the presence of others, relegated to a netherworld of smut. He fears this may be so, irrespective of how fortunate his situation may be in reality. He hates and fears those others—such as his siblings—whom he believes to be entirely free of similar evilness, and he fears that they or his parents will discover what he is really like, and then demean him as Cinderella was by her family. Because he wants others—most of all, his parents—to believe in his innocence, he is delighted that "everybody" believes in Cinderella's. This is one of the great attractions of this fairy tale. Since people give credence to Cinderella's goodness, they will also believe in his, so the child hopes. And "Cinderella" nourishes this hope, which is one reason it is such a delightful story.

14   Another aspect which holds large appeal for the child is the vileness of the stepmother and stepsisters. Whatever the shortcomings of a child may be in his own eyes, these pale into insignificance when compared to the stepsisters' and stepmother's falsehood and nastiness. Further, what these stepsisters do to Cinderella justifies whatever nasty thoughts one may have about one's siblings: they are so vile that anything one may wish would happen to them is more than justified. Compared to their behavior,

Cinderella is indeed innocent. So the child, on hearing her story, feels he need not feel guilty about his angry thoughts.

15   On a very different level—and reality considerations coexist easily with fantastic exaggerations in the child's mind—as badly as one's parents or siblings seem to treat one, and much as one thinks one suffers because of it, all this is nothing compared to Cinderella's fate. Her story reminds the child at the same time how lucky he is, and how much worse things could be. (Any anxiety about the latter possibility is relieved, as always in fairy tales, by the happy ending.)

16   The behavior of a five-and-a-half-year-old girl, as reported by her father, may illustrate how easily a child may feel that she is a "Cinderella." This little girl had a younger sister of whom she was very jealous. The girl was very fond of "Cinderella," since the story offered her material with which to act out her feelings, and because without the story's imagery she would have been hard pressed to comprehend and express them. This little girl had used to dress very neatly and liked pretty clothes, but she became unkempt and dirty. One day when she was asked to fetch some salt, she said as she was doing so, "Why do you treat me like Cinderella?"

17   Almost speechless, her mother asked her, "Why do you think I treat you like Cinderella?"

18   "Because you make me do all the hardest work in the house!" was the little girl's answer. Having thus drawn her parents into her fantasies, she acted them out more openly, pretending to sweep up all the dirt, etc. She went even further, playing that she prepared her little sister for the ball. But she went the "Cinderella" story one better, based on her unconscious understanding of the contradictory emotions fused into the "Cinderella" role, because at another moment she told her mother and sister, "You shouldn't be jealous of me just because I am the most beautiful in the family."

19   This shows that behind the surface humility of Cinderella lies the conviction of her superiority to mother and sisters, as if she would think: "You can make me do all the dirty work, and I pretend that I am dirty, but within me I know that you treat me this way because you are jealous of me because I am so much better than you." This conviction is supported by the story's ending, which assures every "Cinderella" that eventually she will be discovered by her prince.

20   Why does the child believe deep within himself that Cinderella deserves her dejected state? This question takes us back to the child's state of mind at the end of the oedipal period.* Before he is caught in oedipal entanglements, the child is convinced that he is lovable, and loved, if all is well within his family relationships. Psychoanalysis describes this stage of complete satisfaction with oneself as "primary narcissism." During this period the child feels certain that he is the center of the universe, so there is no reason to be jealous of anybody.

---

* *Oedipal:* Freud's theory of the Oedipus complex held that at an early stage of development a child wishes to replace the parent of the same sex in order to achieve the exclusive love of the parent of the opposite sex.

21   The oedipal disappointments which come at the end of this developmental stage cast deep shadows of doubt on the child's sense of his worthiness. He feels that if he were really as deserving of love as he had thought, then his parents would never be critical of him or disappoint him. The only explanation for parental criticism the child can think of is that there must be some serious flaw in him which accounts for what he experiences as rejection. If his desires remain unsatisfied and his parents disappoint him, there must be something wrong with him or his desires, or both. He cannot yet accept that reasons other than those residing within him could have an impact on his fate. In this oedipal jealousy, wanting to get rid of the parent of the same sex had seemed the most natural thing in the world, but now the child realizes that he cannot have his own way, and that maybe this is so because the desire was wrong. He is no longer so sure that he is preferred to his siblings, and he begins to suspect that this may be due to the fact that *they* are free of any bad thoughts or wrongdoing such as his.

22   All this happens as the child is gradually subjected to ever more critical attitudes as he is being socialized. He is asked to behave in ways which run counter to his natural desires, and he resents this. Still he must obey, which makes him very angry. This anger is directed against those who make demands, most likely his parents; and this is another reason to wish to get rid of them, and still another reason to feel guilty about such wishes. This is why the child also feels that he deserves to be chastised for his feelings, a punishment he believes he can escape only if nobody learns what he is thinking when he is angry. The feeling of being unworthy to be loved by his parents at a time when his desire for their love is very strong leads to the fear of rejection, even when in reality there is none. This rejection fear compounds the anxiety that others are preferred and also maybe preferable—the root of sibling rivalry.

23   Some of the child's pervasive feelings of worthlessness have their origin in his experiences during and around toilet training and all other aspects of his education to become clean, neat, and orderly. Much has been said about how children are made to feel dirty and bad because they are not as clean as their parents want or require them to be. As clean as a child may learn to be, he knows that he would much prefer to give free rein to his tendency to be messy, disorderly, and dirty.

24   At the end of the oedipal period, guilt about desires to be dirty and disorderly becomes compounded by oedipal guilt, because of the child's desire to replace the parent of the same sex in the love of the other parent. The wish to be the love, if not also the sexual partner, of the parent of the other sex, which at the beginning of the oedipal development seemed natural and "innocent," at the end of the period is repressed as bad. But while this wish as such is repressed, guilt about it and about sexual feelings in general is not, and this makes the child feel dirty and worthless.

25   Here again, lack of objective knowledge leads the child to think that he is the only bad one in all these respects—the only child who has such desires. It makes every child identify with Cinderella, who is relegated to sit among the cinders. Since the child has such "dirty" wishes, that is where he also belongs, and where he would end up if his parents knew of

his desires. This is why every child needs to believe that even if he were thus degraded, eventually he would be rescued from such degradation and experience the most wonderful exaltation—as Cinderella does.

26   For the child to deal with his feelings of dejection and worthlessness aroused during this time, he desperately needs to gain some grasp on what these feelings of guilt and anxiety are all about. Further, he needs assurance on a conscious and an unconscious level that he will be able to extricate himself from these predicaments. One of the greatest merits of "Cinderella" is that, irrespective of the magic help Cinderella receives, the child understands that essentially it is through her own efforts, and because of the person she is, that Cinderella is able to transcend magnificently her degraded state, despite what appear as insurmountable obstacles. It gives the child confidence that the same will be true for him, because the story relates so well to what has caused both his conscious and his unconscious guilt.

27   Overtly "Cinderella" tells about sibling rivalry in its most extreme form: the jealousy and enmity of the stepsisters, and Cinderella's sufferings because of it. The many other psychological issues touched upon in the story are so covertly alluded to that the child does not become consciously aware of them. In his unconscious, however, the child responds to these significant details which refer to matters and experiences from which he consciously has separated himself, but which nevertheless continue to create vast problems for him.

Fairy Tales and a Dose of Reality
Catherine Orenstein

With shows like Joe Millionaire, The Bachelorette, *and* Married in America, *producers of romance-based reality television have reflected (or helped to create, depending on your point of view) our fascination with fairy tales. Which suitor will Trista choose? The nation intently watches the (melo)drama because we have an emotional stake in the right guy marrying the right girl. We love storybook romance, says Catherine Orenstein, partly because we love fairy tales and the promise of happily-ever-after. But is our understanding of these tales accurate? Take a closer look and we find "cruelty, deceit, greed, murder and nasty in-laws." Maybe this is the stuff that draws us to reality TV. Catherine Orenstein is the author of* Little Red Riding Hood Uncloaked: Sex, Morality, and the Evolution of the Fairy Tale *(2002). This article first appeared in the* New York Times *on 3 March 2003.*

1   The most recent crop of reality television shows taps the fantasies we first learned from fairy tales: castles and fortunes, true love and romantic destiny, and above all that most perfect storybook union, the "fairy tale wedding."

"Fairy Tales and a Dose of Reality" by Catherine Orenstein, *New York Times,* March 3, 2003.

On the rose-strewn finale of "The Bachelorette," Trista chose the shy fireman Ryan, who promptly got down on one knee and held out a diamond. "I don't think that I could have imagined a better ending to this fairy tale story," she sighed. Meanwhile, on "Joe Millionaire," 20 would-be Cinderellas competed for the hand of a modern-day Prince Charming.

2   Of course, in addition to pandering to our storybook fantasies, reality television plays to far crasser conceits—lies and manipulation, an ample display of female flesh and a sadistic interest in the rejected suitors' humiliation. Fox's new show "Married by America," which premieres tonight, will take love out of the equation entirely, with viewers picking who gets paired off. In NBC's coming "Race to the Altar," a sort of hybrid of "The Great Race" and "The Bachelor," couples will compete for a fantasy prime-time wedding.

3   Sounds like fairy tales run amok. In fact, though, this reality comes closer to the true storybook than one might imagine. Those who wish for a real-life fairy tale romance might want to read their fairy tales again. The first published *contes de fees*, as they were called by the Parisian aristocracy at the end of the 17th century, did indeed revolve around courtship and weddings, but they told of unions that were anything but sweet and loving. Charles Perrault's 1697 collection, "Tales of Times Past with Morals," better known today as the "Mother Goose Tales," featured cruelty, deceit, greed, murder and nasty in-laws.

4   His pre-Disney Sleeping Beauty is not chastely awakened by a kiss, but rather impregnated by a passing prince and hidden in the woods. Years later the prince's mother tries to eat her. The young bride in Perrault's "Bluebeard" appears to have made a better match by marrying a wealthy widower. Alas, it turns out her groom is a serial killer. One day she discovers the corpses of his former wives hanging in a secret chamber.

5   As for Cinderella, Hollywood's various versions may preach about true love transcending class, but in Perrault's original story Prince Charming falls for Cinderella's gown and slippers but fails to recognize her face. He mistakes her for her stepsisters, and has to rely on shoe size to be sure he gets the right bride.

6   These early fairy tales suggest how much our expectations of love and marriage have changed in three centuries. Perrault's "fairy tale wedding" was not entirely make-believe. It was based on the prevailing aristocratic marriage of the 17th century, the *mariage de raison*, where newlyweds were often strangers, money was more important than romance and love was not the key but rather an impediment to a successful marriage.

7   Orchestrated by parents, marriage was a business affair. Take, for example, the noble but indebted Grignan family, who sold their son to the daughter of a wealthy tax collector for the sum of 400,000 livres. "Console yourselves for a mesalliance,"* urged a cousin of the groom's mother in a 1694 letter, "by the relief you will feel at no longer being harassed by creditors when you sojourn in your large, beautiful, magnificent chateau."

---

* A *mesalliance* is a "marriage with a person of inferior social position." [*American Heritage Dictionary*]

8   The modern romantic understanding of the fairy tale, and especially the romantic ideal of a "fairy tale wedding," owes most to the 20th century, when Americans began to glorify marriage and domesticity. In 1937, Walt Disney's first full-length animated feature, "Snow White and the Seven Dwarfs," showed the cartoon heroine whistling and singing with rabbits and deer while she cooks, darns and scrubs the dwarfs' bachelor pad. Similarly in 1950, the heroine of Disney's "Cinderella" sings and dances with mice and birds while she cleans house and stitches her ball gown, chores that anticipate her future life as happy housewife to Prince Charming.

9   Those films transformed the message of the fairy tale, just as today we continue to spin our own romantic wives' tales, recasting Prince Charming and Cinderella as prime-time bachelors and bachelorettes who court, propose and even wed for cash, beauty and network profits—not to mention America's entertainment. The fantasy is not that reality television is delivering a fairy tale romance, but that there ever was one at all.

Cinderella: *Not* So Morally Superior
Elisabeth Panttaja

In this brief analysis of "Cinderella," Elisabeth Panttaja offers what for some will be an unsettling claim: that Cinderella succeeds not because she is more patient or virtuous than her stepsisters or stepmother (the typical moral of the story) but because she is craftier, willing to employ powerful magic to defeat the forces arrayed against her. Nor can it be said from the evidence of the story, according to Panttaja, that the prince or Cinderella love each other. Is this the same "Cinderella" that you grew up with? The article from which this selection was excerpted appeared originally in Western Folklore *in January 1993. Elisabeth Panttaja taught at Tufts University when the article was written.*

1   It is not surprising . . . that modern criticism of "Cinderella" . . . has been so strangely indifferent to the role that Cinderella's mother plays in the story. In our post-Freudian world, Cinderella's mother is imagined as absent despite the fact that she plays a central part in the unfolding of Cinderella's destiny. Indeed, Cinderella's mother's role is far from marginal: the words and actions of Cinderella's mother are of vital importance in narrative sequencing and the overall "moral" of the story. The Grimms' version of "Cinderella" opens significantly with the dying mother's injunction to the soon-to-be-orphaned girl. On her deathbed, the mother gives Cinderella the following advice: "Dear child, be good and pious. Then the dear Lord shall always assist you, and I shall look down from heaven and take care of you." In fairy tales, the opening scene is always of particular importance, since it is here that the tale sets forth the problem which it will then go on to solve. Cinderella's problem is precisely the fact that her

mother has died. It is this "lack," the lack of the mother, which Cinderella must overcome in the course of the story. The narrative instantly complicates her task by staging the arrival of a powerful mother and her two daughters, who, in the strength of their unity, hope to vanquish the motherless girl. Thus the story quickly amplifies the mother/daughter theme, rubbing salt, if you will, in Cinderella's wound. For just as Cinderella's powerlessness is a result of her mother's death, so the stepsisters' power is associated with their strong, scheming mother. In short order, then, Cinderella finds herself in need of her mother's good advice, and it is through keeping her mother's advice that she manages to overcome her own social isolation and the plots of her enemies. In the end, Cinderella rises to a position of power and influence, and she accomplishes this, apparently, despite her motherless status.

2   But is she really motherless? Not really, since the twig that she plants on her mother's grave grows into a tree that takes care of her, just as her mother promised to do. The mother, then, is figured in the hazel tree and in the birds that live in its branches. Early in the story, the tree offers solace to the grieving girl; later, it gives her the dresses she needs to attend the ball. Likewise, the two pigeons who live in the tree expose the false brides as they ride away, with bleeding feet, on the prince's horse, and they lead the flock of birds who help Cinderella sort the lentils that the stepmother throws on the hearth. In addition, the fleeing Cinderella is said to find safety in a dovecote and a pear tree ("a beautiful tall tree covered with the most wonderful pears"). Since these places of refuge continue the bird/tree symbolism, it is quite possible that we are meant to see the mother's influence also at work in the rather mysterious way that Cinderella manages to avoid too-early detection. Thus, at every turn in the narrative, the magical power of the mother vies with the forces arrayed against Cinderella, whether they be the selfish designs of the stepmother and stepsisters or the futile attempts of the father and prince to capture and identify her. In the end, the mother, despite death, reigns supreme. Not only does she take her revenge on her daughter's enemies by plucking out the eyes of the stepsisters, but, more importantly, she succeeds in bringing about her daughter's advantageous marriage. The happy ending proves that it is the mother, after all, who has been the power of the story. Cinderella's success resides in the fact that, while apparently motherless, she is in fact well-mothered. In spite of death, the mother/daughter dyad has kept its bonds intact. At its most basic level, the story is about this mother/daughter relationship. It is about the daughter's loyalty to the (good) mother's words and the mother's continuing, magical influence in the (good) daughter's life.

3   Unlike the narratives favored by psychoanalysis, which are about maternal absence and disempowerment, this tale tells a story about a strong mother/daughter relationship that actively shapes events. Cinderella's mother performs a specific social function vis-à-vis her daughter—she assists in her coming out. Her gifts are directed toward a specific goal—to help Cinderella into an advantageous marriage. From

this perspective, what is most interesting about Cinderella's mother is her similarity to the stepmother. These two women share the same devotion to their daughters and the same long-term goals: each mother wants to ensure a future of power and prestige for her daughter, and each is willing to resort to extreme measures to achieve her aim. Thus, Cinderella's mother is a paradoxical figure: while her power is associated at the outset with the power of the Christian god and while she seems to instruct Cinderella in the value of long-suffering self-sacrifice, she is also a wily competitor. She plots and schemes, and she wins. She beats the stepmother at the game of marrying off daughters. She does for Cinderella exactly what the wicked stepmother wishes to do for her own daughters— she gets her married to the "right" man.

4   Considering the similarities in their goals and strategies, the idea that Cinderella and her mother are morally superior to the stepsisters and their mother is shot through with contradictions. Throughout the tale, there exists a structural tension between the character that is drawn thematically (the pious Cinderella) and the character that acts in the narrative (the shrewd, competitive Cinderella). The superficial moral of the story would have us believe that Cinderella's triumph at the ball is a reward for her long-suffering patience. But while Cinderella's piety does play an important role in the forging of her supernatural alliance, it plays almost no role in the important practical business of seducing the prince. Indeed, the battle for the prince's attention is not waged at the level of character at all but at the level of clothes. Cinderella wins the battle because her mother is able, through magic, to provide raiment so stunning that no ordinary dress can compete. Cinderella's triumph at the ball has less to do with her innate goodness and more to do with her loyalty to the dead mother and a string of subversive acts: she disobeys the stepmother, enlists forbidden helpers, uses magic powers, lies, hides, dissembles, disguises herself, and evades pursuit. The brutal ending of the tale, in which Cinderella allows the mother (in the form of two pigeons) to peck out the eyes of the stepsisters, further complicates the story's moral thematics.

5   Just as there is a structural tension between the tale's thematization of Cinderella's goodness and the actual plot, so there is a tension between plot and the alleged theme of romantic love. I say "alleged" here because although modern readers and critics have sought to enshrine romantic love as a central value of the tale, there is actually nothing in the text itself to suggest either that Cinderella loves the prince or that the prince loves her. The prince marries Cinderella because he is enchanted (literally) by the sight of her in her magical clothes. What is interesting about these clothes, at least in the Grimms' version, is that, far from simply enhancing a natural but hidden beauty, they actually create it. In the Grimms' version, Cinderella is described as "deformed," while the sisters are described as "fair," so we can only conclude that the power of Cinderella's clothes is indeed miraculous, since they turn a deformed girl into a woman whose beauty surpasses that of the already fair. Thus, the prince's choice of Cinderella can be explained

neither by her piety, which he has never experienced, nor by her own beauty, which does not exist. It is the mother's magic which brings about the desired outcome, an outcome in which the prince has actually very little choice. The prince's oft-repeated statement, "She's my partner," as well as his obsessive tracking down of the true bride, suggests that he is operating under a charm rather than as an autonomous character, and the fact that both these motifs are repeated three times is further evidence that magic, not free choice, is at work here.

6   This is not surprising: the enchantment of a potential marriage partner is one of the most common motifs in fairy tales and mythology. The motif of an enchanted or somehow disguised bride or bridegroom usually appears in tales that depict some kind of unusual marriage, either the marriage of a god or demon to a human (Cupid and Psyche) or the marriage of a poor or ordinary mortal to a member of the deity or the nobility (Beauty and the Beast). The idea, of course, is that one member, by being disguised or by disguising another, can enter into a marriage that he or she would not normally enter into, usually one that crosses class lines. Thus, the enchantment of a prospective bride or bridegroom has more to do with power and manipulation than it does with romance or affection. Rather than talking about Cinderella's love for the prince, then, it is more accurate to say that Cinderella, in alliance with her mother, bewitches the prince in order to gain the power and prestige that will accrue to her upon her marriage to a member of the nobility.

"Cinderella" and the Loss of Father-Love
Jacqueline M. Schectman

Jacqueline M. Schectman, director of training for the Jung Institute of Boston, is a therapist who draws on the theories of Carl Jung (1875–1961) to help clients understand and address the root causes of their unhappiness. Jung was the founder of analytical psychology. A one-time associate of Sigmund Freud, he developed the theory of the collective unconscious: a set of unconscious patterns in the psyche by which we order our world. These patterns emerge from the unconscious as "archetypes" in stories, myths, and religions—as elements we seem to recognize instantly (perhaps without knowing why) and find deeply resonant, whichever culture we call our own. In "Cinderella," at least four archetypes—Father, Mother, wicked Stepmother, and the Shadow—figure prominently.

In her preface to The Stepmother in Fairy Tales: Bereavement and the Feminine Shadow *(1993), the book in which "'Cinderella' and the Loss of Father-Love" appears, Schectman writes: "My approach to fairy tales is a reflection of my work with families and young children in that I tend to read the tales as bridges between inner and outer life, as stories of the struggle to find and define one's place in the world." For Schectman, the archetypal Stepmother is an important—and sympathetic—force both in the tale and in our lives, for "[s]he is a force against which the child can test his growing strength and maturity."*

Throughout her essay, Schectman interweaves her analyst's notes on various clients with her analysis of "Cinderella." It is fascinating to watch how her understanding of her clients' inner lives informs her understanding of "Cinderella," and vice versa.

1   In my work with young children I have always been moved by the child's miraculous ability to find and use just those materials—games, stories, images, even pieces of furniture—best suited for the healing of his or her wounds. So it was with Ginny, the quick and independent sister of a chronically ill child. Given her sister's special needs, Ginny was always second in her parents' hearts and minds; her frequent misbehavior was her only means of briefly holding center stage. In therapy she learned to use her hours in most expressive ways, directing me to play the role of rescuer/protector/friend, Godmother, Good Fairy or the Prince. At not quite four years of age, "Cinderella" was her chosen tale.

> Ginny's favorite made-up game was to run into the waiting room and hide in a space behind her mother's chair. In my part as Prince, I was to enter with an object, meant to be a shoe, in hand. I'd make a show of searching for the proper foot to fit the shoe, then discover Ginny in her niche. Thus found, she'd emerge in triumph from behind the chair, try on the "shoe," and prance around the room, a tiny Cinderella ready to be seen and loved.

2   "Cinderella" is a story for the Stepchild in us all, for the lonely one waiting for her Prince, for the one who feels unseen by those she loves. We weep with Cinderella when we feel harried and abused, when a Stepmother within warns against our dreams. Joy, she seems to say, is gold that will surely turn to lead at the stroke of twelve. Cinderella's triumph at the ball is a victory for all who'd prove Stepmother wrong, who would naysay her mocking, deprecating voice. When Cinderella dances with The Prince she dances for all who dare to wish for love, for recognition, for better days to come.*

3   When we recall the Cinderellas of our youth we probably remember Disney's lovely, laughing film, or the genteel stories of Perrault, in which a graciously forgiving Cinderella brings her sisters to her royal court.** The Grimms' Germanic version that we'll look at here is a darker tale, bloody and vengeful and full of mutilating loss.† Like most Stepmother

---

* A . . . version of this tale, the movie *Pretty Woman*, takes great pleasure in proving the disapproving wrong. The heroine, dressed in her newly purchased clothes, returns to the store where she'd been insulted and ignored the day before. The look of shocked recognition on the saleswomen's faces sends a cheer up in the audience every time the film is shown.

** C. F. Neil Philip, ed., *The Cinderella Story: The Origins and Variations of the Story Known as "Cinderella,"* for the history and evolution of this tale. In 1892, M. R. Cox compiled 345 variants of "Cinderella" in a collection reissued by Kraus Reprinted Limited in 1967.

† Children take great pleasure in the gory details of this tale, in which they find their fantasies of vengeance played out to the full. Adults, on the other hand, are shocked and prefer the prettied versions they recall.

tales, this "Cinderella" is a tale of grief. It begins, fittingly, with Mother's death-bed scene:

> The wife of a wealthy man fell ill, and was close to death. As her end drew near, she called her beloved daughter to her side, and said: "My dear and only child, remember to be pious and be good. God, then, will protect you, and I shall watch from heaven and be ever near." With that she died. The young girl visited her mother's grave each day and wept . . .

4   In this bereavement tale, every member of the family responds to loss. Cinderella weeps and pines in her attachment to her grief; Stepmother and her daughters carry coldness and envy in their hearts, while father meets their cruel, unconscious power with an equally unconscious weakness and withdrawal. Cinderella is not the only orphan in this tale; her stepsisters have suffered loss and will suffer more throughout this tale, as cruelty turns upon itself in a mockery of Mother Love. The story begins with the Good Mother's death, ends with her punishing revenge and is taken up throughout with a desperate search for masculine security and love. When Mother dies, Father's love is lost as well, buried in the coldness of his grief.

> Winter came and went, and with the Spring the man had found another wife. The woman had two daughters of her own, beautiful like she, but vile in temperament and black of heart.

5   Cinderella's father takes a wife to ease his family's pain. Instead, he brings home grief equal to his own; each family amplifies the others' need. This "proud and haughty" Stepmother* has no softness for her husband's child; her widowhood has left her hard and dry. Her husband and the father of her family has gone, and she's raised two daughters as lonely and unhappy as herself. "Beautiful and fair of face" they may well be, but they seem to lack a lens through which to view the beauty that is theirs. It brings them little joy.

6   The bereavement that binds all the women in this tale—Stepmother, her daughters, surely the heroine herself—is that of father-loss. Each plays out an aspect of this loss, Cinderella in her flights from love, her sisters in their wish to win the Prince, Stepmother in her desperate need to see her daughters wed. She has had to raise her family alone, and her pride and haughtiness may well be her defense against the helplessness she has felt along the way. She's determined that her daughters have a better life than she, a life safely in a husband's care. Her stepchild is a mere distraction from her overall campaign, another burden in her overburdened life.

7   Fathers have played minor, seemingly unimportant, roles in the other tales we've looked at here. In "The Laidly Worm . . . ," and in "Snow

---

* So she is described in Perrault's French version of the tale, in which Stepmother is also called "the most disagreeable lady in the whole country" (Philip, 1989), and (Howell, 1985).

White," the widowed fathers seek and find their second wives, and then all but disappear, seemingly enchanted by the witches in their homes. "Hansel and Gretel"'s Woodsman-Father can do little more throughout the tale than wring his hands. In each of these tales, a son or brother or some passing foreign prince has appeared to defeat the Witch, rescue the princess and bring balance and completion to the tale. These young heroes are stepping into Father's shoes, for once-upon-a-time the Old King was a hero too, with a vitally important role in family life.

8   Neumann (1973:198) sees Father as the bearer of "tradition, culture and the development of consciousness," without whom the child might be lost in a maternal uroboric state. In familial terms, one might understand Father as a necessary third to the perfect twoness of the mother-child bond. His presence moves the child from the paradise of mother's arms into an awareness of others in the world, and thus into awareness of himself as separate being. This archetypal Father carries conflict, therefore consciousness, into the child's life.

9   In Freudian terms, the Oedipal father stands between a mother and her son, challenging the child to take him on or to forego instinctual desire. A daughter, too, must give up her desire for her father, but not before experiencing, at a feeling level, the mutuality of that desire. Father's love, returned, is an acknowledgement of her as a sexual being. Samuels (1986) speaks to the importance of this relationship in feminine development:

> [The] erotic element guarantees the significance of the relationship. . .
> The father could not be more different from his daughter; he is male
> and from another generation. This is what gives him his potential to
> stimulate an expansion and deepening of her personality. But he is also
> part of the same family as his daughter; that should make him "safe"
> as regards physical expression of this necessary sexuality and also pro-
> vides a reason for his own emotional investment.

10   Aside from his role in his children's development, father's greatest contribution to a family's life may be in his support of mother in her nurturing and containing role. Ideally, he provides her with a place of rest, with a means of regathering her strength and her stores of loving care. A year ago I joined family and friends in the huge public picnic that marks Boston's celebration of the Fourth of July. A young woman sat among us and nursed her infant child, while her husband knelt beside her, feeding her while she fed their son. The small circle they created for themselves was so protective and complete that neither the surrounding crowd nor the fireworks could disturb their peace. In the absence of Father, this loving and protective third to the mother-child pair, the demands of mothering may make Stepmothers of us all. A depleted, isolated mother has less and less to give her child, and raising one's family alone may well evoke the Witch:

> Janet's husband, a submariner in the nuclear fleet, spent half his year
> at sea, three months on shore, three months on the sub. The first
> month of his sea-time went relatively well; Janet, warmed by the last

weeks of his time with her, felt cared-for and relaxed, and while she missed him she could feel his presence in their home. Her children felt this too, and joined her in her efforts toward a structured family life. By the second month they'd begin to test her limits and her will, and her unsupported weariness would begin to show: the grass would go unmowed, dishes go unwashed, and she'd lose her patience earlier each day. By the time the petty officer returned he'd find his children wild, his home a mess and his wife a screaming hag. They'd repair the damage over several weeks, but by then it was nearly time for him to leave again.

11   Father's absence need not be so stark to bring Stepmother to the scene. His partial withdrawal, born of helplessness and fear, and played out in rigidity of roles, can be just as keenly felt and not so easily addressed:

> Anne was five, her brother seven, when her parents were divorced. Her father, at a loss for how to spend his weekend visit time with her, left her with his new young bride while he and brother washed the car, mowed the lawn and made household repairs. The four would meet only around meals. No one openly complained; father, after all, was a conscientious man trying hard to do his best. As one might guess, his wife and daughter blamed one another for their loneliness and loss, and their shared resentment grew into week-end dread. The stepmother acted out her archetypal role and Anne responded as a weepy, angry stepchild in her father's home.

12   "Cinderella" brings the theme of father-loss into sharp relief. In no other tale is his distance quite so darkly felt, his grief-borne blindness to the women's needs so stark. He takes no protective role in any version of the tale, and in some he is altogether gone. A Spanish "Cinderella"* has it thus:

> All were very happy for some months, until the father had to take a long trip, from which he never returned. With the absence of [Cinderella's] father, things began to change . . .

13   We can imagine the rage and disappointment in Cinderella's home. A widow remarries, seeking that second chance at life: comfort, warmth, an end to loneliness; a partner in parenting her difficult, demanding girls. Instead, she finds herself in sole charge of a grieving child, a child so attached to mourning that ashes seem her natural milieu. The widow, having been betrayed into a caretaker's role, is clearly having none of it; she has no comfort left to give. The child becomes the target of her wrath and her daughters join her in her outraged sense of loss. They've made

---

* Tardy, William T., *Treasury of Children's Classics in Spanish and English,* Lincolnwood, National Textbook Company, 1987.

do with very little loving parent-care, and scarcity has fed their greed. They are not about to share the little that they have.

> ... the sisters plagued her with their insults and their ugly ways. They took her pretty clothes and bade her dress in rags and wooden shoes. "Where is the proud princess now?" they laughed, and had her work from dawn to dusk ...

14   What deprivation lies behind the sisters' mocking cries, their need to taunt the grieving girl? Do they sense in her her mother's parting gift, the ever present nearness of the love they have never known? Like Psyche's sisters, they must destroy this stranger Eros in their midst, that which never has been, never can be, theirs. Love, beginning with a love of self, is an alien invader in their home, always longed for, always pushed away.

15   How does one empathize with ugliness, with the heartless lack of empathy played out by the sisters in this tale? Sitting with such darkness in an analytic hour is the most difficult of therapeutic tasks, for it constellates one's hateful sister when an understanding soulmate is the patient's desperate need:

> Beth, the fourth of seven girls, spent her childhood vying for her mother's ear, her father's eye. She feels today that she was never truly seen or heard. At thirty-five she is talented, quite beautiful, and by her own sad doing, utterly alone. At family gatherings she provokes her sisters and their mates until they turn their backs on her and leave. She undermines her colleagues, challenges her boss, and throws away her lovers whenever they want loving in return. I am often flooded with revulsion as she tells her tales; she seems so totally devoid of the capacity for empathy and love. Finally, at the nadir of my own disgust, I find that I am with her after all. The rage, and the separateness from her I feel are what she suffers through every hour of her life. I have a glimpse into the depth of her misery and pain.

16   The suffering of the "vile and black of heart" can be profound—a hopeless, lonely journey that would seem to have no end. In a gathering following one of my "Stepmother" talks, a young woman handed me this poem, then slipped away:

The Ugly Stepsister

I am an ugly stepsister.
Never have I lovingly done work.
Only cried and wanted to be rescued
By the Prince divinely dancing.
But my feet
They're too big.
Size nine.
Some seem to think

I could have been
    Cinderella if I'd only tried.
She who was born from love
And knew her true worth.
What did I have to sing about?
                —D.M., Vancouver

17   What to sing about, indeed? A young woman growing up needs a mother, well-grounded in her own femininity, with whom she can identify if she's to value the woman in herself. Cinderella's mother, close to her child even in the moment of her death, provides the girl with that sense of self that shines through all her ashes and her tattered clothes. This centeredness provokes the envy that her sisters feel. The sisters, it would seem, lack that model in their lives; they've only known their mother in her darkness, in the incompleteness of her widow's grief. Worse, they've missed the sparkle in their father's eye, the admiring glance that can take a daughter's beauty in and return it to her with delight and love. Without that loving and reflective eye, what can these sisters know of their true worth? Samuels continues:

> Many fathers and daughters fail to achieve this [erotic] link. This is because men tend to be extremely cautious about becoming erotically involved with their daughters (even in fantasy). . . . The father's failure to participate in a mutual attraction and mutual, painful renunciation of erotic fulfillment with his daughter deprives her of psychological enhancement. This can take many forms: mockery of her sexuality, over-strictness, indifference—and, if the symbolic dimension is savagely repressed, actual incest. In the absence of eros or its excess the daughter loses sight of herself as a sexually viable adult, with disastrous consequences. (Samuels, 1986)

18   All that the sisters in this tale know about father is his absence in their lives. Their loss is so profoundly felt it can only be expressed in surface greed, in a need for all the glitter that the world provides:

> One day, when [Cinderella's] father was about to travel to the nearest town, he asked his step-daughters what he might bring them from the fair. "Pretty dresses," said the one, while her sister asked for emeralds and pearls.

19   Their wish, in its essence, is to be remembered while father journeys to and from the fair. The child (of any age) who assaults the returning traveler with cries of "What did you bring for me?" wants to know that he was missed along the way. Cinderella has what seems, at first, to be a different sort of wish, but she, too, needs to be carried in her father's mind; good mothering is never quite enough:

> "Father, bring me the first branch to touch your hat as you ride toward home."

20   Nature herself seems to tap father on the head. He returns with a hazel twig, a symbol of hidden wisdom, divine inspiration and the Earth Goddess's chthonic powers (Cooper, 80). A grateful Cinderella plants the twig on her mother's grave:

> The Hazel twig, watered by Cinderella's many tears, grew to be a handsome tree, and a small white bird nestled in the tree and granted Cinderella's every wish.

21   This bird—the departed mother's spirit, always near—brings Cinderella everything but her father's loving eye. He seems to be oblivious to the abuse she suffers at her sisters' hands, nor does he see the envy eating at his stepdaughters' hearts. Could this father be determined not to see the younger women in his home, in an effort to deny the erotic energy he feels? In "Thousandfurs" (Grimm, #65), a variant on the Cinderella theme, a King is enjoined to incest by his dying wife; he promises to marry no one not as beautiful as she. As his daughter grows to be the beauty that her mother was, she becomes the object of the King's desire, and must protect herself by running off, hidden in a cloak of many furs. In family life, fathers may protect their daughters and themselves from their desires by turning a blind eye, by not seeing the young beauties growing up before their eyes. While father-daughter incest, acted out, may be the worst sort of sexual abuse, this denial of incestuous desire abuses sexuality in its most delicate and nascent state (cf. Samuels, above). When father turns away in fear, the admiring glances of a passing Prince may take on great importance for a Princess coming into bloom:

> Kate remembers the party for her "Sweet Sixteen," one of her first dates with the boy she'd eloped with at eighteen: "I'd had my hair cut short that day in a becoming style and I wore a dance dress I'd picked out for myself. When my father saw me he was furious, and told me I looked ugly, like some sort of tramp. Even I could see that wasn't so, but he had me close to tears. J. arrived just then and he was so impressed he could barely speak; I was a different girl than the one he'd seen that afternoon in school! The look on his face meant everything to me."

22   The longed for Prince may arrive in more pernicious forms. In Chapter One we looked at brother-sister incest as a saving grace. When kept at the level of desire, this intensity of sibling love serves as container for familial eros, for love that has no other place to go. Sadly, separating action from desire is at times too great a task for a child prince to bear. Brother-sister incest, acted out and then repressed, becomes a hidden source of shame in adult life, a shadow on one's erotic life.

> Gwen and her brother Josh grew up with a father who'd learned to keep his feelings under wraps. He viewed his wife and children from an icy distance that left all in a state of aching need. At some time early

in their lives Gwen and Josh discovered comfort in one another's sexual touch. Gwen cannot yet say when this activity began, nor when it ceased to be. She only knows that pleasure, now, is inextricably bound with shame; her body's needs evoke her greatest fears.

23   In our tale, as in the memory above, father's distance keeps everyone in a state of need. As we might expect, the announcement of the Prince's Ball stirs a flurry of excitement in Cinderella's home:

> The king in those days had a son, and the son was looking for a bride. Accordingly, the King ordered that a feast be held to last three days, to which all the beautiful young maidens in the country were to come. When the sisters learned that they would go they began ordering their stepsister about . . . "We will soon be dancing with the King!" Cinderella did as she was told, but longed to go herself . . .

24   Here, indeed, is the answer to all the women's prayers: A young man with eyes for the beauties in his realm, with a heart ready to be won, with a throne to give his bride. The sisters primp and preen and prepare to meet their Prince; Cinderella weeps, and begs her Stepmother for leave to go along. The woman is aghast:

> "You go to the Feast? How can it be? You have no clothes and shoes, but you would dance? Nonsense!"

25   Three times Cinderella cries and pleads, and twice Stepmother sends her off to pick the lentils from the ashes in the hearth. Like Psyche, enjoined by Aphrodite to separate a pile of grain, Cinderella too—with the help of all the creatures of the air—must sort things out before she can hope to meet her Eros in the Prince. This sifting through the ashes of one's life, "The good for the pot, the bad for the crop," is the torturous inner task that must precede true marriages of heart and mind. Note that nothing here is thrown away; the "bad" is recognized, and taken in. This is the work on Shadow, a task so painful only a Stepmother would demand that it be done.

> Paul spent his hour in recital of his lover's faults. They'd had one of their frequent fights and he wanted sympathy from me, support for his anger and his sense of being wronged. Instead, I asked him to examine his part in what transpired. How had he provoked her wrath, what might he have done to bring things to a different end? Such reflections were the last things on his mind and he snarled his disgust with me. What good was I if I couldn't take his side?

26   Cinderella never questions the rightness of her task. Always the good and pious child, she does as she is told, only to be turned away again:

> Cinderella thought: "Now I can go to the feast!" But her stepmother said again: "No Cinderella, you may not go. You have no gown and you cannot dance. The King would only laugh!"

27   Stepmother, in all her harshness, tells Cinderella one more necessary truth: the sackcloth and ashes of her grief are hardly proper dress for a royal ball, nor has she learned to dance while weeping on her mother's grave. If she's to meet The Prince she must put her mournful piety away.

> In the years in which I led discussion groups for single and divorced adults, I watched participants arrive in every stage of need, some still in mourning for the lover (husband, wife) they'd lost, or indeed had never had. Others were more ready to explore their newly "liberated" lives. The former frequently found sympathy and kindly nods of understanding in the group. Just as frequently they left the social hour alone. Something in their bearing said, "Not Yet," in words that all could understand.

28   Cinderella, having served her mourning time, is more ready than anyone can know. She calls upon her source of strength, and wastes no time in dressing for the ball:

> When all had gone, Cinderella repaired to her mother's grave, where she wept and wished beneath the tree:
>
> > *"Tremble, tremble little tree,*
> > *Gold and silver rain on me."*
>
> And the bird let fall a ballgown made of silver and of gold, and dancing shoes embroidered with the finest silk. Quickly Cinderella dressed, and just as quickly made her way to the palace of the King. There no one knew her in her golden gown . . .

29   We can imagine the fury and dismay of the sisters here, as they watch this lovely stranger dancing with the Prince. Why can't they catch his eye? They too have done just as mother said, but her motherly advice to them has been very different than she offered to the stepchild in their home. All of their energies and hopes have gone into selection of their clothes and jewels; into polishing their courtly manners and their nails. Their every hair is perfectly in place, but they've not been asked to do the inner work demanded of this "foreign princess" clothed in gold. How are they to understand the apparent ease with which she's captured the young man's heart? Neither Stepmother nor her daughters can recognize the hard-working maiden within the golden dress; they see only that she has what they have not.

> After years of agonizing work, Gloria is in reunion with her gifted inner Prince. She plays piano with a local band, sings through her days and steals the time to write the poetry she loves. Her husband, however, feels great envy when he sees her living out her gifts; he is tied to work that brings him little joy. While he rationally connects her blossoming with her therapeutic work he is nonetheless enraged; how dare she find the inner fire that still eludes his life?

30   Cinderella's sisters need not have envied her so much; for all her work, she is unprepared for the suddenness of her success, and flies away in fear:

> Cinderella danced until evening fell. But then she begged her leave. The Prince wished to see her home but Cinderella fled from him . . .

31   How can Cinderella trust the love and admiration of the Prince when her own father seems to see her not at all? Like his wife and step-daughters, he's failed to recognize the beautiful young woman dancing at the ball.

> Bridget's father died when she was just thirteen, too soon to see his "little nurse" become the sprightly beauty she would grow to be. Today she is indeed a nurse, and she has married well, to a man who loves her more than she can quite believe. When they meet with friends she com-pares herself to all the other women in the room, and imagines that her husband finds her wanting in some way; they must be more desirable than she. She cannot find that father-voice within herself to say: You are the fairest in *this* land!

32   How is Cinderella's Prince to capture the mysterious, elusive girl? He asks the man who ought to know her best:

> The Prince waited until Cinderella's father came, and told him of the unknown princess hidden in the pigeon-house. Her father thought: "Could it be Cinderella?" At that the old man took an axe and chopped the pigeon-house to bits, but no one was inside.

33   "Can it be Cinderella?" We can hear the shock and wonder in the old man's voice. As the veil of his denial slowly lifts, he must contemplate his daughter in all of her nubility and charm. Can this lovely woman be his little girl? When he attacks the pigeon-house, and then the pear tree into which the Prince has seen the maiden flee, it's as if the very nature of her feminine allure must be destroyed before she leaves him for a younger man! When we ask, "Who gives this bride to wed?" we are asking father no small thing. His sense of loss at such a time may well evoke an angry, vengeful "Stepfather," not unlike the "Stepmother" who is forced to see her sons off into the world.

34   The father Kate recalls could not bear to see her sexuality emerge. When she eloped with the man who'd caught her eye, father's pain and grief made for an encounter he'd regret throughout his life.

> When Kate eloped, her father, furious, summoned her, her husband and his parents to a meeting at his home. He told her husband that he'd made a terrible mistake: his bride was lazy, disobedient, dis-honest and a tramp. "She will be a rope around your neck for life!" The bridegroom was not inclined to "give her back," but the father-daughter rift took many years to heal.

35   Three times Cinderella ventures out to dance, and three times runs away, to hide once more among the ashes by the hearth. This retreat until the time is right, until the world feels safe enough for love, is part of the connection to the earth Cinderella demonstrates throughout this tale. There is safety in her dirty rags, and she'll hide in them until her doubts and fears release her into life.

> Anne's first forays into sexuality were frightening and harsh; she needed time then to withdraw into herself, to feel into her fear and rage, to learn to be more conscious of the woman she'd become. Accordingly, she made herself as unattractive as her natural beauty would allow: cropped her hair, gained thirty pounds, dressed in shapeless, faded clothes. She remained thus, to her family's dismay, for several years. When a gentle Prince appeared, with the capacity to see the woman hidden in the rags, she allowed herself to venture forth, to see and to be seen. The Prince has come and gone, but Anne has thrown her rags away.

36   Cinderella's Prince has made his choice, and as the festival comes to an end he determines not to let his disappearing partner go again:

> [The Prince] . . . had seen that the palace steps were smeared with tar and pitch, and when she fled one of her golden slippers remained, caught in the sticky tar. The Prince held the slipper in his hand, and felt he would surely find the maiden now.
>   When morning came, he took the golden slipper to Cinderella's house, and showed it to her father, saying: "I will only wed the maid who fits this shoe." Then the sisters had some hope, for they had dainty feet.

37   Now begins the darkest portion of this tale, for while Cinderella hides herself and waits, her sisters try to fit themselves into her tiny shoe. As they try the slipper on their soft, uncalloused feet we hear that most dangerous of sounds, the well-intentioned voice of an ambitious mother-who-knows-best:

> The elder of the two took the shoe into another room to try it on, her mother at her side. Alas, the slipper would not fit. But her mother handed her a knife and said: "Cut off your toe; you'll have no need to walk when you are Queen." This the maiden did, and despite her pain, forced her foot into the tiny shoe. The King's son, seeing her thus shod, carried her away to be his bride.

38   With the advent of an eligible Prince, mothers may see a life of ease ahead for their daughters—better lives, indeed, than they have had! They beseech their daughters to conform, to fit themselves into some preformed, perfect mold. There is freedom in security, they say, and time enough ahead for all your little quirks and dreams, for all the imperfections that make you who you are. There will be a time to take a stand, to run that

race or write that book, time enough for wholeness when you are safely married to The Prince.

39   Perhaps modern women should know better, should know that a woman must accept herself—stand on her own two feet—if she hopes to find a Prince. But for all of that, one can't quite shut out the loud, collective voice that joins the desperate-mother voice within. "Reshape your nose," one hears. "File down your teeth and suck the fat out of your thighs; don't you know the competition's terrible out there?" When one's sense of self depends upon a Prince out in the world, no sacrifice of flesh, no loss of spirit feels too great.

40   What is tragic for the sisters in this tale is that their sacrifices are in vain. The Prince carries each of the pain-wracked maidens off in turn, only to be cautioned by the pigeons perched in Cinderella's magic tree: his bloodied bride is false. Now the younger of the sisters has her turn:

> Then the second sister took the shoe into another room, where her mother waited with a knife. Again, the shoe was just too small, and the mother said, "Cut a bit off your heel . . . "*

and once more, the Prince is warned as he carries the false sister by the hazel tree. Both young women offer up their mutilated feet, but the Prince has no desire for a bloodied, martyred bride.

> Linda recalls her mother when her family was young: "She had a joyful, playful side to her that she completely put away whenever my father was at home. None of us ever saw him laugh, and she assumed, I think, that laughter was not permitted in our house. I know she loved to swim and run and play out in the woods—other people told me this—but she simply let this go in an effort to 'grow up.' Eventually my father found his pleasure far from home; he told my mother that she'd ceased to move him long ago."

41   We must admire the determination of the Prince. He returns each of the injured sisters to her home, and asks Cinderella's father, one more time, for assistance in finding his true bride. Father must finally release his only child, his last reminder of the wife and happy home he'd once enjoyed. His answer is so cruel and final in its disavowal that it serves to free Cinderella

---

* "Cinderella" has its source in seventh-century China, and this version of the tale may be a commentary on the practice of binding female feet. In China, highborn female children had their feet bound into tiny, lotus shapes. "The four smaller toes were folded under the sole, the whole foot was folded so the underside of the heel and toes were brought together." Women with bound feet were the essence of beauty and nobility. "Chinese men were conditioned to intense fetishistic passion for deformed female feet. Chinese poets sang ecstatic praises of the lotus feet that aroused their desire to fever pitch. The crippled woman was considered immeasurably charming by reason of her vulnerability, her suffering and her helplessness—she couldn't even escape an attacker by running away (Walker 319).

from his grasp. If she'd ever hoped to catch her father's eye, to win his love, that hope is surely gone with his reply:

> "These maids have proved themselves untrue. Have you none other here beneath your roof?" "No," said the man; "only a scrawny ser- vant-girl, here before my late wife died. She could not be your bride, I know." But when the Prince persisted, they called Cinderella in.

42   For Cinderella and her Prince, what follows is the moment of surren- der, recognition, and a sense that all is as it's meant to be. Cinderella, her face washed clean of ashes and of grief, tries on the golden shoe that fits her perfectly:

> When Cinderella stood to face her dancing partner once again, the King's son knew her then, and cried out in great joy, "That is my true bride!"

43   Such moments are the stuff of which romantic literature and art are made.* Our beloved—the one we've dreamed of all our lives and have always known within ourselves—suddenly appears, fantasy made flesh. All of our ambivalence is gone, there is nothing left to do but bow to love, and pray that it will last.

44   As the Prince carries Cinderella off, we're told that Stepmother and her daughters become "pale with rage"—and pale, perhaps, with the sisters' loss of blood. One would think the tale could end right there: justice has been done, Cinderella has her man, her vain and selfish sisters have their mutilated feet and empty beds. But the worst is yet to come for the unhap- py sisters in this tale:

> On the wedding day, the false sisters came to join the royal train, hoping to find favor in their sister's eyes. On the way to the church they walked at Cinderella's side, the elder on the left, the younger on the right. The birds pecked out one eye of each. On their return from church, each walked on Cinderella's other side, and the doves pecked out their remaining eyes. Thus the sisters were struck blind, and were punished for their falseness all their days.

45   Blindness has been a theme throughout this tale: Father, blind with hope, seeks a second wife, then shuts his eyes to the redoubled family grief within his home, to his daughters' needs and the abuse being perpetrated out of unmet needs. His blindness in the dark further darkens every facet of his family's life. The stepsisters, blinded by their envy of Cinderella's glowing inner light, attempt to douse it with their cruel and mocking taunts. And Stepmother, who can see very well what *Cinderella* needs to bring her into life, cannot provide her daughters with the guidance they require. She is too close to them to see them as they are, too attached to their "well being" to offer them an honestly reflective eye. As a "good"

---

* Cf. Haule, John, *Divine Madness: Archetypes of Romantic Love,* Boston, Shambhala Press, 1990.

mother she has indeed been blind, closed against the wisdom that the harsh, truth-telling Stepmother can, and does, provide.

46   The pigeons in this tale, embodiments of mother-nurturance through-out, provide the sisters with the sort of cursed gift a Stepmother might give. What might blindness to the outer world mean to the "vile, black-hearted" daughters we have come to know? Their focus has always been "out there," on all the pretty things that shine and glow in the material world, on all the treasures others might possess. They've had no insight, for to peer inside themselves would have revealed an emptiness too terri-ble to bear. Their sunlight gone, perhaps their helpless groping in the dark will provide the inward shift of vision that their souls require, the clear reflective eye always absent from their lives.

47   Cinderella's tale begins with her loving mother's death; her time in rags and ashes prepares her for her life ahead. Her sisters face another sort of death. They can never be the prancing, carefree careless girls they were; their hopes of dancing at another ball are gone. What their lives will be we cannot know, but the necessary darkness that precedes all inner work has come. It is in this darkness that the sisters' tale begins.

Bibliography

Cooper, J.C., *An Illustrated Encyclopedia of Traditional Symbols.* London: Thames and Hudson, Ltd., 1979.

Neumann, Erich, *The Child.* Ralph Manheim, Translator; New York: Harper & Row, 1973.

———. *The Great Mother,* Ralph Manheim, Translator; Princeton: Princeton University Press, 1963.

Walker, Barbara G., *The Woman's Encyclopedia of Myths and Secrets.* San Francisco: Harper & Row, 1983.

Fairy Tales and Modern Stories
Bruno Bettelheim

Bruno Bettelheim (1903-90), a noted psychotherapist, was born in Vienna, Austria. He grad-uated from the University of Vienna (1938), where he studied with Sigmund Freud. Bettelheim was imprisoned by the Nazis at Dachau and Buchenwald from 1938 to 1939. After his release from prison, Bettelheim emigrated to the United States, where he went to work at the University of Chicago. In 1944, he became director of the University's Sonia Shankman Orthogenic School, a treatment facility for severely disturbed children. Bettelheim gained international recognition for his work with autistic children, although not without some controversy over his methods. He published many books on psychotherapy, including Love Is Not Enough: The Treatment of Emotionally Disturbed Children *(1950),* The Children of the Dream *(1969),* The Uses of Enchantment *(1976), and* Freud and Man's Soul *(1982). He also wrote articles on rearing normal children for lay audiences. In addition to a well-known article on his experiences in Nazi concentration camps (1943), Bettelheim published two books on the death camps,* The Informed Heart: Autonomy in a Mass Age *(1960) and* Surviving and Other Essays *(1979), reprinted as* Surviving the Holocaust *(1986). In this essay, taken from* The Uses of Enchantment, *Bettelheim argues that fairy tales can provide children more comfort than "sensible" stories.*

1   The shortcomings of the realistic stories with which many parents have replaced fairy tales is suggested by a comparison of two such stories—"The Little Engine That Could" and "The Swiss Family Robinson"—with the fairy tale of "Rapunzel." "The Little Engine That Could" encourages the child to believe that if he tries hard and does not give up, he will finally succeed. A young adult has recalled how much impressed she was at the age of seven when her mother read her this story. She became convinced that one's attitude indeed affects one's achievements—that if she would now approach a task with the conviction that she could conquer it, she would succeed. A few days later, this child encountered in first grade a challenging situation: she was trying to make a house out of paper, gluing various sheets together. But her house continually collapsed. Frustrated, she began to seriously doubt whether her idea of building such a paper house could be realized. But then the story of "The Little Engine That Could" came to her mind; twenty years later, she recalled how at that moment she began to sing to herself the magic formula "I think I can, I think I can, I think I can . . ." So she continued to work on her paper house, and it continued to collapse. The project ended in complete defeat, with this little girl convinced that she had failed where anybody else could have succeeded, as the Little Engine had. Since "The Little Engine That Could" was a story set in the present, using such common props as engines that pulled trains, this girl had tried to apply its lesson directly in her daily life, without any fantasy elaboration, and had experienced a defeat that still rankled twenty years later.

2   Very different was the impact of "The Swiss Family Robinson" on another little girl. The story tells how a shipwrecked family manages to live an adventurous, idyllic, constructive, and pleasurable life—a life very different from this child's own existence. Her father had to be away from home a great deal, and her mother was mentally ill and spent protracted periods in institutions. So the girl was shuttled from her home to that of an aunt, then to that of a grandmother, and back home again, as the need arose. During these years, the girl read over and over again the story of this happy family who lived on a desert island, where no member could be away from the rest of the family. Many years later, she recalled what a warm, cozy feeling she had when, propped up by a few large pillows, she forgot all about her present predicament as she read this story. As soon as she had finished it, she started to read it over again. The happy hours she spent with the Family Robinson in that fantasy land permitted her not to

be defeated by the difficulties that reality presented to her. She was able to counteract the impact of harsh reality by imaginary gratifications. But since the story was not a fairy tale, it merely gave her a temporary escape from her problems; it did not hold out any promise to her that her life would take a turn for the better.

3   Consider the effect that "Rapunzel" had on a third girl. This girl's mother had died in a car accident. The girl's father, deeply upset by what had happened to his wife (he had been driving the car), withdrew entirely into himself and handed the care of his daughter over to a nursemaid, who was little interested in the girl and gave her complete freedom to do as she liked. When the girl was seven, her father remarried, and, as she recalled it, it was around that time that "Rapunzel" became so important to her. Her stepmother was clearly the witch of the story, and she was the girl locked away in the tower. The girl recalled that she felt akin to Rapunzel because the witch had "forcibly" taken possession of her, as her stepmother had forcibly worked her way into the girl's life. The girl felt imprisoned in her new home, in contrast to her life of freedom with the nursemaid. She felt as victimized as Rapunzel, who, in her tower, had so little control over her life. Rapunzel's long hair was the key to the story. The girl wanted her hair to grow long, but her stepmother cut it short; long hair in itself became the symbol of freedom and happiness to her. The story convinced her that a prince (her father) would come someday and rescue her, and this conviction sustained her. If life became too difficult, all she needed was to imagine herself as Rapunzel, her hair grown long, and the prince loving and rescuing her.

4   "Rapunzel" suggests why fairy tales can offer more to the child than even such a very nice children's story as "The Swiss Family Robinson." In "The Swiss Family Robinson," there is no witch against whom the child can discharge her anger in fantasy and on whom she can blame the father's lack of interest. "The Swiss Family Robinson" offers escape fantasies, and it did help the girl who read it over and over to forget temporarily how difficult life was for her. But it offered no specific hope for the future. "Rapunzel," on the other hand, offered the girl a chance to see the witch of the story as so evil that by comparison even the "witch" stepmother at home was not really so bad. "Rapunzel" also promised the girl that her rescue would be effected by her own body, when her hair grew long. Most important of all, it promised that the "prince" was only temporarily blinded—that he would regain his sight and rescue his princess. This fantasy continued to sustain the girl, though to a less intense degree, until she fell in love and married, and then she no longer needed it. We can understand why at first glance the stepmother, if she had known the meaning of "Rapunzel" to her stepdaughter, would have felt that fairy tales are bad for children. What she would not have known was that unless the stepdaughter had been able to find that fantasy satisfaction through "Rapunzel," she would have tried to break up her father's marriage and that without the hope for the future which the story gave her she might have gone badly astray in life.

5   It seems quite understandable that when children are asked to name their favorite fairy tales, hardly any modern tales are among their choices.

Many of the new tales have sad endings, which fail to provide the escape and consolation that the fearsome events in the fairy tale require if the child is to be strengthened for meeting the vagaries of his life. Without such encouraging conclusions, the child, after listening to the story, feels that there is indeed no hope for extricating himself from his despairs. In the traditional fairy tale, the hero is rewarded and the evil person meets his well-deserved fate, thus satisfying the child's deep need for justice to prevail. How else can a child hope that justice will be done to him, who so often feels unfairly treated? And how else can he convince himself that he must act correctly, when he is so sorely tempted to give in to the asocial proddings of his desires?

An Introduction to Fairy Tales
Maria Tatar

Folklorist Maria Tatar is the author of numerous articles on fairy tale literature and ten scholarly books, one of which is The Annotated Classic Fairy Tales *(2002). The selection that follows is her general introduction to that volume, an overview that will prepare you to read the variants of "Cinderella" to follow. In a recent profile, Tatar said of her life's work: "Fairy tales…face up to the facts of life: nothing is sacred or taboo. Meanwhile they glitter with beauty. I work at the weirdly fascinating intersection of beauty and horror." Tatar teaches folklore at Harvard University.*

1   For many of us childhood books are sacred objects. Often read to pieces, those books took us on voyages of discovery, leading us into secret new worlds that magnify childhood desires and anxieties and address the great existential mysteries. Like David Copperfield, who comforted himself by reading fairy tales, some of us once read "as if for life," using books not merely as consolation but as a way of navigating reality, of figuring out how to survive in a world ruled by adults. In a profound meditation on childhood reading, Arthur Schlesinger, Jr., writes about how the classical tales "tell children what they unconsciously know—that human nature is not innately good, that conflict is real, that life is harsh before it is happy—and thereby reassure them about their own fears and their own sense of self."

2   "What do we ever get nowadays from reading to equal the excitement and the revelation in those first fourteen years?" Graham Greene once asked. Many of us can recall moments of breathless excitement as we settled into our favorite chairs, our secret corners, or our cozy beds, eager to find out how Dorothy would escape the witch, whether the little mermaid would win an immortal soul, or what would become of Mary and Colin in the secret garden. "I hungered for the sharp, frightening, breath-taking, almost painful excitement that the story had given me," Richard Wright observes in recollecting his childhood encounter with the story "Bluebeard and His Seven

Wives." In that world of imagination, we not only escape the drab realities of everyday life but also indulge in the cathartic pleasures of defeating those giants, stepmothers, ogres, monsters, and trolls known as the grown-ups.

3   Yet much as we treasure the stories of childhood, we also outgrow them, cast them off, and dismiss them as childish things, forgetting their power not only to build the childhood world of imagination but also to construct the adult world of reality. Fairy tales, according to the British illustrator Arthur Rackham, have become "part of our everyday thought and expression, and help to shape our lives." There is no doubt, he adds, "that we should be behaving ourselves very differently if Beauty had never been united to her Beast...or if Sister Anne hadn't seen anybody coming; or if 'Open Sesame!' hadn't cleared the way, or Sindbad sailed." Whether we are aware of it or not, fairy tales have modeled behavioral codes and developmental paths, even as they provide us with terms for thinking about what happens in our world.

4   Part of the power of these stories derives not just from the words but also from the images that accompany them. In my own childhood copy of the Grimms' fairy tales, held together by rubber bands and tape, there is one picture worth many thousands of words. Each time I open the book to that page, I feel a rush of childhood memories and experience, for a few moments, what it was like to be a child. The images that accompanied "Cinderella," "Little Red Riding Hood," or "Jack and the Beanstalk" in volumes of classic fairy tales from an earlier era have an aesthetic power that produces an emotional hold rarely encountered in the work of contemporary illustrators, and for this reason I have returned to earlier times and places for the images accompanying the stories in this volume.

5   Fairy tales are up close and personal, telling us about the quest for romance and riches, for power and privilege, and, most important, for a way out of the woods back to the safety and security of home. Bringing myths down to earth and inflecting them in human rather than heroic terms, fairy tales put a familiar spin on the stories in the archive of our collective imagination. Think of Tom Thumb, who miniaturizes David's killing of Goliath in the Bible, Odysseus' blinding of the Cyclops in *The Odyssey,* and Siegfried's conquest of the dragon Fafner in Richard Wagner's *Ring of the Nibelung.* Or of Cinderella, who is sister under the skin to Shakespeare's Cordelia and to Charlotte Brontë's Jane Eyre. Fairy tales take us into a reality that is familiar in the double sense of the term— deeply personal and at the same time centered on the family and its conflicts rather than on what is at stake in the world at large.

6   John Updike reminds us that the fairy tales we read to children today had their origins in a culture of adult storytelling: "They were the television and pornography of their day, the life-lightening trash of preliterate peoples." If we look at the stories in their earliest written forms, we discover preoccupations and ambitions that conform to adult anxieties and desires. Sleeping Beauty may act like a careless, disobedient child when she reaches for the spindle that puts her to sleep, but her real troubles come in the form of a hostile mother-in-law who plans to serve her for dinner with a sauce Robert. "Bluebeard," with its forbidden chamber filled with

the corpses of former wives, engages with issues of marital trust, fidelity, and betrayal, showing how marriage is haunted by the threat of murder. "Rumpelstiltskin" charts a woman's narrow escape from a bargain that could cost the life of her first-born. And "Rapunzel" turns on the perilous cravings of a pregnant woman and on the desire to safeguard a girl's virtue by locking her up in a tower.

7   Fairy tales, once told by peasants around the fireside to distract them from the tedium of domestic chores, were transplanted with great success into the nursery, where they thrive in the form of entertainment and edification for children. These tales, which have come to constitute a powerful cultural legacy passed on from one generation to the next, provide more than gentle pleasures, charming enchantments, and playful delights. They contain much that is "painful and terrifying," as the art historian Kenneth Clark recalled in reminiscing about his childhood encounters with the stories of the Brothers Grimm and Hans Christian Andersen. Arousing dread as well as wonder, fairy tales have, over the centuries, always attracted both enthusiastic advocates, who celebrate their robust charms, and hard-edged critics, who deplore their violence.

8   Our deepest desires as well as our most profound anxieties enter the folk-loric bloodstream and remain in it through stories that find favor with a community of listeners or readers. As repositories of a collective cultural consciousness and unconscious, fairy tales have attracted the attention of psychologists, most notably the renowned child psychologist Bruno Bettelheim. In his landmark study, *The Uses of Enchantment*, Bettelheim argued that fairy tales have a powerful therapeutic value, teaching children that "a struggle against severe difficulties in life is unavoidable." "If one does not shy away," Bettelheim added with great optimism, "but steadfastly meets unexpected and often unjust hardships, one masters all obstacles and at the end emerges victorious."

9   Over the past decades child psychologists have mobilized fairy tales as powerful therapeutic vehicles for helping children and adults solve their problems by meditating on the dramas staged in them. Each text becomes an enabling device, allowing readers to work through their fears and to purge themselves of hostile feelings and damaging desires. By entering the world of fantasy and imagination, children and adults secure for themselves a safe space where fears can be confronted, mastered, and banished. Beyond that, the real magic of the fairy tale lies in its ability to extract pleasure from pain. In bringing to life the dark figures of our imagination as ogres, witches, cannibals, and giants, fairy tales may stir up dread, but in the end they always supply the pleasure of seeing it vanquished.

10   Like Bettelheim, the German philosopher Walter Benjamin applauded the feisty determination of fairy-tale heroes and heroines: "The wisest thing—so the fairy tale taught mankind in olden times, and teaches children to this day—is to meet the forces of the mythical world with cunning and with high spirits." If Bettelheim emphasized the value of "struggle" and "mastery" and saw in fairy tales an "experience in moral education," Benjamin reminded us that the morality endorsed in fairy tales is not with-

out complications and complexities. While we may all agree that promoting "high spirits" is a good thing for the child outside the book, we may not necessarily concur that "cunning" is a quality we wish to encourage by displaying its advantages. Early commentators on fairy tales quickly detected that the moral economy of the fairy tale did not necessarily square with the didactic agendas set by parents. The British illustrator George Cruikshank was appalled by the story "Puss in Boots," which seemed to him "a succession of successful falsehoods—a clever lesson in lying!—a system of imposture rewarded by the greatest worldly advantage!" He found Jack's theft of the giant's treasures morally reprehensible and felt obliged to rewrite the story, turning the robbery into a reappropriation of the dead father's fortune. Cruikshank would have reacted similarly to Aladdin, that prototypical fairytale hero who is described as "headstrong," as an "incorrigible good-for-nothing," and as a boy who will never amount to anything. Wherever we turn, fairy-tale characters always seem to be lying, cheating, or stealing their way to good fortune.

11   In stories for children, we have come to desire and expect clear, positive moral direction, along with straightforward messages. The popular success of William Bennett's *Book of Virtues,* a collection of stories chosen for their ability to transmit "timeless and universal" cultural values, reveals just how invested we are in the notion that moral literature can produce good citizens. Bennett is completely at ease with his list of the virtues we all embrace: self-discipline, compassion, responsibility, friendship, work, courage, perseverance, honesty, loyalty, and faith. But he fails to recognize the complexities of reading, the degree to which children often focus on single details, produce idiosyncratic interpretations, or become passionate about vices as well as virtues.

12   In her memoir *Leaving a Doll's House,* the actress Claire Bloom reminisces about the "sound of Mother's voice as she read to me from Hans Christian Andersen's *The Little Mermaid* and *The Snow Queen*." Although the experience of reading produced "a pleasurable sense of warmth and comfort and safety," Bloom also emphasizes that "these emotionally wrenching tales… instilled in me a longing to be overwhelmed by romantic passion and led me in my teens and early twenties to attempt to emulate these self-sacrificing heroines." That Bloom played the tragic, self-effacing heroine not only on stage but in real life becomes clear from the painful account of her many failed romances and marriages. The stories, to be sure, may merely have reinforced what was already part of Bloom's character and disposition, but it is troubling to read her real-life history in light of her strong identification with figures like Andersen's Little Mermaid. Bloom's recollection of childhood reading reminds us that reading may yield warmth and pleasure, but that there can be real consequences to reading without reflecting on the effect of what is on the page.

13   *The Book of Virtues,* like many anthologies of stories "for children," endorses a kind of mindless reading that fails to interrogate the cultural values embedded in stories written once upon a time, in a different time and place. In its enunciation of a moral beneath each title, it also insists on

reducing every story to a flat one-liner about one virtue or another, failing to take into account Eudora Welty's observation that "there is absolutely everything in great fiction but a clear answer." Even fairy tales, with their naïve sense of justice, their tenacious materialism, their reworking of familiar territory, and their sometimes narrow imaginative range, rarely send unambiguous messages.

14   This lack of ethical clarity did not present a problem for many of the collectors who put fairy tales between the covers of books. When Charles Perrault published his *Tales of Mother Goose* in 1697, he appended at least one moral, sometimes two. Yet those morals often did not square with the events in the story and sometimes offered nothing more than an opportunity for random social commentary and digressions on character. The explicit behavioral directives added by Perrault and others also have a tendency to misfire when they are aimed at children. It did not take Rousseau to discover that when you observe children learning lessons from stories, "you will see that when they are in a position to apply them, they almost always do so in a way opposite to the author's intention." Nearly every former child has learned this lesson through self-observation or through personal experience with children.

15   Do we, then, abandon the notion of finding moral guidance in fairy tales? Is reading reduced to an activity that yields nothing but aesthetic delight or pure pleasure? If fairy tales do not provide us with the tidy morals and messages for which we sometimes long, they still present us with opportunities to think about the anxieties and desires to which the tale gives shape, to reflect on and discuss the values encapsulated in the narrative, and to contemplate the perils and possibilities opened up by the story.

16   Today we recognize that fairy tales are as much about conflict and violence as about enchantment and happily-ever-after endings. When we read "Cinderella," we are fascinated more by her trials and tribulations at the hearth than by her social elevation. We spend more time thinking about the life-threatening chant of the giant in "Jack and the Beanstalk" than about Jack's acquisition of wealth. And Hansel and Gretel's encounter with the seemingly magnanimous witch in the woods haunts our imagination long after we have put the story down.

17   Through the medium of stories, adults can talk with children about what matters in their lives, about issues ranging from fear of abandonment and death to fantasies of revenge and triumphs that lead to happily-ever-after endings. While looking at pictures, reading episodes, and turning pages, adults and children can engage in what the cultural critic Ellen Handler-Spitz calls "conversational reading," dialogues that meditate on the story's effects and offer guidance for thinking about similar matters in the real world. This kind of reading can take many different turns: earnest, playful, meditative, didactic, empathetic, or intellectual.

18   In her recollections of reading "Little Red Riding Hood" with her grandmother, Angela Carter gives us one such scene of reading fairy tales: "My maternal grandmother used to say, 'Lift up the latch and walk in,' when she told it to me when I was a child; and at the conclusion, when the wolf jumps

on Little Red Riding Hood and gobbles her up, my grandmother used to pretend to eat me, which made me squeak and gibber with excited pleasure." Carter's account of her experience with "Little Red Riding Hood" reveals the degree to which the meaning of a tale is generated in its performance. This scene of reading—with its cathartic pleasures—tells us more about what the story means than the "timeless truths" that were enunciated by Charles Perrault in his moral to the first literary version of the tale.

19   Luciano Pavarotti, by contrast, had a very different experience with "Little Red Riding Hood." "In my house," he recalls, "when I was a little boy, it was my grandfather who told the stories. He was wonderful. He told violent, mysterious tales that enchanted me. . . . My favorite one was *Little Red Riding Hood*. I identified with Little Red Riding Hood. I had the same fears as she. I didn't want her to die. I dreaded her death—or what we think death is." Charles Dickens had an even more powerful sentiment about the girl in this story. Little Red Riding Hood was his "first love": "I felt that if I could have married Little Red Riding Hood, I should have known perfect bliss."

20   Each of these three readers responded in very different ways to a story that we are accustomed to considering as a cautionary tale warning about the dangers of straying from the path. Often it is the experience of reading out loud or retelling that produces the most powerful resonances and responses. Since the stories in this collection were once part of an oral tradition and since they are meant to be read aloud and revised, I have sought to recapture the rhythms of oral storytelling in my translations, using phrasing, diction, and pacing that reminds us that these stories were once broadcast, spoken out loud to an audience of young and old.

21   It is the readers of these fairy tales who will reinvigorate them, making them hiss and crackle with narrative energy with each retelling. Hans Christian Andersen, according to his friend Edvard Collin, had a special way of breathing new life into fairy tales:

> Whether the tale was his own or someone else's, the way of telling it was completely his own, and so lively that the children were thrilled. He, too, enjoyed giving his humor free rein, his speaking was without stop, richly adorned with the figures of speech well known to children, and with gestures to match the situation. Even the driest sentence came to life. He did not say, "The children got into the carriage and then drove away," but "They got into the carriage—'goodbye, Dad! Goodbye, Mum!'—the whip cracked smack! smack! and away they went, come on! gee up!"

22   Reading these stories in the fashion of Andersen is a way of reclaiming them, turning them into our cultural stories by inflecting them in new ways and in some cases rescripting what happened "once upon a time."

23   The fairy tales in this volume did not require editorial interventions in an earlier age, precisely because they were brought up to date by their tellers and tailored to the cultural context in which they were told. In presenting the "classic" versions of the tales, this volume is offering foundational texts

that may not necessarily be completely transparent to readers today. They offer the basis for retelling, but in many cases they will call out for parental intervention. The background material on each fairy tale anchors the story in its historical context, revealing the textual peculiarities and ideological twists and turns taken over time at different cultural sites. Knowing that Cinderella lives happily ever after with her stepsisters in some versions of her story and that doves are summoned to peck out the eyes of the stepsisters in others is something that parents will want to know when they read "Cinderella" to their children. That Little Red Riding Hood outwits the wolf in some versions of her story will be an important point to bear in mind when reading Perrault's version of the story, in which the girl is devoured by the wolf. Understanding something about how Bluebeard's wife is sometimes censured for her curiosity and sometimes praised for her resourcefulness will help adults reflect on how to talk about this story with a child.

24   The annotations to the stories are intended to enrich the reading experience, providing cues for points in the story where adult and child can contemplate alternative possibilities, improvise new directions, or imagine different endings. These notes draw attention to moments at which adult and child can engage with issues raised, sometimes simply indulging in the pleasures of the narrative, but sometimes also thinking about the values endorsed in the story and questioning whether the plot has to take the particular turn that it does in the printed version.

25   The illustrations for *The Annotated Classic Fairy Tales* have been drawn largely from the image repertoire of nineteenth-century artists, contemporaries of the collectors and editors of the great national anthologies of fairy tales. Arthur Rackham, Gustave Doré, Edmund Dulac, Walter Crane, Edward Burne-Jones, George Cruikshank, and others produced illustrations that provide not only visual pleasure but also powerful commentaries on the tales, interrupting the flow of the story at critical moments and offering opportunities for further reflection and interpretation. For many of us, the most memorable encounters with fairy tales came in the form of illustrated books. Those volumes, as Walter Benjamin points out, always had "one saving grace: their illustration." The pictures in those anthologies escaped the kind of censorship and bowdlerization to which the texts were often subjected. "They eluded the control of philanthropic theories and quickly, behind the backs of the pedagogues, children and artists came together."

26   The *Annotated Classic Fairy Tales* seeks to reclaim a powerful cultural legacy, creating a storytelling archive for children and adults. While the fairy tales have been drawn from a variety of cultures, they constitute a canon that has gained nearly universal currency in the Western world and that has remained remarkably stable over the centuries. Even those unfamiliar with the details of "The Frog Prince" or "The Little Match Girl" have some sense of what these stories are about and how the salient points in them (attraction and repulsion in the one, compassion in the other) are mobilized in everyday discourse to underscore an argument or to embellish a point. This volume collects the stories that we all think we know—

even when we are unable to retell them—providing also the texts and historical contexts that we often do not have firmly in mind.

27   Disseminated across a wide variety of media, ranging from opera and drama to cinema and advertising, fairy tales have become a vital part of our cultural capital. What keeps them alive and pulsing with vitality and variety is exactly what keeps life pulsing: anxieties, fears, desires, romance, passion, and love. Like our ancestors, who listened to these stories at the fireside, in taverns, and in spinning rooms, we remain transfixed by stories about wicked stepmothers, bloodthirsty ogres, sibling rivals, and fairy godmothers. For us, too, the stories are irresistible, for they offer opportunities to talk, to negotiate, to deliberate, to chatter, and to prattle on endlessly as did the old wives from whom the stories are thought to derive. And from the tangle of that talk and chitchat, we begin to define our own values, desires, appetites, and aspirations, creating identities that will allow us to produce happily-ever-after endings for ourselves and for our children.

The Truth about Cinderella
Martin Daly and Margo Wilson

The First Test: US Child Abuse Reports

1   Our first attempt to measure the impact of step-relationships on the incidence of child abuse made use of a data archive maintained by the American Humane Association (AHA). This organization had assumed the role of central repository for legally mandated child abuse reports in most of the United States, and had a computer file containing tens of thousands of case reports. For each victimized child, the data included basic demographic facts about victim and (alleged) perpetrator, details of the nature of the abuse, the relationship between the victim and the persons *in loco parentis*, and whether the case had been 'validated' in some sort of follow-up investigation beyond the initial report.

2   To compute the age-specific rates of abuse of step-children *versus* others, we also needed data on the living arrangements of children in the population at large. This information was elusive. The US census of population did not distinguish among genetic, adoptive and step-parenthood, and all we could find were estimates based on limited surveys, which almost certainly exaggerated the prevalence of step-relationships because of some unrealistic assumptions that had been made to derive the estimates. But we used them anyway, since they made our comparisons 'conservative': an overestimation of the number of stepfamilies in the population should lead us to underestimate their maltreatment rates and make it more difficult to demonstrate an elevation. But the elevation of risk was dramatic none the less: according to our calculations, a child under three years of age who

lived with one genetic parent and one step-parent in the United States in 1976 was about seven times more likely (the 'odds ratio' in epidemiological parlance) to become a validated child-abuse case in the AHA records than one who dwelt with two genetic parents.

3   There are a number of reasons to be cautious about interpreting this sort of comparison. One is the possibility of biased detection or reportage. Suppose that you lived next door to a child who exhibited recurrent, suspicious bruising, and that you (like everyone else) were familiar with the stereotype of step-parental cruelty. Isn't it possible that your likelihood of assuming the worst and calling a child protection agency might be affected by knowing that the man in the house was a stepfather? Biases of this sort could create the appearance of differential risk where none actually exists. However, there was strong evidence that this was not what was happening in the AHA data. We reasoned that as the severity of child abuse increases, up to the extreme of lethal battering, it should be increasingly unequivocal, so distortions due to biased detection and reportage should diminish. But as we made our abuse criteria increasingly stringent and narrowed the sample down to the most unmistakable cases, the over-representation of stepfamilies did not diminish. Quite the contrary, in fact. By the time we had reduced the cases under consideration from the full file of 87,789 validated maltreatment reports to the 279 fatal child-abuse cases, the estimated rates in step-parent-plus-genetic-parent households had grown to approximately *one hundred times* greater than in two-genetic-parent households.

4   There could be no doubt that the excess risk in stepfamilies was both genuine and huge. But whether it really had anything to do with step-relationship *per se* was not necessarily resolved. Perhaps living with a step-parent was associated with some other factor of more direct relevance.

5   One obvious candidate for such a 'confounding' factor is poverty. If step-parenthood is especially prevalent among the poor (which seemed plausible since marital stability was known to be correlated with income) and if the poor also have high rates of detected child abuse (which they do), then differentials of the sort we had observed might be expected even if step-parent and genetic-parent homes were identically risky within any particular income level. But this initially plausible hypothesis was rejected, for it turned out that the distribution of family incomes in step-parent homes in the United States was virtually identical to that in two-genetic-parent homes. Low-income families were indeed over-represented in the AHA dataset, but the association between abuse and poverty was independent of (was 'orthogonal' to) the association between abuse and step-relationship.

Further Research in Canada

6 We published our US results in a brief journal article in 1980 and in greater detail in 1981, and we turned our attentions elsewhere. But we were never entirely happy with out initial study, for several reasons. The population-

at-large estimates were questionable; the 'abuse' criteria were not necessarily consistent from state to state; and the data were inadequate for testing additional 'confound' hypotheses other than poverty. So a few years later, having moved back home to Canada, we decided to conduct a better controlled, smaller-scale, local study of the same issues.

7   The regional municipality of Hamilton-Wentworth, where we live, is the centre of Canada's steel industry and home to almost half-a-million souls. The local child-protection agencies provided us with information about all cases severe enough to have warranted filing a report with the provincial child-abuse registry, and we surveyed the relevant population-at-large ourselves. About one in every 3,000 Hamilton pre-schoolers residing with both genetic parents was reported to the Ontario child-abuse registry in 1983. The corresponding rate for those living with a step-parent plus a genetic parent was about one in seventy-five, hence forty times greater. This odds ratio was smaller than that which we had found for lethal abuse in the United States, but larger than that for all child abuse, perhaps because the case criterion in our Hamilton study was of intermediate severity.

8   The odds ratio of abuse risk in Hamilton stepfamilies versus genetic-parent families was substantial for children of all ages, but it declined steadily from forty for preschoolers to about ten for teenaged victims. A similar trend had also been apparent in our US study, and we saw an important implication. Most of those who had written on stepfamily conflicts apparently believed that the problems are primarily created by obstreperous adolescents rejecting their custodial parents' new mates; but this could hardly be correct if the elevation of risk from step-parents was maximal for infants. Our hypothesis that the more basic problem is the adult's resentment of pseudo-parental obligation fits the facts much better.

9   Another consistent result from both studies was that excess risk in step-families spanned the gamut of 'abuse' from baby batterings to sexual molestation of older children. This also reinforced our conviction that we were looking at what might be called a 'reverse assay' of parental love. A paucity of heartfelt, individualized concern for the welfare of a child in one's care would seem likely to raise the incidence of any sort of misuse.

10   Still another consistent result was that step-parenthood's impact was statistically independent of poverty's additional effects. Family size, which we had not been able to assess in the US study, proved to be another independent risk factor. Maternal youth was yet another. Evolutionary theories of maternal investment had suggested to us that older mothers might be more selfless than younger. As menopause approaches, investing in the children you already have has less and less negative impact on your expected future reproduction. Evolved maternal psychologies might be expected to reflect this reliable feature of women's life histories. We therefore anticipated that abuse risk would decline steadily as a function of the mother's age at the child's birth, and this expectation was upheld. All in all, although several additional risk factors were identified, step-parenthood held its place as the most important predictor, and its influence was

scarcely diminished when the statistical impacts of all the other risk factors were controlled.

11   It warrants repeating that even severe child abuse is vulnerable to detection biases, but that these biases presumably shrink as the case criterion becomes more extreme. At the limit, we can be reasonably confident that child murders are usually detected and recorded. Admittedly, some failures to help a newborn live may escape detection and some deliberate smotherings may be successfully disguised as 'sudden infant deaths', but there is no reason to suppose that these are numerous, and in any event, the brutal assaultive homicides that are motivated by rage or hatred cannot be disguised in this way. So after completing our study of registered child-abuse cases in Hamilton, we undertook analyses of homicides, using an official government archive containing data on all homicides known to Canadian police departments. Once again, just as we had found in the United States, the over-representation of step-parents as perpetrators of child murder in Canada proved to be even more extreme than their over-representation as perpetrators of non-lethal child abuse. As we reported in an article in *Science* in 1988, a co-residing step-parent was approximately seventy times more likely to kill a child under two years of age than was a co-residing genetic parent, and this odds ratio was still about fifteen for teenage victims.

The Emerging Cross-National Evidence

12   We now know that the story in Great Britain is much the same as in North America: step-parents are hugely over-represented as perpetrators of registered child abuse and even more hugely as child murderers. According to a report produced by the National Society for the Prevention of Cruelty to Children, entitled *Child Abuse Trends in England & Wales 1983–1987*, thirty-two per cent of the 4,037 nationally registered victims of intentionally inflicted physical injuries in that five-year period lived with one natural parent and one substitute parent, whereas a random sample of children with the same age distribution from the population-at-large would have yielded only three per cent. Unlike the situation in North America, stepfamilies in the United Kingdom tend to have slightly lower incomes than two-genetic-parent families, so that the excess of step-parents may in this case be partly an artifact of economic differences. However, when family income was controlled, children in stepfamilies remained nineteen times more likely to be registered as victims of non-accidental physical injuries inflicted by caretakers than were children from two-genetic-parent homes.

13   As for child murder, there was one relevant report dating from before we began our own research. In 1973, forensic psychiatrist P. D. Scott had summarized information on a sample of 'fatal battered-baby cases' perpetrated in anger by British men *in loco paternis*, and despite the fact that the victims averaged just fifteen months of age, fifteen of the twenty-nine killers—fifty-two per cent—were stepfathers. Scott did not attempt to con-

vert these numbers to rates or odds ratios, but relevant population-at-large information can now be derived from a major study of a cohort born in 1970, and it turns out that fewer than one per cent of a sample of children with the same age distribution as the fatally battered babies would be expected to have had a stepfather. In this case, the odds ratio for this particular kind of lethal assault by stepfathers versus genetic fathers was approximately 150.

14   It seemed likely, both from the evidence of these baby batterings and from our evolution-minded hypothesis about step-parental reluctance and resentment, that excess risk from step-parents might be especially severe with regard to angry outbursts. Little children *are* annoying, after all: they cry and soil themselves and sometimes refuse to be consoled. A caretaker with a heartfelt, individualized love for a squalling baby is motivated to tenderly alleviate its distress, but a caretaker who is simply playing the part without emotional commitment—and who might even prefer that the child had never been born—is apt to respond rather differently.

15   Filicides by genetic parents certainly occur. In absolute numbers, they actually exceed the cases perpetrated by step-parents, although the latter occur at much higher per capita rates. But the cases are not similar. The Home Office maintains a case-by-case data archive on homicides in England and Wales, similar to the Canadian archive mentioned above. Although the information in these archives is sparse, consisting solely of numerical codings of a number of standard variables, it still proves revealing as regards the characteristics of killings by genetic *versus* step-parents. Confining our inquiry to cases in which the victims were less than five years of age, in order to exclude all possibility of mutual combat or self-defence on the killer's part, we find a similar pattern in both countries: about eighty per cent of homicidal stepfathers are found to have battered, kicked or bludgeoned their victims to death, whereas the majority of those who killed their genetic offspring did so by less assaultive means. Moreover, in the course of seventeen years of Canadian data and fourteen years of British data, seventy-three of the 390 men who killed their own children did so in the context of a successfully completed suicide, compared to just three of the 197 who killed stepchildren. There is also evidence that diagnosed psychiatric conditions are prevalent among those who kill their genetic children, but not among those who kill stepchildren. In summary, filicidal genetic parents of both sexes are often deeply depressed, are likely to kill the children while they sleep, and may even construe murder-suicide as a humane act of rescue from a cruel world, whereas homicidal step-parents are seldom suicidal and typically manifest their antipathy to their victims in the relative brutality of their lethal acts.

16   In recent years, diverse strands of evidence from a variety of countries have shown that step-parental mistreatment of children is widespread. In New South Wales, Australia, for example, stepfathers have been found to be even more extremely over-represented as the perpetrators of baby batterings than in Canada, the United States, and Great Britain. In Finland, a 1996 report of a questionnaire study of 9,000 fifteen-year-olds indicated that

3.7 percent of girls currently living with a stepfather claimed that he had abused them sexually, compared to 0.2 per cent of those living with their genetic fathers. (The only case of 'mother-son' sexual contact in this study, incidentally, involved a fifteen-year-old boy and his twenty-six-year-old stepmother; in contrast to the girls, all of whom found sexual contact with stepfathers or fathers aversive, 'the boy described the experience as positive'.) Korean schoolchildren living with either a stepfather or a stepmother claim to be beaten at very much higher rates than their two-genetic-parent classmates. Recent studies in Hong Kong, Nigeria, Japan and Trinidad paint similar pictures.

17   It has also become clear that the hazards associated with being a stepchild are not a novel product of the modern age. Using historical archives from the seventeenth to the nineteenth century, the German anthropologist Eckart Voland has shown that Cinderella stories were more than mere fairy tales for European peasants. Voland found that the age-specific mortality of pre-modern Friesian children was elevated in the aftermath of the death of either parent and, more tellingly, that the risk of death was further elevated if the surviving parent remarried.

18   In the face-to-face societies of our ancestors, powerful central authority and social services beyond kin assistance were non-existent, and the situation for stepchildren was probably even worse than in peasant societies. According to one study of contemporary South American hunter-gatherers, the Ache of Paraguay, forty-three per cent of children brought up by a mother and stepfather died before their fifteenth birthdays, compared to nineteen per cent of those brought up by two genetic parents; apparently, deaths by assault and deaths due to deprivation of adequate care were both elevated. Hunter-gatherer societies provide our best model of the social circumstances in which the human animal evolved and to which our psyches are adapted. We hypothesize that it has been a general feature of such societies that step-children are variously disadvantaged—as they are among the Ache—and we know of no contrary evidence.

The Rise of Perrault's "Cinderella"
Bonnie Cullen

In this next selection, art historian Bonnie Cullen explains how, from among the hundreds of "Cinderellas" throughout the world, Charles Perrault's version came to be what many in the West think of as the canonical, or standard, one. Of the seven variants of "Cinderella" named in this article, six appear earlier in the chapter. A longer version of this article first appeared in The Lion and the Unicorn *(Volume 27, 2003).*

1   Why [did] Perrault's story, above all others, [become the dominant version of "Cinderella"]? Considering its origins, there were many contes-

tants for the dominant tale. "Cinderella" is really a large family of tales first analyzed by folklorists in the nineteenth century. Studying more than 300 related narratives from Europe and Asia, Marian Roalfe Cox identified Cinderella stories according to the presence of certain themes: an abused child, rescue through some reincarnation of the dead mother, recognition, and marriage.

2   The earliest known Cinderella story is actually a literary version from ninth-century China. Already it has the familiar elements. Yeh-hsien (Cinderella) has lost both her father and mother and seeks consolation from a pet fish. Her cruel stepmother eats the fish and buries the bones. A man comes from the sky advising her to find and save the bones—she will get whatever she wishes for.

3   When her stepmother and stepsister leave for a festival, Yeh-hsien follows them in a cloak of kingfisher feathers and gold shoes. She loses a shoe, the shoe is found, and given to a king. A search for the foot small enough to fit the shoe ensues. Yeh-hsien is finally shown to be the rightful owner and marries the king (Ting 4–5).

4   In most early Cinderella tales, the dead mother hovers protectively, reincarnated as a cow, a fish, or a tree. Her relationship with the grieving daughter is as significant as the girl's triumph. Occasionally the protagonist is male. The shoe is not always the means of identification, although it is extremely common, as is the use of some magic garment (Philip).

5   By the sixteenth century, Cinderella appears in print in the West. One major debut is in Basile's seventeenth-century collection, *Il Pentamerone (Lo cunto de li cunti),* as the feisty "Gatta Cenerentola" or "Cat Cinderella." Zezolla (Cinderella) kills her wicked stepmother with the help of a governess, but when the governess marries Zezolla's father, the girl is mistreated again. A fairy in a tree supplies magic clothes and a coach for a feast where Zezolla captures a king's heart.

6   In Basile's tale, the dead mother is no longer a significant presence, although she might be vaguely identified with the fairy. While close to some oral versions, his bawdy narrative is full of intricate metaphors and clearly written for an adult audience (Canepa 14–15). The book was published in Neapolitan dialect, which probably limited its dissemination in print (Canepa 12; Opie and Opie 20–21), although Basile's stories may have passed into the oral repertoire and traveled in other languages.

7   During the ancien régime of Louis the XIV, folktales were transformed into a new literary genre, the fairy tale. Narrated as a kind of conversational game in the salons of the *précieuses,* by the end of the century they were being written down (Zipes, *Beauties* 1–9; Warner 167–70). Two distinct versions of "Cinderella" issued from the pens of Charles Perrault and the Countess d'Aulnoy.

8   Marie-Catherine Le Jumel de Barneville, Baronne d'Aulnoy, was a feminist and writer, the first to publish her stories as "fairy tales," or literary versions of popular folktales. Her Cinderella, "Finette Cendron," is both altruistic and spirited. When their parents abandon Finette and her sisters, she engineers daring escapes for all three. They plot against

her, but Finette remains loyal. With a godmother's help she finds some magnificent clothing and triumphs at the ball. She loses a shoe and gallops back to claim it, but refuses to marry the prince until her parents' kingdom, which they lost, is restored (d'Aulnoy, *Fairy Tales* 227–45).*

9   Perrault's "Cendrillon" is quite a different lady. He dubs her chief virtue "la bonne grace," i.e., in the face of adversity she is generous, long-suffering, charming and good-humored; the ideal bride, from the gentleman's perspective.

10   A bland protagonist perhaps, but Perrault exhibits his wit. Cendrillon plays her own tricks on the sisters, asking one if she can borrow a dress to see the mysterious princess at the next ball. He also writes tongue-in-cheek. The slipper, evoking female virginity, is made of glass in his tale. Not only is it fragile and extremely pure, but Perrault hints that visual proof will be necessary.

11   Perrault's position as a member of the French Academy may have led him to adopt this tone for tales of the peasant class (Warner 168–70). He also shifts the spotlight to the fairy godmother, giving her a dominant role. In the ancien régime, fairies were equated with powerful women at court (232–34). D'Aulnoy's fairy is sympathetic and dignified, asking Finette to be her lady's maid and comb her hair. Her magic is in providing the nec-

---

*An example of Finette's resourcefulness: Held captive in a castle, Finette devises a plan when a hungry ogre orders her and her two sisters to cook for him and his ogress (instead of eating them straight-away). It is the last request he makes:

"But," said [the ogre], turning to Finette, "when you have lit the fire, how can you tell if the oven be hot enough?" "My lord," she answered, "I throw butter in, and then I taste it with my tongue." "Very well," he said, "light the fire then." The oven was as big as a stable, for the ogre and ogress ate more bread than two armies. The princess made an enormous fire, which blazed like a fur-nace; and the ogre, who was standing by, ate a hundred lambs and a hundred sucking pigs while waiting for the new bread. [Finette's sisters] Fleur d'Amour and Belle-de-Nuit kneaded the dough. "Well," said the great ogre, "is the oven hot?" "My lord," replied Finette, "you will see presently." And so saying she threw a thousand pounds of butter into the oven. "I should try it with my tongue," she said, "but I am too little." "I am big enough," said the ogre, and bending down he went so far into the oven that he could not draw back again, so that he was burned to the bones. When the ogress came to the oven she was mightily astonished to find a mountain of cinders instead of her husband.

Fleur d'Amour and Belle-de-Nuit, who saw that she was in great distress, comforted her as they could, but they feared lest her grief should be consoled only too soon, and that regaining her appetite she would put them in a salad, as she had meant to do before. So they said to her: "Take courage, madam; you will find some king or some marquis who will be happy to marry you." At that she smiled a little, showing her teeth, which were longer than your finger. When they saw she was in a good humour, Finette said: "If you would but leave off wearing those horrible bear-skins, and dress a little more fashionably! We could arrange your hair beautifully, and you would be like a star." "Come then," she said, "let us see what you can do; but be sure that if I find any ladies more beautiful than myself I shall hack you into little bits." Thereupon the three princesses took off her cap, and began to comb and curl her hair, entertaining her all the while with their chatter. Then Finette took a hatchet, and with a great blow from behind, severed her head from her body.

For the complete version of d'Aulnoy's "Finette Cendron," go to http://www.surlalunefairytales.com/authors/aulnoy/1892/finettecendron.html.

essary items, whether or not she is present. Perrault's elaborate description of rat-and-pumpkin tricks is a spoof: his fairy godmother is a witch.

· · ·

12   When literary Cinderellas began to appear in English in the eighteenth century, it was Madame d'Aulnoy's story that took the lead. [An early version of her work appeared] in *A Collection of Novels and Tales, Written by that Celebrated Wit of France, the Countess d'Anois* (1721–22). Perrault's *Contes* did not appear in English until 1729.

13   By the nineteenth century, the tables had turned, apparently. Only seven English editions of d'Aulnoy's tales survive in the British Library; not all contain "Finette." There are over thirty editions of Perrault's "Cinderella" as a separate volume, besides its inclusion with the tales. Perrault's story was also adapted for pantomime and plays.

14   Perrault's version faced new competition, however. Searching for an antidote to bourgeois life—the stale "getting and spending," as Wordsworth put it—Romantics turned to nature. Might not the oral tales of country folk contain some primal wisdom? How closely they transcribed their originals is debated, but the Grimm brothers believed they were collecting rather than writing stories as they prepared their editions of *Die Kinder- und Hausmärchen* in 1812 (Warner 188–93). Their "Cinderella," "Aschenputtel," is indeed close to folk versions such as the Scottish tale, "Rashin Coatie" (Opie and Opie 117–18).

15   Mourning and revenge underlie "Aschenputtel": the heroine plants a tree on her mother's grave and tends it lovingly. A bird in the tree answers her calls for help. She begs for a dress, attends the feast and attracts the prince. The sisters cheat at the slipper test, cutting off parts of their feet, but birds reveal their deceit and at the wedding, peck out the sisters' eyes.

16   "Primal" tales had their opponents. With the first English translation, in volume two of *German Popular Stories* (1826), the brutal eye-pecking disappeared. During the previous century, the market for printed tales had expanded through chapbooks, devoured by a new audience of young readers as well as adults. By the end of the eighteenth century there was a movement in England to sanitize children's literature. Mrs. Trimmer, reviewing children's books for middle-class families; argued that the often brutal tales "excite . . . groundless fears" and "serve no moral purpose" (2: 185–86). This explains the intrusion of religious motifs, such as praying and church architecture, in chapbook illustration from the early nineteenth century, and the relative scarcity of expensive editions at the time.

17   Fairy tales would not go away, however. Those who wanted to imbue them with bourgeois morality faced equally vociferous champions of "pure" tales. "A child," Ruskin wrote, "should not need to chose between right and wrong. It should not be capable of wrong . . . " Innocent, children could be "fortif[ied] . . . against the glacial cold of selfish science" with the "inextinguishable life" of the folk tradition (83). As Zipes points out, arguments about fairy tales became part of the greater "Condition

of England" debate on the effects of the Industrial Revolution (*Victorian Fairy Tales* xvi–xxix).

18   In the case of "Cinderella," it was a somewhat revised Perrault that prevailed in Victorian England.

. . .

19   One reason Perrault's tale [did so] was its suitability for a modern audience. During the nineteenth century, the market for literary fairy tales in England was increasingly urban and middleclass. Perrault focuses on the social sphere, rather than the forest. He delineates hairdos, costume, behavior at the ball and reactions to Cendrillon's appearance with the ironic tone of a society reporter.

20   D'Aulnoy's Finette is busy slaying ogres and galloping through the mud, while in "Aschenputtel" there is blood from the sisters' mutilated feet. Romantics like Ruskin favored the rugged terrain of folktales, but as Mrs. Trimmer's remarks indicate, "polite" readers were concerned about "improving" young minds to function effectively in society.

21   More important, perhaps, Perrault's tale prevailed in English because it was the best vehicle for Victorian notions of femininity. D'Aulnoy's heroine liberates herself through female power, both magical and human. Folk Cinderellas like Aschenputtel also take action, advised by incarnations of their lost mothers. Perrault's Cendrillon is the least active, and he shifts the spotlight to her fairy godmother, whose magic is as amusing as it is powerful.

22   Whether or not the oral fairy tale had been a female genre, as Warner argues, by the nineteenth century the fairy tale in print was increasingly dominated by male writers and illustrators in an industry controlled by male publishers. That even some women writers followed the "party line" with canonical Cinderellas shows how powerful a formula it was for the middleclass market of nineteenth-century England.

23   It is interesting to note that Disney's revival of "Cinderella," which repeats the Victorian interpretation of Perrault's story, came out in 1950: a time when women, indispensable in the workforce during the war years, were being urged back home with imagery of ideal wives and mothers. There have been attempts to reclaim the tale in recent years in both print and film. Yet the canonical tale, with its Victorian ideology, persists.

Works Cited

Canepa, Nancy L. *From Court to Forest. Giambattista Basile's Lo Cunto de li Cunti and the Birth of the Literary Fairy Tale.* Detroit: Wayne State UP, 1999.

Cox, Marian Roalfe. *Cinderella; Three Hundred and Forty-five Variants.* Publications of the Folk-lore Society (no. 31). London, 1893.

D'Aulnoy, Marie Catherine Baronne. *The Fairy Tales of Madame D'Aulnoy.* Trans. Annie Macdonnell and Miss Lee. London: Lawrence and Bullen, 1892.

Opie, Iona, and Peter Opie. *The Classic Fairy Tales.* Oxford: Book Club Associates by arrangement with Oxford UP, 1992.

7   But to succeed on both the feminist and the fantasy level, the new Cinderella has developed rules and conventions as strict as a Joseph Campbell template.* She should be pretty, but in a class-president way, not a head-cheerleader way. She should be able to stand up for herself (recall the *Crouching Tiger* moves of *Shrek's* Princess Fiona). She must be socially conscious—a result, says Meg Cabot, author of the *Princess Diaries* books, of Princess Diana's charitable work. And she should above all not want to be a princess—at least until she changes her mind. In *Diaries* . . . it's not the girl who must prove herself worthy of princess-hood; princesshood must prove itself worthy of the girl.

8   There's something a little have-your-tiara-and-disdain-it-too about making your protagonists ambivalent about the very fantasy that people paid $9 to see them live out. But that may make the fantasy more palatable to parents and filmmakers: men and, especially, women who are educated profession-als. "I don't want to sound like an archfeminist," says Sherry Lansing, chair-man of Paramount, which produced *Prince*, "but it really is important that it imparts contemporary values. It's a good love that allows both people to remain whole in it." Still, the fantasy couple that this earnestness yields in *Prince* is more yuppie than romantic: she, committing to years of med school; he, giving up his love of car racing to strap on a necktie and negotiate labor disputes. Goodbye, Chuck and Di; hello, Abbey and Jed Bartlet.†

9   But it's easy for someone who has been through college to say a diploma and career are not cure-alls. The movies' audience of young girls makes the filmmakers much more message conscious—at least as far as the girls are con-cerned. The princes in these stories have fewer options than their Cinderellas. Edvard and Charmont are both reluctant to become king, but they learn, through the love of a good woman, to mature into the role and use it for good. The girls fight to control their destiny; the boys good-naturedly learn to accept theirs. Of course, they're not the target audience. "It's nice to have something that's not toxic or repellent to men," says Nina Jacobson, a top executive at Disney (*Diaries'* studio). "But we know we don't need guys to make a movie like that successful." You just need a feisty girl, a prophylactic dose of skepti-cism and a fabulous ball gown—about which no ambivalence is necessary.

---

*Joseph Campbell (1904–1987) is best known for his work in comparative mythology. In *The Hero with a Thousand Faces* (1949), he traces how heroes in myths and folklore thousands of years old, from cultures around the world, progress through recognizable stages on their journeys away from the ordinary world, to a magical realm of adventure and severe challenge, then back to the ordinary. The classic versions of "Cinderella" that you have read in this chapter illustrate important features of what Campbell called a "monomyth"; here Poniewozik is suggesting, ironically, that the newer, filmed versions of "Cinderella" are similarly formulaic, though in ways calculated to sell tickets.

†Chuck and Di: As the older son of Queen Elizabeth II, Charles, Prince of Wales, is next in line to become King of England. "Di" is Diana, to whom Charles was married, then divorced. Jed (Josiah) and Abbey Bartlet: president and First Lady of the United States in the long-running television series *The West Wing*. Poniewozik is suggesting that Charles and Diana, a traditional royal couple, have given way in the popular imagination—or, at least, in the projected fantasies of the movie industry—to Abbey and Josiah Bartlet. Abbey is a Harvard Medical School graduate and practicing physician who will not hesitate to correct her husband.

Cinderella and Princess Culture
Peggy Orenstein

Confronted with a daughter who enjoyed dressing as Cinderella and other storybook princesses, Peggy Orenstein set out to investigate "princess" culture and discovered an enormous corporate money-making machine. As a feminist, Orenstein warily approached the director of consumer products at Disney, Inc., responsible for the packaging of the Magic Kingdom's many princesses into a single merchandising juggernaut. She came away partially, if not entirely, assured that children can take on play identities that feminists once regarded as sexist and still "pass through" to an adulthood free of early gender stereotypes. Orenstein is a contributing writer for the New York Times Magazine, *from which the following was excerpted. The original selection, titled "What's Wrong with Cinderella?" appeared on December 24, 2006. Her memoir* Waiting for Daisy: A Tale of Two Continents, Three Religions, Five Infertility Doctors, An Oscar, An Atomic Bomb, A Romantic Night and One Woman's Quest to Become a Mother *(2007) was a* New York Times *best seller.*

1   I finally came unhinged in the dentist's office—one of those ritzy pediatric practices tricked out with comic books, DVDs and arcade games—where I'd taken my 3-year-old daughter for her first exam. Until then, I'd held my tongue. I'd smiled politely every time the supermarket-checkout clerk greeted her with "Hi, Princess"; ignored the waitress at our local breakfast joint who called the funny-face pancakes she ordered her "princess meal"; made no comment when the lady at Longs Drugs said, "I bet I know your favorite color" and handed her a pink balloon rather than letting her choose for herself. Maybe it was the dentist's Betty Boop inflection that got to me, but when she pointed to the exam chair and said, "Would you like to sit in my special princess throne so I can sparkle your teeth?" I lost it.

2   "Oh, for God's sake," I snapped. "Do you have a princess drill, too?"

3   She stared at me as if I were an evil stepmother.

4   "Come on!" I continued, my voice rising. "It's 2006, not 1950. This is Berkeley, Calif. Does every little girl really have to be a princess?"

5   My daughter, who was reaching for a Cinderella sticker, looked back and forth between us. "Why are you so mad, Mama?" she asked. "What's wrong with princesses?"

6   Diana* may be dead and Masako† disgraced, but here in America, we are in the midst of a royal moment. To call princesses a "trend" among girls is like calling Harry Potter a book. Sales at Disney Consumer Products, which started the craze six years ago by packaging nine of its

---

*Diana Spencer married to Prince Charles of England in a royal wedding broadcast around the world in 1981. The marriage unraveled and the pair divorced in 1996. She died in a car crash in Paris in 1997.

†Masako Owada, a Harvard- and Oxford-trained diplomat (and not of royal blood), married the heir to the Japanese throne in 1993. Ten years into her marriage, the pressures of her position caused "physical and mental fatigue," forcing her to retreat from public view for a time.

female characters under one royal rubric, have shot up to $3 billion, globally, this year, from $300 million in 2001. There are now more than 25,000 Disney Princess items. "Princess," as some Disney execs call it, is not only the fastest-growing brand the company has ever created; they say it is on its way to becoming the largest girls' franchise on the planet.

7   Meanwhile in 2001, Mattel brought out its own "world of girl" line of princess Barbie dolls, DVDs, toys, clothing, home décor and myriad other products. At a time when Barbie sales were declining domestically, they became instant best sellers. Shortly before that, Mary Drolet, a Chicago-area mother and former Claire's and Montgomery Ward executive, opened Club Libby Lu, now a chain of mall stores based largely in the suburbs in which girls ages 4 to 12 can shop for "Princess Phones" covered in faux fur and attend "Princess-Makeover Birthday Parties." Saks bought Club Libby Lu in 2003 for $12 million and has since expanded it to 87 outlets; by 2005, with only scant local advertising, revenues hovered around the $46 million mark, a 53 percent jump from the previous year.* Pink, it seems, is the new gold.

8   Even Dora the Explorer,[†] the intrepid, dirty-kneed adventurer, has ascended to the throne: in 2004, after a two-part episode in which she turns into a "true princess," the Nickelodeon and Viacom consumer-products division released a satin-gowned "Magic Hair Fairytale Dora," with hair that grows or shortens when her crown is touched. Among other phrases the bilingual doll utters: "Vámonos! Let's go to fairy-tale land!" and "Will you brush my hair?"

9   As a feminist mother—not to mention a nostalgic product of the Grranimals[‡] era—I have been taken by surprise by the princess craze and the girlie-girl culture that has risen around it. What happened to William wanting a doll and not dressing your cat in an apron? . . . I watch my fellow mothers, women who once swore they'd never be dependent on a man, smile indulgently at daughters who warble "So This Is Love" or insist on being called Snow White. I wonder if they'd concede so readily to sons who begged for combat fatigues and mock AK-47s.

10   More to the point, when my own girl makes her daily beeline for the dress-up corner of her preschool classroom—something I'm convinced she does largely to torture me—I worry about what playing Little Mermaid is teaching her. I've spent much of my career writing about experiences that undermine girls' well-being, warning parents that a preoccupation with body and beauty (encouraged by films, TV, magazines and, yes, toys) is perilous to their daughters' mental and physical health. Am I now supposed to shrug and forget all that? If trafficking in stereotypes doesn't matter at 3, when does it matter? At 6? Eight? Thirteen?

---

*Saks Incorporated closed its Club Libby Lu stores in January 2009.

†Dora the Explorer is a cartoon character in a Nickelodeon program geared toward young children.

‡Grranimals were a clothing line for children in the 1970s.

11   On the other hand, maybe I'm still surfing a washed-out second wave of feminism in a third-wave world. Maybe princesses are in fact a sign of progress, an indication that girls can embrace their predilection for pink without compromising strength or ambition; that, at long last, they can "have it all." Or maybe it is even less complex than that: to mangle Freud, maybe a princess is sometimes just a princess. And, as my daughter wants to know, what's wrong with that?

12   The rise of the Disney princesses reads like a fairy tale itself, with Andy Mooney, a former Nike executive, playing the part of prince, riding into the company on a metaphoric white horse in January 2000 to save a consumer-products division whose sales were dropping by as much as 30 percent a year. Both overstretched and underfocused, the division had triggered price wars by granting multiple licenses for core products (say, Winnie-the-Pooh undies) while ignoring the potential of new media. What's more, Disney films like "A Bug's Life" in 1998 had yielded few merchandising opportunities—what child wants to snuggle up with an ant?

13   It was about a month after Mooney's arrival that the magic struck. That's when he flew to Phoenix to check out his first "Disney on Ice" show. "Standing in line in the arena, I was surrounded by little girls dressed head to toe as princesses," he told me last summer in his palatial office, then located in Burbank, and speaking in a rolling Scottish burr. "They weren't even Disney products. They were generic princess products they'd appended to a Halloween costume. And the light bulb went off. Clearly there was latent demand here. So the next morning I said to my team, 'O.K., let's establish standards and a color palette and talk to licensees and get as much product out there as we possibly can that allows these girls to do what they're doing anyway: projecting themselves into the characters from the classic movies.'"

14   Mooney picked a mix of old and new heroines to wear the Pantone pink No. 241 corona: Cinderella, Sleeping Beauty, Snow White, Ariel, Belle, Jasmine, Mulan and Pocahontas. It was the first time Disney marketed characters separately from a film's release, let alone lumped together those from different stories. To ensure the sanctity of what Mooney called their individual "mythologies," the princesses never make eye contact when they're grouped: each stares off in a slightly different direction as if unaware of the others' presence.

15   It is also worth noting that not all of the ladies are of royal extraction. Part of the genius of "Princess" is that its meaning is so broadly constructed that it actually has no meaning. Even Tinker Bell was originally a Princess, though her reign didn't last. "We'd always debate over whether she was really a part of the Princess mythology," Mooney recalled. "She really wasn't." Likewise, Mulan and Pocahontas, arguably the most resourceful of the bunch, are rarely depicted on Princess merchandise, though for a different reason. Their rustic garb has less bling potential than that of old-school heroines like Sleeping Beauty. (When Mulan does appear, she is typically in the kimonolike hanfu, which makes her miserable in the movie, rather than her liberated warrior's gear.)

16   The first Princess items, released with no marketing plan, no focus groups, no advertising, sold as if blessed by a fairy godmother. To this day, Disney conducts little market research on the Princess line, relying instead on the power of its legacy among mothers as well as the instant-read sales barometer of the theme parks and Disney Stores. "We simply gave girls what they wanted," Mooney said of the line's success, "although I don't think any of us grasped how much they wanted this. I wish I could sit here and take credit for having some grand scheme to develop this, but all we did was envision a little girl's room and think about how she could live out the princess fantasy. The counsel we gave to licensees was: What type of bedding would a princess want to sleep in? What kind of alarm clock would a princess want to wake up to? What type of television would a princess like to see? It's a rare case where you find a girl who has every aspect of her room bedecked in Princess, but if she ends up with three or four of these items, well, then you have a very healthy business."

17   Every reporter Mooney talks to asks some version of my next question: Aren't the Princesses, who are interested only in clothes, jewelry and cadging the handsome prince, somewhat retrograde role models?

18   "Look," he said, "I have friends whose son went through the Power Rangers phase who castigated themselves over what they must've done wrong. Then they talked to other parents whose kids had gone through it. The boy passes through. The girl passes through. I see girls expanding their imagination through visualizing themselves as princesses, and then they pass through that phase and end up becoming lawyers, doctors, mothers or princesses, whatever the case may be."

19   Mooney has a point: There are no studies proving that playing princess directly damages girls' self-esteem or dampens other aspirations. On the other hand, there is evidence that young women who hold the most conventionally feminine beliefs—who avoid conflict and think they should be perpetually nice and pretty—are more likely to be depressed than others and less likely to use contraception. What's more, the 23 percent decline in girls' participation in sports and other vigorous activity between middle and high school has been linked to their sense that athletics is unfeminine. And in a survey released last October by Girls Inc., school-age girls overwhelmingly reported a paralyzing pressure to be "perfect": not only to get straight A's and be the student-body president, editor of the newspaper and captain of the swim team but also to be "kind and caring," "please everyone, be very thin and dress right." Give those girls a pumpkin and a glass slipper and they'd be in business.